Sources of the Pentateuch

ANTONY F. CAMPBELL and MARK A. O'BRIEN

To our parents

William Orr Campbell
Laura Nancy Caroline Mary Loughnan
John Thomas O'Brien
Cecilia May Flanagan

Contents

Preface

Until recently, the source hypothesis enjoyed the status of classical certainty in most of modern biblical scholarship. For a century or so, it served to organize a mass of data into a relatively simple conceptual structure, thereby providing an overall system within which numerous other observations could be made. Its assumptions became accepted as a framework within which study of the Pentateuch proceeded.

There is great value in being able to work with a set of assumptions that simplifies the range of data in an area as vast as the Pentateuch. One can take comfort in the security of assumptions that are felt to be widely accepted and not to need constant reexamination. There is, however, a correspondingly great danger of blindness and falsehood in the complacent acceptance of simplicity and security. Comfortable as the past may have been, such complacency can no longer hold the field. The source hypothesis has been under challenge and reexamination for some years.

In situations of challenge, the temptation always exists of flight to another equally unexamined set of assumptions: out with the old, in with the new, let comfort be restored. Yielding to this temptation leaves the mass of data unexamined, the old assumptions unchallenged because untested, and the new paradigms fragile for lack of vigorous comparison.

The aim of this book is to enable assumptions about the Pentateuch to be vigorously and thoroughly challenged. We do not set out to advocate a source-critical model for the Pentateuch. We do set out to present one example of a source-critical model as clearly and intelligibly as possible. For this purpose, we have chosen Martin Noth's view of the sources in the source hypothesis, as presented in his *History of Pentateuchal Traditions*.[1]

A successful challenge to any scholarly position must always confront the opposition in its strongest form. Anything less is unworthy and unproductive. There have been many views on the best model of the source hypothesis. Often, and rightly, the models may be practically incompatible. Confusion between these views troubles and clouds discussion of the new alternatives offered. The multiplicity of studies on the pentateuchal text makes it easy to lose sight of the aim of these approaches, which is to bring a simplicity of understanding to a complex process of growth.[2]

---

1. M. Noth, *A History of Pentateuchal Traditions*, trans. B. W. Anderson (Englewood Cliffs, N.J.: Prentice-Hall, 1972; reprint, Chico, Calif.: Scholars Press, 1981; German original, 1948).

2. Any attempt to poke fun at the complexity of analyses of biblical text must ultimately reckon with the reality that, in all approaches, comparable depth will generate comparable complexity.

We are wedded to neither the source-critical model nor Noth's analysis of the sources. For several years, we have been working on our own understanding of the origins of the pentateuchal text. It is our conviction, however, that for understanding how the source hypothesis works as a hypothesis—the solutions it brings to problems in the biblical text and the problems it raises in its turn—Noth's is the most useful analysis to offer.

One of the reasons for this is precisely that Noth's analysis is not particularly personal to him and certainly not idiosyncratic. In *A History of Pentateuchal Traditions*, where his source analysis is presented briefly at the beginning, his interest is in "the origins and first stages of growth which were decisive for the development of the whole," rather than in the literary analysis of sources in the later stages of pentateuchal development. For Noth the history of scholarship had reached a point where source questions "certainly do not require fresh examination as much as does the preliterary history of the Pentateuchal tradition." So although his presentation of the sources has innovative aspects, it is in many ways a summary of the consensus reached by Noth's time—even if "generally accepted solutions have not been reached in every regard."[3]

Noth's analysis is of value for this book precisely because it represents a more-or-less consensus position. Yet it is personal in the sense that it summarizes the views he gained from his own work on the Pentateuch: "It is my concern here only to present clearly the *results* of one particular investigation, thus taking a definite stand in the arena of the continuing lively debate over the literary-critical analysis of the Penta-

teuch, and at the same time introducing into the discussion one or two new views which have resulted from working through the material."[4] These new views of Noth's concerned, in particular, the understanding of how the sources were combined and the recovery of greater continuity in P and J.

The recent challenges to the source hypothesis will be discussed in the introduction. Some of these come from new models for understanding the processes of growth assumed to lie behind the present text of the Pentateuch. The concept of early continuous sources has been questioned, with the development of traditions seen as proceeding largely independently until the literary activity of the deuteronomic movement. The priority and antiquity of the Yahwist narrative also has been questioned in several recent studies.

It is important to recognize that new ways of understanding the process of growth behind the pentateuchal text are not the only challenge to a source-critical model for the Pentateuch. Another significant challenge comes from those concerned with the proper interpretation of the biblical text as literature and with an appropriate literary grasp of the canons of its style. Many features of the Old Testament text that would once have been exploited as evidence for multiple sources and authorship may now be accounted for on grounds of literary style, emphasis, and sensitivity.

The move to literary interpretation is not a matter of minor detail and personal aptitude or skill. It brings with it a massive shift in attitude, where attention is focused on the significance and artistry of the text as it now stands. In past generations, features that apparently indicated

---

3. Noth, *Pentateuchal Traditions*, 1.
4. Ibid., 5–6. What makes Noth's presentation of added value is the possibility of comparing it with his

later study in his commentaries on the books of Exodus (1959), Leviticus (1962), and Numbers (1966).

discontinuity in the text tended to turn the interpreter's gaze toward the origins and growth process of the text as the place for an appropriate explanation. The shift in attitude requires the interpreter to realize that often the explanation for such features can be better found in the meaning and significance they contribute to the text, viewed as a whole.

Historians have the task of identifying the reasons for the backward-looking, source-oriented view of so much of past interpretation. Was the conviction of the "clarity of Scripture" latently active, so that the present text was thought not to need interpretation? Alternatively, had the results of critical study engendered the conviction that the present text, having no author, had no meaning?[5] Was it principally the result of a high-level demarcation dispute, with the academics concerned for the past of the text and leaving to the preachers the exposition of its meaning in its present form? Was the source-oriented interpretation sometimes symptomatic of the flight from the churchly toward the scholarly? Or was it no more than the outcome of different skills applied in different disciplines? By the time that the necessary ancient languages had been acquired, along with biblical archaeology, history, and geography, little time or energy remained for formal training in literature.

It is not surprising that the contemporary literary challenge is being spearheaded by professionals in the literature field or others whose initial training was in literary studies. At the same time, it would be a great pity if the excesses evident in past generations of exegetes were to be matched with equal excesses by new, opposing generations of litterateurs. One does not

have to read very far into the Old Testament text to realize that not all repetitions and other pointers to discontinuity can be attributed to subtlety of literary style.

Martin Noth's scholarship dates from the middle of this century. His is clearly a source-oriented, not a discourse-oriented, approach to the biblical text. Nowadays, contemplating his comments, one finds at times that alternative explanations cry out for a hearing. We have not taken it on ourselves in this book to refute Noth or to set his misconceptions to rights. Our primary aim has been to make his view of the text easily intelligible, so that others can move on from there.

Where it has seemed important, we have gone beyond Noth's own comments to point out some of the observations that he would have taken for granted. Often Noth's comments presuppose knowledge of the scholarship that was commonplace in his day. Just as often, Noth presupposes an acute and informed reading of the text. Without any attempt at being exhaustive, we have tried, where appropriate, to point to some of the features in the text that may well have influenced Noth's judgment. We sometimes emphasize occasions where other ways of accounting for the features of a text would now be given greater sway.

One of the values of this approach should be to show whether or not a powerful challenge to the source-critical model can be mounted on literary grounds. At many points it will be obvious that as competent a scholar and source critic as Noth is, he has clearly failed to see alternative ways of accounting for some features of the present text. In many cases, it will be just as obvious that these points are relatively minor

---

5. In such a case, a search for apparently authorless meaning might have seemed objectionable as an act of irrationally blind faith. The rediscovery and reevalua-

tion of the redactor as author legitimates this aspect of the quest for meaning in the final text—without predetermining the outcome of that quest.

details, having no bearing at all on the source analysis being discussed. How far such conclusions can be generalized is a matter for continuing study.

The options available at present for understanding the origins and growth of the Pentateuch probably boil down to five.[6] First is the conclusion that the history of the text is just too complicated to be reconstructed, and so the only route to follow is that of dealing exclusively with the present text. Second is the hypothesis of continuous redaction: the text has not been built up from extensive sources but from an original narrative which has been added to in various ways at various times. A third understands the features of the text as resulting from the combining of extensive sources, in a process in which the substantial bulk of the sources has been preserved (as in Noth's view—allowing for often substantial later additions, such as the legal codes). Fourth would be those source hypotheses in which the process of combination is markedly different from that proposed by Noth. Finally, fifth is the tracing of groups of independent traditions over time until they are ultimately combined into the present text, without their having formed sources or a comprehensive narrative.

When looking at these options, it is important to distinguish between matters that are substantial enough to affect the acceptability or validity of a particular option and matters that allow for various ways of looking at the text without affecting the specific option under consideration. It is always important to be aware of the limits of any hypothesis, and it is no less important for hypotheses in pentateuchal studies. There is considerable hard evidence available for reflection when deciding between

options. In the source-critical hypothesis, reflected in the texts presented in this book, the criteria are such that in limited areas a consensus on matters of detail should not be expected. There are chapters where, in Noth's judgment, a satisfactory analysis into sources cannot be achieved.[7] There are other areas where source analysis will depend on issues of interpretation and intuitive satisfaction, allowing for a number of possibly satisfactory positions.

There is a tendency to speak of "the Yahwist" and "the Priestly writer" as though these were established identities. At the broad level this is legitimate enough; anything else would be pedantry. But in fact, at any level, there is always some scholar's identification of text at the back of any statement about a source; there has to be some notional idea of the continuity or extent of the text in any statement about P or J. In matters of detail, specifics are called for. A statement cannot just be about J; it has to be about Eissfeldt's or Hölscher's or Noth's J or the author's J, and so on. It would be a pity if a book such as this, in laying out a particular position with clarity, led to that position's being canonized and universalized. Within broad guidelines which may perhaps find a certain consensus, there will always be as much latitude in areas of the source hypothesis as there is in the interpretation of a text.

This is well illustrated by the changes in the drift of Noth's own positions over a number of years. The changes go in contrasting directions. As we point out in the notes to chapter 3, where the Yahwist is concerned, in his 1948 *History of Pentateuchal Traditions* Noth relegated a number of passages to secondary status that in his later commentaries he left as original to the Yahwist. The attitude behind these shifts in judgment

---

6. These options can be situated in relation to the three basic hypotheses that are outlined in chapter 1.

7. E.g., Exodus 33 and Numbers 12.

may be seen from a remark in his unfinished 1968 volume on 1 Kings where, disputing his judgment in 1943, he comments that the possibility for dividing up a text source-critically does not generate the necessity for doing so.[8]

Where the Priestly writer is concerned, the reverse occurred. Substantial blocks of text that in 1948 Noth attributed to P have been relegated to secondary status in his later commentaries. For example, Exodus 29 is original in 1948 and secondary in 1958; much of Exodus 35–40 is original in 1948, whereas almost the whole of it is secondary a decade later. Similarly, most of Leviticus 8 is original in 1948, and all of it is secondary in the 1962 commentary. It may not be out of place to draw attention to Noth's conviction that the combination of the tent complex and the temple complex of traditions was the new and particular contribution of the Priestly writer and that these detailed instructions for the sanctuary were the climax of P's document.[9] With this focus, interest would naturally attach to the instructions (Exodus 25–29), and the subsequent lengthy insistence on compliance might well seem secondary—a compliance taken for granted by the original writer.[10]

The comments just made provide an oversimplified view of complex positions based on a wide range of factors. They may serve, however, to point out the risk of canonizing a single position and to show how widely differing positions can be held within the overall parameters of a source hypothesis as an explanation for the factors in the pentateuchal text.

---

8. "A literary-critical possibility is however still not a literary-critical necessity; and only in the latter case is there sufficient basis for literary-critical operations" (*Könige* [BKAT 9/1; Neukirchen: Neukirchener Verlag, 1968] 245–46). As far back as 1948, Noth expressed the view that it should be "a principle of any sound criticism of the Pentateuch not to assume literary disunity unless the occurrence of variants, of obvious seams and secondary connections, and the like, *compels* such an assumption" (*Pentateuchal Traditions*, 24). The notion of what is compelling may change with time.

9. See Noth's comments: "Now P—and this is apparently what is new with him and particular to him—has combined the complex of ideas associated with the אהל מועד [tent of meeting] and the quite different complex of ideas attached to the Jerusalem temple and its ark" (see *Pentateuchal Traditions*, 245; retranslated here from the German original (1948) to bring out Noth's emphasis on P's own contribution). Also: "Israel appears at Sinai so that Moses may receive on the mountain detailed instructions for making the sanctuary and the things it is to contain as well as for establishing the legitimate cult. This is indeed a fundamental event for P, whose whole description leads up to it and *virtually comes to a conclusion with it*" (M. Noth, *Exodus* [OTL; Philadelphia: Westminster, 1962] 17, emphasis ours).

A quite different emphasis on the part of K. Elliger and N. Lohfink happens to parallel a reduced emphasis on the Sinai traditions. They focus P's interest on the conquest of Canaan and allocate diminished amounts of the Sinai sanctuary text as original to P. See K. Elliger, "Sinn und Ursprung der priesterlichen Geschichtserzählung," *ZTK* 49 (1952) 121–43; and N. Lohfink, "Die Priesterschrift und die Geschichte," *Congress Volume: Göttingen, 1977* (VTSup 29; Leiden: E. J. Brill, 1978) 189–225. The text references for P according to Noth, Elliger, and Lohfink are listed comparatively in Antony F. Campbell, *The Study Companion to Old Testament Literature: An Approach to the Writings of Pre-Exilic and Exilic Israel* (A Michael Glazier Book; Old Testament Studies 2; Collegeville, Minn.: Liturgical Press, 1989/1992) 88–91. Lohfink built on Elliger's text with his own observations and those of older commentaries, as well as more recent studies; see "Priesterschrift und die Geschichte," 198 n. 29.

In material of this kind, which is notoriously difficult to date, a scholar's conception of a source may well be influential in some of the decisions about what is original and what is secondary. Ideally, the conception of the source will have been drawn from a wide representation of its material, and the decisions based on this conception will be applied to localized areas, thus avoiding circular argument. In practice, the danger of circular argument is difficult to eliminate.

10. Detailed evidence for the growth of the text is primary here, of course, and is discussed in chapter 2.

In the light of this complexity and uncertainty, it might well be asked why scholars bother pursuing such evanescent structures as early traditions or ancient sources for the Pentateuch. The mountaineer's response to the "why climb the mountain" question—"because it is there"—may be paraphrased for our question: because there are features in the biblical text that need explanation. But there is more to it than that. Explanations have implications.

First, within the realm of faith, the nature of the biblical text has a bearing on the nature of divine revelation. Is God's self-disclosure within the Scriptures understood to have been univocal and direct, as far divorced from the dynamics of daily human experience as the blinding light of the Damascus road? Or is God's self-disclosure in the Bible thoroughly embedded in the ambiguity and uncertainty of so much human living? The biblical text, as we understand it today, bears witness both to the struggles of many generations in coming to grips with their experience of God in their lives and to the attempt to give that experience adequate articulation. Views are expressed and traditions told, modifications are made, contradictory positions are proposed, composite texts are compiled, prophetic texts are updated, and so on—and all the while, faith is eternally questing for understanding.

In this context, a major aspect of the significance of the Bible is not in answering questions and problems of human living or in propounding God's self-revelation. Rather, its significance is as a model of the dialogue with God necessary in exploring issues of human living and endeavoring to grasp, crystallize, and express the experience of God's self-disclosure. The Bible as model of dialogue encounters God deeply embedded in the ambiguity and uncertainty of so much human living. As model, it excludes little of the range of human experience. As model, it is richly manifold and multifaceted in its witness to the experience of God.

Second, the pursuit of pentateuchal sources is born of a certain fidelity to those patient authors, editors, transmitters, scribes, or copyists who produced the biblical texts.[11] The features in the texts that allow traditions to be traced, sources to be analyzed, and so on, hardly exist by chance. It would have been all too easy for the copyist's pen to have reduced them to uniformity. Today we may argue over the significance of the diversity and duality in the text, but we are faithful to the spirit of its authors in trying to recover in all its contours the meaning of the text they created, shaped, and gave to us.

Third, the task of recovering the meaning of the text in all its contours gives dimension and depth to the theology of ancient Israel. Israel's faith in its quest for understanding embraced a rich variety of theological positions, whether along the gamut of Job and the wisdom literature, or of deuteronomic and priestly theologies, or of Yahwist and Priestly narratives, or many others. However we understand the stages in the Pentateuch—as sources, blocks of tradition, redactional activity, and so on—they can give us insight into the development of Israel's understanding of itself and of its God. Despite the fragility of the conclusions we may reach, the task is hugely worthwhile.

Finally, when given appropriate weight, awareness of the processes of growth inherent in the creation of the biblical text can give contour and color to the understanding of the text in its final form. Just as the light of dawn in Job is seen bringing forth the contours of the earth,

---

11. There are valuable reflections on these creators, preservers, and transmitters in Shemaryahu Talmon, "The Textual Study of the Bible—A New Outlook," in *Qumran and the Biblical Text*, ed. F. M. Cross and S. Talmon (Cambridge: Harvard University Press, 1975) 321–400; see 336–37.

"like clay under the seal," and then bringing out its colors, "dyed like a garment" (Job 38:12-14), so knowledge of the threads being woven into the fabric of a text may enable the interpreter significantly to enrich its meaning. God knows, it does not always happen that way—but it can!

Aims of This Book

1. Our first aim is to present as clearly as possible the text of the pentateuchal sources, as identified by Noth in *A History of Pentateuchal Traditions*. Although we are using the NRSV for the basic text, all translation is controlled by context. When text is moved from the context of the present biblical text to the context of a separate source, a change in translation may be necessary. When this is required, a translation has been provided appropriate to the new context, with a note and the NRSV text in square brackets.

2. Where there are gaps in the continuity of the sources, we provide an explanation for these, in accordance with Noth's understanding of the source hypothesis.

3. Where it seems helpful, we provide notes pointing to issues of structure or interpretation, particularly where these issues are significant for the source hypothesis or might be easily overlooked. This aspect of the notes has deliberately been restricted to a minimum. This volume is not intended as a commentary or as an exercise in advocacy for the source hypothesis.[12]

4. As far as possible, we provide notes commenting on material regarded as secondary within a source. This is part of the task of analysis of the interplay between source and subsequent tradition. Here, too, we have been selective and deliberately refrained from the temptation to treat issues exhaustively. Sometimes there are issues of clear evidence in the text—repetitions, oddities of syntax, and the like—which it is useful to point out, even though they may be susceptible of various interpretations. At other times, decisions to regard material as secondary are largely a matter of informed intuition, shaped by contemporary sensitivity; these are easily subject to change or to different evaluation.

5. We aim to contribute to continuing improvement in the understanding and interpretation of composite texts through close study both of the factors evident in the artful composition of such texts and of the implications present for their meaning and use. Three composite texts are examined: the flood, the opening of the Joseph story, and the deliverance at the sea. Attention is paid to both the unity and the duality present, to the ways in which the apparent achievement of unity has been facilitated, and to the ways in which the various elements combined in the final text may function to give meaning.

6. We present the text of the sources, as identified by Noth. Therefore paragraphing and punctuation must represent the source, not the combined text in the NRSV. Primacy has been given to punctuating the source. Punctuation for the supplementary material has been handled on a case-by-case basis, in order to treat each appropriately. This may range from no initial capitalization and no final period to repeating quo-

---

12. Precisely because this is substantially a presentation of the source hypothesis as understood by Noth, it is inappropriate in the notes on the texts to enter into a full discussion of the more recent challenges to the source hypothesis. The size of the book also rendered this impossible.

tation marks, capitals, and so on. The issue is particularly noticeable in the P document.

Subheads are used as indicators and guides to the text. Especially in the Priestly document, they indicate where key passages begin; they may not apply to all text that follows.

Details of Presentation

1. Breaks in the continuity of a source.

Where gaps occur within a source, they are indicated by three bold-faced ellipsis points (• • •), between paragraphs or within paragraphs, as appropriate.

Where fragments are preserved within such a gap, they are indented from the margin on the line following the ellipses. See, for example, Gen 31:18 and 33:18a in chapter 2 (pp. 32, 33).

2. Breaks in the continuity of the present biblical text.

The three ellipsis points (• • •) are used only for gaps postulated within a source. Breaks in the continuity of sequence in the canonical biblical text are indicated in three ways.

a. by a break in the sequence of the verse numbers:

7:6 Noah was six hundred years old when the flood of waters came on the earth.

11 In the six hundredth year of Noah's life, in the second month, on the seventeenth day of the month, on that day all the fountains of the great deep burst forth, and the windows of the heavens were opened.

The verse numbers indicate that vv. 7-10 are not included in P.

b. by an "a" or "b" with the verse number, indicating that one or the other half of the verse is omitted:

7: 16aAnd those that entered, male and female of all flesh, went in as God had commanded him.

The second half of v. 16 is not included in P.

c. by a superscripted asterisk (*) with the verse number, indicating that a part of the verse, which may be more or less than half, is omitted:

37: 2*This is the story of the family of Jacob.

Joseph, being seventeen years old, was shepherding the flock with his brothers; and Joseph brought a bad report of them to their father.

Part of v. 2 is not included in P.

Genesis 13 in P (pp. 28–29) provides an example of all three conditions:

13:6 And [Heb.; NRSV, so that] the land could not support both of them living together; for their possessions were so great that they could not live together. 11bSo [Heb.; NRSV, thus] they separated from each other. 12*Abram settled in the land of Canaan, while Lot settled among the cities of the Plain.

a. Verses 7-10 are not included in P.
b. Verse 11a is not included in P.
c. Part of v. 12 is not included in P.

Where the NRSV has "so that" in v. 6 and "thus" in v. 11b, the literal understanding of the Hebrew in this new context is "and" and "so," respectively.

The omitted verses or parts of verses will be found in one of the other chapters, in either the sources or the nonsource material.

3. Supplementary material within sources.

Where supplementary material is identified within a source, it is printed in italic text and indented. If it is only one or two words, it is simply italicized.

For example, from Genesis 46 in P (p. 34):

Jacob and all his offspring with him, ⁷his sons, and his sons' sons with him, his daughters, and his sons' daughters; all his offspring he brought with him into Egypt.

8 Now these are the names of the Israelites, Jacob and his offspring, who came to Egypt. Reuben, Jacob's firstborn, ⁹and the children of Reuben: Hanoch, Pallu, Hezron, and Carmi. ¹⁰The children of Simeon: Jemuel, Jamin, Ohad, Jachin, Zohar, and Shaul, the son of a Canaanite woman.

Verses 8ff. are supplementary within the P source.

4. Secondary additions within supplementary material.

If material is considered to be secondary within what is already supplementary, it is also printed in italics but is indented farther from the margin.

For example, from Exodus 12 in P (p. 40):

40 The time that the Israelites had lived in Egypt was four hundred thirty years. ⁴¹At the end of four hundred thirty years, on that very day, all the companies of the LORD went out from the land of Egypt.

⁴²That was for the LORD a night of vigil, to bring them out of the land of Egypt. That same night is a vigil to be kept for the LORD by all the Israelites throughout their generations. 43 The LORD said to Moses and Aaron: This is the ordinance for the passover: no foreigner shall eat of it, ⁴⁴but any slave who has been purchased may eat of it after he has been circumcised; ⁴⁵no bound or hired servant may eat of it.

Verses 40-41 are considered to be P, vv. 43ff. are considered supplements to P, and v. 42 is considered a secondary addition placed in front of the supplement.

5. The non-J variants in the "Elohist" material.

Within the "Elohist" text, covered in chapter 4, a slightly different variation occurs. According to Noth, there are texts in this material that stand out clearly from the J narrative but which he is unwilling to identify with the Elohist. We have left these in Roman type but indented them farther. Any secondary additions identified in these variant texts are farther indented and italicized. See, for example, Gen 15:1-16*; Exod 1:15-21*; Exod 32:1b-4a, 21-24 (pp. 166–67, 183–84, 189–90).

6. The Toledoth Book.

Restricted parts of the Priestly document (chap. 2) are considered by Noth to derive from what is called the "Toledoth book" (see p. 23 n. 4). Within a paragraph, these are marked off by a bullet (•) at the beginning and end. Where a whole paragraph is derived from the Toledoth book, the bullet appears on the margin at the beginning of the paragraph.

7. The use of Greek letters in biblical references.

Occasionally in the notes, the Greek letters α and β are used in text references. They usually refer to cases where the same Greek letters have been used by Noth in his listing of the text in *A History of Pentateuchal Traditions*. They are understood as follows.

Verse halves are denoted by "a" and "b," following the major division of a verse in the Hebrew punctuation (or cantillation marks). Subdivisions within any half-verse are indicated by the Greek letters α and β, following the principal secondary punctuation divisions in the Hebrew. As a rule, this punctuation follows the sense of the verse, so that someone unfamiliar with Hebrew will frequently be able to decide from the context what part of the verse is meant. Thus v. 7aα indicates the beginning of the first half of v. 7, v. 7bβ indicates the end of the second half of v. 7, and v. 7aβbα indicates the middle of v. 7. These are used rarely, where precision or correlation with Noth's listing may be helpful.

Finally, it is appropriate to note that this book is fully the work of both authors. We have hammered out our part of the text together, to the point where often we are no longer sure who originated what. We are happy to bear joint responsibility for the outcome.

Abbreviations

AnBib	Analecta biblica
ATANT	Abhandlungen zur Theologie des Alten und Neuen Testaments
ATD	Das Alte Testament Deutsch
AusBR	*Australian Biblical Review*
BKAT	Biblischer Kommentar: Altes Testament
BZAW	Beihefte zur *ZAW*
CBQ	*Catholic Biblical Quarterly*
CBQMS	Catholic Biblical Quarterly—Monograph Series
DtrH	Deuteronomistic History
HSM	Harvard Semitic Monographs
ICC	International Critical Commentary
JB	Jerusalem Bible
JBL	*Journal of Biblical Literature*
JSOTSup	Journal for the Study of the Old Testament—Supplement Series
NAB	New American Bible
NEB	New English Bible
NIV	New International Version
NRSV	New Revised Standard Version
OTL	Old Testament Library
RSV	Revised Standard Version
SBLMS	Society of Biblical Literature Monograph Series
SBLSP	Society of Biblical Literature Seminar Papers
TBü	Theologische Bücherei
VT	*Vetus Testamentum*
VTSup	Vetus Testamentum, Supplements
WBC	Word Biblical Commentary
WMANT	Wissenschaftliche Monographien zum Alten und Neuen Testament
ZAW	*Zeitschrift für die alttestamentliche Wissenschaft*
ZTK	*Zeitschrift für Theologie und Kirche*

CHAPTER 1

Introduction: Pentateuchal Source Criticism

Early Discovery of Sources

Biblical scholarship from the patristic period until the late Middle Ages was, in general, not concerned with questions about the authorship or history of the biblical text.[1] Some interest had been shown in the early synagogue and church, but the development of a historical perspective with its concern for the particular circumstances of a text's composition had not yet occurred. There was little awareness that the text stemmed from a time and place quite different from that of a patristic or medieval interpreter and that the manner of its composition might have been different from what such an interpreter would have expected.

This began to change under the impact of the Renaissance and the Reformation. A renewed interest in the classical world and its literature was accompanied by a new awareness of how it differed from the contemporary world. The study of ancient languages was put on a more scientific footing, with the result that ancient documents could be examined in a way that was not available to earlier generations.

When this new, historically oriented and critically alert analysis was applied to the Pentateuch it was found to contain numerous duplications, a broad diversity of style, and contrasting viewpoints. It was primarily the discovery of duplication extending across a considerable body of text that led to the claim in the seventeenth century that the Pentateuch had its own history of composition. An early proponent of this hypothesis was Richard Simon (1638–1712), who argued that the Pentateuch had been compiled from a number of documents.[2] Some of these docu-

---

1. This review of the history of research is indebted particularly to H.-J. Kraus, *Geschichte der historisch-kritischen Erforschung des Alten Testaments*, 3d ed. (Neukirchen: Neukirchener Verlag, 1982). Other resources consulted here and available to students are O. Eissfeldt, *The Old Testament: An Introduction* (Oxford: Basil Blackwell, 1965); G. Fohrer, *Introduction to the Old Testament* (London: SPCK, 1968); J. H. Hayes, *An Introduction to Old Testament Study* (Nashville: Abingdon, 1979); and A. de Pury and Th. Römer, "Le Pentateuque en question: Position du problème et brève histoire de la recherche," in *Le Pentateuque en question: Les origines et la composition des cinq premiers livres de la Bible à la lumière des recherches récentes*, ed. A. de Pury (Le Monde de la Bible; Geneva: Labor et Fides, 1989) 9–80.

2. The terms "source" and "document" are used rather freely in biblical scholarship. In this presentation, document refers to a written record of undetermined length and purpose. Source refers to an extended continuous narrative, which is probably but not necessarily written and which has a discernible purpose. Source is used in a different sense by historians and exegetes. The former use it to refer primarily to a text from which the history of Israel may be reconstructed. In the pentateuchal context, the latter use it to refer primarily to a text that was one of the building blocks of the present text.

ments derived from Moses, but it was Ezra, in the post-exilic period, who produced the Pentateuch in its final form. Subsequently, Jean Astruc (1684–1766) claimed there were two sources, one that used *Elohim* (God) and the other, YHWH (LORD). Astruc argued, against the position of Simon, that Moses had compiled the Pentateuch from these two sources and ten additional fragments.[3] Two aspects of Astruc's analysis were significant for subsequent pentateuchal criticism: (1) his appeal to variation in the divine names as a sign of different sources; and (2) his employment of a combination of approaches which were later developed into the source and fragment hypotheses.

Given the subsequent history of the study of pentateuchal sources and the way that they became an issue of division between conservatives and liberals, it is interesting to note that the sources were used by Astruc as an argument to defend the claim of Moses' authorship of the Pentateuch. Because there was duplication and diversity within the text, it had not come from one author; but if a variety of sources and traditions had been used in putting the text together, then it could have come from one person. Therefore, according to Astruc the Pentateuch could have originated with Moses if one envisaged him functioning partly as a compiler of sources and partly as an author. Of significance here is not so much the question of Mosaic authorship of the Pentateuch as the general agreement that the text of the Pentateuch was more complex than had earlier been thought. The focus of attention had become firmly fixed on the peculiar literary phenomena of the Pentateuch.

Struggle to Characterize: Sources or Fragments?

As knowledge of the complexity of the text of the Pentateuch became increasingly refined, moves were made to formulate a comprehensive hypothesis which would account, if possible, for all of the literary phenomena observed. A direction had already been pointed out by Simon's proposal that the duplication and diversity in the text was due to different documents and traditions stemming from different periods of Israel's history.[4] For a comprehensive hypothesis to be successful, therefore, it would need to clarify the nature and extent of these documents and traditions and the process of their combination to form the present text.

Two principal ideas were to the fore during the eighteenth and nineteenth centuries. In one, which has come to be called the *early source hypothesis*,[5] the notion presented was of sources—texts of sustained length with narrative continuity and purpose—which were combined to form a single text. The principal advocates of the early source hypothesis were Johann Gottfried Eichhorn (1752–1827) and Karl-David Ilgen (1763–1834). Eichhorn distinguished two sources, an Elohist and a Yahwist, whereas Ilgen identified two Elohist sources and one Yahwist.[6]

---

3. For a full discussion of the early period of historical analysis of the Pentateuch, see Kraus, *Geschichte*. Attention is drawn to Simon and Astruc here because of their significance for the later formulation of the source hypothesis in its classical form of the four sources, J, E, D, P.

4. Simon formulated the interesting hypothesis that there was a chain of tradition reaching from Moses to Ezra (see Kraus, *Geschichte*, 67; also de Pury and Römer, "Pentateuque en question," 14). Because of this, he may be regarded as a seminal figure in not only the development of source criticism but also in the development of traditio-historical criticism.

5. A number of authors would use the term "documentary hypothesis."

6. In the classical formulation of the source hypothesis in the late nineteenth century, these two Elohist sources came to be identified as a Priestly source (P) and an Elohistic source (E).

In the other, called the *fragment hypothesis*, the diversity of the material and the difficulty of tracing the continuity of the documents led to the notion of originally independent fragments or traditions. These fragments were not elements of longer works; they were what was remembered about a particular figure or place. A leading advocate of this hypothesis was the English scholar Alexander Geddes (1737–1802), who was followed by the German Johann Severin Vater (1771–1826). For a time, Wilhelm Martin Leberecht de Wette (1780–1849) was also a supporter of the fragment hypothesis, although he subsequently accepted both documents and fragments in the composition of the Pentateuch. De Wette holds a prominent position in the development of pentateuchal criticism because of his widely accepted proposal that Deuteronomy was the law book for the reform of Josiah (2 Kings 22–23). The proposed date for the reform of 621 B.C.E. became accepted as a reliable reference point for constructing a chronology of the pentateuchal sources.

These separate hypotheses did not emerge because of fundamental differences in methodology, for both employed literary-critical analysis of the text, but because of the different texts to which this analysis was applied. The early source hypothesis began with the narrative sections of the Pentateuch and claimed that the duplications discovered there revealed the existence of originally independent parallel sources. The fragment hypothesis took as its point of departure the legal codes of the Pentateuch. The difficulty of finding parallel strands in this material, coupled with its apparent lack of internal organization, led to the proposal that the codes were compiled from small collections or fragments of laws. This explanation was then applied

to the rest of the Pentateuch. But the fragment hypothesis found it difficult to account for the more structured nature of the narrative sections of the Pentateuch.

As might be expected, a move was made to reconcile the conflicting explanations by combining their strengths and avoiding their weaknesses. This was the *supplementary hypothesis*. As it was formulated initially by Heinrich Georg August Ewald (1803–1875), this hypothesis envisaged a basic Elohistic (i.e., Priestly) document which was supplemented by Yahwistic fragments. Ewald later modified this by positing two Elohistic documents which were combined and supplemented by a Yahwistic redactor. The modification effectively placed him back within the orbit of the source hypothesis. The supplementary hypothesis was taken up by Friedrich Tuch in his 1858 commentary on Genesis. Tuch returned to the position of one Elohistic source and proposed that it was supplemented by a Yahwistic redactor who, on occasion, also made use of the name *Elohim*.

The debate between these competing hypotheses in the eighteenth and nineteenth centuries is important. First, the limited nature of a hypothesis needs to be recognized. On this point, the remarks of Georg Fohrer are worth quoting:

> None of these so-called hypotheses can be accepted to the exclusion of the others. In actual practice, none has ever been employed by itself; rather one or another has been preferred, while other hypotheses have served to explain individual problems.[7]

A hypothesis is a conceptual structure which serves to organize and render intelligible a mass of otherwise disparate and disordered observations. The observations are based on the study

---

7. Fohrer, *Introduction to the Old Testament*, 113–14.

of phenomena in the biblical text. The hypotheses are attempts to make the best possible sense of these observations. The limits of a hypothesis are experienced when it is able to make sense of a substantial proportion of the phenomena observed but not of all of them. Given the complexity of the observations, mirroring the complexity of life, appeal may be made to several hypotheses or conceptualizations, separately or in various combinations, to explain what is observed in the text.

In the sphere of pentateuchal studies, the various hypotheses reflect scholarly attempts to conceptualize and bring order to a diversity of literary phenomena. Although each hypothesis seeks to be as comprehensive as possible, it is limited by a number of factors. For one thing, there is the amount of literary phenomena that has been identified at any particular stage of research. It is unlikely that anyone can claim to have identified all the relevant literary phenomena in a text like the Pentateuch. There is also the subjective factor inherent in all scientific research. Related to this is the limited ability of any individual or community to generate an insight that will adequately explain all the phenomena under consideration. Finally, there is the problem of validating a theory that can make only a limited appeal to external evidence. One of the difficulties for any pentateuchal hypothesis is the lack of satisfactory comparative material, either within the Old Testament or in ancient Near Eastern literature.

Even though a hypothesis is therefore limited, it may legitimately be called comprehensive insofar as it provides the dominant conceptual model for understanding a text under discussion. Furthermore, recourse to another hypothesis to explain some of the literary phenomena does not necessarily invalidate the original one. One can, for example, envisage the pentateuchal sources as having been supplemented by later redaction without having to abandon the source hypothesis. Invalidation would occur only when the alternative supplanted the original as the dominant conceptual model for explaining the literary phenomena.

Second, the nature of a source emerges as more complex than was initially thought. The early source hypothesis understood the independent sources as unified works, each the product of a single author. The fragment hypothesis failed to supplant the source hypothesis as the favored explanation, but it did raise questions about the nature of the sources: whether existing documents and traditions had been incorporated into them, and whether material had been added to them subsequently. Reflection on these questions raised the possibility that the sources might not be as unified as previously thought, and that they might not have been produced by one author as previously thought. It was only the insights gained by form criticism and traditio-historical criticism in the late nineteenth and early twentieth centuries, however, that permitted a thorough reassessment of the nature and provenance of sources.

Establishment of the Chronology of the Sources

With further analysis and refinement of the hypotheses, a consensus emerged that there were three parallel sources, two of which were Elohistic (i.e., P and E) and one Yahwistic.[8] With the addition of Deuteronomy, a four-source hypothesis emerged. The focus of investigation then shifted to the sequence and dating of these sources and their correlation with a greater

---

8. The major nineteenth-century figures responsible for this development were Hermann Hupfeld, Eduard Riehm, August Dillmann, and Franz Delitzsch.

understanding of the history of Israel. Considerable impetus was given to this by de Wette's proposal that Deuteronomy belonged to Josiah's reform and could therefore be dated securely in 621 B.C.E. Initially, all the sources were judged to predate Deuteronomy (D). The Elohistic source, which was later designated the P source because of its evident priestly interests, was regarded as the earliest or foundational work. This was due to the perception that it supplied the chronological framework for the Pentateuch and contained the bulk of the legislation in Genesis–Numbers. The chronological sequence proposed at this stage was E¹(Priestly source)—E² (Elohist)—J (Yahwist)—D (Deuteronomy).

The major change in this chronology was the recognition that the Priestly document was the latest rather than the earliest of the sources. Although this proposal had been made as early as 1833 by Eduard Reuss, it was the thorough investigations of Karl Heinrich Graf, Abraham Kuenen, and Julius Wellhausen that led to the replacement of the earlier chronology. Wellhausen in particular was responsible for detailing the arguments in favor of the late date for P and making them available to a wide reading public in his famous 1878 publication, *Prolegomena to the History of Ancient Israel.*[9] Briefly the arguments are these: Neither Joshua–2

Kings nor the pre-exilic prophets show any knowledge of the narrative and laws of P. The laws in P give clear evidence of being later than in J, E, and D. For example, J and E sanction a multiplicity of places for worship, whereas D legislates for and forcefully advocates centralization of worship. In P this centralization is presupposed. Current investigation of the history of Israel also made much more sense once the chronological revision was accepted.

The chronological relationship between J and E does not appear to have been a major concern of Wellhausen. Most often he referred to them in their combined form as the JE (Jehovistic) source. Nevertheless, he did point to a number of differences between J and E that inclined him to accept J as the earlier of the two. J shows the least trace of classical prophecy, that is, from Amos onward. In contrast, this influence, according to Wellhausen, is easily recognizable in E.[10] In addition, E has a more refined notion of the deity than J, which readily describes God in anthropomorphic terms, as in the garden story (Genesis 2–3).[11] The chronological sequence of J–E–D–P adopted by Wellhausen and others in the late nineteenth century has come to be called the *classical form of the source hypothesis.* J was generally dated to the tenth or ninth centuries B.C.E., E to the eighth century,

---

9. Julius Wellhausen, *Prolegomena to the History of Ancient Israel* (Meridian Books; Cleveland: World Publishing, 1957). The book appeared in German in 1878 under the title *Geschichte Israels.* The 1883 edition was published as *Prolegomena zur Geschichte Israels,* and this has since become the commonly used title. Wellhausen preferred the abbreviation Q for P, from the Latin "quattuor" (four), because he designated the Priestly source as the book of the four covenants.

10. Wellhausen points to the description of Abraham as a prophet in Genesis 20, Jacob's burial of the teraphim in Gen 35:4, the story of the golden calf, and the reduction of the status of the masseba in Josh 24:27 to that of a witness. According to Wellhausen, all these features reflect the prophetic move to secure

exclusive worship of YHWH against competing deities (*Prolegomena,* 361).

11. Martin Noth expressed reservations about whether J or E was the prior source and whether they can be dated with any certainty. "The question of the relative ages of J and E cannot be determined as easily and certainly as is usually supposed. . . . Moreover, the arguments for an absolute dating of the two sources are exceedingly questionable" (*A History of Pentateuchal Traditions,* trans. B. W. Anderson [Englewood Cliffs, N.J.: Prentice-Hall, 1972; reprint, Chico, Calif.: Scholars Press, 1981] 38 n. 143). However, the majority of source critics have accepted the priority of J and its early date until recently.

D to the seventh century, and P to the sixth or fifth centuries.[12] Wellhausen believed that JE and P extended to the end of Joshua; hence one may legitimately describe this classical form of the hypothesis as applying to the Hexateuch, a position that remained virtually unchallenged until the work of Noth.

By way of anticipation, it is worth noting that the argument from silence employed by Wellhausen to support a late date for P has been used recently by Hans Heinrich Schmid, Martin Rose, and John Van Seters against an early date for J. They argue that Israel's pre-exilic literature reveals little knowledge of the major pentateuchal traditions before the emergence of Deuteronomy in the seventh century.

Concern with Identification of Vocabulary

The source hypothesis in its classical form depended on five literary criteria: (1) duplication and repetition of material, (2) variation in the divine names, (3) contrasting viewpoints in the text, (4) variation in language and style, and (5) evidence of compilation and redaction of parallel accounts. With the hypothesis enjoying wide acceptance, scholars sought out areas that could be further refined. One which initially seemed to offer promise was that of language and style. Commentaries and studies appeared that contained lists of the words and characteristics of style that were believed to be specific to each of the four sources. In English a good example is S. R. Driver's *An Introduction to the Literature of the Old Testament*.[13] As study has progressed, it has increasingly been recognized that although particular words may be specific to a given source in this or that story, they can hardly be restricted to this source in all contexts.[14] With this recognition, reliance on such lists of characteristics has largely vanished, with two notable exceptions—the deuteronomic and priestly material.

These two classes of material may still be identified by such study of specific characteristics. It needs to be emphasized that this is not just a matter of particular words. Almost no group has a monopoly on the vocabulary of a language. What becomes characteristic is the use of specific words in the service of a specific ideology or concern. This is the case for the deuteronomic or deuteronomistic language and for the priestly language.[15]

---

12. Wellhausen, like many source critics of his time, recognized that the sources were not the unified products of single authors. He judged that J and E had each undergone three successive editions (so J[1], J[2], J[3] and E[1], E[2], E[3]) and that P had been supplemented by legislative material (P[s]). In line with Fohrer's remarks cited earlier, Wellhausen employed a type of supplementary hypothesis to account for the complexity of each source.

13. S. R. Driver, *An Introduction to the Literature of the Old Testament* (Edinburgh: T. & T. Clark, 1891; 9th ed., 1913; reprint, New York: Meridian, 1956).

14. Noth himself concluded that "a division of the total material according to linguistic and stylistic considerations is not feasible" (*Pentateuchal Traditions*, 21). He did employ the criterion of the divine names but recognized that it must be used judiciously and supported by other criteria.

15. For useful lists of deuteronomic or deuteronomistic language, see M. Weinfeld, *Deuteronomy and the Deuteronomic School* (Oxford: Clarendon, 1972) 320–65; and H. D. Hoffmann, *Reform und Reformen* (ATANT 66; Zurich: Theologischer Verlag, 1980) 323–66. Useful lists of priestly language may be found in such works as that of Driver, cited earlier. More recent are the studies by R. Polzin, *Late Biblical Hebrew: Toward an Historical Typology of Biblical Hebrew Prose* (HSM 12; Missoula, Mont.: Scholars Press, 1976); and A. Hurvitz, *A Linguistic Study of the Relationship between the Priestly Source and the Book of Ezekiel: A New Approach to an Old Problem* (Cahiers de la Revue Biblique 20; Paris: Gabalda, 1982).

*Need for a Process
of Validation*

The failure of the attempt to discover the characteristic language and style of J and E did not really threaten the source hypothesis at the time. It still rested securely on the four remaining pillars. The failure had even brought some valuable gain in its wake with the new insights into the characteristics of deuteronomic–deuteronomistic and priestly literature.

In 1922, Otto Eissfeldt published a synopsis of the sources, as he understood them, extending from Genesis to Judges.[16] What this synopsis revealed above all was Eissfeldt's conception of the process by which the biblical text was compiled. In the synopsis passages were assigned to one source or another with minimal continuity, if any, within the material taken from any one source. The process of compilation as presented by Eissfeldt could only be imagined as that of an author–compiler with four or five scrolls spread out, selecting now a passage from this one, now a passage from another, without any attempt to maintain the character and integrity of any of the scrolls. As one critic remarked at the time, the publication of such a synopsis would undoubtedly sound the death knell of all source criticism; it revealed in full clarity the absurdity of the process. Although Eissfeldt's synopsis was a near disaster for the source hypothesis,[17] it did show the need for a proper understanding of the process of compilation of the sources and how this could function as a validation of the hypothesis. With Eissfeldt's understanding of the process, recovery of the postulated sources is impossible, ruling out an avenue for the verification of its results.

*Valuable Innovation of
Martin Noth's Position*

In 1948 the German original of Martin Noth's *History of Pentateuchal Traditions* was published. This work attracted widespread interest for its traditio-historical analysis of what were regarded as the foundational traditions of Israel's faith. Noth's analysis was a development and revision of Gerhard von Rad's earlier study, *The Form-Critical Problem of the Hexateuch*.[18] Both were, in turn, a development of the form-critical analysis of the Pentateuch developed by Hermann Gunkel and Hugo Gressmann.

Form-critical analysis had sought to recover the original building blocks of Genesis (Gunkel) and Exodus (Gressmann), the early independent units of tradition that had most likely circulated orally in Israel. Current study of Europe's folk tradition had led to an awareness of the importance of this dimension in the development of Israel's traditions. The work of Gunkel and Gressmann also led to the realization that Wellhausen and others had too bookish a view of how the pentateuchal sources were produced. It was likely that the sources emerged gradually within an Israelite tradition that reached back beyond the introduction of writing and the development of scribal schools. Its origins lay in family gatherings around the hearth, in the village of the clan, at the local shrine.

The tasks undertaken by von Rad and Noth were to trace the development of Israelite tradi-

---

16. O. Eissfeldt, *Hexateuch-Synopse: Die Erzählung der fünf Bücher Mose und des Buches Josua mit dem Anfange des Richterbuches in ihre vier Quellen zerlegt und in deutscher Übersetzung darboten samt einer in Einleitung und Anmerkungen gegebenen Begründung* (Leipzig: Hinrichs, 1922; reprint, Darmstadt: Wissenschaftliche Buchgesellschaft, 1963).

17. Cf. the comments on Eissfeldt's synopsis by de Pury and Römer, "Pentateuque en question," 31.
18. This can be found in English in Gerhard von Rad, *The Problem of the Hexateuch and Other Essays* (London: SCM, 1984) 1–78.

tion from these originally independent units to the later written sources and to outline the criteria that guided this development. According to von Rad (in a position that has since been abandoned), it was the ancient "historical credo" in Deut 6:20-25 and 26:5-9 and Josh 24:2-13 that provided the basic expression of Israel's faith and guided its subsequent development. Noth elaborated on the work of von Rad by identifying in these credal statements five theological themes which express the essential tenets of Israel's faith. They did not appear in Israelite tradition all at once but were gradually joined together in a sequence that can still be determined. The two earliest themes were the guidance out of Egypt and the guidance into the arable land. To these were added, in order, the themes of the promises to the ancestors, the guidance in the wilderness, and the revelation at Sinai.

According to Noth, these themes were elaborated by the originally independent stories, songs, and other literary forms that the form-critical work of Gunkel and Gressmann had recovered. The gradual interaction of the themes saw the formation of an extended narrative, which Noth entitled G (*Grundlage*). This narrative told how the God YHWH had delivered Israel from oppression in Egypt, entered into a covenant with Israel, and led it through the wilderness into the land. These great deeds on Israel's behalf were the fulfillment of the ancient promises to the ancestors. From this foundational narrative, the written sources J, E, and P were derived. Von Rad and Noth's understanding of how the sources were produced also led to a new appreciation of the nature of the sources.

Until then, the sources were viewed principally as a quarry for reconstructing the history of Israelite religion and society. For Wellhausen in particular, the correct formulation of the source hypothesis was a prolegomenon to writing the history of Israel. In contrast, von Rad and Noth emphasized that the sources were theological statements, confessions of the faith of Israel at particular stages in its history.[19]

Noth insisted that the elaboration of Israel's foundational traditions did not cease with the production of the written sources. Each source underwent a certain amount of reworking and expansion as the tradition from which it emerged continued to develop. Within this process, which may be likened to one of supplementation, the particular source exercised a controlling influence, and its essential shape was retained. This is indicated by the way a source can be recovered from the present text. For Noth, therefore, a source is a distillation of the tradition at a particular stage of its development. It then accompanies and guides the further development of that tradition. In this way the form-critical and traditio-historical methods were able to offer a plausible explanation for the sort of phenomena that had obliged earlier critics to postulate additional sources or multiple editions of J or E. The effect of this had been to introduce an unwieldy complexity into the hypothesis, making it difficult to envisage a workable process of compilation.

The impact of Noth's analysis of pentateuchal traditions has unfortunately meant that an important innovation he made to the source hypothesis itself has tended to be overlooked.[20] This innovation is found in the introductory

---

19. This dimension of the sources has been further developed in a number of groundbreaking studies by H. W. Wolff. They are available in English in *The Vitality of Old Testament Traditions*, 2d ed., ed. W. Brueggemann and H. W. Wolff (Atlanta: John Knox, 1982).

20. Bernhard Anderson's introduction to his translation of Noth reflects this tendency to overlook the innovation of his work on the sources in favor of the subsequent analysis of traditions. "Noth's analysis of J, E, and P in the Pentateuch is as refined as that of the most orthodox Wellhausen disciple! However for Noth source analysis is only a provisional starting point. He regards the pre-literary period as decisive in the formation of the Israelite tradition" (*Pentateuchal Traditions*, xv–xvi).

forty pages or so of his work, where he outlines his understanding of the hypothesis and supplies a precise identification of the text of each source. Naturally, in brief preliminaries to a major work of traditio-historical study, Noth was not attempting a thoroughly new and independent study of source criticism. What he did was bring to the study of the sources a new insight into the process of their compilation. From his observation of the text, Noth concluded that the compilers at each stage had used one source as a base, retaining it practically in its entirety, while enriching it from other sources.

In Noth's judgment, the Priestly source (P) had been used as the base for the compilation of the Pentateuch; it had been enriched from the already combined Yahwist and Elohist sources (JE).[21] This meant, for Noth, that practically the whole of P was retained intact within the Pentateuch. Most fortunately, the radical difference between P and JE meant that a very substantial part of the JE material could be added to P without difficulty. P may be likened to a necklace strung with pearls. The thread of the necklace is made up of genealogies, itineraries, and a terse story line, with a strong interest in chronology, features that have long been regarded as characteristic of this source. The pearls are the major stories which are set at strategic points along the thread, stories such as creation and flood, the covenant with Abraham and the burial of Sarah, the plagues and passover, the story of the manna in Exodus 16 and the spy story in Numbers 14.

In contrast to JE, which maximizes the use of dramatic storytelling, P has relatively few stories of this type. Hence P could be enriched by stories from JE, with only a minimum of adjustment being required.

In a similar way, the Yahwist narrative had earlier been used as the base for a combination of Yahwist and Elohist sources. In this case, however, the narrative nature of the two sources was similar, and, as a result, the Elohist source was only used when it supplemented J or offered a real alternative to J's material. Relatively little of the Elohist, therefore, is considered to have survived. The paucity of material attributable to the Elohist has led to considerable debate as to whether such a source ever existed. Many would now believe it more likely that the texts identified by Noth and others as E were traditional variants of material in J.[22]

Noth's understanding of the process of compilation brings two new aspects in its train. First is an emphasis on the importance of the story line. Because J and P—particularly P—have been preserved almost intact, it should be possible to follow their story lines through the text. Gaps, then, must be explained. Second is the possibility of testing the hypothesis for validity. If the hypothesis assumes, as Noth's does, that practically the entire text of a source has been preserved, it is possible to test this by examining the continuity of the source, once identified. Where gaps must be postulated in the source, it must be possible to provide a plausible explana-

---

21. "The P narrative which arose in this way later became the *literary basis of the Pentateuchal narrative.* Contrary to the usual view, the 'redactor' responsible for this literary process did *not* understand it to be his task to combine two formerly separate narratives . . . by simply *adding* them to one another so that through a more or less successful interweaving of the particular narrative elements, aided by some harmonizing redactional additions, the two narratives could be taken up into the resulting literary synthesis in their *entirety.* Instead, he made the P narrative the *basis* of his work and *enriched* it by suitably inserting here and there parts of the other narrative. So viewed, his work becomes far clearer and more intelligible" (*Pentateuchal Traditions,* 11–12).

22. The first to doubt that E was one of the four sources were Paul Volz and Wilhelm Rudolph, *Der Elohist als Erzähler: Ein Irrweg der Pentateuchkritik?* (BZAW 63; Giessen: Töpelmann, 1933). See also Wilhelm Rudolph, *Der "Elohist" von Exodus bis Josua* (BZAW 68; Berlin: de Gruyter, 1938). More recently, C. Westermann has argued that an E source cannot be identified in Genesis (*Genesis 12–36* [Minneapolis: Augsburg, 1985] 571–72).

tion why a particular gap should exist. In this book the texts of Noth's P and J have all such gaps clearly marked and explained in the notes.

The Recent Challenges to the Source Hypothesis

The classical form of the source hypothesis has come under challenge recently from a number of quarters. Each challenge has generated lively debate, but so far no new consensus has emerged that could claim to have decisively replaced the classical formulation. For the sake of convenience the various challenges may be gathered into two groups: (1) those that propose more-or-less radical modifications to the classical form of the hypothesis; and (2) those that argue that the source hypothesis should be discarded altogether. One can discern a link between these two groups in that the more radical modifications lead to the dissolution of the sources as they have been traditionally understood. There is also an intriguing link with the past in that the recent challenges recall, in their own way, the earlier debates between source hypothesis, supplementary hypothesis, and fragment hypothesis.

Modifications to the Source Hypothesis

Redefining P as a redaction rather than a source. Frank Moore Cross, in his influential 1973 study, *Canaanite Myth and Hebrew Epic*, advocated this modification within the classical form of the source hypothesis.[23] According to Cross,

there is material in JE that is presumed in P's framework and theology but has no parallel in P, as one would expect if it had been an independent source. He further claims that there is clear evidence that P knew and used JE. The P stage of redaction created framing elements for the JE material and supplemented it by inserting appropriate additions, as well as some discrete documents. Cross's understanding of the process of compilation is thus in complete contrast to Noth's, which envisaged P as the base narrative, enriched by JE. In effect, Cross's is a new form of the supplementary hypothesis. The notion of P as a stage of pentateuchal redaction has subsequently been argued strongly, in particular by those who propose discarding the source hypothesis altogether.

Rejection of an early date for J. In a 1976 monograph, Hans Heinrich Schmid proposed a drastic revision of the current understanding of the Yahwist source.[24] Schmid took Noth's J as his starting point and proceeded to check the literary forms, style, and theology of a number of key passages.[25] He concluded that the texts examined presuppose classical prophecy of the eighth and seventh centuries B.C.E. and that their theology is closest to that of the deuteronomic–deuteronomistic writings. In support of this conclusion, Schmid pointed to the relative silence of classical prophecy on the pentateuchal traditions. According to Schmid, J is not the product of a Solomonic "Enlightenment." Rather, it is a product of the exilic period and bears a close affiliation to deuteronomic-deuteronomistic literature. Schmid's pupil Martin Rose has since

---

23. F. M. Cross, *Canaanite Myth and Hebrew Epic: Essays in the History of the Religion of Israel* (Cambridge: Harvard University Press, 1973) 293–325, esp. 301 ff.). Ivan Engnell of the Scandinavian school had earlier proposed P and D circles of traditionists who collected and edited oral traditions. For Engnell, then, this was a replacement of the source hypothesis, rather than a modification ("The Pentateuch," in idem,

Critical Essays on the Old Testament [London: SPCK, 1970] 50–67).

24. H. H. Schmid, *Der sogenannte Jahwist: Beobachtungen und Fragen zur Pentateuchforschung* (Zurich: Theologischer Verlag, 1976).

25. These passages are Genesis 15; Exodus 3–4; 7–10; 14; 15; 17; 19–24; Numbers 11; 12; 17.

explored the relationship between J and the Deuteronomistic History (DtrH) and claims that J was composed as a prologue to DtrH to include the beginnings of Israel and the story of creation.[26] It never existed as an independent source. In the hands of Rose, therefore, Schmid's revision of an aspect of the source hypothesis ends up with its dissolution.

Around the same time Schmid's monograph appeared, John Van Seters was also advocating a late date for J, but quite independently of Schmid and in a study that was confined to the Abraham traditions in Genesis.[27] Van Seters's proposal is that there were successive stages of growth of the Abraham story, each stage building upon the preceding one. The first stage, termed pre-Yahwistic, was followed by a second Elohistic stage, and this in turn by a third stage which he identifies as the work of "the Yahwist." This Yahwist made additions to the existing material where appropriate and incorporated a number of larger episodic units. The existing material was also rearranged as part of a major transformation of the story of Abraham. From Van Seters's perspective, the Yahwistic stage of growth reveals considerable powers of conceptualization and literary skill. In a manner reminiscent of von Rad, he regards this stage as the most formative one in the growth of the Pentateuch. His understanding of how the Yahwist story of Abraham emerged is, however, quite different from the tradition-history models constructed by von Rad and Noth.

Van Seters's case for a late, exilic date is based on comparative evidence from the ancient Near East and from literary considerations within the Old Testament itself. Van Seters finds that names, customs, and institutions in the ancestral stories have their closest parallels in ancient Near Eastern societies of the first millennium, not the second millennium as had previously been thought. In short, one cannot recover the epoch of Israel's ancestors from the stories of Abraham. The evidence reveals that the portrait of Abraham was in reality an artificial reconstruction by first-millennium Israelites. The most likely period for this would have been the exile, when there was an "archaizing" tendency, a desire to forge links with the distant past. In a more recent and wide-ranging study of ancient historiography, Van Seters holds that the work of the Yahwist resembles that of the Greek historian Herodotus, a factor that lends support to his proposal of a late date for the Yahwist.[28]

According to Van Seters, the literary forms employed in the Yahwistic story of Abraham also point to the exilic period. Even though one may be able to show that the Yahwist used royal, prophetic, or cultic forms from the pre-exilic period, these were reworked to suit the new situation of the exile. He also believes, like Rose, that the Yahwist was composed as a prologue to the Deuteronomistic History. Unlike Rose, however, Van Seters regards the prologue as postdeuteronomistic.[29] He does not appear to share Schmid and Rose's association of the Yahwist with deuteronomic–deuteronomistic language and thought. Despite the difference, Van Seters's attempt to redefine the Yahwist has the same effect as Schmid and Rose's: it leads to the dis-

---

26. M. Rose, *Deuteronomist und Jahwist: Untersuchungen zu den Berührungspunkten beider Literaturwerke* (ATANT 67; Zurich: Theologischer Verlag, 1981).

27. J. Van Seters, *Abraham in History and Tradition* (New Haven: Yale University Press, 1975).

28. J. Van Seters, *In Search of History: Historiography in the Ancient World and the Origins of Biblical History* (New Haven: Yale University Press, 1983).

29. J. Van Seters, "Joshua 24 and the Problem of Tradition in the Old Testament," in *In the Shelter of Elyon: Essays on Ancient Palestinian Life and Literature in Honor of G. W. Ahlström*, ed. W. Boyd Barrick and John R. Spencer (JSOTSup 31; Sheffield: JSOT, 1984) 139–58, esp. 154.

mantling of this component of the source hypothesis. Because it was composed as a prologue to DtrH, the Yahwist never existed as an independent source.

Rejection of the Source Hypothesis

Replacement by a hypothesis of tradition and redaction history. As noted earlier, one of the major exegetical developments of this century has been the possibility of tracing traditions within the biblical text. Pioneers of this development were von Rad and Noth; the resulting discipline is known as *tradition history.* What this recognizes is the handing down within Israel of memories and material with particular associations. It gives insight into the process of vertical transmission of traditions from one generation to another. Von Rad and Noth regarded the pentateuchal sources as a horizontal cross section, in a given generation, of the traditions existing in Israel. Noth in particular believed that tradition history enabled one to gain an appreciation of the relationship between source and tradition. Understandably, once the source emerged, the tradition associated with it did not cease. It continued to grow, and one can detect evidence of this further growth in the way the source was added to and expanded.

It is somewhat ironic, therefore, that Rolf Rendtorff has employed this same discipline to argue that the source hypothesis is no longer tenable.[30] Rendtorff agrees with von Rad and Noth that the analysis of the composition of the Pentateuch should proceed from the smallest identifiable units to the larger complexes of tradition, such as the ancestors (Genesis 12–50) and exodus (Exodus 1–15), and thence to the present text. For von Rad, it was the historical credo

(Deut 6:20-25; 26:5-9; Josh 24:2-13) that guided the development of the tradition and largely determined the shape of the future sources J and E. For Noth, this determinative function was exercised by the five pentateuchal themes of guidance out of Egypt, guidance into the promised land, promises to the ancestors, guidance in the wilderness, and covenant at Sinai. The product of the elaboration of these traditional themes was a foundational pentateuchal narrative, probably in oral form, from which the sources J and E were later derived.

Rendtorff disagrees with the traditio-historical findings of von Rad and Noth. His analysis of the theologically significant promises in the ancestral and exodus narratives leads him to conclude that the earliest literary links between these complexes of tradition are deuteronomic. Against von Rad, this means what a number of scholars had already shown: the historical credo as such was a late deuteronomic creation, not an early confession. Against Noth, it means there was no early foundational narrative that elaborated the pentateuchal themes and forged a relationship between them. Against the source hypothesis itself, it means there was no such thing as a J or E source. The first extensive pentateuchal narrative was the product of a late deuteronomic redaction.

Rendtorff further disagrees with von Rad and Noth about the compatibility of tradition history and source criticism. Source criticism scrutinizes the present text for duplications and repetitions, changes in the divine name, and so on. It then formulates the hypothesis of originally independent sources that were later combined as an explanation of these phenomena. According to Rendtorff, this operation is incompatible with tradition history, which begins not with the

---

30. R. Rendtorff, *The Problem of the Process of Transmission in the Pentateuch* (JSOTSup 89; Sheffield: JSOT, 1990).

present text but with the smallest independent literary units. These are regarded as the building blocks of the larger narrative and probably circulated originally in oral form. The aim of this approach is to trace the development of the tradition from these units to the present text. Von Rad and Noth were therefore using incompatible approaches for their reconstruction of the history of the text.

There is not only this incompatibility of approaches. Rendtorff also believes that von Rad and Noth were caught in a circular argument. Because they were committed to the source hypothesis, the sources were already presupposed. It is hardly surprising, therefore, that they identified the sources as emerging at certain key stages in the development of Israel's traditions. But one can only affirm the existence of sources when they are "discovered" as part of the findings of a traditio-historical analysis. Rendtorff's own traditio-historical analysis did not yield the sources; rather, it concluded the tradition complexes developed independently until the deuteronomic redaction. This was followed by successive redactions—one of which was what source critics called "P"—until the present text of the Pentateuch was produced. In the course of these successive redactions, various other traditional materials found their way into the text. Rendtorff's understanding of how the Pentateuch developed can thus be seen to echo the earlier fragment hypothesis.

It is questionable whether Rendtorff's charge of incompatibility between tradition history and source criticism can be sustained. Both disciplines employ literary-critical analysis, in the older, technical sense of the term. Source critics employ it to detect duplications, variations in style, and other tensions in the text. Tradition historians employ it to recover the earliest stage of a literary form from the text. Moreover, after an originally oral piece has achieved written form, literary-critical analysis is needed to trace its growth toward the present text. Tradition history becomes redaction history. Rendtorff himself employs literary-critical analysis, and his reconstruction of the history of pentateuchal traditions is effectively a history of the redaction of written traditions. He is skeptical about our ability to trace the earlier oral stages of growth with any certainty.

The real weight of Rendtorff's objection would seem to rest, therefore, on the second point, that von Rad and Noth presupposed the sources rather than discovered them in the course of their traditio-historical analysis. Even if this were the case, however, it would not spell the demise of the source hypothesis. As Rendtorff himself noted, one may affirm the existence of sources if they can be shown to emerge as part of an analysis of Israel's traditions, from their earliest identifiable stage to the present text. This is a task that still needs to be done for the whole of the Pentateuch. Rendtorff's own analysis was restricted to the promises to the ancestors. Following Rendtorff, Erhard Blum has published two studies along these lines, one on Genesis 12–50 and the other on selected pentateuchal texts.[31] In agreement with Rendtorff, Blum finds the pentateuchal source hypothesis unsatisfactory.[32]

Replacement by a literary approach to the Bible. A striking phenomenon in contemporary biblical scholarship has been the surge of interest in the Old Testament as literature, accompanied by new insights into the way this literature

---

31. E. Blum, *Die Komposition der Vätergeschichte* (WMANT 57; Neukirchen: Neukirchener Verlag, 1984); and idem, *Studien zur Komposition des Pentateuch* (BZAW 189; Berlin: Walter de Gruyter, 1990).

32. A proposal that is parallel to Rendtorff and Blum in a number of ways but is quite independent comes from T. L. Thompson, *The Origin Tradition of Ancient Israel*, Vol. 1: *The Literary Formation of Genesis*

works.[33] Attention has been drawn to the way repetition and reduplication function as integral parts of Old Testament storytelling to recapitulate key elements of a story at strategic points or to produce a desired literary effect, such as creating tension by momentarily slowing the pace of a story. Because source criticism was rooted in the observation of such repetitions, one outcome of this literary analysis has been to claim that much of the foundation for source criticism was baseless. What had been claimed as repetitive compilation from different sources need be nothing more than the necessary literary repetition required to produce a particular effect.

In one application of these literary insights to the composition of the Pentateuch as a whole, R. N. Whybray suggests new directions for historical or diachronic analysis of the Pentateuch, correcting what he sees as the limitations of the past.[34] Whybray believes that the new insights into Israelite literature have rendered the traditional source hypothesis obsolete. Nevertheless, he recognizes that the complexity of the Pentateuch and the evidence that it incorporates a number of variant traditions cannot be ignored. His solution is to propose a theory of pentateuchal composition modeled on the artistic techniques discerned in individual narratives. Because an Israelite storyteller can use repeti-

tion, contrast, and tension to compose a rich and complex story, it seems entirely possible to envisage one author creating the Pentateuch as a new and original composition from a variety of contrasting documents and traditions.

Even though Whybray is prepared to accept the existence of traditional material, he believes that the compositional and organizational skill of the author was such that it is now difficult to distinguish between a document that was redacted, a tradition that was completely reworked by the author, or a fictional composition. Whybray's proposal is offered at the end of a long review and discussion of pentateuchal criticism, ranging from Wellhausen to Rendtorff. At this stage, it is only the outline for a comprehensive hypothesis.

Notwithstanding the valuable insights that the new literary approach has given biblical scholarship, it is difficult to see that it can account satisfactorily for the major repetitions and reduplications in the Pentateuch which form the base for a source-critical approach. Advocates of a literary approach believe the new insights into the nature and purpose of Israelite literature show that source criticism should not be used to reconstruct the growth of the text. The phenomena to which source criticism appeals have been claimed by the new literary

---

and Exodus 1–23 (JSOTSup 55; Sheffield: JSOT, 1987). In place of the source hypothesis, Thompson proposes four stages of development. Small units grew into larger compound narratives, such as the Jacob–Esau conflict story and the Jacob–Laban story. The third stage saw the incorporation of this material into "traditional complex-chain narratives" centered on Abraham, Jacob, Joseph, and the exodus. In the fourth stage, the complex-chain narratives became parts of a larger structure called the "*Toledoth* structure." Thompson cautiously dates this narrative structure between the end of the seventh and the middle of the sixth century B.C.E. Thompson's sweep is broad and there is little detailed analysis of texts. He rejects source criticism, tradition criticism, and redaction

criticism and claims to offer a novel approach. This is surprising, because his identification of four stages of growth looks very much like a combination of tradition criticism and redaction criticism.

33. An important study that made the new insights available to a wide reading public was R. Alter, *The Art of Biblical Narrative* (New York: Basic Books, 1981). A more detailed and comprehensive theory of how Israelite literature works has since been proposed by M. Sternberg, *The Poetics of Biblical Narrative: Ideological Literature and the Drama of Reading* (Bloomington: Indiana University Press, 1985).

34. R. N. Whybray, *The Making of the Pentateuch: A Methodological Study* (JSOTSup 53; Sheffield: JSOT, 1987).

analysis as characteristic features of this type of literature, not the telltale signs of a process of combination and redaction of sources. In this view, historical analysis and source criticism are a distortion of the nature and function of Israelite literature. This radical shift of emphasis may be characterized as a movement from a diachronic (historical) reading of the text to a synchronic (ahistorical) reading.[35] So far this synchronic approach has focused principally on individual narratives or blocks of narrative. It has yet to produce a comprehensive analysis of the nature and purpose of the Pentateuch. A characteristic feature of synchronic analysis is its attention to the language and style of a text, as well as to the text's structure, that is, how its parts function in relation to the whole.[36]

Many scholars favoring a literary approach see the undoubted skills of the redactors devoted to composing texts with a literary art that tends to conceal and blend their component traditions. Other scholars find that their experience of the biblical text convinces them that the redactors used their skills to blend traditions while leaving them, as far as possible, intact and identifiable. Differences such as singular and plural, first and third person, predominant verb forms, and others perhaps are blended at the point of junction but not harmonized over a total composition (see, for example, the accounts of the flood and the exodus).

Of the skill and dedication of the redactors of the biblical text there can be no doubt. Gone are the days when some perceived unevenness in the text could be thought to be adequately accounted for by its attribution to a redactor. The literary skill of biblical authors and redactors is increasingly acknowledged. What is still open to debate is whether the modern biblical scholar's claimed ability to identify the sources and component elements of a text is due to the ancient biblical redactor's commitment to preserving these sacred traditions in as intact and as identifiable a manner as possible. If this is so, it witnesses to a literary art that—presumably out of respect for tradition—set itself the task of blending what was different while maintaining its distinctiveness.

Reflections

Sources as Hypothesis

Pentateuchal study is in considerable turmoil as a result of the diachronic analyses of Cross, Schmid, Van Seters, and Rendtorff, on the one hand, and the current advocacy of a synchronic analysis of the text, on the other hand.[37] In the midst of such an unstable situation, it may be well to keep the following reflections in mind.

First, the current challenges to the source hypothesis are not a new phenomenon; as the historical review has shown, there have always been competing hypotheses. The principal ones were the fragment hypothesis and the supplementary hypothesis. These have found new life, albeit in different form, in the recent works of

---

35. Synchronic analysis of the Old Testament reflects the influence of currents in secular literary theory; its forerunners include New Criticism and structuralism. Introductory discussion of some of these areas is available in J. Barton, *Reading the Old Testament: Method in Biblical Study* (London: Darton, Longman & Todd, 1984); and Terry Eagleton, *Literary Theory: An Introduction* (Oxford: Basil Blackwell, 1983).

36. Structure as understood here should not be confused with the analysis of deep structures pursued

by French structuralism. In structuralist terminology this process is called "analyse structurale." The analysis of how the parts of a text function in relation to the whole—what structuralists call the "surface structure" of a text—is termed "analyse structurelle."

37. An extensive review of recent pentateuchal research is provided by S. J. De Vries, "A Review of Recent Research in the Tradition History of the Pentateuch," in the SBLSP, ed. K. H. Richards (Atlanta: Scholars Press, 1987) 459–502.

Rendtorff and Cross. The continuing presence of such rival explanations of the composition of the Pentateuch reinforces a point made during the course of the review, namely, the recognition of the nature of a hypothesis and its limitations. A hypothesis is an attempt to bring order to a diversity of phenomena by offering an explanation of their interrelationships. It is limited by one's ability to identify all the relevant phenomena and to provide an adequate explanation for these phenomena. All hypotheses are provisional and remain open to continued testing against alternative proposals.

A second issue arises from the fact that there is variation between versions of the source hypothesis. This has provoked complaints from some critics who have interpreted it as a sign that the hypothesis itself is fundamentally flawed. Such variation shows, however, that the pentateuchal sources are not textual objects that are recovered definitively and for all time. Variation is part of the provisional and limited nature of any hypothesis. There are, of course, limits to the amount of variation that is tolerable. It is likely that the source hypothesis has endured for so long because, despite internal variations, it has been perceived to offer the most satisfactory overall explanation of the literary phenomena.

A third point concerns validation. This is a problem for any hypothesis, but it is particularly acute in the area of pentateuchal analysis. There are no independent witnesses to the beginnings of Israel's literature. A process of validation must therefore be established that works from within the Pentateuch but avoids as far as possible the danger of circular argument. The historical review drew attention to the contribution Noth's proposal makes to meeting this need for validation. Noth proposed that the redactor of the Pentateuch employed P as the base narrative and enriched it from JE. The same procedure had been employed earlier in the production of the JE narrative: J was used as a base and enriched by E. Noth argued that J and P, particularly P, were thereby preserved substantially intact. The proposal permits a process of validation. The hypothesis requires continuity of the particular source's story line, to greater or lesser degree. One should be able to follow the story lines of P and J. Where gaps have to be postulated, the hypothesis requires us to be able to account for these along the lines of Noth's understanding of the process of redactional enrichment. The validity of the hypothesis will, then, depend to a large degree on the substantial continuity of the sources isolated and on the satisfactory explanation of the gaps.

This appeal is admittedly of limited value, because the sources are postulated as part of the hypothesis. From the point of view of validation, Noth's proposal has a distinct advantage over the rival supplementary and fragment hypotheses, whether in their earlier or more recent forms. The supplementary hypothesis envisages one base source, which was then supplemented by discrete additions. If such a hypothesis were presented with an identifiable base narrative that had subsequently been supplemented without deletions occurring, a degree of validation would be possible. So far, to our knowledge, this has not been attempted. Short of this, the deletions occurring in an assumed base narrative have to be explained without the benefit and control of approximately parallel narratives.

The situation is even more difficult for the fragment hypothesis, which rejects the notion of sources altogether. In its contemporary form, in which it has effectively become a redaction hypothesis, the reconstruction of the process of composition tends to turn for validation to evidence from other books of the Old Testament, for example, to the pre-exilic prophets or the Deuteronomistic History. Arguments from silence, issues of interdependence among texts, and the situation of discrete formulations, such as promises, often are notoriously uncertain.[38] In short, the dependence on hypothetical reconstructions is multiplied. Rendtorff is understandably cautious about our ability to recover the history of the composition of the Pentateuch with any certainty. Such caution is prudent, but it does not lessen the need for hypotheses and the issue of their validation.

The final point to be made concerns the direction of future pentateuchal analysis. Here the experience of the past may shed some light. The historical review shows that there have been three major explanations of the composition of the Pentateuch: the hypothesis of parallel independent sources, the hypothesis of discrete fragments or traditions that were combined by a process of redaction, and the hypothesis of one base source that was supplemented by discrete additions. What is striking is that, although they emerged fairly early in the history of modern criticism of the Pentateuch, each explanation has shown surprising resilience. The source hypothesis has been dominant since Wellhausen but, as the review makes clear, the supplementary and fragment hypotheses have reappeared recently in new and vigorous form. Equally striking is the fact that throughout the whole enterprise, no other explanation has emerged as a serious rival for these three hypotheses. This suggests that the future will see further modifications of each hypothesis and renewed debate between them, at least within the context of a diachronic analysis of the text.

Interplay of Diachronic and Synchronic Dimensions

The past few years have seen a move to replace the traditional historical or diachronic analysis of the text with a synchronic or ahistorical analysis. The move is regarded as necessary by those who consider the two approaches irreconcilable. Such a standoff may be due more to the way each approach has been employed and the claims that have been made for each approach than to an inherent incompatibility between them. Each approach begins with the present text and seeks to identify and explain the literary phenomena of the text. It makes good sense, therefore, to allow each approach to interact with the other, to the overall gain in our understanding of the text.

For example, a synchronic reading of the present text can help to clarify which literary phenomena are evidence of the narrative art of the Old Testament and which are potential evidence of the art of redaction in the Old Testament. This evidence can be clarified further by the interaction of diachronic and synchronic analysis. Scholarly understanding of redaction as a highly skilled literary enterprise has been considerably enhanced over the past few decades. It is now recognized that Old Testament scribes were able to function both as redactors of received material and as authors in their own right.[39]

The source hypothesis can also benefit from a fruitful interplay of diachronic and synchronic

---

38. A good example of clarity in matters of textual interdependence, with implications for the prehistory of the pentateuchal text, is Suzanne Boorer, *The Promise of the Land as Oath: A Key to the Formation of the Pentateuch* (BZAW 205; Berlin: Walter de Gruyter, 1992). From the preface: "They [the results] support most closely Wellhausen's conception and also lend some support to aspects of the paradigm initiated by Noth. However, they stand in direct contradiction to Van Seters' position of a post-Deuteronomistic J and to Rendtorff's conception of a redaction layer spanning the Pentateuch that comprises these Dtr land oath texts" (p. IX).

39. On this, see S. Talmon, "The Textual Study of the Bible—A New Outlook," in *Qumran and the History of the Biblical Text*, ed. F. M. Cross and S. Talmon (Cambridge: Harvard University Press, 1975) 332–81.

analysis. Within the understanding of the hypothesis as formulated by von Rad and Noth, a source may be viewed as drawing on traditions that have been handed down across generations (vertical dimension) and giving them expression in this broader context at this particular stage of their development (horizontal dimension). It represents a certain conceptualization and unification of the leading theological ideas of various traditions. Once the text of a source has been identified, its structure and literary and theological characteristics can be further refined by a synchronic analysis. In short, it can then be treated as a "present text" in its own right. This, in turn, will help to validate or invalidate the proposal that such an independent source originally existed.

Implications for Interpretation

Analysis of the composition of the Pentateuch has now been going on for nearly four centuries and is currently being pursued as vigorously as at any stage in the past. The first implication we may find in this is that the mystery of the Pentateuch's composition is unlikely to be unraveled completely by any particular interpretation. That this is the case seems assured by the richness and complexity of the Pentateuch, as well as by our limited knowledge of ancient Israel and its world. Interpretation is an ongoing process, but it is not without purpose or achievement. The process is fueled by the belief that our understanding of the composition of the Pentateuch can be enhanced. There is no simple key that will unlock the mystery, but there can nevertheless be real progress.

The second implication is the importance of formulating hypotheses that can be validated. These are a vital part of the interpretative process; aided by them, the process can make progress and gain real insight into the composition of the text. Without them, presuppositions can arise that control the interpretation of a text, yet remain untested. In conjunction with this, it is necessary to recognize the limitations of a hypothesis, as well as the inevitable subjective dimension introduced by the interpreter. Interpretation is an activity that engages the interpreter, who as involved subject is capable of revealing but also of inadvertently concealing areas of the text's meaning.

The third implication is the need for openness to various ways of approaching the text, especially recognizing the complementary nature of the diachronic and synchronic approaches. A diachronic analysis of the composition of a text inevitably affects how one understands the present text.[40] A diachronic reading may or may not coincide with a synchronic one, but as an interpretation of the present text, the latter must take it into account. By the same token, a diachronic reading must take a synchronic reading into account when it clashes with the diachronic one. By this sort of interaction, the strengths and weaknesses of various interpretations can be seen with more clarity and appropriate conclusions drawn with more certainty.

Finally, we must recognize the need to enter imaginatively into Israel's world. The traditions that formed part of the structural fabric of society were handed on in their various settings. When, for one reason or another, some of these were selected and written down in a literary

---

40. This has been demonstrated forcefully by S. Boorer in "The Importance of a Diachronic Approach: The Case of Genesis-Kings," *CBQ* 51 (1989) 195–208. By taking the theme of the promise of the land in Genesis–Kings as an example, she shows how the different diachronic interpretations by Wellhausen, Noth, Van Seters, and Rendtorff affect their understanding of the present text.

composition, the transmission in the original setting would not have been impeded. A society as culturally rich and diverse as ancient Israel had multiple channels for carrying and propagating traditions. Some traditions appear to have been almost hermetically sealed off from outside influence and interference—one thinks of the language of deuteronomistic and priestly circles. Others may have been open to cross-fertilization from neighboring traditions and neighboring cultures.

At all times, traditions were commented on, combined, expanded, and reshaped to suit new needs or new situations. Evidence in the biblical text strongly suggests that this happened both in the oral transmission and in written texts. It is to be expected that some material could be transmitted orally with almost perfect and unchanging fidelity, for example, genealogies, significant lists, and so on. Anthropological evidence suggests that in other material—stories, for example—each performance was a new telling of the same story, each performance produced a new text, as it were.

In this context, there is a good possibility that some, if not many, of the biblical narrative texts are not the record of the telling of a story but indications of the salient points of plot and interest around which a story might be woven. What appear as variants within the biblical text may be pointers to other ways in which the same story might be told, on another occasion, in another setting.[41]

In all of this there is a vertical dimension, in which the tradition that keeps the past alive is passed on in order to engender life in the future. At the same time, there is a horizontal dimension, in which the traditions from the past are made accessible and effective for the people of the present.

The Present Volume

There can be little doubt that the source hypothesis is at the center of contemporary discussion of the Pentateuch. For those who adhere to the hypothesis, much effort has gone into refining it and responding to challenges from competing hypotheses. For those who advocate an alternative view, as much effort is spent in arguing that it should be modified substantially or dismantled altogether. This volume is a timely contribution to the discussion. Its aim is to provide teachers and students of the Bible with access to the source hypothesis in a manageable form. It also aims to present the source hypothesis in a form that does justice to the preeminent position it has held, and still holds, in biblical studies. The versions of the sources proposed by Noth have been chosen because his work is widely recognized as the most satisfactory overall presentation of the hypothesis that has been made so far.

Chapters 2, 3, and 4 present the Priestly, Yahwist, and Elohist texts in the versions proposed by Noth. Each chapter is prefaced by a short introduction to the particular source. The accompanying annotations are designed to assist the reader with the explanation of source-critical decisions: why words or passages are included or omitted from the source, and what implications this has for the method of analysis and the meaning of the text. Where possible, these explanations are based on comments by

---

41. See A. F. Campbell, "The Reported Story: Midway between Oral Performance and Literary Art," *Semeia* 46 (1989) 77–85.

Noth. The annotations are as brief as clarity permits and, in general, do not enter into debate or exegesis. The gains to be made by working through Noth's version of the hypothesis in this way are considerable. Readers will be able to make their own judgment about the strengths and weaknesses of the hypothesis, at least in Noth's version. They will be better placed to make an overall assessment of the source hypothesis as such. They will have a useful reference for testing the hypothesis against its major competitors, whether these employ a diachronic or synchronic reading of the text.

The nonsource texts—primarily those that were added under deuteronomistic influence or were additions to the combined sources—are listed with brief comments in chapter 5. Chapter 6 offers studies of three composite texts: the flood story in Genesis 6–9, the beginning of the Joseph story in Genesis 37, and the deliverance at the sea in Exodus 13–14. It provides the opportunity to look at the contributions both of the sources and of their combination into a single literary text. After seeing the sources in the separateness of their traditions, it is valuable to look closely at their skillful shaping into a single text.

CHAPTER 2

The Priestly Document

As envisaged by Martin Noth, the Priestly document is quite different from the Yahwist narrative. Rather than a continuous narrative, on the model of J, the Priestly document can be thought of as a necklace, with its major stories as pearls strung on the thread spun of genealogies, itineraries, and a terse story line.

Such pearls are the accounts of creation and flood, the covenant with Abraham and the burial of Sarah, the promise to Jacob at Bethel, the revelation of God to Moses, the plagues, the passover, the deliverance at the sea, and the manna. The story of Sinai occupies a substantial part of P, with its emphasis on God's instructions for the construction of a sanctuary, the construction in compliance with these instructions, the commissioning of the sanctuary, and the organization of Israel around it, ready for the march into the promised land. The final pearls on this narrative necklace deal with Israel's failure to enter the promised land and the replacement of its "first-generation" leadership. They are the stories of spying out the land, getting water from the rock, and the deaths of Aaron and Moses, succeeded by Eleazar and Joshua.[1]

These might not be the primary constituents of the story of Israel's beginnings as we would tell it today. But the Priestly writer was telling it for a specific audience around the time of Israel's exile—either shortly before it, during the exile itself, or shortly after it. Although many details elude us, the main lines of P's thought seem clear: God set the world in motion in the majestic splendor of the creation account, crowned by God's sabbath which, of all the world, only Israel observed. God's purpose will not fail. God set Israel on the march toward the promised land, splendidly and majestically organized around the sanctuary of God's presence to the people. God's purpose will not fail. Individuals may fail and be replaced, as were even Aaron and Moses; God's purpose will not fail.

In between these two great movements—entry into the world and entry into the land—P ponders the unconditional covenants of God with Noah for humankind and with Abraham for Israel. P looks at the story of Israel's experience of God: the genealogies as threads joining key stories of Israel's becoming a people of God; the itineraries as threads joining key stories of Israel's journey from Egypt to Sinai and toward

---

1. For Noth, "the P narrative is not oriented toward an impending occupation of the land" (*A History of Pentateuchal Traditions*, trans. B. W. Anderson [Englewood Cliffs, N.J.: Prentice-Hall, 1972; reprint, Chico, Calif.: Scholars Press, 1981] 9); for discussion of the text, see n. 109 at the end of this chapter.

the promised land. Above all, at Sinai God becomes permanently present to Israel, dwelling in the sanctuary in Israel's midst.

The Israelites of P's time may have felt abandoned by their God; "our bones are dried up, and our hope is lost; we are cut off completely"

(Ezek 37:11). The Priestly document is a powerful affirmation of faith in God's unconditional commitment to Israel which, although delayed by human fragility, will never be deflected from the ultimate goal of God's love.

The Book of Genesis

THE WHOLE WORLD

Creation

1 In the beginning when God created the heavens and the earth, [2]the earth was a formless void and darkness covered the face of the deep, while a wind from God swept over the face of the waters.[2] [3]Then God said, "Let there be light"; and there was light. [4]And God saw that the light was good; and God separated the light from the darkness. [5]God called the light Day, and the darkness he called Night. And there was evening and there was morning, the first day.

6 And God said, "Let there be a dome in the midst of the waters, and let it separate the waters from the waters." [7]So God made the dome and separated the waters that were under the dome from the waters that were above the dome. And it was so. [8]God called the dome Sky. And there was evening and there was morning, the second day.

9 And God said, "Let the waters under the sky be gathered together into one place, and let the dry land appear." And it was so. [10]God called the dry land Earth, and the waters that were gathered together he called Seas. And God saw that it was good. [11]Then God said, "Let the earth put forth vegetation: plants yielding seed, and fruit trees of every kind on earth that bear fruit with the seed in it." And it was so. [12]The earth brought forth vegetation: plants yielding seed of every kind, and trees of every kind bearing fruit with the seed in it. And God saw that it was good. [13]And there was evening and there was morning, the third day.

14 And God said, "Let there be lights in the dome of the sky to separate the day from the night; and let them be for signs and for seasons and for days and years, [15]and let them be lights

---

2. The Priestly document's presentation of creation is a remarkable statement of faith. It is thought that P was composed around the time of Israel's exile: either in the years immediately before, when the exile was threateningly imminent; in the time of exile itself; or shortly after the end of the exile. In all these situations, the stability of Israel's world was under massive threat. In the exile, king, temple, and land were all lost; all that identified Israel as people of God seemed to have gone. Yet in this creation account, P presents a stately and ordered view of creation, the splendidly majestic work of a God of awesome and unthreatened power. Most remarkable, this creation is crowned with

God's observance of sabbath, a sabbath that is special to Israel alone. (The statement in 2:2 and 3 that God "rested" reads with a strong echo of sabbath in the Hebrew, almost as it were "and God 'sabbathed.' ") In the middle of a destructive world, full of threat and fragility, P's creation account affirms faith in a creator God of sovereign power, the rhythm of whose life Israel was privileged to share through the sabbath (see A. F. Campbell, *The Study Companion to Old Testament Literature: An Approach to the Writings of Pre-exilic and Exilic Israel* [A Michael Glazier Book; Old Testament Studies 2; Collegeville, Minn.: Liturgical Press, 1989/ 1992] chap. 2).

in the dome of the sky to give light upon the earth." And it was so. [16]God made the two great lights—the greater light to rule the day and the lesser light to rule the night—and the stars. [17]God set them in the dome of the sky to give light upon the earth, [18]to rule over the day and over the night, and to separate the light from the darkness. And God saw that it was good. [19]And there was evening and there was morning, the fourth day.

20 And God said, "Let the waters bring forth swarms of living creatures, and let birds fly above the earth across the dome of the sky." [21]So God created the great sea monsters and every living creature that moves, of every kind, with which the waters swarm, and every winged bird of every kind. And God saw that it was good. [22]God blessed them, saying, "Be fruitful and multiply and fill the waters in the seas, and let birds multiply on the earth." [23]And there was evening and there was morning, the fifth day.

24 And God said, "Let the earth bring forth living creatures of every kind: cattle and creeping things and wild animals of the earth of every kind." And it was so. [25]God made the wild animals of the earth of every kind, and the cattle of every kind, and everything that creeps upon the ground of every kind. And God saw that it was good.

26 Then God said, "Let us make humankind in our image, according to our likeness; and let them have dominion over the fish of the sea, and over the birds of the air, and over the cattle, and over all the wild animals of the earth, and over every creeping thing that creeps upon the earth."

[27] So God created humankind in his image,

in the image of God he created them;
male and female he created them.
[28]God blessed them, and God said to them, "Be fruitful and multiply, and fill the earth and subdue it; and have dominion over the fish of the sea and over the birds of the air and over every living thing that moves upon the earth." [29]God said, "See, I have given you every plant yielding seed that is upon the face of all the earth, and every tree with seed in its fruit; you shall have them for food. [30]And to every beast of the earth, and to every bird of the air, and to everything that creeps on the earth, everything that has the breath of life, I have given every green plant for food." And it was so. [31]God saw everything that he had made, and indeed, it was very good. And there was evening and there was morning, the sixth day.

2 Thus the heavens and the earth were finished, and all their multitude. [2]And on the seventh day God finished the work that he had done, and he rested on the seventh day from all the work that he had done. [3]So God blessed the seventh day and hallowed it, because on it God rested from all the work that he had done in creation.

4a These are the generations of the heavens and the earth when they were created.[3]

Genealogy: Adam to Noah

5 •This is the list of the descendants of Adam.•[4] When God created humankind, he made them in the likeness of God. [2]Male and female he created them, and he blessed them and named them "Humankind" when they were created.

---

3. These comments about the "generations" (the "toledoth") usually precede their material like a headline. In this case, the headline follows the creation account, perhaps so as not to interfere with its magnificent opening verse.

4. The bullet is used in this text of the Priestly document to indicate the parts of the "Toledoth book"

that were incorporated into the source by P. Before a paragraph, it denotes the whole paragraph; within a paragraph, it is put before and after the relevant text. The term "Toledoth book" refers to what is believed to have been a collection of genealogies that was available to P and provided a useful framework to the early part of P's document.

• 3 When Adam had lived one hundred thirty years, he became the father of a son in his likeness, according to his image,[5] and named him Seth. [4]The days of Adam after he became the father of Seth were eight hundred years; and he had other sons and daughters. [5]Thus all the days that Adam lived were nine hundred thirty years; and he died.
• 6 When Seth had lived one hundred five years, he became the father of Enosh. [7]Seth lived after the birth of Enosh eight hundred seven years, and had other sons and daughters. [8]Thus all the days of Seth were nine hundred twelve years; and he died.
• 9 When Enosh had lived ninety years, he became the father of Kenan. [10]Enosh lived after the birth of Kenan eight hundred fifteen years, and had other sons and daughters. [11]Thus all the days of Enosh were nine hundred five years; and he died.
• 12 When Kenan had lived seventy years, he became the father of Mahalalel. [13]Kenan lived after the birth of Mahalalel eight hundred and forty years, and had other sons and daughters. [14]Thus all the days of Kenan were nine hundred and ten years; and he died.
• 15 When Mahalalel had lived sixty-five years, he became the father of Jared. [16]Mahalalel lived after the birth of Jared eight hundred thirty years, and had other sons and daughters. [17]Thus all the days of Mahalalel were eight hundred ninety-five years; and he died.

• 18 When Jared had lived one hundred sixty-two years he became the father of Enoch. [19]Jared lived after the birth of Enoch eight hundred years, and had other sons and daughters. [20]Thus all the days of Jared were nine hundred sixty-two years; and he died.
• 21 When Enoch had lived sixty-five years, he became the father of Methuselah. [22]Enoch walked with God after the birth of Methuselah three hundred years, and had other sons and daughters. [23]Thus all the days of Enoch were three hundred sixty-five years. [24]Enoch walked with God; then he was no more, because God took him.
• 25 When Methuselah had lived one hundred eighty-seven years, he became the father of Lamech. [26]Methuselah lived after the birth of Lamech seven hundred eighty-two years, and had other sons and daughters. [27]Thus all the days of Methuselah were nine hundred sixty-nine years; and he died.
• 28 When Lamech had lived one hundred eighty-two years, he became the father of a son;
• • •[6] [30]Lamech lived after the birth of Noah five hundred ninety-five years, and had other sons and daughters. [31]Thus all the days of Lamech were seven hundred seventy-seven years; and he died.
• 32 After Noah was five hundred years old, Noah became the father of Shem, Ham, and Japheth.[7]

---

5. Noth comments that Gen 5:1b-2 and this little addition in 5:3—"in his own likeness, after his image"—enable P to tie what follows to the account of creation.

6. Gen 5:29 is attributed to J. It is different in pattern from the rest of the genealogy, uses YHWH, and has associations with the J narrative. The insertion of this verse required modification of the pattern of the P genealogy, replacing the proper name "Noah" (now given in v. 29) with the common noun "a son"; so the original of v. 28 is assumed to have ended, "he became the father of Noah." Westermann retains v. 28 and the beginning of v. 29, as far as "Noah" (C. Westermann, *Genesis 1–11* [Minneapolis: Augsburg,

1984] 347). Such omissions in the P text are indicated by three ellipsis points, as here. They are given in Noth's enumeration of the P text, where he considers there is a break in its continuity.

7. In the early part of the P text, the genealogies play an important role as the continuous thread on which the major narratives are located; so here, this genealogy moves the action from creation to the flood, from Adam to Noah. The stories of the beginnings of human life (Adam and Eve, Cain and Abel, Lamech) are passed over; instead, the narrative is brought by the genealogy from the newness of the first creation to what is almost "decreation" in the flood and then the repeopling of a world that is now less than perfect.

Flood

6:9 These are the descendants of Noah. Noah was a righteous man, blameless in his generation; Noah walked with God.[8] [10]And Noah had three sons, Shem, Ham, and Japheth.

11 Now the earth was corrupt in God's sight, and the earth was filled with violence.[9] [12]And God saw that the earth was corrupt; for all flesh had corrupted its ways upon the earth. [13]And God said to Noah, "I have determined to make an end of all flesh, for the earth is filled with violence because of them; now I am going to destroy them along with the earth. [14]Make yourself an ark of cypress wood; make rooms in the ark, and cover it inside and out with pitch. [15]This is how you are to make it: the length of the ark three hundred cubits, its width fifty cubits, and its height thirty cubits. [16]Make a roof for the ark, and finish it to a cubit above; and put the door of the ark in its side; make it with lower, second, and third decks. [17]For my part, I am going to bring a flood of waters on the earth, to destroy from under heaven all flesh in which is the breath of life; everything that is on the earth shall die. [18]But I will establish my covenant with you; and you shall come into the ark, you, your sons, your wife, and your sons' wives with you. [19]And of every living thing, of all flesh, you shall bring two of every kind into the ark, to keep them alive with you; they shall be male and female. [20]Of the birds according to their kinds, and of the animals according to their kinds, of every creeping thing of the ground according to its kind, two of every kind shall come in to you, to keep them alive. [21]Also take with you every kind of food that is eaten, and store it up; and it shall serve as food for you and for them." [22]Noah did this; he did all that God commanded him.

7:6 Noah was six hundred years old when the flood of waters came on the earth.

11 In the six hundredth year of Noah's life, in the second month, on the seventeenth day of the month, on that day all the fountains of the great deep burst forth, and the windows of the heavens were opened.

13 On the very same day Noah with his sons, Shem and Ham and Japheth, and Noah's wife and the three wives of his sons entered the ark, [14]they and every wild animal of every kind, and all domestic animals of every kind, and every creeping thing that creeps on the earth, and every bird of every kind—every bird, every winged creature. [15]They went into the ark with Noah, two and two of all flesh in which there was the breath of life. [16a]And those that entered,

---

8. It is worth observing that, in both P (6:9) and J (7:1), Noah's righteousness is emphasized at the start of the account, in relation to the deliverance. At the end, however, in relation to God's unconditional commitment to humankind, there is no mention of righteousness—rather the opposite. See the discussion in chap. 6.

9. P's account of the flood differs from J's in several notable ways. (1) P has no mention of any distinction between clean and unclean animals; this was not revealed until much later, in the cleanliness laws given to Moses on Sinai (see Leviticus 11). For P, one pair from each species is preserved, instead of the seven pairs of clean and one pair of unclean animals in J; food is taken into the ark (Gen 6:21); and there is no final sacrifice.

(2) P's picture of the flood is basically one of decreation. The waters that were put apart to create living space in the creation account (Gen 1:6-8) surge back from above and below to blot out all life that was created (see 7:11 and 8:2a). In J, by contrast, the flood is a massive rainstorm, lasting forty days and forty nights.

(3) P's flood lasts for a year and ten days, from the 17th day of the 2d month of Noah's 600th year to the 27th day of the 2d month of Noah's 601st year (see Gen 7:11 and 8:14). It is structured around a basic period which is one hundred fifty days, rather than forty days. The significance of the symbolism in these figures escapes us now. We can still see, however, that for P the new epoch of the-world-after-the-flood began on New Year's Day of the first year of Noah's seventh century (see Gen 8:13a).

It is easy to hear the echoes of the language and interests of Gen 1:1—2:4a throughout this account.

male and female of all flesh, went in as God had commanded him.[10]

18 The waters swelled and increased greatly on the earth; and the ark floated on the face of the waters. [19]The waters swelled so mightily on the earth that all the high mountains under the whole heaven were covered; [20]the waters swelled above the mountains, covering them fifteen cubits deep. [21]And all flesh died that moved on the earth, birds, domestic animals, wild animals, all swarming creatures that swarm on the earth, and all human beings. [24]And the waters swelled on the earth for one hundred fifty days.

8 But God remembered Noah and all the wild animals and all the domestic animals that were with him in the ark. And God made a wind blow over the earth, and the waters subsided; [2a]the fountains of the deep and the windows of the heavens were closed. [3b]At the end of one hundred fifty days the waters had abated; [4]and in the seventh month, on the seventeenth day of the month, the ark came to rest on the mountains of Ararat. [5]The waters continued to abate until the tenth month; in the tenth month, on the first day of the month, the tops of the mountains appeared.

7 And he [Heb.; NRSV has no pronoun][11] sent out the raven; and it went to and fro until the waters were dried up from the earth.

13a In the six hundred first year, in the first month, the first day of the month, the waters were dried up from the earth.[12] [14]In the second month, on the twenty-seventh day of the month, the earth was dry. [15]Then God said to Noah, [16]"Go out of the ark, you and your wife, and your sons and your sons' wives with you. [17]Bring out with you every living thing that is with you of all flesh—birds and animals and every creeping thing that creeps on the earth—so that they may abound on the earth, and be fruitful and multiply on the earth." [18]So Noah went out with his sons and his wife and his sons' wives. [19]And every animal, every creeping thing, and every bird, everything that moves on the earth, went out of the ark by families.

9 God blessed Noah and his sons, and said to them, "Be fruitful and multiply, and fill the earth.[13] [2]The fear and dread of you shall rest on every animal of the earth, and on every bird of the air, on everything that creeps on the ground, and on all the fish of the sea; into your hand they are delivered. [3]Every moving thing that lives shall be food for you; and just as I gave you the green plants, I give you everything. [4]Only, you shall not eat flesh with its life, that is, its blood. [5]For your own lifeblood I will surely require a reckoning: from every animal I will require it and from human beings, each one for

---

10. In contrast to Noth, K. Elliger, N. Lohfink, and Westermann give Gen 7:17a to P. For Westermann, it is modeled on 7:6a, and the "forty days" are an addition from J; so the original would have read, literally, "And the flood came upon the earth" (*Genesis 1–11*, 437–38). In Westermann's J text, 7:12 is followed directly by 7:17b. These are minor variations in the distribution of the text. See Noth's treatment of J (chap. 3, below).

11. Whenever the NRSV translation is given in brackets, as here, its replacement renders the Hebrew neutrally; in such cases, the NRSV reflects the Hebrew in its final context. In this case, the NRSV has no pronoun, allowing the verb to depend on Noah in the non-P v. 6 of the present or final text. The Hebrew pronoun is included in the verb form; in P, originally,

Noah would probably have been explicitly mentioned here.

12. The flood is the dividing point between an old world, which is not ours, and the changed world now emerging, which is ours. The beginning of this new epoch is traced to New Year's Day of the first year of the seventh century of Noah's life.

13. The echo of the blessing of Gen 1:28 is unmistakable, but it is interrupted here to introduce fear and dread, violence and killing (vv. 2-6). The blessing is resumed in Gen 9:7. It is a strong theological statement that this picture of a diminished and less-than-perfect world is followed by the covenantal affirmation of God's unconditional commitment to humankind and every living creature. It has its parallel, quite differently formulated, in J's Gen 8:20-22.

the blood of another, I will require a reckoning for human life.

⁶ Whoever sheds the blood of a human,
   by a human shall that person's blood be shed;
   for in his own image
      God made humankind.

⁷And you, be fruitful and multiply, abound on the earth and multiply in it."

8 Then God said to Noah and to his sons with him, ⁹"As for me, I am establishing my covenant with you and your descendants after you, ¹⁰and with every living creature that is with you, the birds, the domestic animals, and every animal of the earth with you, as many as came out of the ark. ¹¹I establish my covenant with you, that never again shall all flesh be cut off by the waters of a flood, and never again shall there be a flood to destroy the earth." ¹²God said, "This is the sign of the covenant that I make between me and you and every living creature that is with you, for all future generations: ¹³I have set my bow in the clouds, and it shall be a sign of the covenant between me and the earth. ¹⁴When I bring clouds over the earth and the bow is seen in the clouds, ¹⁵I will remember my covenant that is between me and you and every living creature of all flesh; and the waters shall never again become a flood to destroy all flesh. ¹⁶When the bow is in the clouds, I will see it and remember the everlasting covenant between God and every living creature of all flesh that is on the earth." ¹⁷God said to Noah, "This is the sign of the covenant that I have established between me and all flesh that is on the earth."

• 28 After the flood Noah lived three hundred fifty years. ²⁹All the days of Noah were nine hundred fifty years; and he died.[14]

Genealogy: Noah to Abram

10 •These are the descendants of Noah's sons, Shem, Ham, and Japheth;• children were born to them after the flood.

• 2 The descendants of Japheth: Gomer, Magog, Madai, Javan, Tubal, Meshech, and Tiras. ³The descendants of Gomer: Ashkenaz, Riphath, and Togarmah. ⁴The descendants of Javan: Elishah, Tarshish, Kittim, and Rodanim. ⁵From these the coastland peoples spread. These are the descendants of Japheth in their lands, with their own language, by their families, in their nations.

• 6 The descendants of Ham: Cush, Egypt, Put, and Canaan. ⁷The descendants of Cush: Seba, Havilah, Sabtah, Raamah, and Sabteca. The descendants of Raamah: Sheba and Dedan. ²⁰These are the descendants of Ham, by their families, their languages, their lands, and their nations.

• 22 The descendants of Shem: Elam, Asshur, Arpachshad, Lud, and Aram. ²³The descendants of Aram: Uz, Hul, Gether, and Mash. ³¹These are the descendants of Shem, by their families, their languages, their lands, and their nations.

32 •These are the families of Noah's sons, according to their genealogies, in their nations;• and from these the nations spread abroad on the earth after the flood.

• **11:10** These are the descendants of Shem. When Shem was one hundred years old, he became the father of Arpachshad two years after the flood; ¹¹and Shem lived after the birth of Arpachshad five hundred years, and had other sons and daughters.

• 12 When Arpachshad had lived thirty-five years, he became the father of Shelah; ¹³and

---

14. Noth comments that Gen 9:28-29 is the continuation of the Toledoth book from 5:32, displaced because of the flood account.

Arpachshad lived after the birth of Shelah four hundred three years, and had other sons and daughters.

• 14 When Shelah had lived thirty years, he became the father of Eber; [15]and Shelah lived after the birth of Eber four hundred three years, and had other sons and daughters.

• 16 When Eber had lived thirty-four years, he became the father of Peleg; [17]and Eber lived after the birth of Peleg four hundred thirty years, and had other sons and daughters.

• 18 When Peleg had lived thirty years, he became the father of Reu; [19]and Peleg lived after the birth of Reu two hundred nine years, and had other sons and daughters.

• 20 When Reu had lived thirty-two years, he became the father of Serug; [21]and Reu lived after the birth of Serug two hundred seven years, and had other sons and daughters.

• 22 When Serug had lived thirty years, he became the father of Nahor; [23]and Serug lived after the birth of Nahor two hundred years, and had other sons and daughters.

• 24 When Nahor had lived twenty-nine years, he became the father of Terah; [25]and Nahor lived after the birth of Terah one hundred nineteen years, and had other sons and daughters.

• 26 When Terah had lived seventy years, he became the father of Abram, Nahor, and Haran.[15]

THE ANCESTORS OF ISRAEL

Abraham and Sarah

11:27 Now these are the descendants of Terah. Terah was the father of Abram, Nahor, and Haran; and Haran was the father of Lot.

31 Terah took his son Abram and his grandson Lot son of Haran, and his daughter-in-law Sarai, his son Abram's wife, and they went out together from Ur of the Chaldeans to go into the land of Canaan; but when they came to Haran, they settled there. [32]The days of Terah were two hundred five years; and Terah died in Haran.

12:4b Abram was seventy-five years old when he departed from Haran.[16] [5]Abram took his wife Sarai and his brother's son Lot, and all the possessions that they had gathered, and the persons whom they had acquired in Haran; and they set forth to go to the land of Canaan. And they came [Heb.; NRSV, When they had come] to the land of Canaan.[17]

13:6 And [Heb.; NRSV, so that] the land could not support both of them living together; for their possessions were so great that they could not live together. [11b]So [Heb.; NRSV, thus] they

---

15. This genealogy, spanning Genesis 10 and 11, not only brings us from Noah to Abraham but also peoples the earth, spreading humankind over the face of the known world (10:5, 20, 31, and 32) before focusing on the direct line from Shem to Abraham (11:10 ff.).

16. The accounts of creation and flood have been two pearls on the thread of P's narrative necklace. The next pearl for P is to be the account of the covenant with Abraham. The story line moves economically toward that covenant. It is different from J's narrative. It is assumed that P and P's audience knew the J stories and much of the rest of Israel's traditions. For the

purposes of the P document here, these stories were not of central importance; God's covenant with Abraham was.

17. This is a clear case where context affects translation. The Hebrew conjunction (wĕ) can mean and, but, if, when, since, though, therefore, then, so, or, etc., depending on its context. Here, if the end of Gen 12:5 is read as introducing what follows, it can be translated "when," as in the NRSV. If it is read as concluding a paragraph, it should be translated "and," as here. For "the delicate touch of the redactor," see C. Westermann, *Genesis 12–36* (Minneapolis: Augsburg, 1985) 153.

separated from each other. [12*]Abram settled in the land of Canaan, while Lot settled among the cities of the Plain.

19:29 And it happened [Heb.; NRSV, So it was] that, when God destroyed the cities of the Plain, God remembered Abraham, and sent Lot out of the midst of the overthrow, when he overthrew the cities in which Lot had settled.[18]

16:1a And [Heb.; NRSV, Now] Sarai, Abram's wife, bore him no children. [3]So, after Abram had lived ten years in the land of Canaan, Sarai, Abram's wife, took Hagar the Egyptian, her slave-girl, and gave her to her husband Abram as a wife. [15]Hagar bore Abram a son; and Abram named his son, whom Hagar bore, Ishmael. [16]Abram was eighty-six years old when Hagar bore him Ishmael.

God's Covenant with Abram

17 When Abram was ninety-nine years old, the LORD appeared to Abram, and said to him, "I am God Almighty; walk before me, and be blameless.[19] [2]And I will make my covenant between me and you, and will make you exceedingly numerous." [3]Then Abram fell on his face; and God said to him, [4]"As for me, this is my covenant with you: You shall be the ancestor of a multitude of nations. [5]No longer shall your name be Abram, but your name shall be Abraham; for I have made you the ancestor of a multitude of nations. [6]I will make you exceedingly fruitful; and I will make nations of you, and kings shall come from you. [7]I will establish my covenant between me and you, and your offspring after you throughout their generations, for an everlasting covenant, to be God to you and to your offspring after you. [8]And I will give to you, and to your offspring after you, the land where you are now an alien, all the land of Canaan, for a perpetual holding; and I will be their God."[20]

9 God said to Abraham, "As for you, you shall keep my covenant, you and your offspring after you throughout their generations. [10]This is my covenant, which you shall keep, between me and you and your offspring after you: Every male among you shall be circumcised. [11]You shall circumcise the flesh of your foreskins, and it shall be a sign of the covenant between me and you. [12]Throughout your generations every male among you shall be circumcised when he is eight days old, including the slave born in your house and the one bought with your money from any

---

18. For Noth, it is evident that within the original P source the verse that is now 19:29 belonged with 13:6, 11b, and 12abα. With the combination of the sources, it had to be placed after 18:1—19:28 (*Pentateuchal Traditions*, 13). It is P's notice of the destruction of the cities and the rescue of Lot (cf. Westermann, *Genesis 12–36*, 299, 308).

19. Westermann's comment on this verse is helpful: "P is passing on an ancient patriarchal promise that has come down in which the name of God was given as Yahweh. In the very next sentence, where God introduces himself, he does so by another name; P is thereby putting into perspective the name Yahweh, which has already been in use. At the same time he is indicating the gap between God's revelation to the patriarchs and that made to Israel at the exodus from Egypt" (*Genesis 12–36*, 257; see n. 38, below). The ancient promise is that of posterity, in Gen 17:2.

20. The nature of this covenant is extremely important; it is one of the major pillars of the P document. The covenant is everlasting, promising therefore unending descendants and an everlasting possession of the land. The central element of the covenant is "to be God to you and to your offspring after you" (Gen 17:7). The clause "walk before me, and be blameless" (v. 1b) is understood as a general exhortation rather than a condition of the covenant (cf. Westermann, *Genesis 12–36*, 255–60). In this text, covenant is not divorced from conduct; neither is it conditional on it. Similarly, circumcision is a sign rather than a condition of the covenant. A male who does not bear the sign is outside the covenant community, but this does not affect the unconditional quality of the covenant with Israel. For anxious exiles, wondering whether ultimately they had been abandoned by their God, this affirmation of the unconditional nature of God's commitment to them can only have been heard as a faith statement of utmost importance.

foreigner who is not of your offspring. [13]Both the slave born in your house and the one bought with your money must be circumcised. So shall my covenant be in your flesh an everlasting covenant. [14]Any uncircumcised male who is not circumcised in the flesh of his foreskin shall be cut off from his people; he has broken my covenant."

15 God said to Abraham, "As for Sarai your wife, you shall not call her Sarai, but Sarah shall be her name. [16]I will bless her, and moreover I will give you a son by her. I will bless her, and she shall give rise to nations; kings of peoples shall come from her." [17]Then Abraham fell on his face and laughed, and said to himself, "Can a child be born to a man who is a hundred years old? Can Sarah, who is ninety years old, bear a child?" [18]And Abraham said to God, "O that Ishmael might live in your sight!" [19]God said, "No, but your wife Sarah shall bear you a son, and you shall name him Isaac. I will establish my covenant with him as an everlasting covenant for his offspring after him. [20]As for Ishmael, I have heard you; I will bless him and make him fruitful and exceedingly numerous; he shall be the father of twelve princes, and I will make him a great nation. [21]But my covenant I will establish with Isaac, whom Sarah shall bear to you at this season next year." [22]And when he had finished talking with him, God went up from Abraham.

23 Then Abraham took his son Ishmael and all the slaves born in his house or bought with his money, every male among the men of Abraham's house, and he circumcised the flesh of their foreskins that very day, as God had said to him. [24]Abraham was ninety-nine years old when he was circumcised in the flesh of his foreskin. [25]And his son Ishmael was thirteen years old when he was circumcised in the flesh of his fore-skin. [26]That very day Abraham and his son Ishmael were circumcised; [27]and all the men of his house, slaves born in the house and those bought with money from a foreigner, were circumcised with him.

Birth of Isaac

21:1b And the LORD did for Sarah as he had promised.[21] [2]Sarah conceived and bore Abraham a son in his old age, at the time of which God had spoken to him. [3]Abraham gave the name Isaac to his son whom Sarah bore him. [4]And Abraham circumcised his son Isaac when he was eight days old, as God had commanded him. [5]Abraham was a hundred years old when his son Isaac was born to him.

Abraham's Acquisition of Land: Burial of Sarah

23 Sarah lived one hundred twenty-seven years; this was the length of Sarah's life. [2]And Sarah died at Kiriath-arba (that is, Hebron) in the land of Canaan; and Abraham went in to mourn for Sarah and to weep for her. [3]Abraham rose up from beside his dead, and said to the Hittites, [4]"I am a stranger and an alien residing among you; give me property among you for a burying place, so that I may bury my dead out of my sight." [5]The Hittites answered Abraham, [6]"Hear us, my lord; you are a mighty prince among us. Bury your dead in the choicest of our burial places; none of us will withhold from you any burial ground for burying your dead." [7]Abraham rose and bowed to the Hittites, the people of the land. [8]He said to them, "If you are willing that I should bury my dead out of my sight, hear me, and entreat for me Ephron son of Zohar, [9]so that he may give me the cave of Machpelah, which he owns; it is at the end of his field. For the full price let him give it to me in

---

21. The occurrence of LORD here is explained by Noth as the influence of YHWH in Gen 21:1a, when vv. 1b-5 were inserted here (see *Pentateuchal Traditions*, 17 n.47 and 28 n.88).

your presence as a possession for a burying place." [10]Now Ephron was sitting among the Hittites; and Ephron the Hittite answered Abraham in the hearing of the Hittites, of all who went in at the gate of his city, [11]"No, my lord, hear me; I give you the field, and I give you the cave that is in it; in the presence of my people I give it to you; bury your dead." [12]Then Abraham bowed down before the people of the land. [13]He said to Ephron in the hearing of the people of the land, "If you only will listen to me! I will give the price of the field; accept it from me, so that I may bury my dead there." [14]Ephron answered Abraham, [15]"My lord, listen to me; a piece of land worth four hundred shekels of silver—what is that between you and me? Bury your dead." [16]Abraham agreed with Ephron; and Abraham weighed out for Ephron the silver that he had named in the hearing of the Hittites, four hundred shekels of silver, according to the weights current among the merchants.

17 So the field of Ephron in Machpelah, which was to the east of Mamre, the field with the cave that was in it and all the trees that were in the field, throughout its whole area, passed [18]to Abraham as a possession in the presence of the Hittites, in the presence of all who went in at the gate of his city. [19]After this, Abraham buried Sarah his wife in the cave of the field of Machpelah facing Mamre (that is, Hebron) in the land of Canaan. [20]The field and the cave that is in it passed from the Hittites into Abraham's possession as a burying place.[22]

Death of Abraham

25:7 This is the length of Abraham's life, one hundred seventy-five years. [8]Abraham breathed his last and died in a good old age, an old man and full of years, and was gathered to his people. [9]His sons Isaac and Ishmael buried him in the cave of Machpelah, in the field of Ephron son of Zohar the Hittite, east of Mamre, [10]the field that Abraham purchased from the Hittites. There Abraham was buried, with his wife Sarah. [11a]After the death of Abraham God blessed his son Isaac.

Genealogy: Descendants of Ishmael

• 12 These are the descendants of Ishmael, Abraham's son, whom Hagar the Egyptian, Sarah's slave-girl, bore to Abraham. [13]These are the names of the sons of Ishmael, named in the order of their birth: Nebaioth, the firstborn of Ishmael; and Kedar, Adbeel, Mibsam, [14]Mishma, Dumah, Massa, [15]Hadad, Tema, Jetur, Naphish, and Kedemah. [16]These are the sons of Ishmael and these are their names, by their villages and by their encampments, twelve princes according to their tribes. [17](This is the length of the life of Ishmael, one hundred thirty-seven years; he breathed his last and died, and was gathered to his people.)[23]

Isaac and Rebekah

• 19 These are the descendants of Isaac, Abraham's son: Abraham was the father of

---

22. This issue has to be seen as important in P for it to have been treated at such length. Perhaps it is the beginning of a claim on the land, which will accumulate with each burial (see W. Brueggemann, *Genesis* [Interpretation; Atlanta: John Knox, 1982] 195–97). For Westermann, the importance is its place in the series of stories dealing with the three fundamental moments of family life, which are treated expansively in Genesis 17, 23, and 28: birth (chap. 17), marriage

(chap. 28), and, here, burial (*Genesis 12–36*, 376). If this is correct, the final redactor used P's text in chap. 28 only for the introduction to the marriage story.

23. Just as the P genealogy in Genesis 10 situated the descendants of Shem within a wider world, so here the descendants of Abraham and Sarah are located within a larger extended family. A similar concern for Jacob's descendants will appear in Genesis 36.

Isaac, [20]and Isaac was forty years old when he married Rebekah, daughter of Bethuel the Aramean of Paddan-aram, sister of Laban the Aramean.

• • •[24]

   • 26b Isaac was sixty years old when she bore them.[25]

26:34 When Esau was forty years old, he married Judith daughter of Beeri the Hittite, and Basemath daughter of Elon the Hittite; [35]and they made life bitter for Isaac and Rebekah.

27:46 Then Rebekah said to Isaac, "I am weary of my life because of the Hittite women. If Jacob marries one of the Hittite women such as these, one of the women of the land, what good will my life be to me?"

28 Then Isaac called Jacob and blessed him, and charged him, "You shall not marry one of the Canaanite women. [2]Go at once to Paddan-aram to the house of Bethuel, your mother's father; and take as wife from there one of the daughters of Laban, your mother's brother. [3]May God Almighty bless you and make you fruitful and numerous, that you may become a company of peoples. [4]May he give to you the blessing of Abraham, to you and to your offspring with you, so that you may take possession of the land where you now live as an alien—land that God gave to Abraham." [5]Thus Isaac sent Jacob away; and he went to Paddan-aram, to Laban son of Bethuel the Aramean, the brother of Rebekah, Jacob's and Esau's mother.

[6] Now Esau saw that Isaac had blessed Jacob and sent him away to Paddan-aram to take a wife from there, and that as he blessed him he charged him, "You shall not marry one of the Canaanite women," [7]and that Jacob had obeyed his father and his mother and gone to Paddan-aram. [8]So when Esau saw that the Canaanite women did not please his father Isaac, [9]Esau went to Ishmael and took Mahalath daughter of Abraham's son Ishmael, and sister of Nebaioth, to be his wife in addition to the wives he had.

Jacob and Esau

• • •[26]

   31:18* all the property that he had gained, the livestock in his possession that he had acquired in Paddan-aram, to go to his father Isaac in the land of Canaan.[27]

---

24. This is the first of three places in Genesis where Noth assumes that P's continuity has not been maintained in the process of final compilation; in each case, the more colorful J text is understood to have replaced a plainer P text. Here Gen 25:21-26a replaces P's note of the birth of Esau and Jacob; that originally there was such a note in P is indicated by the phrase "when she bore them," attached to P's chronological note.

25. Gen 25:26b is either a remnant of the P source or a priestly gloss in the combined text. The concern for precise ages and dates is typical of P; see Gen 25:20.

26. This is the second of three places in Genesis where Noth assumes that P's continuity has not been maintained in the process of final compilation; the more colorful J text is understood to have replaced a plainer P text. Here Gen 29:15-30 replaces P's account of Jacob's marriages (cf. Gen 35:22b-26). Precisely why 31:18* and 33:18a should have been the only remnants of this P material retained or why they were inserted into the J text as glosses is not immediately obvious.

27. Gen 31:18* is either a remnant of the P source or a priestly gloss in the combined text. Elements of what is classically recognized as P language are: property that he had gained (## 17-18); in his possession (#27); Paddan-aram (#48); these reference numbers are to the list of characteristic P expressions in S. R. Driver, *An Introduction to the Literature of the Old Testament* (Edinburgh: T. & T. Clark, 1891; 9th ed., 1913; reprint, New York: Meridian, 1956) 130–35. While such lists have lost much of their worth as broadly applicable criteria for identifying other sources, the combination of language and concern are still valid clues to the presence of either deuteronomistic or priestly traditions in specific situations.

33:18a Jacob came safely to the city of Shechem, which is in the land of Canaan, on his way from Paddan-aram.[28]

35:6 Jacob came to Luz (that is, Bethel), which is in the land of Canaan, he and all the people who were with him.

9 God appeared to Jacob again when he came from Paddan-aram, and he blessed him. [10]God said to him, "Your name is Jacob; no longer shall you be called Jacob, but Israel shall be your name." So he was called Israel. [11]God said to him, "I am God Almighty: be fruitful and multiply; a nation and a company of nations shall come from you, and kings shall spring from you. [12]The land that I gave to Abraham and Isaac I will give to you, and I will give the land to your offspring after you." [13a]Then God went up from him. [15]And [Heb.; NRSV, So] Jacob called the place where God had spoken with him Bethel.

Genealogy: Twelve Sons of Jacob

22b Now the sons of Jacob were twelve. [23]The sons of Leah: Reuben (Jacob's firstborn), Simeon, Levi, Judah, Issachar, and Zebulun. [24]The sons of Rachel: Joseph and Benjamin. [25]The sons of Bilhah, Rachel's maid: Dan and Naphtali. [26]The sons of Zilpah, Leah's maid: Gad and Asher. These were the sons of Jacob who were born to him in Paddan-aram.

27 Jacob came to his father Isaac at Mamre, or Kiriath-arba (that is, Hebron), where Abraham and Isaac had resided as aliens. [28]Now the days of Isaac were one hundred eighty years. [29]And Isaac breathed his last; he died and was gathered to his people, old and full of days; and his sons Esau and Jacob buried him.

Genealogy: Descendants of Esau

36 These are the descendants of Esau (that is, Edom). [2]Esau took his wives from the Canaanites: Adah daughter of Elon the Hittite, Oholibamah daughter of Anah son of Zibeon the Hivite, [3]and Basemath, Ishmael's daughter, sister of Nebaioth. [4]Adah bore Eliphaz to Esau; Basemath bore Reuel; [5]and Oholibamah bore Jeush, Jalam, and Korah. These are the sons of Esau who were born to him in the land of Canaan.

6 Then Esau took his wives, his sons, his daughters, and all the members of his household, his cattle, all his livestock, and all the property he had acquired in the land of Canaan; and he moved to a land some distance from his brother Jacob. [7]For their possessions were too great for them to live together; the land where they were staying could not support them because of their livestock. [8]So Esau settled in the hill country of Seir; Esau is Edom.[29]

• 9 These are the descendants of Esau, ancestor of the Edomites, in the hill country of Seir. [10]These are the names of Esau's sons: Eliphaz son of Adah the wife of Esau; Reuel, the son of Esau's wife Basemath. [11]The sons of Eliphaz were Teman, Omar, Zepho, Gatam, and Kenaz. [12](Timna was a concubine of Eliphaz, Esau's son; she bore Amalek to Eliphaz.) These were the sons of Adah, Esau's wife. [13]These were the sons of Reuel: Nahath, Zerah, Shammah, and

---

28. Gen 33:18a is either a remnant of the P source or a priestly gloss in the combined text. Paddan-aram is again a pointer to priestly derivation here. For the understanding of "safely" (Heb., *šālēm*) as Salem, a place name, and "the city of Shechem" as Shechem's city, see Westermann, *Genesis 12–36*, 527–28.

29. For Noth, Gen 36:1-8 is clearly P's work, combining the information on Esau's wives and descendants from the Toledoth book (Gen 36:9-14) with different information about his wives (Gen 26:34; 28:9) and an element originally from the Abraham–Lot story (Gen 13:6).

Mizzah. These were the sons of Esau's wife, Basemath. ¹⁴These were the sons of Esau's wife Oholibamah, daughter of Anah son of Zibeon: she bore to Esau Jeush, Jalam, and Korah.³⁰

Joseph

37 Jacob settled in the land where his father had lived as an alien, the land of Canaan. ²*This is the story of the family of Jacob.

Joseph, being seventeen years old, was shepherding the flock with his brothers; and Joseph brought a bad report of them to their father. • • •³¹

41:46a Joseph was thirty years old when he entered the service of Pharaoh king of Egypt.³²

46:6 And they [Heb.; NRSV, They also] took their livestock and the goods that they had acquired in the land of Canaan, and they came into Egypt, Jacob and all his offspring with him, ⁷his sons, and his sons' sons with him, his daughters, and his sons' daughters; all his offspring he brought with him into Egypt.³³

8 Now these are the names of the Israelites, Jacob and his offspring, who came to Egypt. Reuben, Jacob's firstborn, ⁹and the children of Reuben: Hanoch, Pallu, Hezron, and Carmi. ¹⁰The children of Simeon: Jemuel, Jamin, Ohad, Jachin, Zohar, and Shaul, the son of a Canaanite woman. ¹¹The children of Levi: Gershon, Kohath, and Merari. ¹²The children of Judah: Er, Onan, Shelah, Perez, and Zerah (but Er and Onan died in the land of Canaan); and the children of Perez

*were Hezron and Hamul. ¹³The children of Issachar: Tola, Puvah, Jashub, and Shimron. ¹⁴The children of Zebulun: Sered, Elon, and Jahleel ¹⁵(these are the sons of Leah, whom she bore to Jacob in Paddan-aram, together with his daughter Dinah; in all his sons and his daughters numbered thirty-three). ¹⁶The children of Gad: Ziphion, Haggi, Shuni, Ezbon, Eri, Arodi, and Areli. ¹⁷The children of Asher: Imnah, Ishvah, Ishvi, Beriah, and their sister Serah. The children of Beriah: Heber and Malchiel ¹⁸(these are the children of Zilpah, whom Laban gave to his daughter Leah; and these she bore to Jacob—sixteen persons). ¹⁹The children of Jacob's wife Rachel: Joseph and Benjamin. ²⁰To Joseph in the land of Egypt were born Manasseh and Ephraim, whom Asenath daughter of Potiphera, priest of On, bore to him. ²¹The children of Benjamin: Bela, Becher, Ashbel, Gera, Naaman, Ehi, Rosh, Muppim, Huppim, and Ard ²²(these are the children of Rachel, who were born to Jacob—fourteen persons in all). ²³The children of Dan: Hashum. ²⁴The children of Naphtali: Jahzeel, Guni, Jezer, and Shillem ²⁵(these are the children of Bilhah, whom Laban gave to his daughter Rachel, and these she bore to Jacob—seven persons in all). ²⁶All the persons belonging to Jacob who came into Egypt, who were his own offspring, not including the wives of his sons, were sixty-six persons in all. ²⁷The children of Joseph, who were born to him in Egypt, were two; all the persons of the house of Jacob who came into Egypt were seventy.*³⁴

---

30. Gen 36:15-43 is omitted by Noth as probably an accumulation of additions, either to the P narrative or to the Pentateuch as a whole.

31. This is the last of three places in Genesis where Noth assumes that P's continuity has not been maintained in the process of final compilation; the more colorful J text is understood to have replaced a plainer P text. Here the older (JE) Joseph story replaces P's account of Joseph's stay in Egypt. Gen 37:1-2* and 41:46a are the only traces of a P version of the Joseph story.

32. Gen 41:46a is either a remnant of the P source or a priestly gloss in the combined text. The concern to note the precise age is again typical of P.

33. The "they" and "their" in Gen 46:6 require an appropriate reference to Jacob and his family in the preceding text of an independent P document. In the present text it is provided by 46:5.

34. For comment on this fascinating passage, which interrupts the flow of P's narrative, see C. Westermann, *Genesis 37–50* (Minneapolis: Augsburg, 1986) 158–61.

47:27b And they gained possessions in it, and were fruitful and multiplied exceedingly.[35] [28]Jacob lived in the land of Egypt seventeen years; so the days of Jacob, the years of his life, were one hundred forty-seven years.

48:3 And Jacob said to Joseph, "God Almighty appeared to me at Luz in the land of Canaan, and he blessed me, [4]and said to me, 'I am going to make you fruitful and increase your numbers; I will make of you a company of peoples, and will give this land to your offspring after you for a perpetual holding.' [5]Therefore your two sons, who were born to you in the land of Egypt before I came to you in Egypt, are now mine; Ephraim and Manasseh shall be mine, just as Reuben and Simeon are. [6]As for the offspring born to you after them, they shall be yours. They shall be recorded under the names of their brothers with regard to their inheritance."

49:1a Then Jacob called his sons, [29]and [Heb.; NRSV, Then] he charged them, saying to them, "I am about to be gathered to my people. Bury me with my ancestors—in the cave in the field of Ephron the Hittite, [30]in the cave in the field at Machpelah, near Mamre, in the land of Canaan, in the field that Abraham bought from Ephron the Hittite as a burial site. [31]There Abraham and his wife Sarah were buried; there Isaac and his wife Rebekah were buried; and there I buried Leah—[32]the field and the cave that is in it were purchased from the Hittites." [33]When Jacob ended his charge to his sons, he drew up his feet into the bed, breathed his last, and was gathered to his people.

50:12 Thus his sons did for him as he had instructed them. [13]They carried him to the land of Canaan and buried him in the cave of the field at Machpelah, the field near Mamre, which Abraham bought as a burial site from Ephron the Hittite.

The Book of Exodus

THE CONSTITUTIVE GENERATION OF ISRAEL

Exodus from Egypt

1 These are the names of the sons of Israel who came to Egypt with Jacob, each with his household: [2]Reuben, Simeon, Levi, and Judah, [3]Issachar, Zebulun, and Benjamin, [4]Dan and Naphtali, Gad and Asher. [5]The total number of people born to Jacob was seventy. Joseph was already in Egypt. [6]Then Joseph died, and all his brothers, and that whole generation. [7]But the Israelites were fruitful and prolific; they multiplied and grew exceedingly strong, so that the land was filled with them.[36]

---

35. Here "they" and "it" refer in P back to the immediately preceding Gen 46:6-7, to Jacob and his family whom he brought to Egypt. In their present context in Genesis 47, "they" refers to Israel (the patriarch) and "it" to the land of Egypt in the region of Goshen. Note Westermann's relocation of vv. 27-28 in the text of Genesis 47 (*Genesis 37–50*, 164–72).

36. The nature of the story has changed here. From dealing with individuals and families, the narrative has moved to another plane—that of a nation. This now is the story of Israel's constitutive generation.

13 The Egyptians became ruthless in imposing tasks on the Israelites,[37] [14]and made their lives bitter with hard service in mortar and brick and in every kind of field labor. They were ruthless in all the tasks that they imposed on them.

2:23* The Israelites groaned under their slavery, and cried out. Out of the slavery their cry for help rose up to God. [24]God heard their groaning, and God remembered his covenant with Abraham, Isaac, and Jacob. [25]God looked upon the Israelites, and God took notice of them.

God's Promise to Deliver Israel

6:2 And God [Heb.; NRSV, God also] spoke to Moses and said to him: "I am the LORD. [3]I appeared to Abraham, Isaac, and Jacob as God Almighty, but by my name 'The LORD' I did not make myself known to them. [4]I also established my covenant with them, to give them the land of Canaan, the land in which they resided as aliens. [5]I have also heard the groaning of the Israelites whom the Egyptians are holding as slaves, and I have remembered my covenant. [6]Say therefore to the Israelites, 'I am the LORD, and I will free you from the burdens of the Egyptians and deliver you from slavery to them. I will redeem you with an outstretched arm and with mighty acts of judgment. [7]I will take you as my people, and I will be your God. You shall know that I am the LORD your God, who has freed you from the burdens of the Egyptians. [8]I will bring you into the land that I swore to give to Abraham, Isaac, and Jacob; I will give it to you for a possession. I am the LORD.' " [9]Moses told this to the Israelites; but they would not listen to Moses, because of their broken spirit and their cruel slavery.[38]

10 Then the LORD spoke to Moses, [11]"Go and tell Pharaoh king of Egypt to let the Israelites go out of his land." [12]But Moses spoke to the LORD, "The Israelites have not listened to me; how then shall Pharaoh listen to me, poor speaker that I am?"

13 Thus the LORD spoke to Moses and Aaron, and gave them orders regarding the Israelites and Pharaoh king of Egypt, charging them to free the Israelites from the land of Egypt.

14 The following are the heads of their ancestral houses: the sons of Reuben, the firstborn of Israel: Hanoch, Pallu, Hezron, and Carmi; these are the families of Reuben. [15]The sons of Simeon: Jemuel, Jamin, Ohad, Jachin, Zohar, and Shaul, the son of a Canaanite woman; these are the families of Simeon. [16]The following are the names of the sons of Levi according to their genealogies: Gershon, Kohath, and Merari, and the length of

---

37. This is a good example of how a modern translation of the present text can obscure the features of the sources. In the Hebrew text the Egyptians are named in Exod 1:13 but not in 1:12. The Hebrew of v. 12 is a carefully crafted sentence that does away with the need for a subject to be expressed for any of its four verbs. But translations have felt the need to name the Egyptians in v. 12 and to let that serve for a subject in v. 13 (so, e.g., NAB, NEB, NIV, and RSV). For those pursuing the sequence of the source, the lack of a proper subject in the translation of v. 13 would incorrectly suggest a gap. The NRSV introduces the name into v. 12 but retains the proper name, "the Egyptians," in v. 13, where it rightly reflects the Hebrew.

38. The transition from ancestral stories to the story of the constitutive generation of Israel is marked by a transition in knowledge of God. To the ancestors, God was known as "God Almighty" (El Shaddai); to the nation, God will be known as "the LORD" (YHWH). There is a reference in Exod 6:4 to the covenant with Abraham in Genesis 17. Now God appeals to that covenant, in the context of the groaning in Egypt. Around the time of Israel's later exile, this reference would easily be reapplied to the groaning of those in doubt and despair, if not in actual exile. The promise of deliverance and possession of the land is significant for both contexts, as is the dispirited brokenness of the people.

Levi's life was one hundred thirty-seven years.
[17]The sons of Gershon: Libni and Shimei, by their
families. [18]The sons of Kohath: Amram, Izhar,
Hebron, and Uzziel, and the length of Kohath's
life was one hundred thirty-three years. [19]The
sons of Merari: Mahli and Mushi. These are the
families of the Levites according to their genealo-
gies. [20]Amram married Jochebed his father's sis-
ter and she bore him Aaron and Moses, and the
length of Amram's life was one hundred thirty-
seven years. [21]The sons of Izhar: Korah, Nepheg,
and Zichri. [22]The sons of Uzziel: Mishael, Elza-
phan, and Sithri. [23]Aaron married Elisheba,
daughter of Amminadab and sister of Nahshon,
and she bore him Nadab, Abihu, Eleazar, and
Ithamar. [24]The sons of Korah: Assir, Elkanah,
and Abiasaph; these are the families of the Kora-
hites. [25]Aaron's son Eleazar married one of the
daughters of Putiel, and she bore him Phinehas.
These are the heads of the ancestral houses of the
Levites by their families.

26 It was this same Aaron and Moses to whom
the LORD said, "Bring the Israelites out of the land
of Egypt, company by company." [27]It was they who
spoke to Pharaoh king of Egypt to bring the Israel-
ites out of Egypt, the same Moses and Aaron.

28 On the day when the LORD spoke to Moses
in the land of Egypt, [29]he said to him, "I am the
LORD; tell Pharaoh king of Egypt all that I am
speaking to you." [30]But Moses said in the LORD's
presence, "Since I am a poor speaker, why would
Pharaoh listen to me?"[39]

7 The LORD said to Moses, "See, I have made
you like God to Pharaoh, and your brother
Aaron shall be your prophet. [2]You shall speak all
that I command you, and your brother Aaron
shall tell Pharaoh to let the Israelites go out of
his land. [3]But I will harden Pharaoh's heart, and
I will multiply my signs and wonders in the land
of Egypt. [4]When Pharaoh does not listen to you,
I will lay my hand upon Egypt and bring my
people the Israelites, company by company, out
of the land of Egypt by great acts of judgment.
[5]The Egyptians shall know that I am the LORD,
when I stretch out my hand against Egypt and
bring the Israelites out from among them."[40]
[6]Moses and Aaron did so; they did just as the
LORD commanded them. [7]Moses was eighty

---

39. Texts indented and in italics are considered by
Noth to be priestly supplements to the P source.
Noth's reasons, as given here, are taken from his
1959 Exodus commentary: In Exod 6:13-30, "we have
a great secondary insertion, of which the external distinguishing mark is the almost literal repetition of v.
12 in v. 30, which is preceded in vv. 28 f. by a summary
reference to the call of Moses and the commission
formulated in v. 11. The passage 28-30 thus serves to
pick up the threads of the narrative at the very place
where they had been let drop in v. 12, before the
insertion" (*Exodus* [OTL; Philadelphia: Westminster,
1962] 58). This is an excellent example of what is considered to be highly skillful redactional technique.
When a piece is stitched into the whole cloth of a
narrative, what immediately precedes the insertion is
repeated at the end, to resume the narrative thread.
Naturally, the author of a text can use the same
technique to pick up the story line after a digression.
Where redactional activity is assumed, it is usually

because the insertion expresses a viewpoint at odds
with that of the original. E.g., in Exod 6:13-30, just
before the introduction of Aaron into the narrative, it
is a matter of advancing Aaron's role beyond what
is assigned to him in 7:1, representing a view that
the LORD spoke not just to Moses alone, as in the
preceding text, but to both Moses and Aaron who
were together responsible from the outset for bringing Israel up out of Egypt (cf. vv. 13, 26). As the
Levite genealogy shows, the passage represents Levite
interests.

40. Childs points out the place of Exod 7:3-5 for
understanding the structure of the P text (B. S. Childs,
Exodus [OTL; London: SCM, 1974] 139-40). Pharaoh's heart is hardened so that God may multiply
signs and wonders in Egypt (v. 3). After the plague
sequence, the death of the firstborn and the Passover
will bring about the deliverance of Israel from Egypt
(v. 4). The Egyptians come to know the LORD in the
deliverance at the sea (v. 5; cf. Exod 14:4).

years old and Aaron eighty-three when they spoke to Pharaoh.

The Plagues

8 The LORD said to Moses and Aaron,[41] [9]"When Pharaoh says to you, 'Perform a wonder,' then you shall say to Aaron, 'Take your staff and throw it down before Pharaoh, and it will become a snake.' " [10]So Moses and Aaron went to Pharaoh and did as the LORD had commanded; Aaron threw down his staff before Pharaoh and his officials, and it became a snake. [11]Then Pharaoh summoned the wise men and the sorcerers; and they also, the magicians of Egypt, did the same by their secret arts. [12]Each one threw down his staff, and they became snakes; but Aaron's staff swallowed up theirs. [13]Still Pharaoh's heart was hardened, and he would not listen to them, as the LORD had said.

19 The LORD said to Moses, "Say to Aaron, 'Take your staff and stretch out your hand over the waters of Egypt—over its rivers, its canals, and its ponds, and all its pools of water—so that they may become blood; and there shall be blood throughout the whole land of Egypt, even in vessels of wood and in vessels of stone.' "

[20]* Moses and Aaron did just as the LORD commanded. [21b]And there was blood throughout the whole land of Egypt. [22]But the magicians of Egypt did the same by their secret arts; so Pharaoh's heart remained hardened, and he would not listen to them; as the LORD had said.

8:5 And the LORD said to Moses, "Say to Aaron, 'Stretch out your hand with your staff over the rivers, the canals, and the pools, and make frogs come up on the land of Egypt.' " [6]So Aaron stretched out his hand over the waters of Egypt; and the frogs came up and covered the land of Egypt. [7]But the magicians did the same by their secret arts, and brought frogs up on the land of Egypt.[42]

• • •[43]

15* And he [Heb.; NRSV, and] would not listen to them, just as the LORD had said.

16 Then the LORD said to Moses, "Say to Aaron, 'Stretch out your staff and strike the dust of the earth, so that it may become gnats throughout the whole land of Egypt.' " [17]And they did so; Aaron stretched out his hand with his staff and struck the dust of the earth, and gnats came on humans and animals alike; all the dust of the earth turned into gnats throughout the whole land of Egypt. [18]The magicians tried to produce gnats by their secret arts, but they could not. There were gnats on both humans and animals. [19]And the magicians said to Pharaoh, "This is the finger of God!" But Pharaoh's heart was hardened, and he would not listen to them, just as the LORD had said.[44]

9:8 Then the LORD said to Moses and Aaron, "Take handfuls of soot from the kiln, and let Moses throw it in the air in the sight of Pharaoh. [9]It shall become fine dust all over the land of Egypt, and shall cause festering boils on

---

41. As a supplement to Noth's P text for the plagues, it is helpful to read the treatment by Childs (*Exodus*, 130–53, esp. 130–42). Noth argues for only two sources, P and J, in the plague narrative, attributing most of the traditional E material to J; Childs argues for three sources. However, the P text here and in Childs (despite a confusing sentence) is practically identical; Childs has Exod 7:20a and 8:11b for Noth's 7:20aα and 8:11aβb, and Childs includes 9:35b. Otherwise, what Childs attributes to E will be found in Noth's J.

Each plague in P has three elements: (1) God com-

mands Moses to tell Aaron to stretch out his staff and bring about the plague; (2) the command is complied with and the plague ensues; (3) Pharaoh's heart is hardened and he does not listen (see Childs, *Exodus*, 138).

42. Exod 8:5-7 is numbered 8:1-3 in the Hebrew.

43. The preceding J text in v. 15 (with a different verb) notes that Pharaoh hardened his heart; it replaces P's comment. In the P text, the proper name "Pharaoh" needs to be supplied.

44. Exod 8:15-19 is numbered 8:11-15 in the Hebrew.

humans and animals throughout the whole land of Egypt." [10]So they took soot from the kiln, and stood before Pharaoh, and Moses threw it in the air, and it caused festering boils on humans and animals. [11]The magicians could not stand before Moses because of the boils, for the boils afflicted the magicians as well as all the Egyptians. [12]But the LORD hardened the heart of Pharaoh, and he would not listen to them, just as the LORD had spoken to Moses.

11:9 The LORD said to Moses, "Pharaoh will not listen to you, in order that my wonders may be multiplied in the land of Egypt." [10]Moses and Aaron performed all these wonders before Pharaoh; but the LORD hardened Pharaoh's heart, and he did not let the people of Israel go out of his land.[45]

The Passover

12 The LORD said to Moses and Aaron in the land of Egypt:

[2]This month shall mark for you the beginning of months; it shall be the first month of the year for you.[46]

[3]Tell the whole congregation of Israel that on the tenth of this month they are to take a lamb for each family, a lamb for each household. [4]If a household is too small for a whole lamb, it shall join its closest neighbor in obtaining one; the lamb shall be divided in proportion to the number of people who eat of it. [5]Your lamb shall be without blemish, a year-old male; you may take it from the sheep or from the goats. [6]You shall keep it until the fourteenth day of this month; then the whole assembled congregation of Israel shall slaughter it at twilight. [7]They shall take some of the blood and put it on the two doorposts and the lintel of the houses in which they eat it. [8]They shall eat the lamb that same night; they shall eat it roasted over the fire with unleavened bread and bitter herbs. [9]Do not eat any of it raw or boiled in water, but roasted over the fire, with its head, legs, and inner organs. [10]You shall let none of it remain until the morning; anything that remains until the morning you shall burn. [11]This is how you shall eat it: your loins girded, your sandals on your feet, and your staff in your hand; and you shall eat it hurriedly. It is the passover of the LORD. [12]For I will pass through the land of Egypt that night, and I will strike down every firstborn in the land of Egypt, both human beings and animals; on all

---

45. It is indicative of the minor fluctuations of judgment within the overall source hypothesis that, in his commentary, Noth has no hesitation in assigning Exod 11:9-10 to P, although he displays considerable hesitancy over the contents of chap. 11 (*Exodus*, 92–94). It is taken for granted that there has been a considerable amount of ongoing redactional activity within the P traditions. Some of this can be clearly identified; in this case, the identification of such redaction is more a matter of opinion and instinctive judgment. It seems that Noth often followed a consensus in the introductory section of his *History of Pentateuchal Traditions*; the commentaries on Exodus, Leviticus, and Numbers bear witness to his own studied judgments later. In this book, as a rule, there is neither space nor need to explore the factors that might have influenced Noth in such cases. The comment by Childs is valuable: "The final two verses in ch. 11 formally bring the plague narrative to a conclusion by picking up the vocabulary of the introduction in ch. 7. Lest one consider the plagues a failure by not accomplishing their purpose of freeing Israel, the narrative begins and ends with a theological justification. It belonged to the judgment of God on Pharaoh that he continued his resistance in order to allow God to multiply his signs and wonders. Only when this had been done would God stretch out his hand and bring Israel out of the land in triumph" (*Exodus*, 161–62).

46. The purpose here is "to provide a definite ruling that the year begins in the spring, a custom taken over in Israel from Mesopotamia in the eighth or seventh century BC, instead of in the autumn as in ancient Israel (cf. 23.26; 34.22)" (Noth, *Exodus*, 94–95). Note the natural flow from Exod 12:1 to 12:3, if v. 2 is omitted. If it is an addition, however, it is placed precisely where it needs to be in terms of defining "the month" specified in vv. 3 and 6.

the gods of Egypt I will execute judgments: I am the LORD. [13]The blood shall be a sign for you on the houses where you live: when I see the blood, I will pass over you, and no plague shall destroy you when I strike the land of Egypt.

14 This day shall be a day of remembrance for you. You shall celebrate it as a festival to the LORD; throughout your generations you shall observe it as a perpetual ordinance. [15]Seven days you shall eat unleavened bread; on the first day you shall remove leaven from your houses, for whoever eats leavened bread from the first day until the seventh day shall be cut off from Israel. [16]On the first day you shall hold a solemn assembly, and on the seventh day a solemn assembly; no work shall be done on those days; only what everyone must eat, that alone may be prepared by you. [17]You shall observe the festival of unleavened bread, for on this very day I brought your companies out of the land of Egypt: you shall observe this day throughout your generations as a perpetual ordinance. [18]In the first month, from the evening of the fourteenth day until the evening of the twenty-first day, you shall eat unleavened bread. [19]For seven days no leaven shall be found in your houses; for whoever eats what is leavened shall be cut off from the congregation of Israel, whether an alien or a native of the land. [20]You shall eat nothing leavened; in all your settlements you shall eat unleavened bread.

28 The Israelites went and did just as the LORD had commanded Moses and Aaron.[47]

40 The time that the Israelites had lived in Egypt was four hundred thirty years. [41]At the end of four hundred thirty years, on that very day, all the companies of the LORD went out from the land of Egypt.

[42]That was for the LORD a night of vigil, to bring them out of the land of Egypt. That same night is a vigil to be kept for the LORD by all the Israelites throughout their generations.[48]

43 The LORD said to Moses and Aaron: This is the ordinance for the passover: no foreigner shall eat of it, [44]but any slave who has been purchased may eat of it after he has been circumcised; [45]no bound or hired servant may eat of it. [46]It shall be eaten in one house; you shall not take any of the animal outside the house, and you shall not break any of its bones. [47]The whole congregation of Israel shall celebrate it. [48]If an alien who resides with you wants to celebrate the passover to the LORD, all his males shall be circumcised; then he may draw near to celebrate it; he shall be regarded as a native of the land. But no uncircumcised person shall eat of it; [49]there shall be one law for the native and for the alien who resides among you.

50 All the Israelites did just as the LORD had commanded Moses and Aaron. [51]That very day the LORD brought the Israelites out of the land of Egypt, company by company.[49]

Deliverance: the Crossing of the Sea

14 Then the LORD said to Moses: [2]Tell the Israelites to turn back and camp in front of Pi-hahiroth, between Migdol and the sea, in front of Baal-zephon; you shall camp opposite it, by the sea. [3]Pharaoh will say of the Israelites, 'They are wandering aimlessly in the land; the wilderness has closed in on them.' [4]I will harden

---

47. For Noth, Exod 12:28, in telling of Israel's compliance with God's commands, includes implicitly God's action against the firstborn (cf. 12:12-13), otherwise unmentioned in P (cf. Noth, *Exodus*, 97).

48. Noth regards Exod 12:42 as an addition within the supplement to P. In part, it is meant to explain a later phrase—a vigil for YHWH (see Noth, *Exodus*, 100).

49. These regulations about admission to the Passover sacrifice reflect the later times of life in Israel (Noth, *Exodus*, 100–101); the echo of Exod 12:41 in 12:51 indicates that they are meant to be associated with the Passover from the outset (see Childs, *Exodus*, 201–2).

Pharaoh's heart, and he will pursue them, so that I will gain glory for myself over Pharaoh and all his army; and the Egyptians shall know that I am the LORD. And they did so.[50]

8 The LORD hardened the heart of Pharaoh king of Egypt and he pursued the Israelites, who were going out boldly. 9*And they overtook them camped by the sea, all Pharaoh's horses and chariots, his chariot drivers and his army, by Pi-hahiroth, in front of Baal-zephon.[51] 10*As Pharaoh drew near, the Israelites cried out to the LORD.

15 Then the LORD said to Moses, "Why do you cry out to me? Tell the Israelites to go forward. 16But you lift up your staff, and stretch out your hand over the sea and divide it, that the Israelites may go into the sea on dry ground. 17Then I will harden the hearts of the Egyptians so that they will go in after them; and so I will gain glory for myself over Pharaoh and all his army, his chariots, and his chariot drivers. 18And the Egyptians shall know that I am the LORD, when I have gained glory for myself over Pharaoh, his chariots, and his chariot drivers."

21* Then Moses stretched out his hand over the sea, and the waters were divided. 22The Israelites went into the sea on dry ground, the waters forming a wall for them on their right and on their left. 23The Egyptians pursued, and went into the sea after them, all of Pharaoh's horses, chariots, and chariot drivers.

26 Then the LORD said to Moses, "Stretch out your hand over the sea, so that the water may come back upon the Egyptians, upon their chariots and chariot drivers." 27*So Moses stretched out his hand over the sea. 28The waters returned and covered the chariots and the chariot drivers, the entire army of Pharaoh that had followed them into the sea; not one of them remained. 29But the Israelites walked on dry ground through the sea, the waters forming a wall for them on their right and on their left.

Israel in the Wilderness

Itinerary: From the Red Sea to Sin

15:22* And [Heb.; NRSV, Then] Moses ordered Israel to set out from the Red Sea. 27And [Heb.; NRSV, Then] they came to Elim, where there were twelve springs of water and seventy palm trees; and they camped there by the water.[52]

16 The whole congregation of the Israelites set out from Elim; and Israel came to the wilderness of Sin, which is between Elim and Sinai, on the fifteenth day of the second month after they had departed from the land of Egypt.

The Manna

2 The whole congregation of the Israelites complained against Moses and Aaron in the wilderness. 3The Israelites said to them, "If only we had died by the hand of the LORD in the land of Egypt, when we sat by the fleshpots and ate our fill of bread; for you have brought us out

---

50. For a discussion of the P and J accounts of the deliverance at the sea, see chap. 6, below. The instruction to the Israelites to turn back into Egypt and the echoes of Exod 7:3-5 are pointers to this episode's place in P as part of Israel's exodus from Egypt; in J, it is part of the wilderness wandering (cf. Childs, *Exodus*, 222–23).

51. The order of this sentence in the NRSV has been changed slightly to correspond more closely with the Hebrew. For Noth, in his commentary, the phrase "all Pharaoh's horses and chariots, his chariot drivers and his army" is a secondary expansion (translated in parentheses in Noth's German original *Das zweite Buch Mose* 81 [ATD 5; Göttingen: Vandenhoeck & Ruprecht, 1959]; not, however, in *Exodus*); its odd position is not easily accounted for.

52. From here on, the thread of the P narrative is constituted by the itinerary notices, like signposts along the way toward the promised land.

into this wilderness to kill this whole assembly with hunger."

6 So Moses and Aaron said to all the Israelites, "In the evening you shall know that it was the LORD who brought you out of the land of Egypt, ⁷and in the morning you shall see the glory of the LORD, because he has heard your complaining against the LORD. For what are we, that you complain against us?"

*⁸And Moses said, "When the LORD gives you meat to eat in the evening and your fill of bread in the morning, because the LORD has heard the complaining that you utter against him—what are we? Your complaining is not against us but against the LORD."*⁵³

9 Then Moses said to Aaron, "Say to the whole congregation of the Israelites, 'Draw near to the LORD, for he has heard your complaining.' " ¹⁰And as Aaron spoke to the whole congregation of the Israelites, they looked toward the wilderness, and the glory of the LORD appeared in the cloud. ¹¹The LORD spoke to Moses and said, ¹²"I have heard the complaining of the Israelites; say to them, 'At twilight you shall eat meat, and in the morning you shall have your fill of bread; then you shall know that I am the LORD your God.' "

13 In the evening quails came up and covered the camp; and in the morning there was a layer of dew around the camp. ¹⁴When the layer of dew lifted, there on the surface of the wilderness was a fine flaky substance, as fine as frost on the ground. ¹⁵When the Israelites saw it, they said to one another, "What is it?" For they did not know what it was. Moses said to them, "It is the bread that the LORD has given you to eat. ¹⁶This is what the LORD has commanded: 'Gather as much of it as each of you needs, an omer to a person according to the number of persons, all

providing for those in their own tents.' " ¹⁷The Israelites did so, some gathering more, some less. ¹⁸But when they measured it with an omer, those who gathered much had nothing over, and those who gathered little had no shortage; they gathered as much as each of them needed. ¹⁹And Moses said to them, "Let no one leave any of it over until morning." ²⁰But they did not listen to Moses; some left part of it until morning, and it bred worms and became foul. And Moses was angry with them. ²¹Morning by morning they gathered it, as much as each needed; but when the sun grew hot, it melted.

22 On the sixth day they gathered twice as much food, two omers apiece. When all the leaders of the congregation came and told Moses, ²³he said to them, "This is what the LORD has commanded: 'Tomorrow is a day of solemn rest, a holy sabbath to the LORD; bake what you want to bake and boil what you want to boil, and all that is left over put aside to be kept until morning.' " ²⁴So they put it aside until morning, as Moses commanded them; and it did not become foul, and there were no worms in it. ²⁵Moses said, "Eat it today, for today is a sabbath to the LORD; today you will not find it in the field. ²⁶Six days you shall gather it; but on the seventh day, which is a sabbath, there will be none." ²⁷On the seventh day some of the people went out to gather, and they found none.

32 Moses said, "This is what the LORD has commanded: 'Let an omer of it be kept throughout your generations, in order that they may see the food with which I fed you in the wilderness, when I brought you out of the land of Egypt.' " ³³And Moses said to Aaron, "Take a jar, and put an omer of manna in it, and place it before the LORD, to be kept throughout your generations." ³⁴As the LORD commanded Moses, so Aaron

---

53. Noth comments: "Verse 8 looks to be a secondary variant to v. 7a*bb*; the incomplete sentence 8a in it is a variant of 7a*b*, and 7b recurs in another form in 8b" (*Exodus*, 134).

placed it before the covenant, for safekeeping. [35a]The Israelites ate manna forty years, until they came to a habitable land.

Sinai

Itinerary: From Sin to Sinai

17:1* From the wilderness of Sin the whole congregation of the Israelites journeyed by stages, as the LORD commanded. They camped at Rephidim.

19:2a And they [Heb.; NRSV, They had] journeyed from Rephidim, entered the wilderness of Sinai, and camped in the wilderness. [1]On the third new moon after the Israelites had gone out of the land of Egypt, on that very day, they came into the wilderness of Sinai.[54]

Ascent of the Mountain by Moses

24:15b And the cloud covered the mountain. [16]The glory of the LORD settled on Mount Sinai, and the cloud covered it for six days; on the seventh day he called to Moses out of the cloud. [17]Now the appearance of the glory of the LORD was like a devouring fire on the top of the mountain in the sight of the people of Israel. [18]Moses entered the cloud, and went up on the mountain. Moses was on the mountain for forty days and forty nights.[55]

---

54. In Noth's judgment, the present text order came about secondarily; what is now Exod 19:1 was placed first due to the particular suitability of the date it contained as a solemn opening for the Sinai narrative. From the point of view of content, Noth believes v. 1 belongs after v. 2a, because the itinerary notices normally come first. The NRSV's "They had" reflects the position following v. 1.

Although much more tradition has accumulated around Sinai than P put there, it is still entirely possible that P too preferred the solemn sequence of the final text arrangement. In fact, in his commentary Noth attributes this move to P (*Exodus*, 155). The order here is from Noth's *Pentateuchal Traditions*.

55. At this point we are confronted by one of the major enigmas of the P document: in the surviving P text there is no account of a covenant at Sinai. The facts are simple and there is little debate about them. P has Israel arrive at Sinai in Exod 19:1-2a (or 2a, 1). The next P text is 24:15b-18, in which the cloud covers the mountain and, on the seventh day, Moses is summoned to enter the cloud where he will receive the extensive instructions for the sanctuary (Exodus 25-29). The two tablets of the "testimony" (the term used in Heb. and RSV) receive just one verse (31:18).

The interpretation of these facts is not simple and is disputed. For those who see P as the final major redaction of the Pentateuch, the covenant is given in the JE text and only P's areas of special interest have been added. In this case, it is strange that, if P placed store by the Sinai covenant, not a word was consecrated to it in P's own thought and language, especially given P's extensive coverage of the Sinai traditions.

For those who see P as an independent document, it is possible to argue that the P account of the Sinai covenant was suppressed in favor of the more colorful JE account, as is postulated for earlier points in P. In this case, it is strange that a redactional process using P as a base narrative should have sacrificed the entire P version of so critical a passage, again given P's extensive coverage of the Sinai traditions.

Finally, for those who see P as an independent document, it is also possible to argue that in the fragile and uncertain times around the exile, P chose to rely on the solidly unconditional covenants with Noah (Gen 9:1-17) and Abraham (Gen 17:1-8) rather than the Sinai covenant, burdened with law and, in the previous generation or two, with the quasi-legalistic deuteronomic rhetoric of blessing and curse (see Campbell, *Study Companion*, 72-73). The seven-day preparation and forty-day stay lend weight to the view that P's text here is a total presentation of Moses' experience on the mountain at Sinai (cf. Noth, *Exodus*, 200). Afterward, in P, God simply speaks to Moses (at the tent of meeting; cf. Exod 25:22: there "I will deliver to you all my commands for the Israelites").

In any hypothesis, it is important to see what P associates with Sinai: Israel, splendidly and majestically organized around the sanctuary of God's presence in their midst, on the march toward the promised land. It is not possible to interpret P adequately without taking due account of the specifically P material at Sinai. It is impressive in its sheer mass; it is impressive in its location at the heart of divine revelation; and it is P's own work (see Campbell, *Study Companion*, 73-74, 79-83).

God's Call for an Offering for
the Sanctuary

25 The LORD said to Moses: [2]Tell the Israelites to take for me an offering; from all whose hearts prompt them to give you shall receive the offering for me. [3]This is the offering that you shall receive from them: gold, silver, and bronze, [4]blue, purple, and crimson yarns and fine linen, goats' hair, [5]tanned rams' skins, fine leather, acacia wood, [6]oil for the lamps, spices for the anointing oil and for the fragrant incense, [7]onyx stones and gems to be set in the ephod and for the breastpiece. [8]And have them make me a sanctuary, so that I may dwell among them. [9]In accordance with all that I show you concerning the pattern of the tabernacle and of all its furniture, so you shall make it.[56]

Instructions for the Ark

10 They shall make an ark of acacia wood; it shall be two and a half cubits long, a cubit and a half wide, and a cubit and a half high. [11]You shall overlay it with pure gold, inside and outside you shall overlay it, and you shall make a molding of gold upon it all around. [12]You shall cast four rings of gold for it and put them on its four feet, two rings on the one side of it, and two rings on the other side. [13]You shall make poles of acacia wood, and overlay them with gold. [14]And you shall put the poles into the rings on the sides of the ark, by which to carry the ark. [15]The poles shall remain in the rings of the ark; they shall not be taken from it. [16]You shall

put into the ark the covenant that I shall give you. [17] Then you shall make a mercy seat of pure gold; two cubits and a half shall be its length, and a cubit and a half its width. [18]You shall make two cherubim of gold; you shall make them of hammered work, at the two ends of the mercy seat. [19]Make one cherub at the one end, and one cherub at the other; of one piece with the mercy seat you shall make the cherubim at its two ends. [20]The cherubim shall spread out their wings above, overshadowing the mercy seat with their wings. They shall face one to another; the faces of the cherubim shall be turned toward the mercy seat. [21]You shall put the mercy seat on the top of the ark; and in the ark you shall put the covenant that I shall give you. [22]There I will meet with you, and from above the mercy seat, from between the two cherubim that are on the ark of the covenant, I will deliver to you all my commands for the Israelites.

Instructions for the Table

23 You shall make a table of acacia wood, two cubits long, one cubit wide, and a cubit and a half high. [24]You shall overlay it with pure gold, and make a molding of gold around it. [25]You shall make around it a rim a handbreadth wide, and a molding of gold around the rim. [26]You shall make for it four rings of gold, and fasten the rings to the four corners at its four legs. [27]The rings that hold the poles used for carrying the table shall be close to the rim. [28]You shall make the poles of acacia wood, and overlay

---

56. What follows are instructions, with all the detail of architectural blueprints, for making the sanctuary and its equipment—ark, table, lampstand, tabernacle, altar, court, lamp—and the priestly garments, and for the priestly consecration and the offerings (Exodus 25–29). After these come an equally detailed account of the carrying out of these instructions in the construction of the sanctuary: ark, table, lampstand, tabernacle, altar, court, priestly garments, and the setting up of the tabernacle (chaps. 35–40; see n. 67, below).

These are made according to the heavenly model or "pattern" (*tabnit*), shown Moses on Sinai (Exod 25:9). God's purpose in having Israel make this sanctuary is "so that I may dwell among them" (25:8)—hence its significance for P. The detail of command and compliance is a measure of the seriousness given to the matter of God's presence in Israel's midst. "The presence of God which had once dwelt on Sinai now accompanies Israel in the tabernacle on her desert journey" (Childs, *Exodus*, 536).

them with gold, and the table shall be carried with these. [29]You shall make its plates and dishes for incense, and its flagons and bowls with which to pour drink offerings; you shall make them of pure gold. [30]And you shall set the bread of the Presence on the table before me always.

Instructions for the Lampstand

31 You shall make a lampstand of pure gold. The base and the shaft of the lampstand shall be made of hammered work; its cups, its calyxes, and its petals shall be of one piece with it; [32]and there shall be six branches going out of its sides, three branches of the lampstand out of one side of it and three branches of the lampstand out of the other side of it; [33]three cups shaped like almond blossoms, each with calyx and petals, on one branch, and three cups shaped like almond blossoms, each with calyx and petals, on the other branch—so for the six branches going out of the lampstand. [34]On the lampstand itself there shall be four cups shaped like almond blossoms, each with its calyxes and petals. [35]There shall be a calyx of one piece with it under the first pair of branches, a calyx of one piece with it under the next pair of branches, and a calyx of one piece with it under the last pair of branches—so for the six branches that go out of the lampstand. [36]Their calyxes and their branches shall be of one piece with it, the whole of it one hammered piece of pure gold. [37]You shall make the seven lamps for it; and the lamps shall be set up so as to give light on the space in front of it. [38]Its snuffers and trays shall be of pure gold. [39]It, and all these utensils, shall be made from a talent of pure gold. [40]And see that you make them according to the pattern for them, which is being shown you on the mountain.

Instructions for the Tabernacle

26 Moreover you shall make the tabernacle with ten curtains of fine twisted linen, and blue, purple, and crimson yarns; you shall make them

with cherubim skillfully worked into them. [2]The length of each curtain shall be twenty-eight cubits, and the width of each curtain four cubits; all the curtains shall be of the same size. [3]Five curtains shall be joined to one another; and the other five curtains shall be joined to one another. [4]You shall make loops of blue on the edge of the outermost curtain in the first set; and likewise you shall make loops on the edge of the outermost curtain in the second set. [5]You shall make fifty loops on the one curtain, and you shall make fifty loops on the edge of the curtain that is in the second set; the loops shall be opposite one another. [6]You shall make fifty clasps of gold, and join the curtains to one another with the clasps, so that the tabernacle may be one whole.

7 You shall also make curtains of goats' hair for a tent over the tabernacle; you shall make eleven curtains. [8]The length of each curtain shall be thirty cubits, and the width of each curtain four cubits; the eleven curtains shall be of the same size. [9]You shall join five curtains by themselves, and six curtains by themselves, and the sixth curtain you shall double over at the front of the tent. [10]You shall make fifty loops on the edge of the curtain that is outermost in one set, and fifty loops on the edge of the curtain that is outermost in the second set.

11 You shall make fifty clasps of bronze, and put the clasps into the loops, and join the tent together, so that it may be one whole. [12]The part that remains of the curtains of the tent, the half curtain that remains, shall hang over the back of the tabernacle. [13]The cubit on the one side, and the cubit on the other side, of what remains in the length of the curtains of the tent, shall hang over the sides of the tabernacle, on this side and that side, to cover it. [14]You shall make for the tent a covering of tanned rams' skins and an outer covering of fine leather.

15 You shall make upright frames of acacia wood for the tabernacle. [16]Ten cubits shall be the length of a frame, and a cubit and a half the

width of each frame. [17]There shall be two pegs in each frame to fit the frames together; you shall make these for all the frames of the tabernacle. [18]You shall make the frames for the tabernacle: twenty frames for the south side; [19]and you shall make forty bases of silver under the twenty frames, two bases under the first frame for its two pegs, and two bases under the next frame for its two pegs; [20]and for the second side of the tabernacle, on the north side twenty frames, [21]and their forty bases of silver, two bases under the first frame, and two bases under the next frame; [22]and for the rear of the tabernacle westward you shall make six frames. [23]You shall make two frames for corners of the tabernacle in the rear; [24]they shall be separate beneath, but joined at the top, at the first ring; it shall be the same with both of them; they shall form the two corners. [25]And so there shall be eight frames, with their bases of silver, sixteen bases; two bases under the first frame, and two bases under the next frame.

26 You shall make bars of acacia wood, five for the frames of the one side of the tabernacle, [27]and five bars for the frames of the other side of the tabernacle, and five bars for the frames of the side of the tabernacle at the rear westward. [28]The middle bar, halfway up the frames, shall pass through from end to end. [29]You shall overlay the frames with gold, and shall make their rings of gold to hold the bars; and you shall overlay the bars with gold. [30]Then you shall erect the tabernacle according to the plan for it that you were shown on the mountain.

Instructions for Setting Up the Tabernacle

31 You shall make a curtain of blue, purple, and crimson yarns, and of fine twisted linen; it shall be made with cherubim skillfully worked into it. [32]You shall hang it on four pillars of acacia overlaid with gold, which have hooks of gold and rest on four bases of silver. [33]You shall hang the curtain under the clasps, and bring the ark of the covenant in there, within the curtain; and the curtain shall separate for you the holy place from the most holy. [34]You shall put the mercy seat on the ark of the covenant in the most holy place. [35]You shall set the table outside the curtain, and the lampstand on the south side of the tabernacle opposite the table; and you shall put the table on the north side.

36 You shall make a screen for the entrance of the tent, of blue, purple, and crimson yarns, and of fine twisted linen, embroidered with needlework. [37]You shall make for the screen five pillars of acacia, and overlay them with gold; their hooks shall be of gold, and you shall cast five bases of bronze for them.

Instructions for the Altar

27 You shall make the altar of acacia wood, five cubits long and five cubits wide; the altar shall be square, and it shall be three cubits high. [2]You shall make horns for it on its four corners; its horns shall be of one piece with it, and you shall overlay it with bronze. [3]You shall make pots for it to receive its ashes, and shovels and basins and forks and firepans; you shall make all its utensils of bronze. [4]You shall also make for it a grating, a network of bronze; and on the net you shall make four bronze rings at its four corners. [5]You shall set it under the ledge of the altar so that the net shall extend halfway down the altar. [6]You shall make poles for the altar, poles of acacia wood, and overlay them with bronze; [7]the poles shall be put through the rings, so that the poles shall be on the two sides of the altar when it is carried. [8]You shall make it hollow, with boards. They shall be made just as you were shown on the mountain.

Instructions for the Court

9 You shall make the court of the tabernacle. On the south side the court shall have hangings of fine twisted linen one hundred cubits long for

that side; [10]its twenty pillars and their twenty bases shall be of bronze, but the hooks of the pillars and their bands shall be of silver. [11]Likewise for its length on the north side there shall be hangings one hundred cubits long, their pillars twenty and their bases twenty, of bronze, but the hooks of the pillars and their bands shall be of silver. [12]For the width of the court on the west side there shall be fifty cubits of hangings, with ten pillars and ten bases. [13]The width of the court on the front to the east shall be fifty cubits. [14]There shall be fifteen cubits of hangings on the one side, with three pillars and three bases. [15]There shall be fifteen cubits of hangings on the other side, with three pillars and three bases. [16]For the gate of the court there shall be a screen twenty cubits long, of blue, purple, and crimson yarns, and of fine twisted linen, embroidered with needlework; it shall have four pillars and with them four bases. [17]All the pillars around the court shall be banded with silver; their hooks shall be of silver, and their bases of bronze. [18]The length of the court shall be one hundred cubits, the width fifty, and the height five cubits, with hangings of fine twisted linen and bases of bronze. [19]All the utensils of the tabernacle for every use, and all its pegs and all the pegs of the court, shall be of bronze.

Instructions for the Lamp

20 You shall further command the Israelites to bring you pure oil of beaten olives for the light, so that a lamp may be set up to burn regularly. [21]In the tent of meeting, outside the curtain that is before the covenant, Aaron and his sons shall tend it from evening to morning before the LORD. It shall be a perpetual ordinance to be observed throughout their generations by the Israelites.

Instructions for the Priestly Garments

28 Then bring near to you your brother Aaron, and his sons with him, from among the Israelites, to serve me as priests—Aaron and Aaron's sons, Nadab and Abihu, Eleazar and Ithamar. [2]You shall make sacred vestments for the glorious adornment of your brother Aaron. [3]And you shall speak to all who have ability, whom I have endowed with skill, that they make Aaron's vestments to consecrate him for my priesthood. [4]These are the vestments that they shall make: a breastpiece, an ephod, a robe, a checkered tunic, a turban, and a sash. When they make these sacred vestments for your brother Aaron and his sons to serve me as priests, [5]they shall use gold, blue, purple, and crimson yarns, and fine linen.

6 They shall make the ephod of gold, of blue, purple, and crimson yarns, and of fine twisted linen, skillfully worked. [7]It shall have two shoulder-pieces attached to its two edges, so that it may be joined together. [8]The decorated band on it shall be of the same workmanship and materials, of gold, of blue, purple, and crimson yarns, and of fine twisted linen. [9]You shall take two onyx stones, and engrave on them the names of the sons of Israel, [10]six of their names on the one stone, and the names of the remaining six on the other stone, in the order of their birth. [11]As a gem-cutter engraves signets, so you shall engrave the two stones with the names of the sons of Israel; you shall mount them in settings of gold filigree. [12]You shall set the two stones on the shoulder-pieces of the ephod, as stones of remembrance for the sons of Israel; and Aaron shall bear their names before the LORD on his two shoulders for remembrance. [13]You shall make settings of gold filigree, [14]and two chains of pure gold, twisted like cords; and you shall attach the corded chains to the settings.

15 You shall make a breastpiece of judgment, in skilled work; you shall make it in the style of the ephod; of gold, of blue and purple and crimson yarns, and of fine twisted linen you shall make it. [16]It shall be square and doubled, a span in length and a span in width. [17]You shall set in it four rows of stones. A row of carnelian,

chrysolite, and emerald shall be the first row; [18]and the second row a turquoise, a sapphire and a moonstone; [19]and the third row a jacinth, an agate, and an amethyst; [20]and the fourth row a beryl, an onyx, and a jasper; they shall be set in gold filigree. [21]There shall be twelve stones with names corresponding to the names of the sons of Israel; they shall be like signets, each engraved with its name, for the twelve tribes. [22]You shall make for the breastpiece chains of pure gold, twisted like cords; [23]and you shall make for the breastpiece two rings of gold, and put the two rings on the two edges of the breastpiece. [24]You shall put the two cords of gold in the two rings at the edges of the breastpiece; [25]the two ends of the two cords you shall attach to the two settings, and so attach it in front to the shoulder-pieces of the ephod. [26]You shall make two rings of gold, and put them at the two ends of the breastpiece, on its inside edge next to the ephod. [27]You shall make two rings of gold, and attach them in front to the lower part of the two shoulder-pieces of the ephod, at its joining above the decorated band of the ephod. [28]The breast-piece shall be bound by its rings to the rings of the ephod with a blue cord, so that it may lie on the decorated band of the ephod, and so that the breastpiece shall not come loose from the ephod. [29]So Aaron shall bear the names of the sons of Israel in the breastpiece of judgment on his heart when he goes into the holy place, for a continual remembrance before the LORD. [30]In the breast-piece of judgment you shall put the Urim and the Thummim, and they shall be on Aaron's heart when he goes in before the LORD; thus Aaron shall bear the judgment of the Israelites on his heart before the LORD continually.

31 You shall make the robe of the ephod all of blue. [32]It shall have an opening for the head in the middle of it, with a woven binding around the opening, like the opening in a coat of mail, so that it may not be torn. [33]On its lower hem you shall make pomegranates of blue, purple, and crimson yarns, all around the lower hem, with bells of gold between them all around—[34]a golden bell and a pomegranate alternating all around the lower hem of the robe. [35]Aaron shall wear it when he ministers, and its sound shall be heard when he goes into the holy place before the LORD, and when he comes out, so that he may not die.

36 You shall make a rosette of pure gold, and engrave on it, like the engraving of a signet, "Holy to the LORD." [37]You shall fasten it on the turban with a blue cord; it shall be on the front of the turban. [38]It shall be on Aaron's forehead, and Aaron shall take on himself any guilt incurred in the holy offering that the Israelites consecrate as their sacred donations; it shall always be on his forehead, in order that they may find favor before the LORD.

39 You shall make the checkered tunic of fine linen, and you shall make a turban of fine linen, and you shall make a sash embroidered with needlework.

40 For Aaron's sons you shall make tunics and sashes and headdresses; you shall make them for their glorious adornment. [41]You shall put them on your brother Aaron, and on his sons with him, and shall anoint them and ordain them and consecrate them, so that they may serve me as priests. [42]You shall make for them linen undergarments to cover their naked flesh; they shall reach from the hips to the thighs; [43]Aaron and his sons shall wear them when they go into the tent of meeting, or when they come near the altar to minister in the holy place; or they will bring guilt on themselves and die. This shall be a perpetual ordinance for him and for his descendants after him.

Instructions for the
Priestly Consecration

29 Now this is what you shall do to them to consecrate them, so that they may serve me as priests.[57] Take one young bull and two rams without blemish, [2]and unleavened bread, unleavened cakes mixed with oil, and unleavened wafers spread with oil. You shall make them of choice wheat flour. [3]You shall put them in one basket and bring them in the basket, and bring the bull and the two rams. [4]You shall bring Aaron and his sons to the entrance of the tent of meeting, and wash them with water. [5]Then you shall take the vestments, and put on Aaron the tunic and the robe of the ephod, and the ephod, and the breastpiece, and gird him with the decorated band of the ephod; [6]and you shall set the turban on his head, and put the holy diadem on the turban. [7]You shall take the anointing oil, and pour it on his head and anoint him. [8]Then you shall bring his sons, and put tunics on them, [9]and you shall gird them with sashes and tie headdresses on them; and the priesthood shall be theirs by a perpetual ordinance. You shall then ordain Aaron and his sons.

10 You shall bring the bull in front of the tent of meeting. Aaron and his sons shall lay their hands on the head of the bull, [11]and you shall slaughter the bull before the LORD, at the entrance of the tent of meeting, [12]and shall take some of the blood of the bull and put it on the horns of the altar with your finger, and all the rest of the blood you shall pour out at the base of the altar. [13]You shall take all the fat that covers the entrails, and the appendage of the liver, and the two kidneys with the fat that is on them, and turn them into smoke on the altar. [14]But the flesh of the bull, and its skin, and its dung, you shall burn with fire outside the camp; it is a sin offering.

15 Then you shall take one of the rams, and Aaron and his sons shall lay their hands on the head of the ram, [16]and you shall slaughter the ram, and shall take its blood and dash it against all sides of the altar. [17]Then you shall cut the ram into its parts, and wash its entrails and its legs, and put them with its parts and its head, [18]and turn the whole ram into smoke on the altar; it is a burnt offering to the LORD; it is a pleasing odor, an offering by fire to the LORD.

19 You shall take the other ram; and Aaron and his sons shall lay their hands on the head of the ram, [20]and you shall slaughter the ram, and take some of its blood and put it on the lobe of Aaron's right ear and on the lobes of the right ears of his sons, and on the thumbs of their right hands, and on the big toes of their right feet, and dash the rest of the blood against all sides of the altar. [21]Then you shall take some of the blood that is on the altar, and some of the anointing oil, and sprinkle it on Aaron and his vestments and on his sons and his sons' vestments with him; then he and his vestments shall be holy, as well as his sons and his sons' vestments.

22 You shall also take the fat of the ram, the fat tail, the fat that covers the entrails, the appendage of the liver, the two kidneys with the fat that is on them, and the right thigh (for it is a ram of ordination), [23]and one loaf of bread, one cake of bread made with oil, and one wafer, out of the basket of unleavened bread that is

---

57. In his Exodus commentary, Noth treats all of 29:1—31:17 as secondary expansions of the P document. As far as Exod 29:1-46 is concerned, there are two principal reasons for this treatment: (1) a shift in concern from the sanctuary and its contents (chaps. 25–28) to the ordination celebration for Aaron and his sons; and (2) a number of divergences, although insignificant, in the details of the priests' dress from those in chap. 28. There is also the confusing order of the sections within 29:26-46 (*Exodus*, 229). Lohfink includes as original only Exod 29:43-46 following on 26:1-30 ("Die Priesterschrift und die Geschichte," in *Congress Volume: Göttingen, 1977* [VTSup 29; Leiden: E. J. Brill, 1978] 198; see Campbell, *Study Companion*, 89).

before the LORD; [24]and you shall place all these on the palms of Aaron and on the palms of his sons, and raise them as an elevation offering before the LORD. [25]Then you shall take them from their hands, and turn them into smoke on the altar on top of the burnt offering of pleasing odor before the LORD; it is an offering by fire to the LORD.

26 You shall take the breast of the ram of Aaron's ordination and raise it as an elevation offering before the LORD; and it shall be your portion. [27]You shall consecrate the breast that was raised as an elevation offering and the thigh that was raised as an elevation offering from the ram of ordination, from that which belonged to Aaron and his sons. [28]These things shall be a perpetual ordinance for Aaron and his sons from the Israelites, for this is an offering; and it shall be an offering by the Israelites from their sacrifice of offerings of well-being, their offering to the LORD.

29 The sacred vestments of Aaron shall be passed on to his sons after him; they shall be anointed in them and ordained in them. [30]The son who is priest in his place shall wear them seven days, when he comes into the tent of meeting to minister in the holy place.

31 You shall take the ram of ordination, and boil its flesh in a holy place; [32]and Aaron and his sons shall eat the flesh of the ram and the bread that is in the basket, at the entrance of the tent of meeting. [33]They themselves shall eat the food by which atonement is made, to ordain and consecrate them, but no one else shall eat of them, because they are holy. [34]If any of the flesh for the ordination, or of the bread, remains until the morning, then you shall burn the remainder with fire; it shall not be eaten, because it is holy.

35 Thus you shall do to Aaron and to his sons, just as I have commanded you; through seven days you shall ordain them. [36]Also every day you shall offer a bull as a sin offering for atonement. Also you shall offer a sin offering for the altar, when you make atonement for it, and shall anoint it, to consecrate it. [37]Seven days you shall make atonement for the altar, and consecrate it, and the altar shall be most holy; whatever touches the altar shall become holy.

Instructions for the Offerings

38 Now this is what you shall offer on the altar: two lambs a year old regularly each day. [39]One lamb you shall offer in the morning, and the other lamb you shall offer in the evening; [40]and with the first lamb one-tenth of a measure of choice flour mixed with one-fourth of a hin of beaten oil, and one-fourth of a hin of wine for a drink offering. [41]And the other lamb you shall offer in the evening, and shall offer with it a grain offering and its drink offering, as in the morning, for a pleasing odor, an offering by fire to the LORD. [42]It shall be a regular burnt offering throughout your generations at the entrance of the tent of meeting before the LORD, where I will meet with you, to speak to you there. [43]I will meet with the Israelites there, and it shall be sanctified by my glory; [44]I will consecrate the tent of meeting and the altar; Aaron also and his sons I will consecrate, to serve me as priests. [45]I will dwell among the Israelites, and I will be their God. [46]And they shall know that I am the LORD their God, who brought them out of the land of Egypt that I might dwell among them; I am the LORD their God.

Further Instructions

30 *You shall make an altar on which to offer incense; you shall make it of acacia wood.*[58] [2]*It*

---

58. Noth, in his commentary, dismisses Exodus 30–31 in rather summary fashion. They are "various passages of mixed content," and the case for their being a supplement to the P narrative "is generally agreed" (*Exodus*, 234), their sections "introduced by a stereotyped formula which is not necessary in the context

shall be one cubit long, and one cubit wide; it shall be square, and shall be two cubits high; its horns shall be of one piece with it. [3]*You shall overlay it with pure gold, its top, and its sides all around and its horns; and you shall make for it a molding of gold all around.* [4]*And you shall make two golden rings for it; under its molding on two opposite sides of it you shall make them, and they shall hold the poles with which to carry it.* [5]*You shall make the poles of acacia wood, and overlay them with gold.* [6]*You shall place it in front of the curtain that is above the ark of the covenant, in front of the mercy seat that is over the covenant, where I will meet with you.* [7]*Aaron shall offer fragrant incense on it; every morning when he dresses the lamps he shall offer it,* [8]*and when Aaron sets up the lamps in the evening, he shall offer it, a regular incense offering before the* LORD *throughout your generations.* [9]*You shall not offer unholy incense on it, or a burnt offering, or a grain offering; and you shall not pour a drink offering on it.* [10]*Once a year Aaron shall perform the rite of atonement on its horns. Throughout your generations he shall perform the atonement for it once a year with the blood of the atoning sin offering. It is most holy to the* LORD.

11 The LORD *spoke to Moses:* [12]*When you take a census of the Israelites to register them, at registration all of them shall give a ransom for their lives to the* LORD, *so that no plague may come upon them for being registered.* [13]*This is what each one who is registered shall give: half a shekel according to the shekel of the sanctuary (the shekel is twenty gerahs), half a shekel as an offering to the* LORD. [14]*Each one who is registered, from twenty years old and upward, shall give the* LORD's *offering.* [15]*The rich shall not give more, and the poor shall not give less, than the half shekel, when you bring this offering to the* LORD *to make atonement for your lives.* [16]*You shall take the atonement money from the Israelites and shall designate it for the service of the tent of meeting; before the* LORD *it will be a reminder to the Israelites of the ransom given for your lives.*

17 The LORD *spoke to Moses:* [18]*You shall make a bronze basin with a bronze stand for washing. You shall put it between the tent of meeting and the altar, and you shall put water in it;* [19]*with the water Aaron and his sons shall wash their hands and their feet.* [20]*When they go into the tent of meeting, or when they come near the altar to minister, to make an offering by fire to the* LORD, *they shall wash with water, so that they may not die.* [21]*They shall wash their hands and their feet, so that they may not die: it shall be a perpetual ordinance for them, for him and for his descendants throughout their generations.*

22 The LORD *spoke to Moses:* [23]*Take the finest spices: of liquid myrrh five hundred shekels, and of sweet-smelling cinnamon half as much, that is, two hundred fifty, and two hundred fifty of aromatic cane,* [24]*and five hundred of cassia— measured by the sanctuary shekel—and a hin of olive oil;* [25]*and you shall make of these a sacred*

---

and points to the secondary character of the passage" (*Exodus*, 236). Questions of order are important to the judgment that these chapters are secondary; so Noth believes the proper place for the instructions on the altar of incense would have been in chaps. 25–27, and that prescriptions for use that go beyond the descriptive form of chaps. 25–28 are added (*Exodus*, 234–35). He expresses surprise that the bronze basin was not among the items in chaps. 25–27; given its existence in the post-exilic temple, a short insertion here was required (30:17-21; see *Exodus*, 237). Exodus 31:1-11 is considered secondary because it includes the altar of incense, the basin, the anointing oil, and the incense in the list (*Exodus*, 239).

To a large extent, decisions on what is or is not secondary in these chapters depend on the place of tradition in the composition of P. To simplify: if the Priestly writer was responsible for the shaping of chaps. 25–28, it is highly likely that the later chapters are from a second priestly hand; but if chaps. 25–28 were already traditional and the Priestly writer was responsible for chaps. 35–40, a quite different picture would emerge.

anointing oil blended as by the perfumer; it shall be a holy anointing oil. *26With it you shall anoint the tent of meeting and the ark of the covenant, 27and the table and all its utensils, and the lampstand and its utensils, and the altar of incense, 28and the altar of burnt offering with all its utensils, and the basin with its stand; 29you shall consecrate them, so that they may be most holy; whatever touches them will become holy. 30You shall anoint Aaron and his sons, and consecrate them, in order that they may serve me as priests. 31You shall say to the Israelites, "This shall be my holy anointing oil throughout your generations. 32It shall not be used in any ordinary anointing of the body, and you shall make no other like it in composition; it is holy, and it shall be holy to you. 33Whoever compounds any like it or whoever puts any of it on an unqualified person shall be cut off from the people."*

34 The LORD *said to Moses: Take sweet spices, stacte, and onycha, and galbanum, sweet spices with pure frankincense (an equal part of each), 35and make an incense blended as by the perfumer, seasoned with salt, pure and holy; 36and you shall beat some of it into powder, and put part of it before the covenant in the tent of meeting where I shall meet with you; it shall be for you most holy. 37When you make incense according to this composition, you shall not make it for yourselves; it shall be regarded by you as holy to the* LORD. *38Whoever makes any like it to use as perfume shall be cut off from the people.*

31 The LORD *spoke to Moses: 2See, I have called by name Bezalel son of Uri son of Hur, of the tribe of Judah: 3and I have filled him with divine spirit, with ability, intelligence, and knowledge in every kind of craft, 4to devise artistic designs, to work in gold, silver, and bronze, 5in cutting stones for setting, and in carving wood,*

in every kind of craft. 6Moreover, I have appointed with him Oholiab son of Ahisamach, of the tribe of Dan; and I have given skill to all the skillful, so that they may make all that I have commanded you: 7the tent of meeting, and the ark of the covenant, and the mercy seat that is on it, and all the furnishings of the tent, 8the table and its utensils, and the pure lampstand with all its utensils, and the altar of incense, 9and the altar of burnt offering with all its utensils, and the basin with its stand, 10and the finely worked vestments, the holy vestments for the priest Aaron and the vestments of his sons, for their service as priests, 11and the anointing oil and the fragrant incense for the holy place. They shall do just as I have commanded you.

12 The LORD *said to Moses: 13You yourself are to speak to the Israelites: "You shall keep my sabbaths, for this is a sign between me and you throughout your generations, given in order that you may know that I, the* LORD, *sanctify you. 14You shall keep the sabbath, because it is holy for you; everyone who profanes it shall be put to death; whoever does any work on it shall be cut off from among the people. 15Six days shall work be done, but the seventh day is a sabbath of solemn rest, holy to the* LORD; *whoever does any work on the sabbath day shall be put to death. 16Therefore the Israelites shall keep the sabbath, observing the sabbath throughout their generations, as a perpetual covenant. 17It is a sign forever between me and the people of Israel that in six days the* LORD *made heaven and earth, and on the seventh day he rested, and was refreshed."*

The Tablets of the Law

18 When God finished speaking with Moses on Mount Sinai, he gave him the two tablets of the covenant, tablets of stone, written with the finger of God.[59]

---

59. The Hebrew word translated as "covenant" here by the NRSV is not the usual *běrît* but *'ēdût*, which is traditionally translated "testimony."

*Moses' Call for an Offering
for the Sanctuary*

35 Moses assembled all the congregation of the Israelites and said to them:[60]

These are the things that the LORD has commanded you to do:

²Six days shall work be done, but on the seventh day you shall have a holy sabbath of solemn rest to the LORD; whoever does any work on it shall be put to death. ³You shall kindle no fire in all your dwellings on the sabbath day.

⁴Moses said to all the congregation of the Israelites:[61]

This is the thing that the LORD has commanded: ⁵Take from among you an offering to the LORD; let whoever is of a generous heart bring the LORD's offering: gold, silver, and bronze; ⁶blue, purple, and crimson yarns, and fine linen; goats' hair, ⁷tanned rams' skins, and fine leather; acacia wood, ⁸oil for the light, spices for the anointing oil and for the fragrant incense, ⁹and onyx stones and gems to be set in the ephod and the breastpiece.

10 All who are skillful among you shall come and make all that the LORD has commanded.[62]

the tabernacle, ¹¹its tent and its covering, its clasps and its frames, its bars, its pillars, and its bases; ¹²the ark with its poles, the mercy seat, and the curtain for the screen; ¹³the table with its poles and all its utensils, and the bread of the Presence; ¹⁴the lampstand also for the light, with its utensils and its lamps, and the oil for the light; ¹⁵and the altar of incense, with its poles, and the anointing oil and the fragrant incense, and the screen for the entrance, the entrance of the tabernacle; ¹⁶the altar of burnt offering, with its grating of bronze, its poles, and all its utensils, the basin with its stand; ¹⁷the hangings of the court, its pillars and its bases, and the screen for the gate of the court; ¹⁸the pegs of the tabernacle and the pegs of the court, and their cords; ¹⁹the finely worked vestments for ministering in the holy place, the

---

60. In his Exodus commentary, Noth treats almost the whole of Exodus 35–40 as secondary. Only the following is tentatively retained:

39:32 In this way all the work of the tabernacle of the tent of meeting was finished; the Israelites had done everything just as the LORD had commanded Moses. ⁴²Just as the LORD had commanded Moses, so the Israelites had done all of the work. ⁴³When Moses saw that they had done all the work just as the LORD had commanded, he blessed them.

40:17 In the first month in the second year, on the first day of the month, the tabernacle was set up. (See *Exodus*, 282)

Lohfink retains slightly more for his P: Exod 35:4-5a, 10, 20-22a, 29; 36:2-3a, 8*; 39:32-33a, 42-43; 40:17, 33b-35 ("Priesterschrift und die Geschichte," 198).

These are good examples of fluctuations in the identification of parts of a given source, which may be important for the history of Israelite theology but do not in any way affect the essentials of the source hypothesis as such.

61. With the repetition of the introductory formula (Exod 35:1 and 35:4), the position before the beginning of the compliance with God's instructions, and the repetition of the sabbath command (considered secondary in 31:12-17), it is easy to see why these verses are considered secondary (*Exodus*, 275).

It is far from easy to decide whether this view is correct. The decision is ultimately whether this reference to sabbath coheres with the grand unified design visible in the P document, and so is attributed as original to P, or whether it reveals a narrower and more intensely focused concern, and so is attributed to a later hand.

A decision may be impossible. It may well be judged appropriate to mention sabbath before specifying the work to be undertaken. It is possible that 31:12-17, differently formulated, is the secondary tradition. It is impossible to deny an author the occasional narrower and more intensely focused concern, even if it conflicts with a grand unified design. To paraphrase Noth, from another context: all this is subject to considerable reservations, for the nature of the material scarcely allows of any more certain conclusions (*Leviticus* [OTL; Philadelphia: Westminster, 1965; rev. trans., 1977] 15).

62. The NRSV, RSV, and NAB include the tabernacle in Exod 35:10; in the Hebrew, followed by Noth, it begins v. 11.

holy vestments for the priest Aaron, and the vestments of his sons, for their service as priests.[63]

20 Then all the congregation of the Israelites withdrew from the presence of Moses. [21]And they came, everyone whose heart was stirred, and everyone whose spirit was willing, and brought the LORD's offering to be used for the tent of meeting, and for all its service, and for the sacred vestments. [22]So they came, both men and women; all who were of a willing heart brought brooches and earrings and signet rings and pendants, all sorts of gold objects, everyone bringing an offering of gold to the LORD. [23]And everyone who possessed blue or purple or crimson yarn or fine linen or goats' hair or tanned rams' skins or fine leather, brought them. [24]Everyone who could make an offering of silver or bronze brought it as the LORD's offering; and everyone who possessed acacia wood of any use in the work, brought it. [25]All the skillful women spun with their hands, and brought what they had spun in blue and purple and crimson yarns and fine linen; [26]all the women whose hearts moved them to use their skill spun the goats' hair. [27]And the leaders brought onyx stones and gems to be set in the ephod and the breastpiece.

[28]*and spices and oil for the light, and for the anointing oil, and for the fragrant incense.*[64]

[29]All the Israelite men and women whose hearts made them willing to bring anything for the work that the LORD had commanded by Moses to be done, brought it as a freewill offering to the LORD.

Construction of the Sanctuary

30 Then Moses said to the Israelites: See, the LORD has called by name Bezalel son of Uri son of Hur, of the tribe of Judah; [31]he has filled him with divine spirit

with skill, intelligence, and knowledge in every kind of craft[65]

[32]to devise artistic designs, to work in gold, silver, and bronze, [33]in cutting stones for setting, and in carving wood, in every kind of craft.

[34]And he has inspired him to teach, both him and Oholiab son of Ahisamach, of the tribe of Dan. [35]He has filled them with skill to do every kind of work done by an artisan or by a designer or by an embroiderer in blue, purple, and crimson yarns, and in fine linen, or by a weaver—by any sort of artisan or skilled designer.

36 Bezalel and Oholiab and every skillful one to whom the LORD has given skill and understanding to know how to do any work in the construction of the sanctuary shall work in accordance with all that the LORD has commanded.[66]

2 Moses then called Bezalel and Oholiab and every skillful one to whom the LORD had given skill, everyone whose heart was stirred to come to do the work; [3]and they received from Moses all the freewill offerings that the Israelites had brought for doing the work on the sanctuary. They still kept bringing him freewill offerings every morning, [4]so that all the artisans who were doing every sort of task on the sanctuary came, each from the task being performed, [5]and said to Moses, "The people are bringing much more than enough for doing the work that the LORD

---

63. This is considered as probably secondary because the items to be made are listed here between the command for a collection and the report that the collection has been taken up (cf. Noth, *Exodus*, 275). It refers to the altar of incense, the basin, anointing oil, and incense, which were earlier regarded as secondary (Exod 30:1-38).

64. This list includes reference to items earlier regarded as secondary (cf. Exod 30:22-38; 31:11).

65. Verses 30-33 are to be found also in the sec-

ondary Exod 31:1-5, spoken there by God to Moses. The half-verse considered secondary here may have been felt to interrupt the movement from the gift of the divine spirit to its exercise (the infinitive "to devise").

66. Exodus 35:34—36:1 is not found in Exodus 31. Noth points out that the teaching activity referred to in 35:34 does not happen; he suggests the text may no longer be fully intact (*Exodus*, 276).

has commanded us to do." [6]So Moses gave command, and word was proclaimed throughout the camp: "No man or woman is to make anything else as an offering for the sanctuary." So the people were restrained from bringing; [7]for what they had already brought was more than enough to do all the work.[67]

Construction of the Ark

37 Bezalel made the ark of acacia wood; it was two and a half cubits long, a cubit and a half wide, and a cubit and a half high.[68] [2]He overlaid it with pure gold inside and outside, and made a molding of gold around it. [3]He cast for it four rings of gold for its four feet, two rings on its one side and two rings on its other side. [4]He made poles of acacia wood, and overlaid them with gold, [5]and put the poles into the rings on the sides of the ark, to carry the ark. [6]He made a mercy seat of pure gold; two cubits and a half was its length, and a cubit and a half its width. [7]He made two cherubim of hammered gold; at the two ends of the mercy seat he made them, [8]one cherub at the one end, and one cherub at the other end; of one piece with the mercy seat he made the cherubim at its two ends. [9]The cherubim spread out their wings above, overshadowing the mercy seat with their wings. They faced one another; the faces of the cherubim were turned toward the mercy seat.

Construction of the Table

10 He also made the table of acacia wood, two cubits long, one cubit wide, and a cubit and a half high. [11]He overlaid it with pure gold, and made a molding of gold around it. [12]He made around it a rim a handbreadth wide, and made a molding of gold around the rim. [13]He cast for it four rings of gold, and fastened the rings to the four corners at its four legs. [14]The rings that held the poles used for carrying the table were close to the rim. [15]He made the poles of acacia wood to carry the table, and overlaid them with gold. [16]And he made the vessels of pure gold that were to be on the table, its plates and dishes for incense, and its bowls and flagons with which to pour drink offerings.

Construction of the Lampstand

17 He also made the lampstand of pure gold. The base and the shaft of the lampstand were made of hammered work; its cups, its calyxes, and its petals were of one piece with it. [18]There were six branches going out of its sides, three branches of the lampstand out of one side of it and three branches of the lampstand out of the other side of it; [19]three cups shaped like almond blossoms, each with calyx and petals, on one branch, and three cups shaped like almond blossoms, each with calyx and petals, on the other branch—so for the six branches going out of the lampstand. [20]On the lampstand itself there were four cups shaped like almond blossoms, each with its calyxes and petals. [21]There was a calyx of one piece with it under the first pair of branches, a calyx of one piece with it under the next pair of branches, and a calyx of one piece

---

67. Although Exodus 35–40 appears, at first sight, to be an almost verbatim repetition of the instructions in chaps. 25–29, there are a number of significant differences. These have occasioned debate over the age of chaps. 35–40. In his commentary, Noth argues that, because chaps. 35–39 combine the basic and additional material in chaps. 25–31, it is clear that chaps. 35–39 are secondary (*Exodus*, 274–75). See the discussions in Childs, *Exodus*, 529–37, and John I. Durham, *Exodus* (WBC; Waco, Tex.: Word Books, 1987) 350–53, 368–71, 473–75. As usual, the text here follows Noth's *Pentateuchal Traditions*.

68. In Noth's judgment, a later redactor wanted the tabernacle constructed before the ark, the table, and the lampstand. As evidence that Exod 37:1-24 (29) originally preceded 36:8, maintaining the same order as in chaps. 25–26, Noth adduces the naming of Bezalel in 37:1, as belonging at the start of the sequence. Exodus 36:8 would have originally begun with a simple "and he made," as in 36:14, 20, 31, 35, etc. With the rearrangement in the present text, a new beginning was inserted at 36:1, modeled on 36:2 (*Pentateuchal Traditions*, 18 n. 56).

with it under the last pair of branches. ²²Their calyxes and their branches were of one piece with it, the whole of it one hammered piece of pure gold. ²³He made its seven lamps and its snuffers and its trays of pure gold. ²⁴He made it and all its utensils of a talent of pure gold.

25 He made the altar of incense of acacia wood, one cubit long, and one cubit wide; it was square, and was two cubits high; its horns were of one piece with it. ²⁶He overlaid it with pure gold, its top, and its sides all around, and its horns; and he made for it a molding of gold all around, ²⁷and made two golden rings for it under its molding, on two opposite sides of it, to hold the poles with which to carry it. ²⁸And he made the poles of acacia wood, and overlaid them with gold.

29 He made the holy anointing oil also, and the pure fragrant incense, blended as by the perfumer.[69]

Construction of the Tabernacle

36:8 All those with skill among the workers made the tabernacle with ten curtains; they were made of fine twisted linen, and blue, purple, and crimson yarns, with cherubim skillfully worked into them. ⁹The length of each curtain was twenty-eight cubits, and the width of each curtain four cubits; all the curtains were of the same size.

10 He joined five curtains to one another, and the other five curtains he joined to one another. ¹¹He made loops of blue on the edge of the outermost curtain of the first set; likewise he made them on the edge of the outermost curtain of the second set; ¹²he made fifty loops on the one curtain, and he made fifty loops on the edge of the curtain that was in the second set; the loops were opposite one another. ¹³And he made fifty clasps of gold, and joined the curtains one to the other with clasps; so the tabernacle was one whole.

14 He also made curtains of goats' hair for a tent over the tabernacle; he made eleven curtains. ¹⁵The length of each curtain was thirty cubits, and the width of each curtain four cubits; the eleven curtains were of the same size. ¹⁶He joined five curtains by themselves, and six curtains by themselves. ¹⁷He made fifty loops on the edge of the outermost curtain of the one set, and fifty loops on the edge of the other connecting curtain. ¹⁸He made fifty clasps of bronze to join the tent together so that it might be one whole. ¹⁹And he made for the tent a covering of tanned rams' skins and an outer covering of fine leather.

20 Then he made the upright frames for the tabernacle of acacia wood. ²¹Ten cubits was the length of a frame, and a cubit and a half the width of each frame. ²²Each frame had two pegs for fitting together; he did this for all the frames of the tabernacle. ²³The frames for the tabernacle he made in this way: twenty frames for the south side; ²⁴and he made forty bases of silver under the twenty frames, two bases under the first frame for its two pegs, and two bases under the next frame for its two pegs. ²⁵For the second side of the tabernacle, on the north side, he made twenty frames ²⁶and their forty bases of silver, two bases under the first frame and two bases under the next frame. ²⁷For the rear of the tabernacle westward he made six frames. ²⁸He made two frames for corners of the tabernacle in the rear. ²⁹They were separate beneath, but joined at the top, at the first ring; he made two of them in this way, for the two corners. ³⁰There were eight frames with their bases of silver: sixteen bases, under every frame two bases.

31 He made bars of acacia wood, five for the frames of the one side of the tabernacle, ³²and five bars for the frames of the other side of the tabernacle, and five bars for the frames of the tab-

---

69. These are again items regarded as secondary earlier (cf. Exod 30:1-5, 22-25).

ernacle at the rear westward. [33]He made the middle bar to pass through from end to end halfway up the frames. [34]And he overlaid the frames with gold, and made rings of gold for them to hold the bars, and overlaid the bars with gold.

35 He made the curtain of blue, purple, and crimson yarns, and fine twisted linen, with cherubim skillfully worked into it. [36]For it he made four pillars of acacia, and overlaid them with gold; their hooks were of gold, and he cast for them four bases of silver. [37]He also made a screen for the entrance to the tent, of blue, purple, and crimson yarns, and fine twisted linen, embroidered with needlework; [38]and its five pillars with their hooks. He overlaid their capitals and their bases with gold, but their five bases were of bronze.

Construction of the Altar

38 He made the altar of burnt offering also of acacia wood; it was five cubits long, and five cubits wide; it was square, and three cubits high. [2]He made horns for it on its four corners; its horns were of one piece with it, and he overlaid it with bronze. [3]He made all the utensils of the altar, the pots, the shovels, the basins, the forks, and the firepans: all its utensils he made of bronze. [4]He made for the altar a grating, a network of bronze, under its ledge, extending halfway down. [5]He cast four rings on the four corners of the bronze grating to hold the poles; [6]he made the poles of acacia wood, and overlaid them with bronze. [7]And he put the poles through the rings on the sides of the altar, to carry it with them; he made it hollow, with boards.

8 He made the basin of bronze with its stand of bronze, from the mirrors of the women who served at the entrance to the tent of meeting.[70]

Construction of the Court

9 He made the court; for the south side the hangings of the court were of fine twisted linen, one hundred cubits long; [10]its twenty pillars and their twenty bases were of bronze, but the hooks of the pillars and their bands were of silver. [11]For the north side there were hangings one hundred cubits long; its twenty pillars and their twenty bases were of bronze, but the hooks of the pillars and their bands were of silver. [12]For the west side there were hangings fifty cubits long, with ten pillars and ten bases; the hooks of the pillars and their bands were of silver. [13]And for the front to the east, fifty cubits. [14]The hangings for one side of the gate were fifteen cubits, with three pillars and three bases. [15]And so for the other side; on each side of the gate of the court were hangings of fifteen cubits, with three pillars and three bases. [16]All the hangings around the court were of fine twisted linen. [17]The bases for the pillars were of bronze, but the hooks of the pillars and their bands were of silver; the overlaying of their capitals was also of silver, and all the pillars of the court were banded with silver. [18]The screen for the entrance to the court was embroidered with needlework in blue, purple, and crimson yarns and fine twisted linen. It was twenty cubits long and, along the width of it, five cubits high, corresponding to the hangings of the court. [19]There were four pillars; their four bases were of bronze, their hooks of silver, and the overlaying of their capitals and their bands of silver. [20]All the pegs for the tabernacle and for the court all around were of bronze.

Summary

21 These are the records of the tabernacle, the tabernacle of the covenant, which were

---

70. Again, this is an item considered secondary earlier (cf. Exod 30:18).

drawn up at the commandment of Moses, the work of the Levites being under the direction of Ithamar son of the priest Aaron. [22]Bezalel son of Uri son of Hur, of the tribe of Judah, made all that the LORD commanded Moses.

[23]*And with him was Oholiab son of Ahisamach, of the tribe of Dan, engraver, designer, and embroiderer in blue, purple, and crimson yarns, and in fine linen.*[71]

[24]All the gold that was used for the work, in all the construction of the sanctuary, the gold from the offering, was twenty-nine talents and seven hundred thirty shekels, measured by the sanctuary shekel. [25]The silver from those of the congregation who were counted was one hundred talents and one thousand seven hundred seventy-five shekels, measured by the sanctuary shekel; [26]a beka a head (that is, half a shekel, measured by the sanctuary shekel), for everyone who was counted in the census, from twenty years old and upward, for six hundred three thousand, five hundred fifty men. [27]The hundred talents of silver were for casting the bases of the sanctuary, and the bases of the curtain; one hundred bases for the hundred talents, a talent for a base. [28]Of the thousand seven hundred seventy-five shekels he made hooks for the pillars, and overlaid their capitals and made bands for them. [29]The bronze that was contributed was seventy talents, and two thousand four hundred shekels; [30]with it he made the bases for the entrance of the tent of meeting, the bronze altar and the bronze grating for it and all the utensils of the altar, [31]the bases all around the court, and the bases of the gate of the court, all the pegs of the tabernacle, and all the pegs around the court.

Making of the Priestly Garments

39 Of the blue, purple, and crimson yarns they made finely worked vestments, for minis-tering in the holy place; they made the sacred vestments for Aaron; as the LORD had commanded Moses.

[2]He made the ephod of gold, of blue, purple, and crimson yarns, and of fine twisted linen. [3]Gold leaf was hammered out and cut into threads to work into the blue, purple, and crimson yarns and into the fine twisted linen, in skilled design. [4]They made for the ephod shoulder-pieces, joined to it at its two edges. [5]The decorated band on it was of the same materials and workmanship, of gold, of blue, purple, and crimson yarns, and of fine twisted linen; as the LORD had commanded Moses.

[6]The onyx stones were prepared, enclosed in settings of gold filigree and engraved like the engravings of a signet, according to the names of the sons of Israel. [7]He set them on the shoulder-pieces of the ephod, to be stones of remembrance for the sons of Israel; as the LORD had commanded Moses.

[8]He made the breastpiece, in skilled work, like the work of the ephod, of gold, of blue, purple, and crimson yarns, and of fine twisted linen. [9]It was square; the breastpiece was made double, a span in length and a span in width when doubled. [10]They set in it four rows of stones. A row of carnelian, chrysolite, and emerald was the first row; [11]and the second row, a turquoise, a sapphire, and a moonstone; [12]and the third row, a jacinth, an agate, and an amethyst; [13]and the fourth row, a beryl, an onyx, and a jasper; they were enclosed in settings of gold filigree. [14]There were twelve stones with names corresponding to the names of the sons of Israel; they were like signets, each engraved with its name, for the twelve tribes. [15]They made on the breastpiece chains of pure gold, twisted like cords; [16]and they made two settings of gold filigree and two gold rings, and put the two rings on the two edges of the breastpiece; [17]and they put

---

71. See above. Exod 35:35.

the two cords of gold in the two rings at the edges of the breastpiece. [18]Two ends of the two cords they had attached to the two settings of filigree; in this way they attached it in front to the shoulder-pieces of the ephod. [19]Then they made two rings of gold, and put them at the two ends of the breastpiece, on its inside edge next to the ephod. [20]They made two rings of gold, and attached them in front to the lower part of the two shoulder-pieces of the ephod, at its joining above the decorated band of the ephod. [21]They bound the breastpiece by its rings to the rings of the ephod with a blue cord, so that it should lie on the decorated band of the ephod, and that the breastpiece should not come loose from the ephod; as the LORD had commanded Moses.

[22] He also made the robe of the ephod woven all of blue yarn; [23]and the opening of the robe in the middle of it was like the opening in a coat of mail, with a binding around the opening, so that it might not be torn. [24]On the lower hem of the robe they made pomegranates of blue, purple, and crimson yarns, and of fine twisted linen. [25]They also made bells of pure gold, and put the bells between the pomegranates on the lower hem of the robe all around, between the pomegranates; [26]a bell and a pomegranate, a bell and a pomegranate all around on the lower hem of the robe for ministering; as the LORD had commanded Moses.

[27] They also made the tunics, woven of fine linen, for Aaron and his sons, [28]and the turban of fine linen, and the headdresses of fine linen, and the linen undergarments of fine twisted linen, [29]and the sash of fine twisted linen, and of blue, purple, and crimson yarns, embroidered with needlework; as the LORD had commanded Moses.

[30] They made the rosette of the holy diadem of pure gold, and wrote on it an inscription, like the engraving of a signet, "Holy to the LORD." [31]They tied to it a blue cord, to fasten it on the turban above; as the LORD had commanded Moses.

[32] In this way all the work of the tabernacle of the tent of meeting was finished; the Israelites had done everything just as the LORD had commanded Moses.

[33]*Then they brought the tabernacle to Moses, the tent and all its utensils, its hooks, its frames, its bars, its pillars, and its bases;* [34]*the covering of tanned rams' skins and the covering of fine leather, and the curtain for the screen;* [35]*the ark of the covenant with its poles and the mercy seat;* [36]*the table with all its utensils, and the bread of the Presence;* [37]*the pure lampstand with its lamps set on it and all its utensils, and the oil for the light;* [38]*the golden altar, the anointing oil and the fragrant incense, and the screen for the entrance of the tent;* [39]*the bronze altar, and its grating of bronze, its poles, and all its utensils; the basin with its stand;* [40]*the hangings of the court, its pillars, and its bases, and the screen for the gate of the court, its cords, and its pegs; and all the utensils for the service of the tabernacle, for the tent of meeting;* [41]*the finely worked vestments for ministering in the holy place, the sacred vestments for the priest Aaron, and the vestments of his sons to serve as priests.* [42]*The Israelites had done all of the work just as the LORD had commanded Moses.*[72]

[43]When Moses saw that they had done all the work just as the LORD had commanded, he blessed them.

---

72. Verses 33-42 list in detail all the items that had been made. Noth comments: "It may be asked whether, in the general statements of vv. 32, 42 f., there is still the residue of a short account from the original P narrative, which said that the instructions given to Moses in chs. 25 ff. were all carried out correctly and well. The P narrative certainly must once have contained such an account" (*Exodus*, 280). See p. 53 n. 60, above.

Setting Up of the Tabernacle

40 The LORD spoke to Moses: [2]On the first day of the first month you shall set up the tabernacle of the tent of meeting.

[3]You shall put in it the ark of the covenant and you shall screen the ark with the curtain. [4]You shall bring in the table, and arrange its setting; and you shall bring in the lampstand, and set up its lamps. [5]You shall put the golden altar for incense before the ark of the covenant, and set up the screen for the entrance of the tabernacle. [6]You shall set the altar of burnt offering before the entrance of the tabernacle of the tent of meeting, [7]and place the basin between the tent of meeting and the altar, and put water in it. [8]You shall set up the court all around, and hang up the screen for the gate of the court.

[9]Then you shall take the anointing oil, and anoint the tabernacle and all that is in it, and consecrate it and all its furniture, so that it shall become holy.

[10]You shall also anoint the altar of burnt offering and all its utensils, and consecrate the altar, so that the altar shall be most holy. [11]You shall also anoint the basin with its stand, and consecrate it. [12]Then you shall bring Aaron and his sons to the entrance of the tent of meeting, and shall wash them with water; [13]and put on Aaron the sacred vestments, and you shall anoint him and consecrate him, so that he may serve me as priest. [14]You shall bring his sons also and put tunics on them, [15]and anoint them, as you anointed their father, that they may serve me as priests: and their anointing shall admit them to a perpetual priesthood throughout all generations to come.

[16] Moses did everything just as the LORD had commanded him.[73]

[17] In the first month in the second year, on the first day of the month, the tabernacle was set up. [18]Moses set up the tabernacle; he laid its bases, and set up its frames, and put in its poles, and raised up its pillars; [19]and he spread the tent over the tabernacle, and put the covering of the tent over it; as the LORD had commanded Moses. [20]He took the covenant and put it into the ark, and put the poles on the ark, and set the mercy seat above the ark; [21]and he brought the ark into the tabernacle, and set up the curtain for screening, and screened the ark of the covenant, as the LORD had commanded Moses. [22]He put the table in the tent of meeting, on the north side of the tabernacle, outside the curtain, [23]and set the bread in order on it before the LORD; as the LORD had commanded Moses. [24]He put the lampstand in the tent of meeting, opposite the table on the south side of the tabernacle, [25]and set up the lamps before the LORD; as the LORD had commanded Moses.

[26]He put the golden altar in the tent of meeting before the curtain, [27]and offered fragrant incense on it; as the LORD had commanded Moses.

[28]He also put in place the screen for the entrance of the tabernacle. [29]He set the altar of burnt offering at the entrance of the tabernacle of the tent of meeting.

and offered on it the burnt offering and the grain offering as the LORD had commanded Moses. [30]He set the basin between the tent of meeting and the altar, and put water in it for washing, [31]with which Moses and Aaron and his sons washed their hands and their feet. [32]When they went into the tent of meeting, and when they approached the altar, they washed; as the LORD had commanded Moses.[74]

---

73. In his Exodus commentary, Noth claims 40:17 as original to P but regards vv. 1-16 and 18-33 as secondary, because they "presuppose the secondary additions to the P narrative" (*Exodus*, 282–83). Here the concern with vv. 3-8 and 10-16 seems to be that they spell out the details implicit in what is commanded in vv. 2 and 9. The anointing here anticipates the anointing of Leviticus 8.

74. In his commentary, Noth remarks: "The details of vv. 18-33 could stem from a later writer to whom the brief observation in v. 17 seemed insufficient and who took the material for his description from chs. 25-31" (*Exodus*, 283). Again, Leviticus 8–9 is anticipated. Here it seems that only the specifically secondary items have been singled out; for the altar, see Exod 30:1-10, and for the basin, 30:17-21.

³³He set up the court around the tabernacle and the altar, and put up the screen at the gate of the court. So Moses finished the work.

34 Then the cloud covered the tent of meeting, and the glory of the LORD filled the tabernacle. *³⁵Moses was not able to enter the tent of meeting because the cloud settled upon it, and the glory of the LORD filled the tabernacle. ³⁶Whenever the* *cloud was taken up from the tabernacle, the Israelites would set out on each stage of their journey; ³⁷but if the cloud was not taken up, then they did not set out until the day that it was taken up. ³⁸For the cloud of the LORD was on the tabernacle by day, and fire was in the cloud by night, before the eyes of all the house of Israel at each stage of their journey.*⁷⁵

The Book of Leviticus

Commissioning of the Sanctuary

Ordination of Aaron and His Sons

8 The LORD spoke to Moses, saying:⁷⁶ ²Take Aaron and his sons with him, the vestments, the anointing oil, the bull of sin offering, the two rams, and the basket of unleavened bread; ³and assemble the whole congregation at the entrance of the tent of meeting. ⁴And Moses did as the LORD commanded him. When the congregation was assembled at the entrance of the tent of meeting, ⁵Moses said to the congregation, "This is what the LORD has commanded to be done."

6 Then Moses brought forward Aaron. *and his sons and washed them with water*⁷⁷ ⁷He put the tunic on him, fastened the sash around him, clothed him with the robe, and put the ephod on him. He then put the decorated band of the ephod around him, tying the ephod

---

75. "Here too things are presupposed which are later narrated once again" (Noth, *Exodus*, 283). The comments on the cloud as signal to stay or depart are out of place here and belong with Num 9:15-23. For Noth, this anticipation may be a pointer to a later concern to complete the account of the sanctuary within the confines of the Book of Exodus. Certainly, the material does function proleptically; it is a satisfying flash-forward to how things will be when all is finally done. The more material that comes between Exodus 40 and Numbers 10, the more necessary these comments become. Here God is in Israel's midst, whatever their journey.

76. A significant aspect in Noth's understanding of the P source is the conviction that it is a narrative document. The extensive collections of laws in Leviticus 1-7, 11-15, and 17-26 do not belong within the Priestly document (see *Pentateuchal Traditions*, 8-9); hence only the narrative sections are attributed to P here.

Noth argues that Leviticus 1-7 is in its appropriate place, before the narrative in Leviticus 8-9 of the first sacrifices. "But it so obviously breaks the narrative connection which unquestionably exists between Exodus *25-31 and *35-40 on the one hand, and Leviticus 8-9 on the other, that it is in general justifiably excluded from the original P narrative" (*Pentateuchal Traditions*, 8). Leviticus 16:1 explicitly connects with Lev 10:1-7, suggesting that chaps. 11-15 have been appropriately inserted before Leviticus 16; and Leviticus 17-26 has been appropriately inserted right after Leviticus 16 (*Pentateuchal Traditions*, 9).

In his 1962 commentary, in fact, Noth attributes Leviticus 9 alone to the original P source: "Only the story of the first great sacrifices in ch. 9 belongs to the original P-narrative. . . . If Lev. 8-10 are to be regarded as the literary kernel of the whole book, then it must be stated that this kernel is formed by a portion of the P-narrative already amplified by later additions. The remaining content of the book clearly did not belong to the original or expanded P-narrative" (Noth, *Leviticus*, 13).

77. The translation has been slightly adjusted here to allow the appropriate separation of the verse. The concern is with the shift from Aaron alone (v. 6aα and 7ff.) to Aaron and his sons in the rest of v. 6 (Noth, *Leviticus*, 69).

to him with it. [8]He placed the breastpiece on him, and in the breastpiece he put the Urim and the Thummim. [9]And he set the turban on his head, and on the turban, in front, he set the golden ornament, the holy crown, as the LORD commanded Moses.

10 Then Moses took the anointing oil. *and anointed the tabernacle and all that was in it, and consecrated them. [11]He sprinkled some of it on the altar seven times, and anointed the altar and all its utensils, and the basin and its base, to consecrate them.*[78]

[12]He poured some of the anointing oil on Aaron's head and anointed him, to consecrate him. [13]And Moses brought forward Aaron's sons, and clothed them with tunics, and fastened sashes around them, and tied headdresses on them, as the LORD commanded Moses.

14 He led forward the bull of sin offering; and Aaron and his sons laid their hands upon the head of the bull of sin offering, [15]and it was slaughtered. Moses took the blood and with his finger put some on each of the horns of the altar, purifying the altar; then he poured out the blood at the base of the altar. Thus he consecrated it, to make atonement for it. [16]Moses took all the fat that was around the entrails, and the appendage of the liver, and the two kidneys with their fat, and turned them into smoke on the altar. [17]But the bull itself, its skin and flesh and its dung, he burned with fire outside the camp, as the LORD commanded Moses.

18 Then he brought forward the ram of burnt offering. Aaron and his sons laid their hands on the head of the ram, [19]and it was slaughtered. Moses dashed the blood against all sides of the altar. [20]The ram was cut into its parts, and Moses turned into smoke the head and the parts and

the suet. [21]And after the entrails and the legs were washed with water, Moses turned into smoke the whole ram on the altar; it was a burnt offering for a pleasing odor, an offering by fire to the LORD, as the LORD commanded Moses.

22 Then he brought forward the second ram, the ram of ordination. Aaron and his sons laid their hands on the head of the ram, [23]and it was slaughtered. Moses took some of its blood and put it on the lobe of Aaron's right ear and on the thumb of his right hand and on the big toe of his right foot. [24]After Aaron's sons were brought forward, Moses put some of the blood on the lobes of their right ears and on the thumbs of their right hands and on the big toes of their right feet; and Moses dashed the rest of the blood against all sides of the altar. [25]He took the fat—the broad tail, all the fat that was around the entrails, the appendage of the liver, and the two kidneys with their fat—and the right thigh. [26]From the basket of unleavened bread that was before the LORD, he took one cake of unleavened bread, one cake of bread with oil, and one wafer, and placed them on the fat and on the right thigh. [27]He placed all these on the palms of Aaron and on the palms of his sons, and raised them as an elevation offering before the LORD. [28]Then Moses took them from their hands and turned them into smoke on the altar with the burnt offering. This was an ordination offering for a pleasing odor, an offering by fire to the LORD. [29]Moses took the breast and raised it as an elevation offering before the LORD; it was Moses' portion of the ram of ordination, as the LORD commanded Moses.

30 Then Moses took some of the anointing oil and some of the blood that was on the altar and sprinkled them on Aaron and his vestments,

---

78. The reference to the anointing of the tabernacle and its contents here is considered by Noth to be quite unexpected in this context. According to Noth, it obviously rests on secondary additions based on Exod 40:9-11, a rather late passage (*Leviticus*, 69–70). In *Pentateuchal Traditions*, Noth regarded Exod 40:2 and 9 as original to P; in his commentary, all of Exod 40:1-16 is considered secondary.

and also on his sons and their vestments. Thus he consecrated Aaron and his vestments, and also his sons and their vestments.

31 And Moses said to Aaron and his sons, "Boil the flesh at the entrance of the tent of meeting, and eat it there with the bread that is in the basket of ordination offerings, as I was commanded, 'Aaron and his sons shall eat it'; [32]and what remains of the flesh and the bread you shall burn with fire. [33]You shall not go outside the entrance of the tent of meeting for seven days, until the day when your period of ordination is completed. For it will take seven days to ordain you; [34]as has been done today, the LORD has commanded to be done to make atonement for you. [35]You shall remain at the entrance of the tent of meeting day and night for seven days, keeping the LORD's charge so that you do not die; for so I am commanded." [36]Aaron and his sons did all the things that the LORD commanded through Moses.[79]

Public Offering of Sacrifice at the Sanctuary

9 On the eighth day Moses summoned Aaron and his sons and the elders of Israel. [2]He said to Aaron, "Take a bull calf for a sin offering and a ram for a burnt offering, without blemish, and offer them before the LORD. [3]And say to the people of Israel, 'Take a male goat for a sin offering; a calf and a lamb, yearlings without blemish, for a burnt offering; [4]and an ox and a ram for an offering of well-being to sacrifice before the LORD; and a grain offering mixed with oil. For today the LORD will appear to you.' " [5]They brought what Moses commanded to the front of the tent of meeting; and the whole congregation drew near and stood before the LORD. [6]And Moses said, "This is the thing that the LORD commanded you to do, so that the glory of the LORD may appear to you." [7]Then Moses said to Aaron, "Draw near to the altar and sacrifice your sin offering and your burnt offering, and make atonement for yourself and for the people."

and sacrifice the offering of the people, and make atonement for them; as the LORD has commanded."[80]

8 Aaron drew near to the altar, and slaughtered the calf of the sin offering, which was for himself. [9]The sons of Aaron presented the blood to him, and he dipped his finger in the blood and put it on the horns of the altar; and the rest of the blood he poured out at the base of

---

79. In his Leviticus commentary, Noth reverses his position here and regards Leviticus 8 as secondary. "The account of the carrying out of the priests' institution to office in ch. 8 is clearly secondary P material, both as such, and as an appendix to the instructions—themselves added as a later supplement—for this particular institution in Ex. 29" (*Leviticus*, 13). In chap. 8 the people are spectators; in chap. 9, they are participants. "It is indeed quite clear that the narrative in ch. 9 does not presuppose the preceding chapters, which therefore have not occupied this place from the start. . . . This chapter [chap. 9] is the first (and only) piece of 'original P' in Leviticus" (*Leviticus*, 75–76).

In the texts reproduced in this handbook, following Noth's *History of Pentateuchal Traditions*, Exodus 29 is attributed in its entirety to P. In his 1959 Exodus commentary, however, Noth considers the whole of Exodus 29 as a supplement to P. It no longer deals with the furnishings of the sanctuary but with the cultic celebration of the priestly ordination; and "the chapter contains a number of divergencies, albeit insignificant, in the details of the priests' dress from those given in the previous chapter." Furthermore, literary unity is lost after v. 25; in vv. 26-46 "we have to reckon with numerous secondary expansions without being able to establish in detail the sequence in which these additions were made" (*Exodus*, 229). Hence Noth's reversal of his position concerning Leviticus 8.

80. A number of factors are active in this verse. The reason why Lev 9:7b and 9:15a are identified as secondary here is probably the Hebrew phrase translated "the offering of the people" or "the people's offering"—"the very comprehensively used collective 'presentation' (*qorbān*)" (Noth, *Leviticus*, 78). The precise phrase (*qorban hā'ām*) is found only here.

the altar. [10]But the fat, the kidneys, and the appendage of the liver from the sin offering he turned into smoke on the altar, as the LORD commanded Moses; [11]and the flesh and the skin he burned with fire outside the camp.

12 Then he slaughtered the burnt offering. Aaron's sons brought him the blood, and he dashed it against all sides of the altar. [13]And they brought him the burnt offering piece by piece, and the head, which he turned into smoke on the altar. [14]He washed the entrails and the legs and, with the burnt offering, turned them into smoke on the altar.

[15]*Next he presented the people's offering.* He took the goat of the sin offering that was for the people, and slaughtered it, and presented it as a sin offering like the first one. [16]He presented the burnt offering, and sacrificed it according to regulation. [17]He presented the grain offering, and, taking a handful of it, he turned it into smoke on the altar, in addition to the burnt offering of the morning.

18 He slaughtered the ox and the ram as a sacrifice of well-being for the people. Aaron's sons brought him the blood, which he dashed against all sides of the altar, [19]and the fat of the ox and of the ram—the broad tail, the fat that covers the entrails, the two kidneys and the fat on them, and the appendage of the liver. [20]They first laid the fat on the breasts, and the fat was turned into smoke on the altar; [21]and the breasts and the right thigh Aaron raised as an elevation offering before the LORD, as Moses had commanded.

22 Aaron lifted his hands toward the people and blessed them; and he came down after sacri-ficing the sin offering, the burnt offering, and the offering of well-being. [23]Moses and Aaron entered the tent of meeting, and then came out and blessed the people; and the glory of the LORD appeared to all the people.

[24]*Fire came out from the LORD and consumed the burnt offering and the fat on the altar; and when all the people saw it, they shouted and fell on their faces.*[81]

10 *Now Aaron's sons, Nadab and Abihu, each took his censer, put fire in it, and laid incense on it; and they offered unholy fire before the LORD, such as he had not commanded them.* [2]*And fire came out from the presence of the LORD and consumed them, and they died before the LORD.* [3]*Then Moses said to Aaron, "This is what the LORD meant when he said,*

> *'Through those who are near me*
> *I will show myself holy,*
> *and before all the people*
> *I will be glorified.' "*

4 Moses summoned Mishael and Elzaphan, sons of Uzziel the uncle of Aaron, and said to them, "Come forward, and carry your kinsmen away from the front of the sanctuary to a place outside the camp." [5]*They came forward and carried them by their tunics out of the camp, as Moses had ordered.* [6]*And Moses said to Aaron and to his sons Eleazar and Ithamar, "Do not dishevel your hair, and do not tear your vestments, or you will die and wrath will strike all the congregation; but your kindred, the whole house of Israel, may mourn the burning that the LORD has sent.* [7]*You shall not go outside the entrance of the tent of meeting, or you will die; for the anointing oil of the LORD is on you." And they did as Moses had ordered.*

---

81. In his commentary on Leviticus, Noth is emphatic that v. 24a must be a later addition; v. 24b, on the other hand, he accepts as original, noting that it makes good sense in reference to the glory of the LORD. Verse 24a aims at a vivid depiction of God's acceptance of the sacrifice, but it is incompatible with the preceding narrative in which the offering of the sacrifices, including their burning on the altar, was completed and finished. "The narrative must have run otherwise if it was originally working up to the conclusion of v. 24a" (*Leviticus*, 81–82).

8 And the LORD spoke to Aaron: [9]Drink no wine or strong drink, neither you nor your sons, when you enter the tent of meeting, that you may not die; it is a statute forever throughout your generations. [10]You are to distinguish between the holy and the common, and between the unclean and the clean; [11]and you are to teach the people of Israel all the statutes that the LORD has spoken to them through Moses.

12 Moses spoke to Aaron and to his remaining sons, Eleazar and Ithamar: Take the grain offering that is left from the LORD's offerings by fire, and eat it unleavened beside the altar, for it is most holy; [13]you shall eat it in a holy place, because it is your due and your sons' due, from the offerings by fire to the LORD; for so I am commanded. [14]But the breast that is elevated and the thigh that is raised, you and your sons and daughters as well may eat in any clean place; for they have been assigned to you and your children from the sacrifices of the offerings of well-being of the people of Israel. [15]The thigh that is raised and the breast that is elevated they shall bring, together with the offerings by fire of the fat, to raise for an elevation offering before the LORD; they are to be your due and that of your children forever, as the LORD has commanded.

16 Then Moses made inquiry about the goat of the sin offering, and—it had already been burned! He was angry with Eleazar and Ithamar, Aaron's remaining sons, and said, [17]"Why did you not eat the sin offering in the sacred area? For it is most holy, and God has given it to you that you may remove the guilt of the congregation, to make atonement on

their behalf before the LORD. [18]Its blood was not brought into the inner part of the sanctuary. You should certainly have eaten it in the sanctuary, as I commanded." [19]And Aaron spoke to Moses, "See, today they offered their sin offering and their burnt offering before the LORD; and yet such things as these have befallen me! If I had eaten the sin offering today, would it have been agreeable to the LORD?" [20]And when Moses heard that, he agreed.[82]

16 The LORD spoke to Moses after the death of the two sons of Aaron, when they drew near before the LORD and died. [2]The LORD said to Moses:

Tell your brother Aaron not to come just at any time into the sanctuary inside the curtain before the mercy seat that is upon the ark, or he will die; for I appear in the cloud upon the mercy seat. [3]Thus shall Aaron come into the holy place: with a young bull for a sin offering and a ram for a burnt offering. [4]He shall put on the holy linen tunic, and shall have the linen undergarments next to his body, fasten the linen sash, and wear the linen turban; these are the holy vestments. He shall bathe his body in water, and then put them on. [5]He shall take from the congregation of the people of Israel two male goats for a sin offering, and one ram for a burnt offering.

6 Aaron shall offer the bull as a sin offering for himself, and shall make atonement for himself and for his house. [7]He shall take the two goats and set them before the LORD at the entrance of the tent of meeting; [8]and Aaron shall cast lots on the two goats, one lot for the LORD and the other lot for Azazel. [9]Aaron shall present the goat on which the lot fell for the LORD, and offer it as a

---

82. Leviticus 10 divides into two parts: vv. 1-7, relating a cultic incident connected to chap. 9; and vv. 8-20, containing instructions correcting or filling out the sacrificial actions of chap. 9. "In the second part it is quite obvious that we are dealing with detailed later additions to ch. 9; but even the first part, to which the second is loosely joined, could hardly have been an original part of the P-narrative, especially as it is clearly linked on to the mention of the fire which came out from the divine glory . . . and which is already secondary in ch. 9" (Noth, *Leviticus*, 83).

sin offering; [10]but the goat on which the lot fell for Azazel shall be presented alive before the LORD to make atonement over it, that it may be sent away into the wilderness to Azazel.

11 Aaron shall present the bull as a sin offering for himself, and shall make atonement for himself and for his house; he shall slaughter the bull as a sin offering for himself. [12]He shall take a censer full of coals of fire from the altar before the LORD, and two handfuls of crushed sweet incense, and he shall bring it inside the curtain [13]and put the incense on the fire before the LORD, that the cloud of the incense may cover the mercy seat that is upon the covenant, or he will die. [14]He shall take some of the blood of the bull, and sprinkle it with his finger on the front of the mercy seat, and before the mercy seat he shall sprinkle the blood with his finger seven times.

15 He shall slaughter the goat of the sin offering that is for the people and bring its blood inside the curtain, and do with its blood as he did with the blood of the bull, sprinkling it upon the mercy seat and before the mercy seat. [16]Thus he shall make atonement for the sanctuary, because of the uncleannesses of the people of Israel, and because of their transgressions, all their sins; and so he shall do for the tent of meeting, which remains with them in the midst of their uncleannesses. [17]No one shall be in the tent of meeting from the time he enters to make atonement in the sanctuary until he comes out and has made atonement for himself and for his house and for all the assembly of Israel. [18]Then he shall go out to the altar that is before the LORD and make atonement on its behalf, and shall take some of the blood of the bull and of the blood of the goat, and put it on each of the horns of the altar. [19]He shall sprinkle some of the blood on it with his finger seven times, and cleanse it and hallow it from the uncleannesses of the people of Israel.

20 When he has finished atoning for the holy place and the tent of meeting and the altar, he shall present the live goat. [21]Then Aaron shall lay both his hands on the head of the live goat, and confess over it all the iniquities of the people of Israel, and all their transgressions, all their sins, putting them on the head of the goat, and sending it away into the wilderness by means of someone designated for the task. [22]The goat shall bear on itself all their iniquities to a barren region; and the goat shall be set free in the wilderness.

23 Then Aaron shall enter the tent of meeting, and shall take off the linen vestments that he put on when he went into the holy place, and shall leave them there. [24]He shall bathe his body in water in a holy place, and put on his vestments; then he shall come out and offer his burnt offering and the burnt offering of the people, making atonement for himself and for the people. [25]The fat of the sin offering he shall turn into smoke on the altar. [26]The one who sets the goat free for Azazel shall wash his clothes and bathe his body in water, and afterward may come into the camp. [27]The bull of the sin offering and the goat of the sin offering, whose blood was brought in to make atonement in the holy place, shall be taken outside the camp; their skin and their flesh and their dung shall be consumed in fire. [28]The one who burns them shall wash his clothes and bathe his body in water, and afterward may come into the camp.

29 This shall be a statute to you forever: In the seventh month, on the tenth day of the month, you shall deny yourselves, and shall do no work, neither the citizen nor the alien who resides among you. [30]For on this day atonement shall be made for you, to cleanse you; from all your sins you shall be clean before the LORD. [31]It is a sabbath of complete rest to you, and you shall deny yourselves; it is a statute forever. [32]The priest who is anointed and consecrated as priest in his father's place shall make atonement, wearing the linen vestments, the holy vestments. [33]He shall make atonement for the sanctuary, and he shall make atonement for the tent of meeting and for the altar, and he shall make atonement for the priests and for all the people of the assembly.

[34]This shall be an everlasting statute for you, to make atonement for the people of Israel once in the year for all their sins. And Moses did as the LORD had commanded him.[83]

The Book of Numbers

Organization of Israel around the Sanctuary

Census of the People

1 The LORD spoke to Moses in the wilderness of Sinai,[84] in the tent of meeting, on the first day of the second month, in the second year after they had come out of the land of Egypt, saying: [2]Take a census of the whole congregation of Israelites, in their clans, by ancestral houses, according to the number of names, every male individually; [3]from twenty years old and

---

83. On Leviticus 16, Noth concludes in his commentary: the original chapter "in spite of many connections with the P-narrative, did not belong to the original substance of P, but was only worked in at some later stage (with the introductory sentence v. 2aα). This chapter has had its own early history and must be interpreted from within—especially as its content is somewhat unusual and peculiar to itself" (*Leviticus*, 118). As he commented earlier, "It is evident at the first glance that the chapter is in its present form the result of a probably fairly long previous history that has left its traces in a strange lack of continuity and unity about the whole. The position is indeed so complicated that all attempts hitherto at factual and literary analysis have not led to at all convincing results. But the fact itself, that the chapter came into being through an elaborate process of growth, is generally recognized and accepted" (*Leviticus*, 117).

Leviticus 16:1 links up loosely with the incident of 10:1-7, and so is associated with the P narrative at a stage where it is already enlarged with secondary material. Chapter 16 has the appropriate cleansing ritual needed after the unholy incident of 10:1-7. In Noth's view, chaps. 11–15 were inserted between chaps. 10 and 16 at a later stage. Leviticus 16:1 is itself secondary to the independent introductory clause beginning v. 2, which situates what follows within the giving of the law to Moses and so is anchored in the Sinai situation. Perhaps, therefore, 16:2 ff. was part of a narrative complex before v. 1 tied it to 10:1-7. It may have been associated with the priestly ordination and first sacrifices, but this is quite unsure (Noth, *Leviticus*, 117-18; consultation of the German is helpful: *Das dritte Buch Mose* [ATD 6; Göttingen: Vandenhoeck & Ruprecht, 1962]).

Noth's comment on the nature of the non-narrative portions of Leviticus is worth repeating: "For the non-narrative portions of Leviticus, there is therefore a plausible hypothesis about how they came to be incorporated in the P-narrative or Pentateuch-narrative, as the case may be. Yet they were none of them composed or written down in the first place with a view to this arrangement, but existed previously in their own right. They have, moreover, no connection with the 'ancient sources.' But they look so independent over against P, both in language and by a variety of differences in their ideas, that we are forbidden to assume them to have been planned and formulated as an expansion of P" (*Leviticus*, 14). A. Cholewinski regards the Holiness Code (Leviticus 17–26) as a deliberate corrective polemic against P, particularly to make clear that a covenant was concluded between God and Israel at Sinai (*Heiligkeitsgesetz und Deuteronomium: Eine vergleichende Studie* [AnBib 66; Rome: Biblical Institute, 1976] esp. 334–44).

84. Noth suggests that if the Book of Numbers were studied on its own, its "unsystematic collection of innumerable pieces of tradition of very varied content, age and character" would lead to something like the fragment hypothesis. But the book cannot be treated in isolation; it belongs within the Pentateuch and needs to be approached in the light of results achieved elsewhere. "In view of the peculiar nature of Numbers, however, the application of these results must be carried through with caution and restraint. It is certainly not practicable simply to proceed to a division of the textual material among the Pentateuchal sources J, E and P (and, in any event, it would have to be a question of secondary forms of these sources)" (M. Noth, *Numbers* [OTL; London: SCM, 1968] 4–5).

upward, everyone in Israel able to go to war. You and Aaron shall enroll them, company by company. [4]A man from each tribe shall be with you, each man the head of his ancestral house. [5]These are the names of the men who shall assist you:

> From Reuben, Elizur son of Shedeur.
> [6]From Simeon, Shelumiel son of Zurishaddai.
> [7]From Judah, Nahshon son of Amminadab.
> [8]From Issachar, Nethanel son of Zuar.
> [9]From Zebulun, Eliab son of Helon.
> [10]From the sons of Joseph:
> from Ephraim, Elishama son of Ammihud;
> from Manasseh, Gamaliel son of Pedahzur.
> [11]From Benjamin, Abidan son of Gideoni.
> [12]From Dan, Ahiezer son of Ammishaddai.
> [13]From Asher, Pagiel son of Ochran.
> [14]From Gad, Eliasaph son of Deuel.
> [15]From Naphtali, Ahira son of Enan.

[16]These were the ones chosen from the congregation, the leaders of their ancestral tribes, the heads of the divisions of Israel.

17 Moses and Aaron took these men who had been designated by name, [18]and on the first day of the second month they assembled the whole congregation together. They registered themselves in their clans, by their ancestral houses, according to the number of names from twenty years old and upward, individually, [19]as the LORD commanded Moses. So he enrolled them in the wilderness of Sinai.

20 The descendants of Reuben, Israel's firstborn, their lineage, in their clans, by their ancestral houses, according to the number of names, individually, every male from twenty years old and upward, everyone able to go to war: [21]those enrolled of the tribe of Reuben were forty-six thousand five hundred.

22 The descendants of Simeon, their lineage, in their clans, by their ancestral houses, those of them that were numbered, according to the number of names, individually, every male from twenty years old and upward, everyone able to

go to war: [23]those enrolled of the tribe of Simeon were fifty-nine thousand three hundred.

24 The descendants of Gad, their lineage, in their clans, by their ancestral houses, according to the number of the names, from twenty years old and upward, everyone able to go to war: [25]those enrolled of the tribe of Gad were forty-five thousand six hundred fifty.

26 The descendants of Judah, their lineage, in their clans, by their ancestral houses, according to the number of names, from twenty years old and upward, everyone able to go to war: [27]those enrolled of the tribe of Judah were seventy-four thousand six hundred.

28 The descendants of Issachar, their lineage, in their clans, by their ancestral houses, according to the number of names, from twenty years old and upward, everyone able to go to war: [29]those enrolled of the tribe of Issachar were fifty-four thousand four hundred.

30 The descendants of Zebulun, their lineage, in their clans, by their ancestral houses, according to the number of names, from twenty years old and upward, everyone able to go to war: [31]those enrolled of the tribe of Zebulun were fifty-seven thousand four hundred.

32 The descendants of Joseph, namely, the descendants of Ephraim, their lineage, in their clans, by their ancestral houses, according to the number of names, from twenty years old and upward, everyone able to go to war: [33]those enrolled of the tribe of Ephraim were forty thousand five hundred.

34 The descendants of Manasseh, their lineage, in their clans, by their ancestral houses, according to the number of names, from twenty years old and upward, everyone able to go to war: [35]those enrolled of the tribe of Manasseh were thirty-two thousand two hundred.

36 The descendants of Benjamin, their lineage, in their clans, by their ancestral houses, according to the number of names, from twenty years old and upward, everyone able to go to

war: [37]those enrolled of the tribe of Benjamin were thirty-five thousand four hundred.

38 The descendants of Dan, their lineage, in their clans, by their ancestral houses, according to the number of names, from twenty years old and upward, everyone able to go to war: [39]those enrolled of the tribe of Dan were sixty-two thousand seven hundred.

40 The descendants of Asher, their lineage, in their clans, by their ancestral houses, according to the number of names, from twenty years old and upward, everyone able to go to war: [41]those enrolled of the tribe of Asher were forty-one thousand five hundred.

42 The descendants of Naphtali, their lineage, in their clans, by their ancestral houses, according to the number of names, from twenty years old and upward, everyone able to go to war: [43]those enrolled of the tribe of Naphtali were fifty-three thousand four hundred.

44 These are those who were enrolled, whom Moses and Aaron enrolled with the help of the leaders of Israel, twelve men, each representing his ancestral house. [45]So the whole number of the Israelites, by their ancestral houses, from twenty years old and upward, everyone able to go to war in Israel— [46]their whole number was six hundred three thousand five hundred fifty. [47]The Levites, however, were not numbered by their ancestral tribe along with them.

48 The LORD had said to Moses: [49]Only the tribe of Levi you shall not enroll, and you shall not take a census of them with the other Israelites. [50]Rather you shall appoint the Levites over the tabernacle of the covenant, and over all its equipment, and over all that belongs to it; they are to carry the tabernacle and all its equipment, and they shall tend it, and shall camp around the tab-ernacle. [51]When the tabernacle is to set out, the Levites shall take it down; and when the tabernacle is to be pitched, the Levites shall set it up. And any outsider who comes near shall be put to death. [52]The other Israelites shall camp in their respective regimental camps, by companies; [53]but the Levites shall camp around the tabernacle of the covenant, that there may be no wrath on the congregation of the Israelites; and the Levites shall perform the guard duty of the tabernacle of the covenant. [54]The Israelites did so; they did just as the LORD commanded Moses.[85]

Establishment of the Camp around the Sanctuary

2 The LORD spoke to Moses and Aaron, saying: [2]The Israelites shall camp each in their respective regiments, under ensigns by their ancestral houses; they shall camp facing the tent of meeting on every side. [3]Those to camp on the east side toward the sunrise shall be of the regimental encampment of Judah by companies. The leader of the people of Judah shall be Nahshon son of Amminadab, [4]with a company as enrolled of seventy-four thousand six hundred. [5]Those to camp next to him shall be the tribe of Issachar. The leader of the Issacharites shall be Nethanel son of Zuar, [6]with a company as enrolled of fifty-four thousand four hundred. [7]Then the tribe of Zebulun: The leader of the Zebulunites shall be Eliab son of Helon, [8]with a company as enrolled of fifty-seven thousand four hundred. [9]The total enrollment of the camp of Judah, by companies, is one hundred eighty-six thousand four hundred. They shall set out first on the march.

10 On the south side shall be the regimental encampment of Reuben by companies. The

---

85. Noth, in his commentary on Numbers, remarks that vv. 48-54 depend on v. 47 and anticipate the theme of the organization of the camp and of the Levites, which is not introduced until later. The addi-tion wants "to see the special position of the Levites at least briefly mentioned and envisaged at this point" (*Numbers*, 17).

leader of the Reubenites shall be Elizur son of Shedeur, [11]with a company as enrolled of forty-six thousand five hundred. [12]And those to camp next to him shall be the tribe of Simeon. The leader of the Simeonites shall be Shelumiel son of Zurishaddai, [13]with a company as enrolled of fifty-nine thousand three hundred. [14]Then the tribe of Gad: The leader of the Gadites shall be Eliasaph son of Reuel, [15]with a company as enrolled of forty-five thousand six hundred fifty. [16]The total enrollment of the camp of Reuben, by companies, is one hundred fifty-one thousand four hundred fifty. They shall set out second.

17 The tent of meeting, with the camp of the Levites, shall set out in the center of the camps; they shall set out just as they camp, each in position, by their regiments.

18 On the west side shall be the regimental encampment of Ephraim by companies. The leader of the people of Ephraim shall be Elishama son of Ammihud, [19]with a company as enrolled of forty thousand five hundred. [20]Next to him shall be the tribe of Manasseh. The leader of the people of Manasseh shall be Gamaliel son of Pedahzur, [21]with a company as enrolled of thirty-two thousand two hundred. [22]Then the tribe of Benjamin: The leader of the Benjaminites shall be Abidan son of Gideoni, [23]with a company as enrolled of thirty-five thousand four hundred. [24]The total enrollment of the camp of Ephraim, by companies, is one hundred eight thousand one hundred. They shall set out third on the march.

25 On the north side shall be the regimental encampment of Dan by companies. The leader of the Danites shall be Ahiezer son of Ammishaddai, [26]with a company as enrolled of sixty-two thousand seven hundred. [27]Those to camp next to him shall be the tribe of Asher. The leader of the Asherites shall be Pagiel son of Ochran, [28]with a company as enrolled of forty-one thousand five hundred. [29]Then the tribe of Naphtali: The leader of the

Naphtalites shall be Ahira son of Enan, [30]with a company as enrolled of fifty-three thousand four hundred. [31]The total enrollment of the camp of Dan is one hundred fifty-seven thousand six hundred. They shall set out last, by companies.

32 This was the enrollment of the Israelites by their ancestral houses; the total enrollment in the camps by their companies was six hundred three thousand five hundred fifty. [33]Just as the LORD had commanded Moses, the Levites were not enrolled among the other Israelites.

34 The Israelites did just as the LORD had commanded Moses: They camped by regiments, and they set out the same way, everyone by clans, according to ancestral houses.

Concerning the Levites

3 This is the lineage of Aaron and Moses at the time when the LORD spoke with Moses on Mount Sinai. [2]These are the names of the sons of Aaron: Nadab the firstborn, and Abihu, Eleazar, and Ithamar; [3]these are the names of the sons of Aaron, the anointed priests, whom he ordained to minister as priests. [4]Nadab and Abihu died before the LORD when they offered illicit fire before the LORD in the wilderness of Sinai, and they had no children. Eleazar and Ithamar served as priests in the lifetime of their father Aaron.

5 Then the LORD spoke to Moses, saying: [6]Bring the tribe of Levi near, and set them before Aaron the priest, so that they may assist him. [7]They shall perform duties for him and for the whole congregation in front of the tent of meeting, doing service at the tabernacle; [8]they shall be in charge of all the furnishings of the tent of meeting, and attend to the duties for the Israelites as they do service at the tabernacle. [9]You shall give the Levites to Aaron and his descendants; they are unreservedly given to him from among the Israelites. [10]But you shall make a register of Aaron and his descendants; it is they who shall attend to the priesthood, and any outsider who comes near shall be put to death.

11 Then the LORD spoke to Moses, saying: 12I hereby accept the Levites from among the Israelites as substitutes for all the firstborn that open the womb among the Israelites. The Levites shall be mine, 13for all the firstborn are mine; when I killed all the firstborn in the land of Egypt, I consecrated for my own all the firstborn in Israel, both human and animal; they shall be mine. I am the LORD.[86]

Enrollment of the Levites

14 Then the LORD spoke to Moses in the wilderness of Sinai, saying: 15Enroll the Levites by ancestral houses and by clans. You shall enroll every male from a month old and upward. 16So Moses enrolled them according to the word of the LORD, as he was commanded. 17The following were the sons of Levi, by their names: Gershon, Kohath, and Merari. 18These are the names of the sons of Gershon by their clans: Libni and Shimei. 19The sons of Kohath by their clans: Amram, Izhar, Hebron, and Uzziel. 20The sons of Merari by their clans: Mahli and Mushi. These are the clans of the Levites, by their ancestral houses.

21 To Gershon belonged the clan of the Libnites and the clan of the Shimeites; these were the clans of the Gershonites. 22Their enrollment, counting all the males from a month old and upward, was seven thousand five hundred. 23The clans of the Gershonites were to camp behind the tabernacle on the west, 24with Eliasaph son of Lael as head of the ancestral house of the Gershonites. 25The responsibility of the sons of Gershon in the tent of meeting was to be the tabernacle, the tent with its covering, the screen for the entrance of the tent of meeting, 26the hangings of the court, the screen for the entrance of the court that is around the tabernacle and the altar, and its cords—all the service pertaining to these.

27 To Kohath belonged the clan of the Amramites, the clan of the Izharites, the clan of the Hebronites, and the clan of the Uzzielites; these are the clans of the Kohathites. 28Counting all the males, from a month old and upward, there were eight thousand six hundred, attending to the duties of the sanctuary. 29The clans of the Kohathites were to camp on the south side of the tabernacle, 30with Elizaphan son of Uzziel as head of the ancestral house of the clans of the Kohathites. 31Their responsibility was to be the ark, the table, the lampstand, the altars, the vessels of the sanctuary with which the priests minister, and the screen—all the service pertaining to these. 32Eleazar son of Aaron the priest was to be chief over the leaders of the Levites.

and to have oversight of those who had charge of the sanctuary.[87]

33 To Merari belonged the clan of the Mahlites and the clan of the Mushites: these are the clans of Merari. 34Their enrollment, counting

---

86. Of Numbers 3–4, Noth says: "It is now no longer possible to reconstruct, even with minimal certainty, the literary development of this complex of tradition and there is a lack of reliable points of reference even for the construction of a relative chronology of the individual elements. . . . A hard and fast judgment is particularly difficult, because the early and even the late history of the Levitical office is obscure" (*Numbers*, 31).

Where Num 3:1-13 is concerned, 3:1-4 is an isolated passage. There are repeated new beginnings in 3:5, 11, and 14; 3:11-13 corrects vv. 5-10, and the passage is taken up again in 3:40-51, which Noth regards as secondary even to 3:11-13 (*Numbers*, 30–31, 40). In his Numbers commentary Noth regards 3:1-4 and 3:11-13 as secondary, the latter because it gives a "favourably disposed correction of the preceding and is surely to be seen in this sense as a later addition" (*Numbers*, 33–34). "The preceding," i.e., vv. 5-10, he is prepared, in the commentary, to attribute to the original P. Noth sees P debasing the Levites: "P presumes the existence of the 'Levites', but denies to them even the modest cultic functions of Ezek. 44 and writes them off with theoretical tasks which can have had meaning only in Israel's former wilderness period" (*Numbers*, 33).

87. Verse 32b is a clarifying note, spelling out the responsibility given to the Aaronides in the first half of the verse.

all the males from a month old and upward, was six thousand two hundred. ³⁵The head of the ancestral house of the clans of Merari was Zuriel son of Abihail; they were to camp on the north side of the tabernacle. ³⁶The responsibility assigned to the sons of Merari was to be the frames of the tabernacle, the bars, the pillars, the bases, and all their accessories—all the service pertaining to these; ³⁷also the pillars of the court all around, with their bases and pegs and cords.

38 Those who were to camp in front of the tabernacle on the east—in front of the tent of meeting toward the east—were Moses and Aaron and Aaron's sons, having charge of the rites within the sanctuary, whatever had to be done for the Israelites; and any outsider who came near was to be put to death. ³⁹The total enrollment of the Levites whom Moses and Aaron enrolled at the commandment of the LORD, by their clans, all the males from a month old and upward, was twenty-two thousand.

Ransom of the Firstborn

40 Then the LORD said to Moses: Enroll all the firstborn males of the Israelites, from a month old and upward, and count their names. ⁴¹But you shall accept the Levites for me—I am the LORD—as substitutes for all the firstborn among the Israelites, and the livestock of the Levites as substitutes for all the firstborn among the livestock of the Israelites. ⁴²So Moses enrolled all the firstborn among the Israelites, as the LORD commanded him. ⁴³The total enrollment, all the firstborn males from a month old and upward, counting the number of names, was twenty-two thousand two hundred seventy-three.

44 Then the LORD spoke to Moses, saying: ⁴⁵Accept the Levites as substitutes for all the firstborn among the Israelites, and the livestock of the Levites as substitutes for their livestock; and the Levites shall be mine. I am the

LORD. ⁴⁶As the price of redemption of the two hundred seventy-three of the firstborn of the Israelites, over and above the number of the Levites, ⁴⁷you shall accept five shekels apiece, reckoning by the shekel of the sanctuary, a shekel of twenty gerahs. ⁴⁸Give to Aaron and his sons the money by which the excess number of them is redeemed. ⁴⁹So Moses took the redemption money from those who were over and above those redeemed by the Levites; ⁵⁰from the firstborn of the Israelites he took the money, one thousand three hundred sixty-five shekels, reckoned by the shekel of the sanctuary; ⁵¹and Moses gave the redemption money to Aaron and his sons, according to the word of the LORD, as the LORD had commanded Moses.

Tasks and Duties of the Levites

4 The LORD spoke to Moses and Aaron, saying: ²Take a census of the Kohathites separate from the other Levites, by their clans and their ancestral houses, ³from thirty years old up to fifty years old, all who qualify to do work relating to the tent of meeting. ⁴The service of the Kohathites relating to the tent of meeting concerns the most holy things.

5 When the camp is to set out, Aaron and his sons shall go in and take down the screening curtain, and cover the ark of the covenant with it; ⁶then they shall put on it a covering of fine leather, and spread over that a cloth all of blue, and shall put its poles in place. ⁷Over the table of the bread of the Presence they shall spread a blue cloth, and put on it the plates, the dishes for incense, the bowls, and the flagons for the drink offering; the regular bread also shall be on it; ⁸then they shall spread over them a crimson cloth, and cover it with a covering of fine leather, and shall put its poles in place. ⁹They shall take a blue cloth, and cover the lampstand for the light, with its lamps, its snuffers, its trays, and all the vessels for oil with which it is supplied; ¹⁰and

they shall put it with all its utensils in a covering of fine leather, and put it on the carrying frame. [11]*Over the golden altar they shall spread a blue cloth, and cover it with a covering of fine leather, and shall put its poles in place.*[88] [12]And they shall take all the utensils of the service that are used in the sanctuary, and put them in a blue cloth, and cover them with a covering of fine leather, and put them on the carrying frame. [13]They shall take away the ashes from the altar, and spread a purple cloth over it; [14]and they shall put on it all the utensils of the altar, which are used for the service there, the firepans, the forks, the shovels, and the basins, all the utensils of the altar; and they shall spread on it a covering of fine leather, and shall put its poles in place. [15]When Aaron and his sons have finished covering the sanctuary and all the furnishings of the sanctuary, as the camp sets out, after that the Kohathites shall come to carry these, but they must not touch the holy things, or they will die. These are the things of the tent of meeting that the Kohathites are to carry.

[16] *Eleazar son of Aaron the priest shall have charge of the oil for the light, the fragrant incense, the regular grain offering, and the anointing oil, the oversight of all the tabernacle and all that is in it, in the sanctuary and in its utensils.*

[17] *Then the* LORD *spoke to Moses and Aaron, saying:* [18]*You must not let the tribe of the clans of the Kohathites be destroyed from among the Levites.* [19]*This is how you must deal with them in order that they may live and not die when they* come near to the most holy things: Aaron and his sons shall go in and assign each to a particular task or burden. [20]But the Kohathites must not go in to look on the holy things even for a moment; otherwise they will die.

[21] Then the LORD spoke to Moses, saying: [22]Take a census of the Gershonites also, by their ancestral houses and by their clans; [23]from thirty years old up to fifty years old you shall enroll them, all who qualify to do work in the tent of meeting. [24]This is the service of the clans of the Gershonites, in serving and bearing burdens: [25]They shall carry the curtains of the tabernacle, and the tent of meeting with its covering, and the outer covering of fine leather that is on top of it, and the screen for the entrance of the tent of meeting, [26]and the hangings of the court, and the screen for the entrance of the gate of the court that is around the tabernacle and the altar, and their cords, and all the equipment for their service; and they shall do all that needs to be done with regard to them. [27]All the service of the Gershonites shall be at the command of Aaron and his sons, in all that they are to carry, and in all that they have to do; and you shall assign to their charge all that they are to carry. [28]This is the service of the clans of the Gershonites relating to the tent of meeting.

And their responsibilities are to be under the oversight of Ithamar son of Aaron the priest.

[29] As for the Merarites, you shall enroll them by their clans and their ancestral houses; [30]from thirty years old up to fifty years old you shall

---

88. By the time of his Numbers commentary (1966), Noth had come to regard not only Num 3:40-51 as secondary (as noted above in connection with 3:3-11) but also all of chap. 4 (*Numbers*, 40-41). It treats a subject already dealt with in 3:25-26, 31, 37-38, and it has connections with Exodus 25 ff. that are lacking in the chap. 3 treatment. There is a further downplaying in chap. 4 of the Levites (*Numbers*, 41). In his *History of Pentateuchal Traditions* (represented here), some of the material considered as secondary is derived from secondary sections of Exodus 25-31, e.g., the golden altar (cf. Exod 30:1-10) and the anointing oil and incense (cf. Exod 30:22-38). The references to Ithamar (Num 4:28b, 33b) come after the close of the respective sections and so are likely to be additional (*Numbers*, 43). Noth considers Num 4:16-20, coming after the end of the Kohathite section, "a still more recent addition," with the special duties of the priest Eleazar and the further precautions about the Kohathites (*Numbers*, 43).

enroll them, everyone who qualifies to do the work of the tent of meeting. [31]This is what they are charged to carry, as the whole of their service in the tent of meeting: the frames of the tabernacle, with its bars, pillars, and bases, [32]and the pillars of the court all around with their bases, pegs, and cords, with all their equipment and all their related service; and you shall assign by name the objects that they are required to carry. [33]This is the service of the clans of the Merarites, the whole of their service relating to the tent of meeting.

under the hand of Ithamar son of Aaron the priest.

34 So Moses and Aaron and the leaders of the congregation enrolled the Kohathites, by their clans and their ancestral houses, [35]from thirty years old up to fifty years old, everyone who qualified for work relating to the tent of meeting; [36]and their enrollment by clans was two thousand seven hundred fifty. [37]This was the enrollment of the clans of the Kohathites, all who served at the tent of meeting, whom Moses and Aaron enrolled according to the commandment of the LORD by Moses.

38 The enrollment of the Gershonites, by their clans and their ancestral houses, [39]from thirty years old up to fifty years old, everyone who qualified for work relating to the tent of meeting— [40]their enrollment by their clans and their ancestral houses was two thousand six hundred thirty. [41]This was the enrollment of the clans of the Gershonites, all who served at the tent of meeting, whom Moses and Aaron enrolled according to the commandment of the LORD.

42 The enrollment of the clans of the Merarites, by their clans and their ancestral houses, [43]from thirty years old up to fifty years old, everyone who qualified for work relating to the tent of meeting— [44]their enrollment by their clans was three thousand two hundred. [45]This is the enrollment of the clans of the Merarites, whom Moses and Aaron enrolled according to the commandment of the LORD by Moses.

46 All those who were enrolled of the Levites, whom Moses and Aaron and the leaders of Israel enrolled, by their clans and their ancestral houses, [47]from thirty years old up to fifty years old, everyone who qualified to do the work of service and the work of bearing burdens relating to the tent of meeting, [48]their enrollment was eight thousand five hundred eighty. [49]According to the commandment of the LORD through Moses they were appointed to their several tasks of serving or carrying; thus they were enrolled by him, as the LORD commanded Moses.[89]

Offerings of Israelite Tribal Representatives

7 On the day when Moses had finished setting up the tabernacle, and had anointed and consecrated it with all its furnishings, and had anointed and consecrated the altar with all its utensils, [2]the leaders of Israel, heads of their ancestral houses, the leaders of the tribes, who were over those who were enrolled, made offerings. [3]They brought their offerings before the LORD, six covered wagons and twelve oxen, a wagon for every two of the leaders, and for each one an ox; they presented them before the tabernacle. [4]Then the LORD said to Moses: [5]Accept these from them, that they may be used in doing the service of the tent of meeting, and give them to the Levites, to each according to

89. Numbers 5 and 6 contain various and quite different laws, "with no recognizably close relationships, as far as subject-matter is concerned, either with each other or with what precedes and follows" (Noth, *Numbers*, 44). Noth suggests that these laws are inserted at this point, because the narrative is nearing the end of the period at Sinai and this is the obvious place at which to introduce any legal material still to be associated with Sinai. He adds that "they come from a comparatively late period, even if they do contain older traditional material" (*Numbers*, 45).

his service. *6So Moses took the wagons and the oxen, and gave them to the Levites. 7Two wagons and four oxen he gave to the Gershonites, according to their service; 8and four wagons and eight oxen he gave to the Merarites, according to their service, under the direction of Ithamar son of Aaron the priest. 9But to the Kohathites he gave none, because they were charged with the care of the holy things that had to be carried on the shoulders.*

10 The leaders also presented offerings for the dedication of the altar at the time when it was anointed; the leaders presented their offering before the altar. 11The LORD said to Moses: They shall present their offerings, one leader each day, for the dedication of the altar.

12 The one who presented his offering the first day was Nahshon son of Amminadab, of the tribe of Judah; 13his offering was one silver plate weighing one hundred thirty shekels, one silver basin weighing seventy shekels, according to the shekel of the sanctuary, both of them full of choice flour mixed with oil for a grain offering; 14one golden dish weighing ten shekels, full of incense; 15one young bull, one ram, one male lamb a year old, for a burnt offering; 16one male goat for a sin offering; 17and for the sacrifice of well-being, two oxen, five rams, five male goats, and five male lambs a year old. This was the offering of Nahshon son of Amminadab.

18 On the second day Nethanel son of Zuar, the leader of Issachar, presented an offering; 19he presented for his offering one silver plate weighing one hundred thirty shekels, one silver basin weighing seventy shekels, according to the shekel of the sanctuary, both of them full of choice flour mixed with oil for a grain offering; 20one golden dish weighing ten shekels, full of incense; 21one young bull, one ram, one male lamb a year old, as a burnt offering; 22one male goat as a sin offering; 23and for the sacrifice of well-being, two oxen, five rams, five male goats, and five male lambs a year old. This was the offering of Nethanel son of Zuar.

24 On the third day Eliab son of Helon, the leader of the Zebulunites: 25his offering was one silver plate weighing one hundred thirty shekels, one silver basin weighing seventy shekels, according to the shekel of the sanctuary, both of them full of choice flour mixed with oil for a grain offering; 26one golden dish weighing ten shekels, full of incense; 27one young bull, one ram, one male lamb a year old, for a burnt offering; 28one male goat for a sin offering; 29and for the sacrifice of well-being, two oxen, five rams, five male goats, and five male lambs a year old. This was the offering of Eliab son of Helon.

30 On the fourth day Elizur son of Shedeur, the leader of the Reubenites: 31his offering was one silver plate weighing one hundred thirty shekels, one silver basin weighing seventy shekels, according to the shekel of the sanctuary, both of them full of choice flour mixed with oil for a grain offering; 32one golden dish weighing ten shekels, full of incense; 33one young bull, one ram, one male lamb a year old, for a burnt offering; 34one male goat for a sin offering; 35and for the sacrifice of well-being, two oxen, five rams, five male goats, and five male lambs a year old. This was the offering of Elizur son of Shedeur.

36 On the fifth day Shelumiel son of Zurishaddai, the leader of the Simeonites: 37his offering was one silver plate weighing one hundred thirty shekels, one silver basin weighing seventy shekels, according to the shekel of the sanctuary, both of them full of choice flour mixed with oil for a grain offering; 38one golden dish weighing ten shekels, full of incense; 39one young bull, one ram, one male lamb a year old, for a burnt offering; 40one male goat for a sin offering; 41and for the sacrifice of well-being, two oxen, five rams, five male goats, and five male lambs a year old. This was the offering of Shelumiel son of Zurishaddai.

42 On the sixth day Eliasaph son of Deuel, the leader of the Gadites: 43his offering was one silver plate weighing one hundred thirty shekels, one silver basin weighing seventy shekels, according to the shekel of the sanctuary, both of them full of choice flour mixed with oil for a grain offering; [44]one golden dish weighing ten shekels, full of incense; [45]one young bull, one ram, one male lamb a year old, for a burnt offering; [46]one male goat for a sin offering; [47]and for the sacrifice of well-being, two oxen, five rams, five male goats, and five male lambs a year old. This was the offering of Eliasaph son of Deuel.

[48] On the seventh day Elishama son of Ammihud, the leader of the Ephraimites: [49]his offering was one silver plate weighing one hundred thirty shekels, one silver basin weighing seventy shekels, according to the shekel of the sanctuary, both of them full of choice flour mixed with oil for a grain offering; [50]one golden dish weighing ten shekels, full of incense; [51]one young bull, one ram, one male lamb a year old, for a burnt offering; [52]one male goat for a sin offering; [53]and for the sacrifice of well-being, two oxen, five rams, five male goats, and five male lambs a year old. This was the offering of Elishama son of Ammihud.

[54] On the eighth day Gamaliel son of Pedahzur, the leader of the Manassites: [55]his offering was one silver plate weighing one hundred thirty shekels, one silver basin weighing seventy shekels, according to the shekel of the sanctuary, both of them full of choice flour mixed with oil for a grain offering; [56]one golden dish weighing ten shekels, full of incense; [57]one young bull, one ram, one male lamb a year old, for a burnt offering; [58]one male goat for a sin offering; [59]and for the sacrifice of well-being, two oxen, five rams, five male goats, and five male lambs a year old. This was the offering of Gamaliel son of Pedahzur.

[60] On the ninth day Abidan son of Gideoni, the leader of the Benjaminites: [61]his offering was one silver plate weighing one hundred thirty shekels, one silver basin weighing seventy shekels, according to the shekel of the sanctuary, both of them full of choice flour mixed with oil for a grain offering; [62]one golden dish weighing ten shekels,

full of incense; [63]one young bull, one ram, one male lamb a year old, for a burnt offering; [64]one male goat for a sin offering; [65]and for the sacrifice of well-being, two oxen, five rams, five male goats, and five male lambs a year old. This was the offering of Abidan son of Gideoni.

[66] On the tenth day Ahiezer son of Ammishaddai, the leader of the Danites: [67]his offering was one silver plate weighing one hundred thirty shekels, one silver basin weighing seventy shekels, according to the shekel of the sanctuary, both of them full of choice flour mixed with oil for a grain offering; [68]one golden dish weighing ten shekels, full of incense; [69]one young bull, one ram, one male lamb a year old, for a burnt offering; [70]one male goat for a sin offering; [71]and for the sacrifice of well-being, two oxen, five rams, five male goats, and five male lambs a year old. This was the offering of Ahiezer son of Ammishaddai.

[72] On the eleventh day Pagiel son of Ochran, the leader of the Asherites: [73]his offering was one silver plate weighing one hundred thirty shekels, one silver basin weighing seventy shekels, according to the shekel of the sanctuary, both of them full of choice flour mixed with oil for a grain offering; [74]one golden dish weighing ten shekels, full of incense; [75]one young bull, one ram, one male lamb a year old, for a burnt offering; [76]one male goat for a sin offering; [77]and for the sacrifice of well-being, two oxen, five rams, five male goats, and five male lambs a year old. This was the offering of Pagiel son of Ochran.

[78] On the twelfth day Ahira son of Enan, the leader of the Naphtalites: [79]his offering was one silver plate weighing one hundred thirty shekels, one silver basin weighing seventy shekels, according to the shekel of the sanctuary, both of them full of choice flour mixed with oil for a grain offering; [80]one golden dish weighing ten shekels, full of incense; [81]one young bull, one ram, one male lamb a year old, for a burnt offering; [82]one male goat for a sin offering; [83]and for the

sacrifice of well-being, two oxen, five rams, five male goats, and five male lambs a year old. This was the offering of Ahira son of Enan.

84 This was the dedication offering for the altar, at the time when it was anointed, from the leaders of Israel: twelve silver plates, twelve silver basins, twelve golden dishes, [85] each silver plate weighing one hundred thirty shekels and each basin seventy, all the silver of the vessels two thousand four hundred shekels according to the shekel of the sanctuary, [86] the twelve golden dishes, full of incense, weighing ten shekels apiece according to the shekel of the sanctuary, all the gold of the dishes being one hundred twenty shekels; [87] all the livestock for the burnt offering twelve bulls, twelve rams, twelve male lambs a year old, with their grain offering; and twelve male goats for a sin offering; [88] and all the livestock for the sacrifice of well-being twenty-four bulls, the rams sixty, the male goats sixty, the male lambs a year old sixty. This was the dedication offering for the altar, after it was anointed.

89 When Moses went into the tent of meeting to speak with the LORD, he would hear the voice speaking to him from above the mercy seat that was on the ark of the covenant from between the two cherubim; thus it spoke to him.[90]

Separation of the Levites

8:5 The LORD spoke to Moses, saying: [6]Take the Levites from among the Israelites and cleanse them. [7]Thus you shall do to them, to cleanse them: sprinkle the water of purification on them, have them shave their whole body with a razor and wash their clothes, and so cleanse themselves. [8]Then let them take a young bull and its grain offering of choice flour mixed with oil, and you shall take another young bull for a sin offering. [9]You shall bring the Levites before the tent of meeting, and assemble the whole congregation of the Israelites. [10]When you bring the Levites before the LORD, the Israelites shall lay their hands on the Levites, [11]and Aaron shall present the Levites before the LORD as an elevation offering from the Israelites, that they may do the service of the LORD. [12]The Levites shall lay their hands on the heads of the bulls, and he shall offer the one for a sin offering and the other for a burnt offering to the LORD, to make atonement for the Levites. [13]Then you shall have the Levites stand before Aaron and his sons, and you shall present them as an elevation offering to the LORD.

14 Thus you shall separate the Levites from among the other Israelites, and the Levites shall be mine. [15]Thereafter the Levites may go in to do service at the tent of meeting, once you have cleansed them and presented them as an elevation offering. [16]For they are unreservedly given to me from among the Israelites; I have taken them for myself, in place of all that open the womb, the firstborn of all the Israelites. [17]For all the firstborn among the Israelites are mine, both human and animal. On the day that I struck down all the firstborn in the land of Egypt I consecrated them for myself, [18]but I have taken the Levites in place of all the firstborn among the Israelites. [19]Moreover, I have given the Levites as a gift to Aaron and his sons from among the Israelites, to do the service for the Israelites at the tent of meeting, and to make atonement for the Israelites, in order that there

---

90. Leviticus 7, with its detailed description of the fantastically rich gifts offered by representatives of the twelve tribes for the dedication of the altar, is characterized by Noth as "one of the very late additions to the P-narrative." Although it is set "on the day" when the tabernacle and altar had been anointed and consecrated, that day was at least a month in the past (cf. Exod 40:2, 17 and Num 1:1, 18). The chapter is dependent on passages that Noth already has regarded as secondary, such as Exod 40:9-10 and Num 4:4-33 (at least in the Numbers commentary). Such wealth and precious metals could not have been thought to be available in the wilderness (*Numbers*, 63).

may be no plague among the Israelites for coming too close to the sanctuary.

20 Moses and Aaron and the whole congregation of the Israelites did with the Levites accordingly; the Israelites did with the Levites just as the LORD had commanded Moses concerning them. [21]The Levites purified themselves from sin and washed their clothes; then Aaron presented them as an elevation offering before the LORD, and Aaron made atonement for them to cleanse them. [22]Thereafter the Levites went in to do their service in the tent of meeting in attendance on Aaron and his sons. As the LORD had commanded Moses concerning the Levites, so they did with them.

23 The LORD spoke to Moses, saying: [24]This applies to the Levites: from twenty-five years old and upward they shall begin to do duty in the service of the tent of meeting; [25]and from the age of fifty years they shall retire from the duty of the service and serve no more. [26]They may assist their brothers in the tent of meeting in carrying out their duties, but they shall perform no service. Thus you shall do with the Levites in assigning their duties.[91]

Passover Regulations

9 The LORD spoke to Moses in the wilderness of Sinai, in the first month of the second year after they had come out of the land of Egypt, saying: [2]Let the Israelites keep the passover at its appointed time. [3]On the fourteenth day of this month, at twilight, you shall keep it at its appointed time; according to all its statutes and all its regulations you shall keep it. [4]So Moses told the Israelites that they should keep the passover. [5]They kept the passover in the first month, on the fourteenth day of the month, at twilight, in the wilderness of Sinai. Just as the LORD had commanded Moses, so the Israelites did. [6]Now there were certain people who were unclean through touching a corpse, so that they could not keep the passover on that day. They came before Moses and Aaron on that day, [7]and said to him, "Although we are unclean through touching a corpse, why must we be kept from presenting the LORD's offering at its appointed time among the Israelites?" [8]Moses spoke to them, "Wait, so that I may hear what the LORD will command concerning you."

9 The LORD spoke to Moses, saying: [10]Speak to the Israelites, saying: Anyone of you or your descendants who is unclean through touching a corpse, or is away on a journey, shall still keep the passover to the LORD. [11]In the second month on the fourteenth day, at twilight, they shall keep it; they shall eat it with unleavened bread and bitter herbs. [12]They shall leave none of it until morning, nor break a bone of it; according to all the statute for the passover they shall keep it. [13]But anyone who is clean and is not on a journey, and yet refrains from keeping the passover, shall be cut off from the people for not presenting the LORD's offering at its appointed time; such a one shall bear the consequences for the sin. [14]Any alien residing among you who wishes to keep the passover to the LORD shall do so according to the statute of the passover and according to its regulation; you shall have one statute for both the resident alien and the native.[92]

---

91. This passage offers a variance relaxing the stricter conditions of age laid down in Num 4:2-3, where thirty to fifty years old was specified. For Noth, "this must surely be understood as a later correction," resulting from an appreciable lack of Levitical strength (*Numbers*, 69).

92. Num 9:1-14 provides for a celebration of the Passover exactly one month after the due date, where certain impediments have occurred. Noth comments, "The secondary character of the passage relegates it to those additions to the P-narrative which certainly come from the post-exilic period. In this period there is also the supposition, which is quite anachronistic as far as the Mosaic period is concerned, that individuals can be absent on a long journey" (*Numbers*, 70–71).

Israel's Journey toward the Land

God's Guidance

15 On the day the tabernacle was set up, the cloud covered the tabernacle, the tent of the covenant; and from evening until morning it was over the tabernacle, having the appearance of fire. [16]It was always so: the cloud covered it by day and the appearance of fire by night. [17]Whenever the cloud lifted from over the tent, then the Israelites would set out; and in the place where the cloud settled down, there the Israelites would camp. [18]At the command of the LORD the Israelites would set out, and at the command of the LORD they would camp. As long as the cloud rested over the tabernacle, they would remain in camp. [19]Even when the cloud continued over the tabernacle many days, the Israelites would keep the charge of the LORD, and would not set out. [20]Sometimes the cloud would remain a few days over the tabernacle, and according to the command of the LORD they would remain in camp; then according to the command of the LORD they would set out. [21]Sometimes the cloud would remain from evening until morning; and when the cloud lifted in the morning, they would set out, or if it continued for a day and a night, when the cloud lifted they would set out. [22]Whether it was two days, or a month, or a longer time, that the cloud continued over the tabernacle, resting upon it, the Israelites would remain in camp and would not set out; but when it lifted they would set out. [23]At the command of the LORD they would camp, and at the command of the LORD they would set out. They kept the charge of the LORD, at the command of the LORD by Moses.

10 The LORD spoke to Moses, saying: [2]Make two silver trumpets; you shall make them of hammered work; and you shall use them for summoning the congregation, and for breaking camp. [3]When both are blown, the whole congregation shall assemble before you at the entrance of the tent of meeting. [4]But if only one is blown, then the leaders, the heads of the tribes of Israel, shall assemble before you. [5]When you blow an alarm, the camps on the east side shall set out; [6]when you blow a second alarm, the camps on the south side shall set out. An alarm is to be blown whenever they are to set out. [7]But when the assembly is to be gathered, you shall blow, but you shall not sound an alarm. [8]The sons of Aaron, the priests, shall blow the trumpets; this shall be a perpetual institution for you throughout your generations. [9]When you go to war in your land against the adversary who oppresses you, you shall sound an alarm with the trumpets, so that you may be remembered before the LORD your God and be saved from your enemies. [10]Also on your days of rejoicing, at your appointed festivals, and at the beginnings of your months, you shall blow the trumpets over your burnt offerings and over your sacrifices of well-being; they shall serve as a reminder on your behalf before the LORD your God: I am the LORD your God.[93]

Itinerary: From Sinai to Paran

11 In the second year, in the second month, on the twentieth day of the month, the cloud lifted from over the tabernacle of the covenant. [12]Then the Israelites set out by stages from the wilderness of Sinai, and the cloud settled down in the wilderness of Paran.

[13]They set out for the first time at the command of the LORD by Moses. [14]The standard of the camp of Judah set out first, company by company, and over the whole company was Nahshon son of Amminadab. [15]Over the company of the tribe

---

93. Noth suggests that these trumpets derive from the post-exilic temple. He views the idea that the trumpets served as a prayer (remembrance) before God as certainly resting on later interpretation (*Numbers*, 76).

of Issachar was Nethanel son of Zuar; ¹⁶and over the company of the tribe of Zebulun was Eliab son of Helon.

17 Then the tabernacle was taken down, and the Gershonites and the Merarites, who carried the tabernacle, set out. ¹⁸Next the standard of the camp of Reuben set out, company by company; and over the whole company was Elizur son of Shedeur. ¹⁹Over the company of the tribe of Simeon was Shelumiel son of Zurishaddai, ²⁰and over the company of the tribe of Gad was Eliasaph son of Deuel.

21 Then the Kohathites, who carried the holy things, set out; and the tabernacle was set up before their arrival. ²²Next the standard of the Ephraimite camp set out, company by company, and over the whole company was Elishama son of Ammihud. ²³Over the company of the tribe of Manasseh was Gamaliel son of Pedahzur, ²⁴and over the company of the tribe of Benjamin was Abidan son of Gideoni.

*25 Then the standard of the camp of Dan, acting as the rear guard of all the camps, set out, company by company, and over the whole company was Ahiezer son of Ammishaddai. ²⁶Over the company of the tribe of Asher was Pagiel son of Ochran, ²⁷and over the company of the tribe of Naphtali was Ahira son of Enan. ²⁸This was the order of march of the Israelites, company by company, when they set out.*⁹⁴

Spying Out the Land

13 The LORD said to Moses, ²"Send men to spy out the land of Canaan, which I am giving

to the Israelites; from each of their ancestral tribes you shall send a man, every one a leader among them." ³So Moses sent them from the wilderness of Paran, according to the command of the LORD,

all of them leading men among the Israelites. ⁴These were their names: From the tribe of Reuben, Shammua son of Zaccur; ⁵from the tribe of Simeon, Shaphat son of Hori; ⁶from the tribe of Judah, Caleb son of Jephunneh; ⁷from the tribe of Issachar, Igal son of Joseph; ⁸from the tribe of Ephraim, Hoshea son of Nun; ⁹from the tribe of Benjamin, Palti son of Raphu; ¹⁰from the tribe of Zebulun, Gaddiel son of Sodi; ¹¹from the tribe of Joseph (that is, from the tribe of Manasseh), Gaddi son of Susi; ¹²from the tribe of Dan, Ammiel son of Gemalli; ¹³from the tribe of Asher, Sethur son of Michael; ¹⁴from the tribe of Naphtali, Nahbi son of Vophsi; ¹⁵from the tribe of Gad, Geuel son of Machi. ¹⁶These were the names of the men whom Moses sent to spy out the land. And Moses changed the name of Hoshea son of Nun to Joshua. ¹⁷ᵃMoses sent them⁹⁵ to spy out the land of Canaan.

21 So they went up and spied out the land from the wilderness of Zin to Rehob, near Lebo-hamath.

25 At the end of forty days they returned from spying out the land. ²⁶*And they came to Moses and Aaron and to all the congregation of the Israelites in the wilderness of Paran; they brought back word to them and to all the congregation, and showed them the fruit of the land.

---

94. Noth comments that Num 10:13-28 "probably does not belong to the basic form of P." Although it follows the data of chap. 2, it introduces a new element in vv. 17 and 21, according to which the sanctuary was carried in two parts: the Gershonites carry the externals and the Kohathites carry the holy things. In doing this, it modified Num 2:17 along lines indicated in chap. 4, which was secondary for Noth in the Numbers commentary (*Numbers*, 76–77).

95. The list of leaders is regarded as secondary, because it is in tension with the list in Num 1:5-15 and, in comparison with the latter, "the present list gives the impression of being freely composed" (Noth, *Numbers*, 103). In his commentary, Noth includes v. 2bβ—"every one a leader among them"—as part of the secondary passage.

32 And [Heb.; NRSV, So] they brought to the Israelites an unfavorable report of the land that they had spied out, saying, "The land that we have gone through as spies is a land that devours its inhabitants; and all the people that we saw in it are of great size. ³³There we saw the Nephilim *(the Anakites come from the Nephilim)* ⁹⁶ ³³and to ourselves we seemed like grasshoppers, and so we seemed to them."

14:1a Then all the congregation raised a loud cry. ²And all the Israelites complained against Moses and Aaron; the whole congregation said to them, "Would that we had died in the land of Egypt! Or would that we had died in this wilderness! ³Why is the LORD bringing us into this land to fall by the sword? Our wives and our little ones will become booty; would it not be better for us to go back to Egypt?"

5 Then Moses and Aaron fell on their faces before all the assembly of the congregation of the Israelites. ⁶And Joshua son of Nun and Caleb son of Jephunneh, who were among those who had spied out the land, tore their clothes ⁷and said to all the congregation of the Israelites, "The land that we went through as spies is an exceedingly good land. ⁸If the LORD is pleased with us, he will bring us into this land and give it to us, a land that flows with milk and honey. ⁹Only, do not rebel against the LORD; and do not fear the people of the land, for they are no more than bread for us; their protection is removed from them, and the LORD is with us; do not fear them." ¹⁰But the whole congregation threatened to stone them.

Then the glory of the LORD appeared at the tent of meeting to all the Israelites.

26 And the LORD spoke to Moses and to Aaron, saying: ²⁷How long shall this wicked congregation complain against me? *I have heard the complaints of the Israelites, which they complain against me.*⁹⁷ ²⁸Say to them, "As I live," says the LORD, "I will do to you the very things I heard you say: ²⁹your dead bodies shall fall in this very wilderness; and of all your number, included in the census, from twenty years old and upward, who have complained against me."⁹⁸

³⁰Not one of you shall come into the land in which I swore to settle you, except Caleb son of Jephunneh and Joshua son of Nun. ³¹But your little ones, who you said would become booty, I will bring in, and they shall know the land that you have despised. ³²But as for you, your dead bodies shall fall in this wilderness. ³³And your children shall be shepherds in the wilderness for forty years, and shall suffer for your faithlessness, until the last of your dead bodies lies in the wilderness.

³⁴According to the number of the days in which you spied out the land, forty days, for every day

---

96. Here the Anakites (*běnê ʿănāq*) are derived from the Nephilim (giants). By contrast, in Num 13:22 and 13:28 (both J) a different phrase is used for the Anakites (*yělidê hāʿănāq*, which Noth renders "necklace people"). The addition is missing from the Greek and appears to be an explanatory gloss. The Nephilim are otherwise only mentioned in Gen 6:4 (Noth, *Numbers*, 107).

97. Noth's comment is that this sentence in Num 14:27b "comes after the event and is an addition" (*Numbers*, 110).

98. The analysis here assumes an understanding of Num 14:29 as a complete sentence: "Your dead bodies shall fall in this very wilderness—all your number included in the census, from twenty years old and upward, who have complained against me." Cf. JB, NEB, and NIV.

a year, you shall bear your iniquity, forty years, and you shall know my displeasure.[99]
³⁵I the LORD have spoken; surely I will do thus to all this wicked congregation gathered together against me: in this wilderness they shall come to a full end, and there they shall die.

36 And the men whom Moses sent to spy out the land, who returned and made all the congregation complain against him by bringing a bad report about the land—³⁷the men who brought an unfavorable report about the land died by a plague before the LORD. ³⁸But Joshua son of Nun and Caleb son of Jephunneh alone remained alive, of those men who went to spy out the land.

Rebellion of Korah

16:1a *Now Korah took* [NRSV rearranged to mirror Hebrew]

son of Izhar son of Kohath son of Levi
²**two hundred fifty Israelite men, leaders of the congregation, chosen from the assembly, well-known men.* ³*They assembled against Moses and against Aaron, and said to them, "You have gone too far! All the congregation are holy, everyone of them, and the LORD is among them. So why then do you exalt yourselves above the assembly of the*

LORD?" ⁴*When Moses heard it, he fell on his face.* ⁵*Then he said to Korah and all his company, "In the morning the LORD will make known who is his, and who is holy, and who will be allowed to approach him; the one whom he will choose he will allow to approach him.* ⁶*Do this: take censers, Korah and all your company,* ⁷*and tomorrow put fire in them, and lay incense on them before the LORD; and the man whom the LORD chooses shall be the holy one."*
You Levites have gone too far!"
⁸*Then Moses said to Korah, "Hear now, you Levites!* ⁹*Is it too little for you that the God of Israel has separated you from the congregation of Israel, to allow you to approach him in order to perform the duties of the LORD's tabernacle, and to stand before the congregation and serve them?* ¹⁰*He has allowed you to approach him, and all your brother Levites with you; yet you seek the priesthood as well!* ¹¹*Therefore you and all your company have gathered together against the LORD. What is Aaron that you rail against him?"*
16 *And Moses said to Korah, "As for you and all your company, be present tomorrow before the LORD, you and they and Aaron;* ¹⁷*and let each one of you take his censer, and*

---

99. While the grand lines of source division may be relatively clear, Noth has never been one to shirk naming the places where uncertainty prevails. In tracing possible levels of growth within a single source, informed intuition may be a significant factor. Such intuition operates within the parameters of a particular academic culture; judgments can be expected to vary as the culture changes. The parameters are changing at present and it is no longer enough simply to say why something is out of place. Increasing importance is being given to the task of examining what seems out of place, so as to grasp the good reasons for why it is where it is and how it may make good sense there.

It is interesting to observe the carefully tentative way that Noth treats Num 14:30-34 in his commentary. In v. 34, the forty years in the wilderness is rather artificially tied to the forty days spent spying out the

land. Noth comments cautiously, "One might wonder whether v. 34 is not a speculative element only added later." Verse 30 is considered definitely as an addition, "since it begins with remarkable abruptness and mentions Caleb before Joshua" (*Numbers*, 110). If vv. 30 and 34 are secondary, the question has to be asked about vv. 31-33; the frequency of repetitions in the section raises the possibility of other later expansions. Noth remarks that if vv. 31-32 were also secondary, it would be particularly interesting because it would remove any mention even here of the future entry into the land in the original P narrative. In line with this, vv. 36-38 have Joshua and Caleb remain alive, but no mention is made of their inheriting some of the land. It is implied that the children will enter in due course (v. 33), but no more is said. All of this is congruent with the lack of interest in the conquest in the original P narrative (Noth, *Numbers*, 110–11).

*put incense on it, and each one of you present his censer before the LORD, two hundred fifty censers; you also, and Aaron, each his censer." *[18]*So each man took his censer, and they put fire in the censers and laid incense on them, and they stood at the entrance of the tent of meeting with Moses and Aaron. *[19]*Then Korah assembled the whole congregation against them at the entrance of the tent of meeting. And the glory of the LORD appeared to the whole congregation.*

*20 Then the LORD spoke to Moses and to Aaron, saying: *[21]*Separate yourselves from this congregation, so that I may consume them in a moment. *[22]*They fell on their faces, and said, "O God, the God of the spirits of all flesh, shall one person sin and you become angry with the whole congregation?"*

*23 And the LORD spoke to Moses, saying: *[24]**Say to the congregation: Get away! *[27]**So they got away from Korah.*[100] *[35]*And fire came out from the LORD and consumed the two hundred fifty men offering the incense.*

36 Then the LORD spoke to Moses, saying:[101] *[37]*Tell Eleazar son of Aaron the priest to take the censers out of the blaze; then scatter the fire far and wide. *[38]*For the censers of these sinners have become holy at the cost of their lives. Make them into hammered plates as a covering for the altar, for they presented them before the LORD and they became holy. Thus they shall be a sign to the Israelites. *[39]*So Eleazar the priest took the bronze censers that had been presented by those who were burned; and they were hammered out as a covering for the altar—*[40]*a reminder to the Israelites that no outsider, who is not of the descendants of Aaron, shall approach to offer incense before the LORD, so as not to become like Korah and his company—just as the LORD had said to him through Moses.*

*41 On the next day, however, the whole congregation of the Israelites rebelled against Moses and against Aaron, saying, "You have killed the people of the LORD." *[42]*And when the congregation had assembled against them, Moses and Aaron turned toward the tent of meeting; the cloud had covered it and the glory of the LORD appeared. *[43]*Then Moses and Aaron came to the front of the tent of meeting, *[44]*and the LORD spoke to Moses, saying, *[45]*"Get away from this congregation, so that I may consume them in a moment." And they fell on their faces. *[46]*Moses said to Aaron, "Take your censer, put fire on it from the altar and lay incense on it, and carry it quickly to the congregation and make atonement for them. For wrath has gone out from the LORD; the plague has begun." *[47]*So Aaron took it as Moses had ordered, and ran into the middle of the assembly, where the plague had already begun among the people. He put on the incense,*

---

100. Korah and his two hundred and fifty are in front of the tent of meeting (Num 16:18-19), not at Korah's dwelling. In the Dathan and Abiram story, Dathan and Abiram are punished when they and their homes (tents) are swallowed up (see Num 16:25-34* in chap. 3, below). Noth remarks that at the end of v. 24 and again at the beginning of v. 27, "the Korah story is quite incongruously mixed up with the Dathan-Abiram story" (*Numbers*, 127–28).

The understanding of the Hebrew here is not easily rendered in English. In both vv. 24 and 27, there is a preposition "round about" (*missābib*), which it is difficult to fit into the English cadence. Of v. 24 Noth remarks that the mention of "the dwelling of Korah" and of the names "Dathan and Abiram" has to be "a completely secondary fusion" at an interface of the two narrative versions (*Numbers*, 127). Verse 27a he describes as "yet another editorial addition linking Korah and Dathan-Abiram" (*Numbers*, 128). The biblical text given here is the most satisfactory representation possible from the NRSV. Note the NAB's translation of v. 24: "Withdraw from the space around the Dwelling" (i.e., the tabernacle). (Note: the understanding here presumes that in the translation of the text, in both German and English editions of Noth's *Numbers*, the bracket in v. 24 should be extended to include Dathan and Abiram.)

101. Num 16:36-50 is numbered 17:1-15 in Hebrew.

and made atonement for the people. [48]*He stood between the dead and the living; and the plague was stopped.* [49]*Those who died by the plague were fourteen thousand seven hundred, besides those who died in the affair of Korah.* [50]*When the plague was stopped, Aaron returned to Moses at the entrance of the tent of meeting.*

Aaron's Staff

17 *The* LORD *spoke to Moses, saying:*[102] [2]*Speak to the Israelites, and get twelve staffs from them, one for each ancestral house, from all the leaders of their ancestral houses. Write each man's name on his staff,* [3]*and write Aaron's name on the staff of Levi. For there shall be one staff for the head of each ancestral house.* [4]*Place them in the tent of meeting before the covenant, where I meet with you.* [5]*And the staff of the man whom I choose shall sprout; thus I will put a stop to the complaints of the Israelites that they continually make against you.* [6]*Moses spoke to the Israelites; and all their leaders gave him staffs, one for each leader, according to their ancestral houses, twelve staffs; and the staff of Aaron was among theirs.* [7]*So Moses placed the staffs before the* LORD *in the tent of the covenant.*

8 *When Moses went into the tent of the covenant on the next day, the staff of Aaron for the house of Levi had sprouted. It put forth buds, produced blossoms, and bore ripe almonds.* [9]*Then Moses brought out all the staffs from before the* LORD *to all the Israelites; and they looked, and each man took his staff.* [10]*And the* LORD *said to Moses, "Put back the staff of Aaron before the covenant, to be kept as a warning to rebels, so that you may make an end of their complaints against me, or else they will die."* [11]*Moses did so; just as the* LORD *commanded him, so he did.*

Priests and Levites

12 *The Israelites said to Moses, "We are perishing; we are lost, all of us are lost!*

[13]*Everyone who approaches the tabernacle of the* LORD *will die. Are we all to perish?"*

18 *The* LORD *said to Aaron: You and your sons and your ancestral house with you shall bear responsibility for offenses connected with the sanctuary, while you and your sons alone shall bear responsibility for offenses connected with the priesthood.* [2]*So bring with you also your brothers of the tribe of Levi, your ancestral tribe, in order that they may be joined to you, and serve you while you and your sons with you are in front of the tent of the covenant.* [3]*They shall perform duties for you and for the whole tent. But they must not approach either the utensils of the sanctuary or the altar, otherwise both they and you will die.* [4]*They are attached to you in order to perform the duties of the tent of meeting, for all the service of the tent; no outsider shall approach you.* [5]*You yourselves shall perform the duties of the sanctuary and the duties of the altar, so that wrath may never again come upon the Israelites.* [6]*It is I who now take your brother Levites from among the Israelites; they are now yours as a gift, dedicated to the* LORD, *to perform the service of the tent of meeting.* [7]*But you and your sons with you shall diligently perform your priestly duties in all that concerns the altar and the area behind the curtain. I give your priesthood as a gift; any outsider who approaches shall be put to death.*

8 *The* LORD *spoke to Aaron: I have given you charge of the offerings made to me, all the holy gifts of the Israelites; I have given them to you and your sons as a priestly portion due you in perpetuity.* [9]*This shall be yours from the most holy things, reserved from the fire: every offering of theirs that they render to me as a most holy thing, whether grain offering, sin offering, or guilt offering, shall belong to you and your sons.* [10]*As a most holy thing you shall eat it; every male may eat it; it shall be holy to you.* [11]*This also is yours: I have given to you,*

---

102. Num 17:1-13 is numbered 17:16-28 in Hebrew.

together with your sons and daughters, as a perpetual due, whatever is set aside from the gifts of all the elevation offerings of the Israelites; everyone who is clean in your house may eat them. [12]All the best of the oil and all the best of the wine and of the grain, the choice produce that they give to the LORD, I have given to you. [13]The first fruits of all that is in their land, which they bring to the LORD, shall be yours; everyone who is clean in your house may eat of it. [14]Every devoted thing in Israel shall be yours. [15]The first issue of the womb of all creatures, human and animal, which is offered to the LORD, shall be yours; but the firstborn of human beings you shall redeem, and the firstborn of unclean animals you shall redeem. [16]Their redemption price, reckoned from one month of age, you shall fix at five shekels of silver, according to the shekel of the sanctuary (that is, twenty gerahs). [17]But the firstborn of a cow, or the firstborn of a sheep, or the firstborn of a goat, you shall not redeem; they are holy. You shall dash their blood on the altar, and shall turn their fat into smoke as an offering by fire for a pleasing odor to the LORD; [18]but their flesh shall be yours, just as the breast that is elevated and as the right thigh are yours. [19]All the holy offerings that the Israelites present to the LORD I have given to you, together with your sons and daughters, as a perpetual due; it is a covenant of salt forever before the LORD for you and your descendants as well. [20]Then the LORD said to Aaron: You shall have no allotment in their land, nor shall you have any share among them; I am your share and your possession among the Israelites.

21 To the Levites I have given every tithe in Israel for a possession in return for the ser-

vice that they perform, the service in the tent of meeting. [22]From now on the Israelites shall no longer approach the tent of meeting, or else they will incur guilt and die. [23]But the Levites shall perform the service of the tent of meeting, and they shall bear responsibility for their own offenses; it shall be a perpetual statute throughout your generations. But among the Israelites they shall have no allotment, [24]because I have given to the Levites as their portion the tithe of the Israelites, which they set apart as an offering to the LORD. Therefore I have said of them that they shall have no allotment among the Israelites.

25 Then the LORD spoke to Moses, saying: [26]You shall speak to the Levites, saying: When you receive from the Israelites the tithe that I have given you from them for your portion, you shall set apart an offering from it to the LORD, a tithe of the tithe. [27]It shall be reckoned to you as your gift, the same as the grain of the threshing floor and the fullness of the wine press. [28]Thus you also shall set apart an offering to the LORD from all the tithes that you receive from the Israelites; and from them you shall give the LORD's offering to the priest Aaron. [29]Out of all the gifts to you, you shall set apart every offering due to the LORD; the best of all of them is the part to be consecrated. [30]Say also to them: When you have set apart the best of it, then the rest shall be reckoned to the Levites as produce of the threshing floor, and as produce of the wine press. [31]You may eat it in any place, you and your households; for it is your payment for your service in the tent of meeting. [32]You shall incur no guilt by reason of it, when you have offered the best of it. But you shall not profane the holy gifts of the Israelites, on pain of death.[103]

---

103. In his *History of Pentateuchal Traditions*, Noth provides a division between earlier and later passages within Numbers 16–18; but he comments that even the basic level gives the impression of being second-ary within the P narrative, inserted immediately before the final theme concluding the narrative, the deaths of Miriam, Aaron, and Moses. He notes three reasons for this judgment: (1) here Moses and Aaron appear

Itinerary: To Zin

20:1*The Israelites, the whole congregation, came into the wilderness of Zin in the first month. Miriam died there, and was buried there.

Water from the Rock

2 Now there was no water for the congregation; so they gathered together against Moses and against Aaron

³The people quarreled with Moses,[104]

and said,

Would that we had died when our kindred died before the LORD!

⁴"Why have you brought the assembly of the LORD into this wilderness for us and our livestock to die here?"

⁵Why have you brought us up out of Egypt, to bring us to this wretched place? It is no place for

grain, or figs, or vines, or pomegranates; and there is no water to drink.

⁶Then Moses and Aaron went away from the assembly to the entrance of the tent of meeting; they fell on their faces, and the glory of the LORD appeared to them. ⁷The LORD spoke to Moses, saying:

⁸Take the staff, and assemble the congregation, you and your brother Aaron

And you shall [Heb; NRSV, and] command the rock before their eyes to yield its water;[105]

thus you shall bring water out of the rock for them

thus you shall provide drink for the congregation and their livestock.

⁹So Moses took the staff from before the LORD, as he had commanded him.

¹⁰Moses and Aaron gathered the assembly

---

simply as Levites, which is not normally the case in P; (2) the narrative is related in content to Lev 10:1-7, which is itself secondary; and (3) the challenge to and confirmation of the regulations given at Sinai are hardly likely to have been themes of the original P narrative (see *Pentateuchal Traditions*, 19). Considerations of space preclude a discussion of the levels within the chapters; for this, see Noth, *Numbers*, 118–38.

Numbers 19, which has no reference to the surrounding material, is regarded as an addition. "It is an originally independent unit which has been inserted immediately before the Pentateuchal narrative is resumed once more in 20.1" (Noth, *Numbers*, 139).

104. There are two parallel strands in this material, with two different outcomes: Moses and Aaron are not to enter the promised land (20:12); the names of Kadesh and Meribah are explained (20:13). In Noth's judgment, "the basic form comprises a narrative strand whose choice of vocabulary and way of looking at things are clearly indicative of the 'Priestly writing' (P); it appears in vv. 2, 3b, 4, 6, 7, 8aβbβ, 10, 11b, 12. The rest exhibits such close and in many respects literal conformity with Ex. 17.1-7 that we cannot avoid the idea that a later hand has subsequently inserted into the P-narrative at this point the essentials of the narrative of the water-miracle of Ex. 17" (*Numbers*, 144). There is a slight difference in the text of v. 3 as attributed to P here by Noth (*Pentateuchal Traditions*)

from that given in the quotation from his Numbers commentary.

For v. 3a, see Exod 17:2; v. 5 is a doublet of v. 4 and has echoes of Exod 17:3 (E). Verse 8 includes two sets of doublets. One concerns the means by which the water was brought from the rock: in one case, by Moses' word; in the other, by striking the rock with the staff. The second concerns the actual provision of the water. The reference to the staff in v. 8aα suggests derivation from Exod 17:5, and v. 8bα, one element of the second doublet, provides the sequence to go with that. Verses 9 and 11a continue the theme of striking with the staff. Verse 13 takes the explanation of Meribah from Exod 17:7 and hints at an explanation for Kadesh (see Noth, *Numbers*, 144, 147).

For J and, apparently, E, this story belonged at the start of the wilderness wanderings. P uses the story to explain why Moses and Aaron were denied entry into the promised land. Following the divine instruction to summon water from the rock by a word of command (original P text in v. 8), Moses and Aaron are portrayed disobeying this order and instead upbraiding the assembly for demanding the impossible (v. 10). Nevertheless, the water arrives (v. 11b), but v. 12 insists that the failure of trust will keep Moses and Aaron out of the promised land (*Numbers*, 146–47).

105. This was apparently the command that, according to P, Moses and Aaron failed to obey, and thus they forfeited their entry into the promised land.

together before the rock, and he said to them, "Listen, you rebels, shall we bring water for you out of this rock?"

11Then Moses lifted up his hand and struck the rock twice with his staff.

But water [Heb.; NRSV, Water] came out abundantly, and the congregation and their livestock drank. 12And [Heb.; NRSV, But] the LORD said to Moses and Aaron, "Because you did not trust in me, to show my holiness before the eyes of the Israelites, therefore you shall not bring this assembly into the land that I have given them."

13These are the waters of Meribah, where the people of Israel quarreled with the LORD, and by which he showed his holiness.

Itinerary: To Mount Hor

22b And the Israelites, the whole congregation, came to Mount Hor.

Death of Aaron and Succession

23 Then the LORD said to Moses:

and Aaron at Mount Hor, on the border of the land of Edom, 24"Let Aaron be gathered to his people. For he shall not enter the land that I have given to the Israelites, because you rebelled against my command at the waters of Meribah.[106]

25"Take Aaron and his son Eleazar, and bring them up Mount Hor; 26strip Aaron of his vestments, and put them on his son Eleazar. But Aaron shall be gathered to his people, and shall die there." 27Moses did as the LORD had commanded; they went up Mount Hor in the sight of the whole congregation. 28Moses stripped Aaron of his vestments, and put them on his son Eleazar; and Aaron died there on the top of the mountain. Moses and Eleazar came down from the mountain. 29When all the congregation saw that Aaron had died, all the house of Israel mourned for Aaron thirty days.

Itinerary: From Mount Hor to the Plains of Moab

21:4* From Mount Hor they set out

22:1b and camped in the plains of Moab across the Jordan from Jericho.

Commissioning of Joshua

27:12 The LORD said to Moses, "Go up this mountain of the Abarim range, and see the land that I have given to the Israelites. 13When you have seen it, you also shall be gathered to your people, as your brother Aaron was, 14because you rebelled against my word in the wilderness of Zin when the congregation quarreled with me. You did not show my holiness before their eyes at the waters." (These are the waters of Meribath-kadesh in the wilderness of Zin.) 15Moses spoke to the LORD, saying, 16"Let the LORD, the God of the spirits of all flesh, appoint someone over the congregation 17who shall go out before them and come in before them, who shall lead them out and bring them in, so that the congregation of the LORD may not be like sheep without a shepherd." 18So the LORD said to Moses, "Take Joshua son of Nun, a man in whom is the spirit, and lay your hand upon him; 19have him stand before Eleazar the priest and all the congregation, and commission him in their sight. 20You shall give him some of your authority, so that all the congregation of the Israelites may obey. 21But he shall stand before Eleazar the priest, who shall inquire for him by the decision of the Urim before the LORD; at his

---

106. The passage seems to be additional. There is an inconsistency between the address to Moses and Aaron at Mount Hor (20:23) before the command to Moses to bring Aaron and his son up Mount Hor (20:25). If both vv. 22 and 23 were original, it would be expected that the geographical location of Mount Hor would have been given in v. 22b, at its first mention. The reference to Meribah assumes the secondary v. 13. Finally, the reference to Aaron being gathered to his people (v. 24a) anticipates v. 26 (see Noth, *Numbers*, 152–53).

word they shall go out, and at his word they shall come in, both he and all the Israelites with him, the whole congregation." ²²So Moses did as the LORD commanded him. He took Joshua and had him stand before Eleazar the priest and the whole congregation; ²³he laid his hands on him and commissioned him—as the LORD had directed through Moses.

Midianite Campaign

31 The LORD spoke to Moses, saying, ²"Avenge the Israelites on the Midianites; afterward you shall be gathered to your people." ³So Moses said to the people , "Arm some of your number for the war, so that they may go against Midian, to execute the LORD's vengeance on Midian. ⁴You shall send a thousand from each of the tribes of Israel to the war." ⁵So out of the thousands of Israel, a thousand from each tribe were conscripted, twelve thousand armed for battle. ⁶Moses sent them to the war, a thousand from each tribe, along with Phinehas son of Eleazar the priest, with the vessels of the sanctuary and the trumpets for sounding the alarm in his hand. ⁷They did battle against Midian, as the LORD had commanded Moses, and killed every male. ⁸They killed the kings of Midian: Evi, Rekem, Zur, Hur, and Reba, the five kings of Midian, in addition to others who were slain by them; and they also killed Balaam son of Beor with the sword. ⁹The Israelites took the women of Midian and their little ones captive; and they took all their cattle, their flocks, and all their goods as booty. ¹⁰All their towns where they had settled, and all their encampments, they burned, ¹¹but they took all the spoil and all the booty, both people and animals. ¹²Then they brought the captives and the booty and the spoil to Moses, to Eleazar the priest, and to the congregation of the Israelites, at the camp on the plains of Moab by the Jordan at Jericho.

¹³ Moses, Eleazar the priest, and all the leaders of the congregation went to meet them outside the camp. ¹⁴Moses became angry with the officers of the army, the commanders of thousands and the commanders of hundreds, who had come from service in the war. ¹⁵Moses said to them, "Have you allowed all the women to live? ¹⁶These women here, on Balaam's advice, made the Israelites act treacherously against the LORD in the affair of Peor, so that the plague came among the congregation of the LORD. ¹⁷Now therefore, kill every male among the little ones, and kill every woman who has known a man by sleeping with him. ¹⁸But all the young girls who have not known a man by sleeping with him, keep alive for yourselves. ¹⁹Camp outside the camp seven days; whoever of you has killed any person or touched a corpse, purify yourselves and your captives on the third and on the seventh day. ²⁰You shall purify every garment, every article of skin, everything made of goats' hair, and every article of wood."

²¹ Eleazar the priest said to the troops who had gone to battle: "This is the statute of the law that the LORD has commanded Moses: ²²gold, silver, bronze, iron, tin, and lead— ²³everything that can withstand fire, shall be passed through fire, and it shall be clean. Nevertheless it shall also be purified with the water for purification; and whatever cannot withstand fire, shall be passed through the water. ²⁴You must wash your clothes on the seventh day, and you shall be clean; afterward you may come into the camp."

²⁵ The LORD spoke to Moses, saying, ²⁶"You and Eleazar the priest and the heads of the ancestral houses of the congregation make an inventory of the booty captured, both human and animal. ²⁷Divide the booty into two parts, between the warriors who went out to battle and all the congregation. ²⁸From the share of the warriors who went out to battle, set aside as tribute for the LORD, one item out

of every five hundred, whether persons, oxen, donkeys, sheep, or goats. [29]Take it from their half and give it to Eleazar the priest as an offering to the LORD. [30]But from the Israelites' half you shall take one out of every fifty, whether persons, oxen, donkeys, sheep, or goats—all the animals—and give them to the Levites who have charge of the tabernacle of the LORD."

[31] Then Moses and Eleazar the priest did as the LORD had commanded Moses:

[32] The booty remaining from the spoil that the troops had taken totaled six hundred seventy-five thousand sheep, [33]seventy-two thousand oxen, [34]sixty-one thousand donkeys, [35]and thirty-two thousand persons in all, women who had not known a man by sleeping with him.

[36] The half-share, the portion of those who had gone out to war, was in number three hundred thirty-seven thousand five hundred sheep and goats, [37]and the LORD's tribute of sheep and goats was six hundred seventy-five. [38]The oxen were thirty-six thousand, of which the LORD's tribute was seventy-two. [39]The donkeys were thirty thousand five hundred, of which the LORD's tribute was sixty-one. [40]The persons were sixteen thousand, of which the LORD's tribute was thirty-two persons. [41]Moses gave the tribute, the offering for the LORD, to Eleazar the priest, as the LORD had commanded Moses.

[42] As for the Israelites' half, which Moses separated from that of the troops, [43]the congregation's half was three hundred thirty-seven thousand five hundred sheep and goats, [44]thirty-six thousand oxen, [45]thirty thousand five hundred donkeys, [46]and sixteen thousand persons. [47]From the Israelites' half Moses took one of every fifty, both of persons and of animals, and gave them to the Levites who had charge of the tabernacle of the LORD; as the LORD had commanded Moses.

[48] Then the officers who were over the thousands of the army, the commanders of thousands and the commanders of hundreds, approached Moses, [49]and said to Moses, "Your servants have counted the warriors who are under our command, and not one of us is missing. [50]And we have brought the LORD's offering, what each of us found, articles of gold, armlets and bracelets, signet rings, earrings, and pendants, to make atonement for ourselves before the LORD." [51]Moses and Eleazar the priest received the gold from them, all in the form of crafted articles. [52]And all the gold of the offering that they offered to the LORD, from the commanders of thousands and the commanders of hundreds, was sixteen thousand seven hundred fifty shekels. [53](The troops had all taken plunder for themselves.) [54]So Moses and Eleazar the priest received the gold from the commanders of thousands and of hundreds, and brought it into the tent of meeting as a memorial for the Israelites before the LORD.[107]

---

107. For Noth, Num 31:1-12, which v. 2 secondarily attaches explicitly to Num 27:12-14 (the concern is in v. 2b, being "gathered to your people"), is probably to be understood as secondary. "The various additions in 31:13-54 may have been only gradually inserted into the completed Pentateuch" (*Pentateuchal Traditions*, 19). In the Numbers commentary, Noth remarks: "It is, however, certain that the chapter [Numbers 31] is one of the very late sections in the Pentateuch. It is not, even as a late addition, to be considered as part of the P-narrative, but represents a supplement to the Pentateuch as a whole, for, in its present content and scope as a whole, it presupposes that variegated chapter Num. 25" (*Numbers*, 229).

The Book of Deuteronomy

*Death of Moses
and Succession of Joshua*

34:1*Then Moses went up from the plains of Moab to Mount Nebo.[108]

• • •

[7]Moses was one hundred twenty years old when he died; his sight was unimpaired and his vigor had not abated. [8]The Israelites wept for Moses in the plains of Moab thirty days; then the period of mourning for Moses was ended.

9 Joshua son of Nun was full of the spirit of wisdom, because Moses had laid his hands on him; and the Israelites obeyed him, doing as the LORD had commanded Moses.[109]

---

108. When the Pentateuch was combined with the Deuteronomistic History, P's report of Moses' death naturally had to be transferred here, at the end of Deuteronomy, after Moses had set the affairs of Israel in order and immediately before the entry into the promised land.

109. For Noth, P ends here. "No traces of a coherent P narrative can be identified beyond Deut. 34. All that we find after Deuteronomy are isolated additions to older texts in the style and thought pattern of P. This is precisely the case also in the Book of Joshua" (*Pentateuchal Traditions*, 10). For comment on Lohfink's P texts in Joshua, see Campbell, *Study Companion*, 82 n. 22.

CHAPTER 3

The Yahwist Narrative

The Yahwist narrative is thought of as a selection from the storehouse of Israel's stories and traditions, arranged and interpreted to express a particular communication concerning Israel in the Yahwist's time. In Martin Noth's identification, it stretches from creation (Gen 2:4b—3:24) to the prophecies of Balaam and beyond. It includes stories of the whole human race (Genesis 2–11), stories of Israel's ancestors (Genesis 12–50), and stories of Israel's constitutive generation, led by Moses (Exodus and Numbers). The Yahwist's purpose in assembling this rich and varied material was to proclaim that Israel was the LORD's chosen mediator to bring salvation and blessing to the troubled humanity described in Genesis 2–11. Genesis 12:1-3, in which this divine purpose is first proclaimed as blessing for Abraham and for "all the families of the earth," is a pivotal text in the Yahwist narrative. It looks forward to the story of Israel as the blessed nation and source of blessing. At the same time, it looks back to the story of humanity in need of blessing.

The stories of Israel's ancestors tell of patriarchs and matriarchs who are fragile bearers of the divine blessing. They often seek to take matters into their own hands, and they are often involved in conflicts that threaten the welfare and future of the family. Yet through all this very human story, the subtle but powerful purpose of the LORD is at work to bring blessing. The Jacob–Esau conflict reaches resolution. The near disastrous conflict between Joseph and his brothers is resolved, and the narrative concludes with the family together in Egypt, rapidly growing into a great and powerful nation. The promise of descendants is being fulfilled.

The story of Israel in Egypt reveals the LORD's loyalty to the promises and a divine power that can fulfill the promises against the most powerful opposition. When the very existence of Israel is threatened by the might of Egypt, the LORD intervenes through the agency of Moses. Israel is led out of Egypt to freedom, and the pursuing oppressor is finally destroyed in the deliverance at the sea. The unique relationship between Israel and the LORD is then sealed in the covenant at Sinai. With the LORD as their God, Israel sets out across the wilderness for the land. Their arrival and settlement in the land would mark the fulfillment of the promise of land to the ancestors.

The journey to the land reveals again the fragility of the bearers of blessing. The fragility of the ancestors was their human weakness: the temptation of individuals to take matters into their own hands rather than trust in the LORD, the attempt by members of a family to dominate others, the tendency to fall into conflict. The fragility of Israel is far more dangerous and damaging. It is the failure by a great and powerful nation to trust its LORD when faced with something it cannot control, namely, the wilderness. Worse still, this failure results in open rebellion against the LORD and Moses.

The astonishing claim of the Yahwist's narrative is that even in such a climate of rebellion and hostility, divine blessing is at work. This is brought out strongly in the story of Balaam in Numbers 22–24. As Israel emerges from its conflict-ridden journey through the wilderness, a foreigner, Balaam, is moved to proclaim to the nations that Israel is unswervingly blessed by God. This blessing is not effective for Balaam's time ("not now . . . not near," Num 24:17). Israel must still complete its journey and occupy the

land. The Yahwist's text points to its realization in the time of David and Solomon, when the conquest of the land was completed and Israel united in peace under one king. The promise of blessing in descendants and land had then become tangible reality for Israel as people of God; for "all the families of the earth," it remained as promise.

According to Noth, the Yahwist's story of Israel and its destiny was preserved relatively intact, except for the account of the conquest. This was presumably discarded when the combined sources were linked with the Deuteronomistic History (Deuteronomy–2 Kings), which had its own account of the conquest in the Book of Joshua.

The Book of Genesis

THE WHOLE HUMAN RACE

Creation

2:4b In the day that the LORD God made the earth and the heavens,[1] [5]when no plant of the field was yet in the earth and no herb of the field had yet sprung up—for the LORD God had not caused it to rain upon the earth, and there was no one to till the ground; [6]but a stream would rise from the earth, and water the whole face of

the ground—[7]then the LORD God formed man from the dust of the ground, and breathed into his nostrils the breath of life; and the man became a living being. [8]And the LORD God planted a garden in Eden, in the east; and there he put the man whom he had formed. [9]Out of the ground the LORD God made to grow every tree that is pleasant to the sight and good for

---

1. The striking differences between the creation accounts in Gen 1:1—2:4a and 2:4b—3:24 provided the initial impetus for the development of the source hypothesis. What is particularly significant for the hypothesis here is the identification of parallel, contrasting accounts of creation.

The J account is told as a dramatic story with a crisis and its resolution. The creator is the "LORD God," who is portrayed in anthropomorphic terms. Creation begins with a barren dry earth out of which the LORD God forms man (Gen 2:7). This initial act is followed by the planting of a garden with trees

(2:8-9) and the forming of all the animals and birds (2:19-20). Creation is completed by the fashioning of woman from man (2:21-23). Transgression of the command disrupts the order of the garden; the crisis in their relationship with the LORD God is resolved by their expulsion from the garden (3:8-24).

This drama of crisis and resolution is not present in the P account, where the divinity, named simply "God," is portrayed as transcendent and all powerful and creates principally by command. Creation in P's narrative is described on a cosmic scale and in an order that differs markedly from that of J.

food, the tree of life also in the midst of the garden, and the tree of the knowledge of good and evil.[2]

10 A river flows out of Eden to water the garden, and from there it divides and becomes four branches. [11]The name of the first is Pishon; it is the one that flows around the whole land of Havilah, where there is gold; [12]and the gold of that land is good; bdellium and onyx stone are there. [13]The name of the second river is Gihon; it is the one that flows around the whole land of Cush. [14]The name of the third river is Tigris, which flows east of Assyria. And the fourth river is the Euphrates.

15 The LORD God took the man and put him in the garden of Eden to till it and keep it. [16]And the LORD God commanded the man, "You may freely eat of every tree of the garden; [17]but of the tree of the knowledge of good and evil you shall not eat, for in the day that you eat of it you shall die."

18 Then the LORD God said, "It is not good that the man should be alone; I will make him a helper as his partner." [19]So out of the ground the LORD God formed every animal of the field and every bird of the air, and brought them to the man to see what he would call them; and whatever the man called every living creature, that was its name. [20]The man gave names to all cattle, and to the birds of the air, and to every animal of the field; but for the man there was not found a helper as his partner. [21]So the LORD God caused a deep sleep to fall upon the man, and he slept; then he took one of his ribs and closed up its place with flesh. [22]And the rib that the LORD God had taken from the man he made

into a woman and brought her to the man. [23]Then the man said,

"This at last is bone of my bones
  and flesh of my flesh;
this one shall be called Woman,
  for out of Man this one was taken."

[24]Therefore a man leaves his father and his mother and clings to his wife, and they become one flesh. [25]And the man and his wife were both naked, and were not ashamed.

3 Now the serpent was more crafty than any other wild animal that the LORD God had made. He said to the woman, "Did God say, 'You shall not eat from any tree in the garden'?" [2]The woman said to the serpent, "We may eat of the fruit of the trees in the garden; [3]but God said, 'You shall not eat of the fruit of the tree that is in the middle of the garden, nor shall you touch it, or you shall die.' " [4]But the serpent said to the woman, "You will not die; [5]for God knows that when you eat of it your eyes will be opened, and you will be like God, knowing good and evil." [6]So when the woman saw that the tree was good for food, and that it was a delight to the eyes, and that the tree was to be desired to make one wise, she took of its fruit and ate; and she also gave some to her husband, who was with her, and he ate. [7]Then the eyes of both were opened, and they knew that they were naked; and they sewed fig leaves together and made loincloths for themselves.

8 They heard the sound of the LORD God walking in the garden at the time of the evening breeze, and the man and his wife hid themselves from the presence of the LORD God among the trees of the garden. [9]But the LORD God called

---

2. The tree of life is not mentioned in the divine injunction in Gen 2:17 or in the crisis in the garden (3:1-13). It reappears, however, in 3:22-24. This can be understood to indicate that the tradition knew two ways of telling the story, one based on the tree of life and the other on the tree of the knowledge of good and evil. J's inclusion of the tree of life serves as a reminder of the alternative version (C. Westermann, *Genesis 1–11* [Minneapolis: Augsburg, 1984] 212–13).

to the man, and said to him, "Where are you?"
[10]He said, "I heard the sound of you in the garden, and I was afraid, because I was naked; and I hid myself." [11]He said, "Who told you that you were naked? Have you eaten from the tree of which I commanded you not to eat?" [12]The man said, "The woman whom you gave to be with me, she gave me fruit from the tree, and I ate." [13]Then the LORD God said to the woman, "What is this that you have done?" The woman said, "The serpent tricked me, and I ate." [14]The LORD God said to the serpent,

"Because you have done this,
    cursed are you among all animals
    and among all wild creatures;
upon your belly you shall go,
    and dust you shall eat
    all the days of your life.
[15]I will put enmity between you and the
        woman,
    and between your offspring and hers;
he will strike your head,
    and you will strike his heel."

[16]To the woman he said,

"I will greatly increase your pangs in
        childbearing;
    in pain you shall bring forth children,
    yet your desire shall be for your husband,
    and he shall rule over you."

[17]And to the man he said,

"Because you have listened to the voice of
        your wife,
    and have eaten of the tree
about which I commanded you,
    'You shall not eat of it,'
cursed is the ground because of you;
    in toil you shall eat of it all the days of
        your life;
[18]thorns and thistles it shall bring forth
        for you;
    and you shall eat the plants of the field.
[19]By the sweat of your face
    you shall eat bread

until you return to the ground,
    for out of it you were taken;
you are dust,
    and to dust you shall return."

20 The man named his wife Eve, because she was the mother of all living. [21]And the LORD God made garments of skins for the man and for his wife, and clothed them.

22 Then the LORD God said, "See, the man has become like one of us, knowing good and evil; and now, he might reach out his hand and take also from the tree of life, and eat, and live forever"—[23]therefore the LORD God sent him forth from the garden of Eden, to till the ground from which he was taken. [24]He drove out the man; and at the east of the garden of Eden he placed the cherubim, and a sword flaming and turning to guard the way to the tree of life.

Cain and Abel

4 Now the man knew his wife Eve, and she conceived and bore Cain, saying, "I have produced a man with the help of the LORD." [2]Next she bore his brother Abel. Now Abel was a keeper of sheep, and Cain a tiller of the ground. [3]In the course of time Cain brought to the LORD an offering of the fruit of the ground, [4]and Abel for his part brought of the firstlings of his flock, their fat portions. And the LORD had regard for Abel and his offering, [5]but for Cain and his offering he had no regard. So Cain was very angry, and his countenance fell. [6]The LORD said to Cain, "Why are you angry, and why has your countenance fallen? [7]If you do well, will you not be accepted? And if you do not do well, sin is lurking at the door; its desire is for you, but you must master it."

8 Cain said to his brother Abel, "Let us go out to the field." And when they were in the field, Cain rose up against his brother Abel, and killed him. [9]Then the LORD said to Cain, "Where is your brother Abel?" He said, "I do not know; am I my brother's keeper?" [10]And the

LORD said, "What have you done? Listen; your brother's blood is crying out to me from the ground! [11]And now you are cursed from the ground, which has opened its mouth to receive your brother's blood from your hand. [12]When you till the ground, it will no longer yield to you its strength; you will be a fugitive and a wanderer on the earth." [13]Cain said to the LORD, "My punishment is greater than I can bear! [14]Today you have driven me away from the soil, and I shall be hidden from your face; I shall be a fugitive and a wanderer on the earth, and anyone who meets me may kill me." [15]Then the LORD said to him, "Not so! Whoever kills Cain will suffer a sevenfold vengeance." And the LORD put a mark on Cain, so that no one who came upon him would kill him. [16]Then Cain went away from the presence of the LORD, and settled in the land of Nod, east of Eden.

17 Cain knew his wife, and she conceived and bore Enoch; and he built a city, and named it Enoch after his son Enoch. [18]To Enoch was born Irad; and Irad was the father of Mehujael, and Mehujael the father of Methushael, and Methushael the father of Lamech. [19]Lamech took two wives; the name of the one was Adah, and the name of the other Zillah. [20]Adah bore Jabal; he was the ancestor of those who live in tents and have livestock. [21]His brother's name was Jubal; he was the ancestor of all those who play the lyre and pipe. [22]Zillah bore Tubal-cain, who made all kinds of bronze and iron tools. The sister of Tubal-cain was Naamah.

23 Lamech said to his wives:
  "Adah and Zillah, hear my voice;
    you wives of Lamech, listen to what
      I say:
  I have killed a man for wounding me,
    a young man for striking me.
  [24]If Cain is avenged sevenfold,
    truly Lamech seventy-sevenfold."[3]

• • •[4]

5:29 He named him Noah, saying, "Out of the ground that the LORD has cursed this one shall bring us relief from our work and from the toil of our hands."[5]

• • •[6]

Flood

6:5 The LORD saw that the wickedness of humankind was great in the earth, and that every inclination of the thoughts of their hearts was only evil continually. [6]And the LORD was sorry that he had made humankind on the earth, and it grieved him to his heart. [7]So the LORD said, "I will blot out from the earth the human beings I have created—people together with animals and creeping things and birds of the air, for I am

---

3. Noth comments that Gen 4:25 is an explanatory gloss in view of 5:3, seeking to smooth the tension between 4:1-2a and 5:3, which identifies Seth as Adam's firstborn. Both 4:25 and 5:3 use *Elohim* for God and *Adam* as a proper name. As a consequence, Noth concludes, 4:26 must also be a learned gloss to 5:6 (see M. Noth, *A History of Pentateuchal Traditions*, trans. B. W. Anderson [Englewood Cliffs, N.J.: Prentice-Hall, 1972; reprint, Chico, Calif.: Scholars Press, 1981] 12 n. 26). There is no passage in J corresponding to P's genealogy from Adam to Noah.

4. The ellipses throughout are given in Noth's text and indicate where he considers there to be a break in the continuity of the J text. The original J text between Gen 4:24 and 5:29 has been suppressed in favor of the Toledoth book of genealogies which was available to P.

5. Noth comments that this is a fragment from the J narrative, preserved because of interest in its explanation of Noah's name (*Pentateuchal Traditions*, 12).

6. Noth omits Gen. 6:1-4, with the comment that it is so isolated a passage that its origin is quite uncertain. It could be from J, a supplement to J, or an addition to the completed Pentateuch (Noth, *Pentateuchal Traditions*, 28 n. 83).

sorry that I have made them." [8]But Noah found favor in the sight of the LORD.[7]

• • •[8]

7 Then the LORD said to Noah, "Go into the ark, you and all your household, for I have seen that you alone are righteous before me in this generation.[9] [2]Take with you seven pairs of all clean animals, the male and its mate; and a pair of the animals that are not clean, the male and its mate, [3b]to keep their kind alive on the face of all the earth.[10] [4]For in seven days I will send rain on the earth for forty days and forty nights; and every living thing that I have made I will blot out from the face of the ground."[11] [5]And Noah did all that the LORD had commanded him.

10 And after seven days the waters of the flood came on the earth. [7*]And Noah went into the ark to escape the waters of the flood.[12]

[16b]And the LORD shut him in. [12]The rain fell on the earth forty days and forty nights.[13]

17b And the waters increased, and bore up the ark, and it rose high above the earth. [22]Everything on dry land in whose nostrils was the breath of life died. [23*]He blotted out every living thing that was on the face of the ground, human beings and animals and creeping things and birds of the air. Only Noah was left, and those that were with him in the ark.

8:6a At the end of forty days,[14] [2b]the rain from the heavens was restrained, [3a]and the waters gradually receded from the earth.

• • •[15]

6b Noah opened the window of the ark that he had made. [8]Then he sent out the dove from him, to see if the waters had subsided from the face of the ground; [9]but the dove found no place

---

7. In the case of the flood story, the parallel J and P sources were combined in a manner different from that employed in the accounts of creation. Instead of being juxtaposed they were interwoven, with P taken as a base and enriched from J. According to Noth, this resulted in some J material being omitted to avoid duplicating the basic P account. The identifying characteristics of each source are given in the following footnotes. Noth has rearranged the order of Gen 7:10, 7:16b, and 8:6a, according to the presumed sequence of the J story.

8. The section of J omitted here would have contained an announcement of the flood and the order to build an ark.

9. As in P, Noah's righteousness is signaled here (and in Gen 6:8) in connection with deliverance from the flood. At the end of the story his righteousness is not an issue; quite the contrary (8:21b).

10. J distinguishes between clean animals, which may be slaughtered for food and sacrifice, and unclean animals, which may not; hence seven pairs and one pair. P does not make the distinction, because it is not revealed until Sinai, and therefore takes one pair of all animals as well as food, and has no sacrifice.

11. J's account of the flood is structured in forty-day and seven-day periods. By contrast, P uses one hundred and fifty-day periods, and the flood lasts for a year and ten days.

12. Noth places an asterisk against Gen 7:7, indicating that part of the verse is to be omitted. Most probably, Noth means to omit "and his sons and his wife and his sons' wives with him," which is understood as a later expansion in P style (cf. Hermann Gunkel, *Genesis*, 8th ed. [Göttingen: Vandenhoeck & Ruprecht, 1969; reprint of 3d ed., 1910] 144).

13. J's flood is the result of a prolonged rainstorm. P's flood, to the contrary, is a form of "decreation," an inrushing from above and below of the waters separated at creation.

14. It has been a commonplace of scholarship to see the sequence Gen 7:23—8:2b-3a as too abrupt; hence the transfer of 8:6a to this position, where it indicates the end of the forty days' rain, begun in 7:12. This reconstruction specifies one basic forty-day period for J's flood, rather than the two forty-day periods implied if 8:6a is not placed in front of 8:2b-3a. There are complications in relation to the series of three seven-day periods as implied by the wording of 8:10 and 12 (cf. Westermann, *Genesis 1–11*, 444). The attempt to explain how the present text was formed and why an initial reference to seven days' waiting should have been lost is a difficult undertaking, complicated by some fluctuations in the Greek manuscripts.

15. Noth judged there was a break in the text here, but the sequence may be considered tolerable.

to set its foot, and it returned to him to the ark, for the waters were still on the face of the whole earth. So he put out his hand and took it and brought it into the ark with him. [10]He waited another seven days, and again he sent out the dove from the ark; [11]and the dove came back to him in the evening, and there in its beak was a freshly plucked olive leaf; so Noah knew that the waters had subsided from the earth. [12]Then he waited another seven days, and sent out the dove; and it did not return to him any more.

13b And Noah removed the covering of the ark, and looked, and saw that the face of the ground was drying.

• • •[16]

20 Then Noah built an altar to the LORD, and took of every clean animal and of every clean bird, and offered burnt offerings on the altar. [21]And when the LORD smelled the pleasing odor, the LORD said in his heart, "I will never again curse the ground because of humankind, for the inclination of the human heart is evil from youth; nor will I ever again destroy every living creature as I have done.

[22]As long as the earth endures,
    seedtime and harvest, cold and heat,
    summer and winter, day and night,
        shall not cease."[17]

Peopling of the Earth

9:18 The sons of Noah who went out of the ark were Shem, Ham, and Japheth. Ham was the father of Canaan. [19]These three were the sons of Noah; and from these the whole earth was peopled.

20 Noah, a man of the soil, was the first to plant a vineyard. [21]He drank some of the wine and became drunk, and he lay uncovered in his tent. [22]And Ham, the father of Canaan, saw the nakedness of his father, and told his two brothers outside. [23]Then Shem and Japheth took a garment, laid it on both their shoulders, and walked backward and covered the nakedness of their father; their faces were turned away, and they did not see their father's nakedness. [24]When Noah awoke from his wine and knew what his youngest son had done to him, [25]he said,

"Cursed be Canaan;
    lowest of slaves shall he be to his
        brothers."
[26]He also said,
"Blessed by the LORD my God be Shem;
    and let Canaan be his slave.
[27]May God make space for Japheth,
    and let him live in the tents of Shem;
    and let Canaan be his slave."

• • •[18]

10:8 Cush became the father of Nimrod; he was the first on earth to become a mighty warrior.

[9]*He was a mighty hunter before the LORD; therefore it is said, "Like Nimrod a mighty hunter before the LORD."*[19]

---

16. The section of J omitted here would have been an account of the departure from the ark.

17. The echo of the pre-flood situation is unmistakable: "every inclination of the thoughts of their hearts was only evil continually" (Gen 6:5), and here "the inclination of the human heart is evil from youth" (8:21). The text demands that we ponder why what was portrayed as the cause of the flood in the first place should now be given as the reason why it will never recur. Because nothing has changed in human nature, the change must be placed in God. What was portrayed previously as intolerable is now portrayed as inevitable—but no longer as a bar to relationship with God.

18. The J material in Genesis 10 is considered by Noth to be a further example of the P base being selectively enriched from the J source, leaving J incomplete in the combined text (*Pentateuchal Traditions*, 12–13; see also Westermann, *Genesis 1–11*, 498–503).

19. The "first" in Gen 10:8 hints at a model role for Nimrod; the saying quoted in v. 9 confirms it explicitly. "The founder king was a man of might and power because he subdued the wild animals" (Westermann [for whom v. 9 was inserted by J], *Genesis 1–11*, 516).

[10]The beginning of his kingdom was Babel, Erech, and Accad, all of them in the land of Shinar. [11]From that land he went into Assyria, and built Nineveh, Rehoboth-ir, Calah, and [12]Resen between Nineveh and Calah; that is the great city. [13]Egypt became the father of Ludim, Anamim, Lehabim, Naphtuhim, [14]Pathrusim, Casluhim, and Caphtorim, from which the Philistines come.

15 Canaan became the father of Sidon his firstborn, and Heth, [16]and the Jebusites, the Amorites, the Girgashites, [17]the Hivites, the Arkites, the Sinites, [18]the Arvadites, the Zemarites, and the Hamathites. Afterward the families of the Canaanites spread abroad. [19]And the territory of the Canaanites extended from Sidon, in the direction of Gerar, as far as Gaza, and in the direction of Sodom, Gomorrah, Admah, and Zeboiim, as far as Lasha.

21 To Shem also, the father of all the children of Eber, the elder brother of Japheth, children were born. [24]Arpachshad became the father of Shelah; and Shelah became the father of Eber. [25]To Eber were born two sons: the name of the one was Peleg, for in his days the earth was divided, and his brother's name was Joktan. [26]Joktan became the father of Almodad, Sheleph, Hazarmaveth, Jerah, [27]Hadoram, Uzal, Diklah, [28]Obal, Abimael, Sheba, [29]Ophir, Havilah, and Jobab; all these were the descendants of Joktan. [30]The territory in which they lived extended from Mesha in the direction of Sephar, the hill country of the east.

Tower of Babel

11 Now the whole earth had one language and the same words. [2]And as they migrated from the east, they came upon a plain in the land of Shinar and settled there. [3]And they said to one another, "Come, let us make bricks, and burn them thoroughly." And they had brick for stone, and bitumen for mortar. [4]Then they said, "Come, let us build ourselves a city, and a tower with its top in the heavens, and let us make a name for ourselves; otherwise we shall be scattered abroad upon the face of the whole earth." [5]The LORD came down to see the city and the tower, which mortals had built. [6]And the LORD said, "Look, they are one people, and they have all one language; and this is only the beginning of what they will do; nothing that they propose to do will now be impossible for them. [7]Come, let us go down, and confuse their language there, so that they will not understand one another's speech." [8]So the LORD scattered them abroad from there over the face of all the earth, and they left off building the city. [9]Therefore it was called Babel, because there the LORD confused the language of all the earth; and from there the LORD scattered them abroad over the face of all the earth.

• • •[20]

28 Haran died before his father Terah in the land of his birth, in Ur of the Chaldeans. [29]Abram and Nahor took wives; the name of Abram's wife was Sarai, and the name of Nahor's wife was Milcah. She was the daughter of Haran the father of Milcah and Iscah. [30]Now Sarai was barren; she had no child.

• • •[21]

---

20. In Noth's view, Gen 11:28-30 has been retained for the sake of certain details; otherwise the J transition from Babel to Abraham has been omitted in favor of the P genealogy (*Pentateuchal Traditions*, 13).

21. The fragmentary nature of the text at this point is highlighted for Noth by the fact that Lot appears below in J's Abraham traditions without any prior introduction.

THE ANCESTORS OF ISRAEL

Abraham and Sarah

12 Now the LORD said to Abram, "Go from your country and your kindred and your father's house to the land that I will show you. [2]I will make of you a great nation, and I will bless you, and make your name great, so that you will be a blessing. [3]I will bless those who bless you, and the one who curses you I will curse; and in you all the families of the earth shall be blessed."[22]

4a So Abram went, as the LORD had told him; and Lot went with him.

• • •[23]

6 Abram passed through the land to the place at Shechem, to the oak of Moreh. At that time the Canaanites were in the land. [7]Then the LORD appeared to Abram, and said, "To your offspring I will give this land." So he built there an altar to the LORD, who had appeared to him. [8]From there he moved on to the hill country on the east of Bethel, and pitched his tent, with Bethel on the west and Ai on the east; and there he built an altar to the LORD and invoked the name of the LORD. [9]And Abram journeyed on by stages toward the Negeb.

10 Now there was a famine in the land. So Abram went down to Egypt to reside there as an alien, for the famine was severe in the land. [11]When he was about to enter Egypt, he said to his wife Sarai, "I know well that you are a woman beautiful in appearance; [12]and when the Egyptians see you, they will say, 'This is his wife'; then they will kill me, but they will let you live. [13]Say you are my sister, so that it may go well with me because of you, and that my life may be spared on your account." [14]When Abram entered Egypt the Egyptians saw that the woman was very beautiful. [15]When the officials of Pharaoh saw her, they praised her to Pharaoh. And the woman was taken into Pharaoh's house. [16]And for her sake he dealt well with Abram; and he had sheep, oxen, male donkeys, male and female slaves, female donkeys, and camels.

17 But the LORD afflicted Pharaoh and his house with great plagues because of Sarai, Abram's wife. [18]So Pharaoh called Abram, and said, "What is this you have done to me? Why did you not tell me that she was your wife? [19]Why did you say, 'She is my sister,' so that I took her for my wife? Now then, here is your wife, take her, and be gone." [20]And Pharaoh gave his men orders concerning him; and they set him on the way, with his wife and all that he had.

13 So Abram went up from Egypt, he and his wife, and all that he had, and Lot with him, into the Negeb.

---

22. Noth, like von Rad, identifies Gen 12:1-3 as a key theological statement by J, which embraces both the subsequent story of Israel and the preceding story of humankind. Abraham, and the nation descended from him, is to be the mediator of divine blessing for the troubled humanity that is described in Genesis 2–11. H. W. Wolff ("The Kerygma of the Yahwist," in *The Vitality of Old Testament Traditions*, ed. W. Brueggemann and H. W. Wolff, 2d ed. [Atlanta: John Knox, 1982] 41–66) traces this theme of blessing in a number of strategic texts throughout J (Gen 12:1-3; 18:18; [22:17-18]; 26:[1-3]12-33; 27:27-29; 28:14; 30:27, 30; 39:5; 41:55-57; Exod 12:31-32; Num 24:9). An area that Wolff finds difficult to account for is J's wilderness wandering stories, where there seems to be no echo of the promise of blessing. The function of these stories within the theological schema of J has subsequently been explored in A. F. Campbell, *The Study Companion to Old Testament Literature: An Approach to the Writings of Pre-exilic and Exilic Israel* (A Michael Glazier Book; Old Testament Studies 2; Collegeville, Minn.: Liturgical Press, 1989/1992), chap. 3.

23. The J report of Abraham's journey to the land has been omitted in favor of the P material with its information about Abraham's age, Sarah and Lot, and the family's considerable wealth.

Separation of Abraham and Lot

2 Now Abram was very rich in livestock, in silver, and in gold. [3]He journeyed on by stages from the Negeb as far as Bethel, to the place where his tent had been at the beginning, between Bethel and Ai, [4]to the place where he had made an altar at the first; and there Abram called on the name of the LORD. [5]Now Lot, who went with Abram, also had flocks and herds and tents, [7]and there was strife between the herders of Abram's livestock and the herders of Lot's livestock. At that time the Canaanites and the Perizzites lived in the land.[24]

8 Then Abram said to Lot, "Let there be no strife between you and me, and between your herders and my herders; for we are kindred. [9]Is not the whole land before you? Separate yourself from me. If you take the left hand, then I will go to the right; or if you take the right hand, then I will go to the left." [10]Lot looked about him, and saw that the plain of the Jordan was well watered everywhere like the garden of the LORD, like the land of Egypt, in the direction of Zoar; this was before the LORD had destroyed Sodom and Gomorrah. [11a]So Lot chose for himself all the plain of the Jordan, and Lot journeyed eastward [12*]and moved his tent as far as Sodom. [13]Now the people of Sodom were wicked, great sinners against the LORD.

14 The LORD said to Abram, after Lot had separated from him, "Raise your eyes now, and look from the place where you are, northward and southward and eastward and westward; [15]for all the land that you see I will give to you and to your offspring forever. [16]I will make your offspring like the dust of the earth; so that if one can count the dust of the earth, your offspring also can be counted. [17]Rise up, walk through the length and the breadth of the land, for I will give it to you."[25] [18]So Abram moved his tent, and came and settled by the oaks of Mamre, which are at Hebron; and there he built an altar to the LORD.

The LORD's Covenant with Abraham

15:1[*] After these things the word of the LORD came to Abram in a vision, "Your reward shall be very great."[26] [2a]But Abram said, "O LORD GOD, what will you give me, for I continue childless, [3b]and so a slave born in my house is to be my heir?" [4]But the word of the LORD came to him, "This man shall not be your heir; no one but your very own issue shall be your heir." [6]And he believed the LORD; and the LORD reckoned it to him as righteousness.

7 Then he said to him, "I am the LORD who brought you from Ur of the Chaldeans, to give you this land to possess." [8]But he said, "O Lord GOD, how am I to know that I shall possess it?"

⁹He said to him, "Bring me a heifer three years old, a female goat three years old, a ram three years old, a turtledove, and a young pigeon." ¹⁰He brought him all these and cut them in two, laying each half over against the other; but he did not cut the birds in two. ¹¹And when birds of prey came down on the carcasses, Abram drove them away.

12 As the sun was going down, a deep sleep fell upon Abram, and a deep and terrifying darkness descended upon him. ¹⁷When the sun had gone down and it was dark, a smoking fire pot and a flaming torch passed between these pieces. ¹⁸On that day the LORD made a covenant with Abram, saying, "To your descendants I give this land, from the river of Egypt to the great river, the river Euphrates."

¹⁹*the land of the Kenites, the Kenizzites, the Kadmonites, ²⁰the Hittites, the Perizzites, the Rephaim, ²¹the Amorites, the Canaanites, the Girgashites, and the Jebusites."*²⁷

• • •²⁸

Birth of Ishmael

16:1b She had an Egyptian slave-girl whose name was Hagar, ²and Sarai said to Abram, "You see that the LORD has prevented me from bearing children; go in to my slave-girl; it may be that I shall obtain children by her." And Abram listened to the voice of Sarai. ⁴He went in to Hagar, and she conceived; and when she saw that she had conceived, she looked with contempt on her mistress. ⁵Then Sarai said to Abram, "May the wrong done to me be on you!

I gave my slave-girl to your embrace, and when she saw that she had conceived, she looked on me with contempt. May the LORD judge between you and me!" ⁶But Abram said to Sarai, "Your slave-girl is in your power; do to her as you please." Then Sarai dealt harshly with her, and she ran away from her.

7 The angel of the LORD found her by a spring of water in the wilderness, the spring on the way to Shur. ⁸And he said, "Hagar, slave-girl of Sarai, where have you come from and where are you going?" She said, "I am running away from my mistress Sarai."²⁹ ¹¹And the angel of the LORD said to her,

"Now you have conceived and shall bear
    a son;
you shall call him Ishmael,
    for the LORD has given heed to your
    affliction.
¹² He shall be a wild ass of a man,
with his hand against everyone,
    and everyone's hand against him;
and he shall live at odds with all his kin."

¹³So she named the LORD who spoke to her, "You are El-roi"; for she said, "Have I really seen God and remained alive after seeing him?" ¹⁴Therefore the well was called Beer-lahai-roi; it lies between Kadesh and Bered.

• • •³⁰

Promise of a Son—Isaac

18 The LORD appeared to him [Heb; NRSV, to Abraham] by the oaks of Mamre, as he sat at the entrance of his tent in the heat of the

---

27. This list of nations fills in the bare geographical description of the promised land in Gen 15:18.

28. The story of Hagar in Genesis 16 is another example of how J and P were interwoven, with the sparse P account in Gen 16:1a, 3, 15-16 being used as a base and enriched from the more dramatic J version. In this process, the J introduction to the story of Hagar has been omitted in favor of P's report that Sarah was barren (v. 1a). J's report of Sarah's barren-

ness occurs in 11:30. It is assumed that the original J introduction would have named Sarah.

29. Noth comments that Gen 16:9, the command to return to her mistress, has been added with a view to the subsequent story of Hagar in 21:8-21. 16:10 for its part is an expansion of a very general nature (*Pentateuchal Traditions*, 28 n. 86).

30. The J account of the birth and naming of Ishmael has been omitted in favor of P in Gen 16:15-16.

day.[31] [2]He looked up and saw three men standing near him. When he saw them, he ran from the tent entrance to meet them, and bowed down to the ground. [3]He said, "My lord, if I find favor with you, do not pass by your servant. [4]Let a little water be brought, and wash your feet, and rest yourselves under the tree. [5]Let me bring a little bread, that you may refresh yourselves, and after that you may pass on—since you have come to your servant." So they said, "Do as you have said." [6]And Abraham hastened into the tent to Sarah, and said, "Make ready quickly three measures of choice flour, knead it, and make cakes." [7]Abraham ran to the herd, and took a calf, tender and good, and gave it to the servant, who hastened to prepare it. [8]Then he took curds and milk and the calf that he had prepared, and set it before them; and he stood by them under the tree while they ate.

[9] They said to him, "Where is your wife Sarah?" And he said, "There, in the tent." [10]Then one said, "I will surely return to you in due season, and your wife Sarah shall have a son." And Sarah was listening at the tent entrance behind him. [11]Now Abraham and Sarah were old, advanced in age; it had ceased to be with Sarah after the manner of women. [12]So Sarah laughed to herself, saying, "After I have grown old, and my husband is old, shall I have pleasure?" [13]The LORD said to Abraham, "Why did Sarah laugh, and say, 'Shall I indeed bear a child, now that I am old?' [14]Is anything too wonderful for the LORD? At the set time I will return to you, in due season, and Sarah shall have a son." [15]But Sarah denied, saying, "I did not laugh"; for she was afraid. He said, "Oh yes, you did laugh."

[16] Then the men set out from there, and they looked toward Sodom; and Abraham went with them to set them on their way. [17]The LORD said, "Shall I hide from Abraham what I am about to do, [18]seeing that Abraham shall become a great and mighty nation, and all the nations of the earth shall be blessed in him?"[32]

> [19]*No, for I have chosen him, that he may charge his children and his household after him to keep the way of the LORD by doing righteousness and justice; so that the LORD may bring about for Abraham what he has promised him."*[33]

[20]Then the LORD said, "How great is the outcry against Sodom and Gomorrah and how very grave their sin! [21]I must go down and see whether they have done altogether according to the outcry that has come to me; and if not, I will know."

[22] So the men turned from there, and went toward Sodom, while Abraham remained standing before the LORD. [23]Then Abraham came near and said, "Will you indeed sweep away the righteous with the wicked? [24]Suppose there are fifty righteous within the city; will you then sweep away the place and not forgive it for the fifty righteous who are in it? [25]Far be it from you to do such a thing, to slay the righteous with

---

31. The pronouns here demand Abraham as antecedent; the name is not in the Hebrew. Noth's J includes Genesis 16, and the mention of Abraham is assumed to have been present in the original ending to this chapter, omitted in favor of P (16:15-16). Alternatively, the reference to the oaks of Mamre can be taken to indicate that Gen 18:1 was originally preceded by 13:18 (cf. Gunkel, *Genesis*, 193). The NRSV then supplies the required identification of Abraham as the "him" to whom the LORD appeared.

32. The language of Gen 18:18 ("nations of the earth" [*hā'āreṣ*]) differs slightly from that of 12:3b and 28:14 ("families of the earth" [*hā'ǎdāmâ*]). Noth judges this as less striking than the differences of formulation in 22:15-18 (for Noth, part of a supplement to E) and 26:3-5 (judged by Noth as an addition in J); see also n. 47, below. Here Noth retains 18:18 for J; it has the same verbal form for "bless" as 12:3 and 28:14.

33. This verse casts Abraham as a divinely commissioned teacher and renders fulfillment of the promise conditional upon his fidelity to this vocation, in contrast to his image in J.

the wicked, so that the righteous fare as the wicked! Far be that from you! Shall not the Judge of all the earth do what is just?" 26And the LORD said, "If I find at Sodom fifty righteous in the city, I will forgive the whole place for their sake." 27Abraham answered, "Let me take it upon myself to speak to the Lord, I who am but dust and ashes. 28Suppose five of the fifty righteous are lacking? Will you destroy the whole city for lack of five?" And he said, "I will not destroy it if I find forty-five there." 29Again he spoke to him, "Suppose forty are found there." He answered, "For the sake of forty I will not do it." 30Then he said, "Oh do not let the Lord be angry if I speak. Suppose thirty are found there." He answered, "I will not do it, if I find thirty there." 31He said, "Let me take it upon myself to speak to the Lord. Suppose twenty are found there." He answered, "For the sake of twenty I will not destroy it." 32Then he said, "Oh do not let the Lord be angry if I speak just once more. Suppose ten are found there." He answered, "For the sake of ten I will not destroy it." 33And the LORD went his way, when he had finished speaking to Abraham; and Abraham returned to his place.

Sodom and Gomorrah

19 The two angels came to Sodom in the evening, and Lot was sitting in the gateway of Sodom. When Lot saw them, he rose to meet them, and bowed down with his face to the ground. 2He said, "Please, my lords, turn aside to your servant's house and spend the night, and wash your feet; then you can rise early and go on your way." They said, "No; we will spend the night in the square." 3But he urged them strongly; so they turned aside to him and entered his house; and he made them a feast, and baked unleavened bread, and they ate. 4But before they lay down, the men of the city, the men of Sodom, both young and old, all the people to the last man, surrounded the house; 5and they called to Lot, "Where are the men who came to you tonight? Bring them out to us, so that we may know them." 6Lot went out of the door to the men, shut the door after him, 7and said, "I beg you, my brothers, do not act so wickedly. 8Look, I have two daughters who have not known a man; let me bring them out to you, and do to them as you please; only do nothing to these men, for they have come under the shelter of my roof." 9But they replied, "Stand back!" And they said, "This fellow came here as an alien, and he would play the judge! Now we will deal worse with you than with them." Then they pressed hard against the man Lot, and came near the door to break it down. 10But the men inside reached out their hands and brought Lot into the house with them, and shut the door. 11And they struck with blindness the men who were at the door of the house, both small and great, so that they were unable to find the door.

12 Then the men said to Lot, "Have you anyone else here? Sons-in-law, sons, daughters, or anyone you have in the city—bring them out of the place. 13For we are about to destroy this place, because the outcry against its people has become great before the LORD, and the LORD has sent us to destroy it." 14So Lot went out and said to his sons-in-law, who were to marry his daughters, "Up, get out of this place; for the LORD is about to destroy the city." But he seemed to his sons-in-law to be jesting.

15 When morning dawned, the angels urged Lot, saying, "Get up, take your wife and your two daughters who are here, or else you will be consumed in the punishment of the city." 16But he lingered; so the men seized him and his wife and his two daughters by the hand, the LORD being merciful to him, and they brought him out and left him outside the city. *17When they had brought them outside, they said, "Flee for your life; do not look back or stop anywhere in the Plain; flee to the hills, or else you will be consumed." 18And Lot said to them, "Oh,*

no, my lords; [19]*your servant has found favor with you, and you have shown me great kindness in saving my life; but I cannot flee to the hills, for fear the disaster will overtake me and I die.* [20]*Look, that city is near enough to flee to, and it is a little one. Let me escape there—is it not a little one?—and my life will be saved!"* [21]*He said to him, "Very well, I grant you this favor too, and will not overthrow the city of which you have spoken.* [22]*Hurry, escape there, for I can do nothing until you arrive there." Therefore the city was called Zoar.*[34]

[23]The sun had risen on the earth when Lot came to Zoar.

24 Then the LORD rained on Sodom and Gomorrah sulfur and fire from the LORD out of heaven; [25]and he overthrew those cities, and all the Plain, and all the inhabitants of the cities, and what grew on the ground.

[26]*But Lot's wife, behind him, looked back, and she became a pillar of salt.*[35]

27 Abraham went early in the morning to the place where he had stood before the LORD; [28]and he looked down toward Sodom and Gomorrah and toward all the land of the Plain and saw the smoke of the land going up like the smoke of a furnace.

30 Now Lot went up out of Zoar and settled in the hills with his two daughters, for he was afraid to stay in Zoar; so he lived in a cave with his two daughters. [31]And the firstborn said to the younger, "Our father is old, and there is not

a man on earth to come in to us after the manner of all the world. [32]Come, let us make our father drink wine, and we will lie with him, so that we may preserve offspring through our father." [33]So they made their father drink wine that night; and the firstborn went in, and lay with her father; he did not know when she lay down or when she rose. [34]On the next day, the firstborn said to the younger, "Look, I lay last night with my father; let us make him drink wine tonight also; then you go in and lie with him, so that we may preserve offspring through our father." [35]So they made their father drink wine that night also; and the younger rose, and lay with him; and he did not know when she lay down or when she rose. [36]Thus both the daughters of Lot became pregnant by their father. [37]The firstborn bore a son, and named him Moab; he is the ancestor of the Moabites to this day. [38]The younger also bore a son and named him Benammi; he is the ancestor of the Ammonites to this day.

20:1a From there Abraham journeyed toward the region of the Negeb, and settled between Kadesh and Shur.[36]

Isaac and Rebekah

Birth of Isaac

21:1a The LORD dealt with Sarah as he had said.

---

34. This section works an etiology of Zo'ar into the story, which includes a pun on the Hebrew word for "little one" (Gen 19:20).

35. The report of the death of Lot's wife is considered by Noth to be a later intrusion into the description of the destruction of Sodom and Gomorrah (cf. *Pentateuchal Traditions*, 195). Nevertheless, the notice of her death here prepares for Gen 19:30-38, where there is no mention of her.

36. Noth comments that Gen 20:1a is clearly a variant of 20:1b. The E story in chap. 20 of Abraham and Abimelech, king of Gerar, has been added to J, an example of J being enriched from the E source. The purpose of 20:1a within the J source itself was to transfer Abraham back to the Negeb (cf. 12:9; 13:1) for the remainder of the narrative, once the stories attached to his sojourn at Hebron had been told (Noth, *Pentateuchal Traditions*, 28 n. 87).

• • •[37]

[7]And she said, "Who would ever have said to Abraham that Sarah would nurse children? Yet I have borne him a son in his old age."

22:20 Now after these things it was told Abraham, "Milcah also has borne children, to your brother Nahor: [21]Uz the firstborn, Buz his brother, Kemuel the father of Aram, [22]Chesed, Hazo, Pildash, Jidlaph, and Bethuel." [23]Bethuel became the father of Rebekah. These eight Milcah bore to Nahor, Abraham's brother. [24]Moreover, his concubine, whose name was Reumah, bore Tebah, Gaham, Tahash, and Maacah.[38]

Rebekah Becomes Isaac's Wife

24 Now Abraham was old, well advanced in years; and the LORD had blessed Abraham in all things. [2]Abraham said to his servant, the oldest of his house, who had charge of all that he had, "Put your hand under my thigh [3]and I will make you swear by the LORD, the God of heaven and earth, that you will not get a wife for my son from the daughters of the Canaanites, among whom I live, [4]but will go to my country and to my kindred and get a wife for my son Isaac." [5]The servant said to him, "Perhaps the woman may not be willing to follow me to this land;

must I then take your son back to the land from which you came?" [6]Abraham said to him, "See to it that you do not take my son back there.

[7]*The LORD, the God of heaven, who took me from my father's house and from the land of my birth, and who spoke to me and swore to me, 'To your offspring I will give this land,' he will send his angel before you, and you shall take a wife for my son from there.*[39]

[8]But if the woman is not willing to follow you, then you will be free from this oath of mine; only you must not take my son back there." [9]So the servant put his hand under the thigh of Abraham his master and swore to him concerning this matter.

[10] Then the servant took ten of his master's camels and departed, taking all kinds of choice gifts from his master; and he set out and went to Aram-naharaim, to the city of Nahor. [11]He made the camels kneel down outside the city by the well of water; it was toward evening, the time when women go out to draw water. [12]And he said, "O LORD, God of my master Abraham, please grant me success today and show steadfast love to my master Abraham. [13]I am standing here by the spring of water, and the daughters of the townspeople are coming out to draw water.

---

37. The P account of the birth of Isaac (Gen 21:1b-5) has been inserted here between J's introduction and conclusion. According to Noth, the insertion was accompanied by the replacement of an original *Elohim* in v. 1b with YHWH, under the influence of v. 1a (*Pentateuchal Traditions*, 28 n. 88; also 17 n. 47; see the P text in chap. 2, above). Verse 6 is an independent addition, being principally a pun on the name Isaac (*Pentateuchal Traditions*, 39 n. 146). It is worth noting here the different ways the parallel P and J promises of a son and reports of Isaac's birth are combined. The two versions of the promise in Gen 17:15-19 (within P's account of the covenant with Abraham) and 18:1-15 (J) were juxtaposed. The reports of Isaac's birth were conflated. In contrast to preceding practice, however, the J variant has been

favored in this case as a base, with the enrichment being supplied from P.

38. Noth comments that it is difficult to be certain about assigning a list such as Gen 22:20-24 to a source. What favors its inclusion in J is the way it prepares for the J story in Genesis 24, in particular with the reference to Rebekah in v. 23a. In Noth's opinion, v. 23a was added by J when the list was incorporated into the source (*Pentateuchal Traditions*, 29 n. 89).

39. For Noth, Gen 24:7 and 24:40b are pious additions, counterbalancing the doubting questions of vv. 5 and 39. They provide firm affirmations of faith and the promise of angelic guidance. An evident supporting factor here is that v. 8 is in tension with v. 7 while following smoothly on vv. 5-6. Verses 25, 30, 61a, and 62b are a series of minor expansions.

[14]Let the girl to whom I shall say, 'Please offer your jar that I may drink,' and who shall say, 'Drink, and I will water your camels'—let her be the one whom you have appointed for your servant Isaac. By this I shall know that you have shown steadfast love to my master."

15 Before he had finished speaking, there was Rebekah, who was born to Bethuel son of Milcah, the wife of Nahor, Abraham's brother, coming out with her water jar on her shoulder. [16]The girl was very fair to look upon, a virgin, whom no man had known. She went down to the spring, filled her jar, and came up. [17]Then the servant ran to meet her and said, "Please let me sip a little water from your jar." [18]"Drink, my lord," she said, and quickly lowered her jar upon her hand and gave him a drink. [19]When she had finished giving him a drink, she said, "I will draw for your camels also, until they have finished drinking." [20]So she quickly emptied her jar into the trough and ran again to the well to draw, and she drew for all his camels. [21]The man gazed at her in silence to learn whether or not the LORD had made his journey successful.

22 When the camels had finished drinking, the man took a gold nose-ring weighing a half shekel, and two bracelets for her arms weighing ten gold shekels, [23]and said, "Tell me whose daughter you are. Is there room in your father's house for us to spend the night?" [24]She said to him, "I am the daughter of Bethuel son of Milcah, whom she bore to Nahor."

[25]She added, "We have plenty of straw and fodder and a place to spend the night."[40]

[26]The man bowed his head and worshiped the LORD [27]and said, "Blessed be the LORD, the God of my master Abraham, who has not forsaken his steadfast love and his faithfulness toward my master. As for me, the LORD has led me on the way to the house of my master's kin."

28 Then the girl ran and told her mother's household about these things. [29]Rebekah had a brother whose name was Laban; and Laban ran out to the man, to the spring.

[30]As soon as he had seen the nose-ring, and the bracelets on his sister's arms, and when he heard the words of his sister Rebekah, "Thus the man spoke to me," he went to the man; and there he was, standing by the camels at the spring.[41]

[31]He said, "Come in, O blessed of the LORD. Why do you stand outside when I have prepared the house and a place for the camels?" [32]So the man came into the house; and Laban unloaded the camels, and gave him straw and fodder for the camels, and water to wash his feet and the feet of the men who were with him. [33]Then food was set before him to eat; but he said, "I will not eat until I have told my errand." He said, "Speak on."

34 So he said, "I am Abraham's servant. [35]The LORD has greatly blessed my master, and he has become wealthy; he has given him flocks and herds, silver and gold, male and female slaves, camels and donkeys. [36]And Sarah my master's wife bore a son to my master when she was old; and he has given him all that he has. [37]My master made me swear, saying, 'You shall not take a wife for my son from the daughters of the Canaanites, in whose land I live; [38]but you shall go to my father's house, to my kindred, and get a

---

40. A factor in Noth's judgment here may well have been the introductory "She added." Although such factors may sometimes point to redactional work, at other times they may be better explained in terms of literary style.

41. Verse 30 is an enhancement of v. 29, with the brother–sister relationship from v. 29a and duplicating v. 29b in slightly different terms. There are various ways of accounting for repetitions such as this, and here Noth regards v. 30 as a minor expansion within the source (*Pentateuchal Traditions*, 29 n. 90).

wife for my son.' [39]I said to my master, 'Perhaps the woman will not follow me.' [40]But he said to me,

> The LORD, before whom I walk, will send his angel with you and make your way successful. You shall get a wife for my son from my kindred, from my father's house.[42]

[41]'Then you will be free from my oath, when you come to my kindred; even if they will not give her to you, you will be free from my oath.'

[42] "I came today to the spring, and said, 'O LORD, the God of my master Abraham, if now you will only make successful the way I am going! [43]I am standing here by the spring of water; let the young woman who comes out to draw, to whom I shall say, "Please give me a little water from your jar to drink," [44]and who will say to me, "Drink, and I will draw for your camels also"—let her be the woman whom the LORD has appointed for my master's son.'

[45] "Before I had finished speaking in my heart, there was Rebekah coming out with her water jar on her shoulder; and she went down to the spring, and drew. I said to her, 'Please let me drink.' [46]She quickly let down her jar from her shoulder, and said, 'Drink, and I will also water your camels.' So I drank, and she also watered the camels. [47]Then I asked her, 'Whose daughter are you?' She said, 'The daughter of Bethuel, Nahor's son, whom Milcah bore to him.' So I put the ring on her nose, and the bracelets on her arms. [48]Then I bowed my head and worshiped the LORD, and blessed the LORD, the God of my master Abraham, who had led me by the right way to obtain the daughter of my master's kinsman for his son. [49]Now then, if you will deal loyally and truly with my master, tell me; and if not, tell me, so that I may turn either to the right hand or to the left."

[50] Then Laban and Bethuel answered, "The thing comes from the LORD; we cannot speak to you anything bad or good. [51]Look, Rebekah is before you, take her and go, and let her be the wife of your master's son, as the LORD has spoken."

[52] When Abraham's servant heard their words, he bowed himself to the ground before the LORD. [53]And the servant brought out jewelry of silver and of gold, and garments, and gave them to Rebekah; he also gave to her brother and to her mother costly ornaments. [54]Then he and the men who were with him ate and drank, and they spent the night there. When they rose in the morning, he said, "Send me back to my master." [55]Her brother and her mother said, "Let the girl remain with us a while, at least ten days; after that she may go." [56]But he said to them, "Do not delay me, since the LORD has made my journey successful; let me go that I may go to my master." [57]They said, "We will call the girl, and ask her." [58]And they called Rebekah, and said to her, "Will you go with this man?" She said, "I will." [59]So they sent away their sister Rebekah and her nurse along with Abraham's servant and his men. [60]And they blessed Rebekah and said to her,

> "May you, our sister, become
>   thousands of myriads;
> may your offspring gain possession
>   of the gates of their foes."
> [61]Then Rebekah and her maids rose up, mounted the camels, and followed the man.[43]

And [Heb.; NRSV, Thus] the servant took Rebekah, and went his way.

---

42. See n. 39, above.

43. Genesis 24:61a covers material in vv. 59 and 61b, giving an initiative to Rebekah here but supplying an entourage of maids in contrast with "her nurse" in v. 59. This could be accounted for in various ways; in Noth's view, it is a minor expansion within the source (*Pentateuchal Traditions*, 29 n. 90).

62 Now Isaac had come from Beer-lahai-roi. *and was settled in the Negeb.*[44]
[63]Isaac went out in the evening to walk in the field; and looking up, he saw camels coming. [64]And Rebekah looked up, and when she saw Isaac, she slipped quickly from the camel, [65]and said to the servant, "Who is the man over there, walking in the field to meet us?" The servant said, "It is my master." So she took her veil and covered herself. [66]And the servant told Isaac all the things that he had done. [67]Then Isaac brought her into his mother Sarah's tent. He took Rebekah, and she became his wife; and he loved her. So Isaac was comforted after his mother's death.

Isaac's Inheritance

25:5 Abraham gave all he had to Isaac.[45] [6]But to the sons of his concubines Abraham gave gifts, while he was still living, and he sent them away from his son Isaac, eastward to the east country. [11b]And Isaac settled at Beer-lahai-roi.

Birth of Esau and Jacob

21 Isaac prayed to the LORD for his wife, because she was barren; and the LORD granted his prayer, and his wife Rebekah conceived. [22]The children struggled together within her; and she said, "If it is to be this way, why do I live?" So she went to inquire of the LORD. [23]And the LORD said to her,

"Two nations are in your womb,
and two peoples born of you shall
be divided;

the one shall be stronger than the other,
the elder shall serve the younger."

[24]When her time to give birth was at hand, there were twins in her womb. [25]The first came out red, all his body like a hairy mantle; so they named him Esau. [26a]Afterward his brother came out, with his hand gripping Esau's heel; so he was named Jacob.

27 When the boys grew up, Esau was a skillful hunter, a man of the field, while Jacob was a quiet man, living in tents. [28]Isaac loved Esau, because he was fond of game; but Rebekah loved Jacob.

29 Once when Jacob was cooking a stew, Esau came in from the field, and he was famished. [30]Esau said to Jacob, "Let me eat some of that red stuff, for I am famished!" (Therefore he was called Edom.) [31]Jacob said, "First sell me your birthright." [32]Esau said, "I am about to die; of what use is a birthright to me?" [33]Jacob said, "Swear to me first." So he swore to him, and sold his birthright to Jacob. [34]Then Jacob gave Esau bread and lentil stew, and he ate and drank, and rose and went his way. Thus Esau despised his birthright.

Isaac and Rebekah among the Philistines

26:1* Now there was a famine in the land. And Isaac went to Gerar, to King Abimelech of the Philistines. [2]The LORD appeared to him [Heb.; NRSV, Isaac] and said,

Do not go down to Egypt; settle in the land that I shall show you.[46]

---

44. Verse 62 poses problems for commentators. Noth's resolution is to see v. 62b as a minor expansion; cf. the J passages 20:1a and 25:11b.

45. Noth comments that it is impossible to decide with certainty about the dry list in Gen 25:1-4, which he omits from his text (*Pentateuchal Traditions*, 29 n. 91). It reads: "25:1 Abraham took another wife, whose name was Keturah. [2]She bore him Zimran, Jokshan, Medan, Midian, Ishbak, and Shuah. [3]Jokshan was the father of Sheba and Dedan. The sons of Dedan were

Asshurim, Letushim, and Leummim. [4]The sons of Midian were Ephah, Epher, Hanoch, Abida, and Eldaah. All these were the children of Keturah."

46. For Noth, the secondary verses in Genesis 26, as in Genesis 24, consist partly of various expansions of a general kind and partly of references to some of the Abraham stories in J (*Pentateuchal Traditions*, 29 n. 92). Here, in v. 2, which refers back to the story of 12:10-20, there is a possible tension between the commands in v. 2b (future) and v. 3a (present).

[3] "Reside in this land as an alien, and I will be with you, and will bless you; for to you and to your descendants I will give all these lands."

And I will fulfill the oath that I swore to your father Abraham. [4] *I will make your offspring as numerous as the stars of heaven, and will give to your offspring all these lands; and all the nations of the earth shall gain blessing for themselves through your offspring,* [5] *because Abraham obeyed my voice and kept my charge, my commandments, my statutes, and my laws.*[47]

6 So Isaac settled in Gerar. [7] When the men of the place asked him about his wife, he said, "She is my sister"; for he was afraid to say, "My wife," thinking, "or else the men of the place might kill me for the sake of Rebekah, because she is attractive in appearance." [8] When Isaac had been there a long time, King Abimelech of the Philistines looked out of a window and saw him fondling his wife Rebekah. [9] So Abimelech called for Isaac, and said, "So she is your wife! Why then did you say, 'She is my sister'?" Isaac said to him, "Because I thought I might die because of her." [10] Abimelech said, "What is this you have done to us? One of the people might easily have lain with your wife, and you would have brought guilt upon us." [11] So Abimelech warned all the people, saying, "Whoever touches this man or his wife shall be put to death."

12 Isaac sowed seed in that land, and in the same year reaped a hundredfold. The LORD blessed him, [13] and the man became rich; he prospered more and more until he became very wealthy. [14] He had possessions of flocks and herds, and a great household, so that the Philistines envied him.

[15] *(Now the Philistines had stopped up and filled with earth all the wells that his father's servants had dug in the days of his father Abraham.)*[48] [16] And Abimelech said to Isaac, "Go away from us; you have become too powerful for us."

17 So Isaac departed from there and camped in the valley of Gerar and settled there.

[18] *Isaac dug again the wells of water that had been dug in the days of his father Abraham; for the Philistines had stopped them up after the death of Abraham; and he gave them the names that his father had given them.*[49] [19] But when Isaac's servants dug in the valley and found there a well of spring water, [20] the herders of Gerar quarreled with Isaac's herders, saying, "The water is ours." So he called the well Esek, because they contended with him. [21] Then they dug another well, and they quarreled over that one also; so he called it Sitnah. [22] He moved from there and dug another well, and they did not quarrel over it; so he called it Rehoboth, saying, "Now the LORD has made room for us, and we shall be fruitful in the land." [23] From there he went up to Beer-sheba.

[24] *And that very night the LORD appeared to him and said, "I am the God of your father Abraham; do not be afraid, for I am with you and will bless you and make your offspring numerous for my*

---

47. A shift in language and thought is a pointer to redactional activity here. Although Gen 26:4 contains the promise of 12:3 and 28:14, it uses "nations" instead of "families," *hā'āreṣ* instead of *hā'ădāmâ* (often rendered "the earth" and "the ground" respectively), and the *hithpael* form of the verb "to bless" instead of the *nifal* form found in 12:3 and 28:14. Whereas in 12:3 and 28:14 the blessing is formulated as a promise, here it is referred to as an oath, sworn to Abraham (v. 3) because of his obedience (v. 5; cf. also 22:15-18). Here, as in 22:15-18, the style, language, and thought are close to that of deuteronomic circles.

48. The tension visible here is between the Philistines' power to plug all the wells (v. 15) and their acknowledgment of Isaac's superior power (v. 16). Note also 21:25-30 in text attributed to E.

49. The theme of v. 15 is resumed here. There is a possible tension between the reuse of the several wells dug and named previously by Abraham (v. 18) and the apparently new wells dug and named by Isaac's servants in vv. 19-22.

servant Abraham's sake." [25]So he built an altar there, called on the name of the LORD, and pitched his tent there.[50]
And there Isaac's servants dug a well.

26 Then Abimelech went to him from Gerar, with Ahuzzath his adviser and Phicol the commander of his army. [27]Isaac said to them, "Why have you come to me, seeing that you hate me and have sent me away from you?" [28]They said, "We see plainly that the LORD has been with you; so we say, let there be an oath between you and us, and let us make a covenant with you [29]so that you will do us no harm, just as we have not touched you and have done to you nothing but good and have sent you away in peace. You are now the blessed of the LORD." [30]So he made them a feast, and they ate and drank. [31]In the morning they rose early and exchanged oaths; and Isaac set them on their way, and they departed from him in peace. [32]That same day Isaac's servants came and told him about the well that they had dug, and said to him, "We have found water!" [33]He called it Shibah; therefore the name of the city is Beer-sheba to this day.

Jacob and Esau

27 When Isaac was old and his eyes were dim so that he could not see, he called his elder son Esau and said to him, "My son"; and he answered, "Here I am."[51] [2]He said, "See, I am old; I do not know the day of my death. [3]Now then, take your weapons, your quiver and your bow, and go out to the field, and hunt game for me. [4]Then prepare for me savory food, such as I like, and bring it to me to eat, so that I may bless you before I die."

5 Now Rebekah was listening when Isaac spoke to his son Esau. So when Esau went to the field to hunt for game and bring it, [6]Rebekah said to her son Jacob, "I heard your father say to your brother Esau, [7]'Bring me game, and prepare for me savory food to eat, that I may bless you before the LORD before I die.' [8]Now therefore, my son, obey my word as I command you. [9]Go to the flock, and get me two choice kids, so that I may prepare from them savory food for your father, such as he likes; [10]and you shall take it to your father to eat, so that he may bless you before he dies." [11]But Jacob said to his mother Rebekah, "Look, my brother Esau is a hairy man, and I am a man of smooth skin. [12]Perhaps my father will feel me, and I shall seem to be mocking him, and bring a curse on myself and not a blessing." [13]His mother said to him, "Let your curse be on me, my son; only obey my word, and go, get them for me." [14]So he went and got them and brought them to his mother; and his mother prepared savory food, such as his father loved. [15]Then Rebekah took the best garments of her elder son Esau, which were with her in the house, and put them on her younger son Jacob; [16]and she put the skins of the kids on his hands and on the smooth part of his neck. [17]Then she handed the savory food, and the bread that she had prepared, to her son Jacob.

18 So he went in to his father, and said, "My father"; and he said, "Here I am; who are you, my son?" [19]Jacob said to his father, "I am Esau

---

50. Verses 24-25a, with their reference to "my servant Abraham," unique here in Genesis, have been seen as moving away from the concern with wells and attaching the renown of Beersheba to this theophany, rather than to the oath establishing peace in vv. 26-33. The formulation seems to have drawn on elements of the theophanies in Genesis 12 and 15; as elsewhere in Genesis 26, Abraham motifs are attracted to Isaac.

51. In contrast to many of his predecessors, Noth found that, despite some evidence of duplication and variation in terminology, there was insufficient evidence for an E version of Genesis 27 (*Pentateuchal Traditions*, 29 n. 93). The following notes identify and comment on the relevant texts. For a brief discussion of the history of exegesis of this chapter, see Westermann, *Genesis 12–36*, 436.

your firstborn. I have done as you told me; now sit up and eat of my game, so that you may bless me." [20]But Isaac said to his son, "How is it that you have found it so quickly, my son?" He answered, "Because the LORD your God granted me success." [21]Then Isaac said to Jacob, "Come near, that I may feel you, my son, to know whether you are really my son Esau or not." [22]So Jacob went up to his father Isaac, who felt him and said, "The voice is Jacob's voice, but the hands are the hands of Esau." [23]He did not recognize him, because his hands were hairy like his brother Esau's hands; so he blessed him.[52] [24]He said, "Are you really my son Esau?" He answered, "I am." [25]Then he said, "Bring it to me, that I may eat of my son's game and bless you." So he brought it to him, and he ate; and he brought him wine, and he drank. [26]Then his father Isaac said to him, "Come near and kiss me, my son." [27]So he came near and kissed him; and he smelled the smell of his garments, and blessed him, and said,

"Ah, the smell of my son
　is like the smell of a field that the
　　LORD has blessed.
[28]May God give you of the dew of heaven,
　and of the fatness of the earth,
　and plenty of grain and wine.
[29]Let peoples serve you,
　and nations bow down to you.
Be lord over your brothers,

and may your mother's sons bow
　down to you.
Cursed be everyone who curses you,
　and blessed be everyone who
　　blesses you!"[53]

30 As soon as Isaac had finished blessing Jacob, when Jacob had scarcely gone out from the presence of his father Isaac, his brother Esau came in from his hunting. [31]He also prepared savory food, and brought it to his father. And he said to his father, "Let my father sit up and eat of his son's game, so that you may bless me." [32]His father Isaac said to him, "Who are you?" He answered, "I am your firstborn son, Esau." [33]Then Isaac trembled violently, and said, "Who was it then that hunted game and brought it to me, and I ate it all before you came, and I have blessed him?—yes, and blessed he shall be!" [34]When Esau heard his father's words, he cried out with an exceedingly great and bitter cry, and said to his father, "Bless me, me also, father!" [35]But he said, "Your brother came deceitfully, and he has taken away your blessing." [36]Esau said, "Is he not rightly named Jacob? For he has supplanted me these two times. He took away my birthright; and look, now he has taken away my blessing." Then he said, "Have you not reserved a blessing for me?" [37]Isaac answered Esau, "I have already made him your lord, and I have given him all his brothers as servants, and with grain and wine I have sustained him. What

---

52. The report of Isaac blessing Jacob in Gen 27:23b anticipates some of v. 27a and seems to come too early in the story. For Noth, this suggests it could conceivably be an addition, but he retains it; he refrains from attributing any of this chapter to E. Westermann discerns ancient ritual procedures in the story involving the transfer of blessing. For him, v. 23b forms the introduction of a blessing ritual that reaches its culmination in the pronouncement of vv. 27-29 (*Genesis 12–36*, 440).

53. The alternation of the divine name has been an important factor in the identification of sources; it occurs here in Gen 27:27b and 27:28. For Noth, the

alternation is in itself insufficient to establish the existence of sources. Therefore, in order to claim v. 28 as evidence of E in this case, one would need to show that it forms part of an independent version of Jacob's theft of his brother's blessing. In Noth's judgment, such supporting evidence is lacking in Genesis 27. In his view, the blessing in vv. 27b-29 has been compiled from a variety of fixed blessing formulas; in particular, v. 28 seems to have been shaped independently of the present context (*Pentateuchal Traditions*, 29 n. 93).

The end of v. 29 recalls the promise of 12:3, except that, whereas here both curse and blessing are given plural weight, there the curse is in the singular.

then can I do for you, my son?" [38]Esau said to his father, "Have you only one blessing, father? Bless me, me also, father!" And Esau lifted up his voice and wept.

39 Then his father Isaac answered him:
"See, away from the fatness of the earth
    shall your home be,
    and away from the dew of heaven on high.
[40]By your sword you shall live,
    and you shall serve your brother;
but when you break loose,
    you shall break his yoke from your neck."

Jacob's Flight from Esau

41 Now Esau hated Jacob because of the blessing with which his father had blessed him, and Esau said to himself, "The days of mourning for my father are approaching; then I will kill my brother Jacob." [42]But the words of her elder son Esau were told to Rebekah; so she sent and called her younger son Jacob and said to him, "Your brother Esau is consoling himself by planning to kill you. [43]Now therefore, my son, obey my voice; flee at once to my brother Laban in Haran, [44]and stay with him a while, until your brother's fury turns away—[45]until your brother's anger against you turns away, and he forgets what you have done to him; then I will send, and bring you back from there. Why should I lose both of you in one day?"

28:10 Jacob left Beer-sheba and went toward Haran. [11]*He came to a certain place and stayed there for the night, because the sun had set.

[13]And the LORD stood beside him[54] and said, "I am the LORD, the God of Abraham your father and the God of Isaac; the land on which you lie I will give to you and to your offspring; [14]and your offspring shall be like the dust of the earth, and you shall spread abroad to the west and to the east and to the north and to the south; and all the families of the earth shall be blessed in you and in your offspring.[55] [15]Know that I am with you and will keep you wherever you go, and will bring you back to this land; for I will not leave you until I have done what I have promised you." [16]Then Jacob woke from his sleep and said, "Surely the LORD is in this place—and I did not know it!"
[19]He called that place Bethel.
    But the name of the city was Luz at the first.[56]

Jacob and Laban

29 Then Jacob went on his journey, and came to the land of the people of the east. [2]As he looked, he saw a well in the field and three flocks of sheep lying there beside it; for out of that well the flocks were watered. The stone on the well's mouth was large, [3]and when all the flocks were gathered there, the shepherds would roll the stone from the mouth of the well, and water the sheep, and put the stone back in its place on the mouth of the well.

4 Jacob said to them, "My brothers, where do you come from?" They said, "We are from Haran." [5]He said to them, "Do you know Laban son of Nahor?" They said, "We do." [6]He said to

---

54. The Hebrew pronoun can be read as either "him" or "it" (cf. NRSV note). In the J text the pronoun clearly refers to Jacob; in the JE combination it can refer either to Jacob or to the ladder (from E).

55. Verse 14 follows the formulation of the promise in Gen 12:3, using the same phrase, "families of *hā'ǎdāmâ*," and the same *nifal* form of the verb "to bless." At the end it adds "and in your offspring." See also nn. 32 and 47, above.

56. Gunkel, e.g., saw v. 19b as a gloss because there was no city in "that place" at the time, Luz being separate from Bethel (Josh 16:2) and only identified with it later. For an indication of recent scholarship that would assign all of v. 19 to the so-called E material on form-critical grounds, see Westermann, *Genesis 12–36*, 453, 458. This is an example where decisions about the attribution of text to sources may vary without affecting the substantials of the source hypothesis.

them, "Is it well with him?" "Yes," they replied, "and here is his daughter Rachel, coming with the sheep." [7]He said, "Look, it is still broad daylight; it is not time for the animals to be gathered together. Water the sheep, and go, pasture them." [8]But they said, "We cannot until all the flocks are gathered together, and the stone is rolled from the mouth of the well; then we water the sheep."

9 While he was still speaking with them, Rachel came with her father's sheep; for she kept them. [10]Now when Jacob saw Rachel, the daughter of his mother's brother Laban, and the sheep of his mother's brother Laban, Jacob went up and rolled the stone from the well's mouth, and watered the flock of his mother's brother Laban. [11]Then Jacob kissed Rachel, and wept aloud. [12]And Jacob told Rachel that he was her father's kinsman, and that he was Rebekah's son; and she ran and told her father.

13 When Laban heard the news about his sister's son Jacob, he ran to meet him; he embraced him and kissed him, and brought him to his house. Jacob told Laban all these things, [14]and Laban said to him, "Surely you are my bone and my flesh!" And he stayed with him a month.

15 Then Laban said to Jacob, "Because you are my kinsman, should you therefore serve me for nothing? Tell me, what shall your wages be?" [16]Now Laban had two daughters; the name of the elder was Leah, and the name of the younger was Rachel. [17]Leah's eyes were lovely, and Rachel was graceful and beautiful. [18]Jacob loved Rachel; so he said, "I will serve you seven years for your younger daughter Rachel." [19]Laban said, "It is better that I give her to you than that I should give her to any other man; stay with me." [20]So Jacob served seven years for Rachel, and they seemed to him but a few days because of the love he had for her.

21 Then Jacob said to Laban, "Give me my wife that I may go in to her, for my time is completed." [22]So Laban gathered together all the people of the place, and made a feast. [23]But in the evening he took his daughter Leah and brought her to Jacob; and he went in to her. [24](Laban gave his maid Zilpah to his daughter Leah to be her maid.) [25]When morning came, it was Leah! And Jacob said to Laban, "What is this you have done to me? Did I not serve with you for Rachel? Why then have you deceived me?" [26]Laban said, "This is not done in our country—giving the younger before the firstborn. [27]Complete the week of this one, and we will give you the other also in return for serving me another seven years." [28]Jacob did so, and completed her week; then Laban gave him his daughter Rachel as a wife. [29](Laban gave his maid Bilhah to his daughter Rachel to be her maid.) [30]So Jacob went in to Rachel also, and he loved Rachel more than Leah. He served Laban for another seven years.

Birth of Jacob's Children

31 When the LORD saw that Leah was unloved, he opened her womb; but Rachel was barren. [32]Leah conceived and bore a son, and she named him Reuben; for she said, "Because the LORD has looked on my affliction; surely now my husband will love me." [33]She conceived again and bore a son, and said, "Because the LORD has heard that I am hated, he has given me this son also"; and she named him Simeon. [34]Again she conceived and bore a son, and said, "Now this time my husband will be joined to me, because I have borne him three sons"; therefore he was named Levi. [35]She conceived again and bore a son, and said, "This time I will praise the LORD"; therefore she named him Judah; then she ceased bearing.

30:1* When Rachel saw that she bore Jacob no children,

• • •⁵⁷

³*and that I too may have children through her."
⁴So she gave him her maid Bilhah as a wife; and
Jacob went in to her. ⁵And Bilhah conceived
and bore Jacob a son.

• • •

⁷Rachel's maid Bilhah conceived again and bore
Jacob a second son. ⁸Then Rachel said, "With
mighty wrestlings I have wrestled with my
sister, and have prevailed"; so she named him
Naphtali.

9 When Leah saw that she had ceased bearing children, she took her maid Zilpah and gave
her to Jacob as a wife. ¹⁰Then Leah's maid
Zilpah bore Jacob a son. ¹¹And Leah said,
"Good fortune!" so she named him Gad.
¹²Leah's maid Zilpah bore Jacob a second son.
¹³And Leah said, "Happy am I! For the women
will call me happy"; so she named him Asher.

14 In the days of wheat harvest Reuben went
and found mandrakes in the field, and brought
them to his mother Leah. Then Rachel said to
Leah, "Please give me some of your son's mandrakes." ¹⁵But she said to her, "Is it a small
matter that you have taken away my husband?
Would you take away my son's mandrakes also?"
Rachel said, "Then he may lie with you tonight
for your son's mandrakes." ¹⁶When Jacob came

from the field in the evening, Leah went out to
meet him, and said, "You must come in to me;
for I have hired you with my son's mandrakes."
So he lay with her that night.

• • •

²⁰*Now my husband will honor me, because I
have borne him six sons"; so she named him
Zebulun.
   *²¹Afterwards she bore a daughter, and named her
Dinah.*⁵⁸

• • •

²⁴And she named him Joseph, saying, "May the
LORD add to me another son!"

25 When Rachel had borne Joseph, Jacob
said to Laban, "Send me away, that I may go to
my own home and country.⁵⁹ ²⁶Give me my
wives and my children for whom I have served
you, and let me go; for you know very well the
service I have given you." ²⁷But Laban said to
him, "If you will allow me to say so, I have
learned by divination that the LORD has blessed
me because of you; ²⁸name your wages, and I
will give it." ²⁹Jacob said to him, "You yourself
know how I have served you, and how your cattle
have fared with me. ³⁰For you had little before I
came, and it has increased abundantly; and the
LORD has blessed you wherever I turned. But
now when shall I provide for my own household

---

57. According to Noth, in Gen 29:31—30:24 the
compiler has used J as the base, replaced occasionally
by E when the E version was preferred; these gaps are
indicated in the text by the ellipses. The etymologies
of the names form the essential content of the passage. Sometimes the compiler preserved both variants
(i.e., Zebulon in 30:20 and Joseph in 30:23-24); sometimes the E form was preferred by the compiler (i.e.,
Dan in 30:6 and Issachar in 30:18; see Noth, *Pentateuchal Traditions*, 29 n. 94).

58. Noth's reason for considering this verse an
addition within J is uncertain. Westermann, noting
there is no etymology for Dinah's name, attributes it to
a redactor, who is here making up the number twelve,
prior to the birth of Benjamin (*Genesis 12–36*, 472, 476).

59. In Gen 30:25-43, which is very difficult in its

details, a division between two sources is not helpful,
in Noth's view. Rather, the text appears to have been
altered by a variety of later additions. These are (1) v.
27; (2) the reference to black lambs within vv. 32, 33b,
35, and 40; (3) the reference to almond and plane rods
and the phrase "exposing the white of the rods" within
v. 37; (4) the reference to "the watering places"
within v. 38. The E variants appear to have been narrated quite differently; cf. 31:7 and below in the Elohist,
chap. 4. Such indications of variant ways of telling a
story are discussed on p. 172. In the enumeration
of the J text, by chapter and verse, Noth takes no
account of his footnoted comments (cf. *Pentateuchal
Traditions*, 29 n. 94). In view of this, it seems unnecessary to go into detailed explanations of these expansions here.

also?" [31]He said, "What shall I give you?" Jacob said, "You shall not give me anything; if you will do this for me, I will again feed your flock and keep it: [32]let me pass through all your flock today, removing from it every speckled and spotted sheep and every black lamb, and the spotted and speckled among the goats; and such shall be my wages. [33]So my honesty will answer for me later, when you come to look into my wages with you. Every one that is not speckled and spotted among the goats and black among the lambs, if found with me, shall be counted stolen." [34]Laban said, "Good! Let it be as you have said." [35]But that day Laban removed the male goats that were striped and spotted, and all the female goats that were speckled and spotted, every one that had white on it, and every lamb that was black, and put them in charge of his sons; [36]and he set a distance of three days' journey between himself and Jacob, while Jacob was pasturing the rest of Laban's flock.

37 Then Jacob took fresh rods of poplar and almond and plane, and peeled white streaks in them, exposing the white of the rods. [38]He set the rods that he had peeled in front of the flocks in the troughs, that is, the watering places, where the flocks came to drink. And since they bred when they came to drink, [39]the flocks bred in front of the rods, and so the flocks produced young that were striped, speckled, and spotted. [40]Jacob separated the lambs, and set the faces of the flocks toward the striped and the completely black animals in the flock of Laban; and he put his own droves apart, and did not put them with Laban's flock. [41]Whenever the stronger of the flock were breeding, Jacob laid the rods in the troughs before the eyes of the flock, that they might breed among the rods, [42]but for the feebler of the flock he did not lay them there; so the feebler were Laban's, and the stronger Jacob's. [43]Thus the man grew exceedingly rich, and had large flocks, and male and female slaves, and camels and donkeys.

Jacob's Flight from Laban

31 Now Jacob heard that the sons of Laban were saying, "Jacob has taken all that was our father's; he has gained all this wealth from what belonged to our father." [3]Then the LORD said to Jacob, "Return to the land of your ancestors and to your kindred, and I will be with you." [17]So Jacob arose, and set his children and his wives on camels; [18*]and he drove away all his livestock.

19a Now Laban had gone to shear his sheep. [20]And Jacob deceived Laban the Aramean, in that he did not tell him that he intended to flee. [21*]So he fled with all that he had, and set his face toward the hill country of Gilead.

22 On the third day Laban was told that Jacob had fled. [23]So he took his kinsfolk with him and pursued him for seven days until he caught up with him in the hill country of Gilead. [25*]Now Jacob had pitched his tent in the hill country. *And Laban with his kinsfolk camped in the hill country of Gilead.*[60] [26*]Laban said to Jacob, [27]"Why did you flee secretly and deceive me and not tell me? I would have sent you away with mirth and songs, with tambourine and lyre, [30a]even though you had to go because you longed greatly for your father's house." [31]Jacob answered Laban, "Because I was afraid, for I thought that you would take your daughters from me by force."

---

60. The reasons for Noth's source decisions here are unexplained. He may have given 31:25a to E to maintain a minimal continuity and regarded this latter part of v. 25b as a repetition from v. 23, added to introduce the confrontation between Jacob and Laban (v. 26 ff.). With the more recent downgrading of E as a source, alternative divisions of the material become attractive. On the textual difficulties of this verse, see Westermann, *Genesis 12–36*, 494.

• • •[61]

36a Then Jacob became angry, and upbraided Laban. [38]"These twenty years I have been with you; your ewes and your female goats have not miscarried, and I have not eaten the rams of your flocks. [39]That which was torn by wild beasts I did not bring to you; I bore the loss of it myself; of my hand you required it, whether stolen by day or stolen by night. [40]It was like this with me: by day the heat consumed me, and the cold by night, and my sleep fled from my eyes."

Reconciliation between Jacob and Laban

46 And Laban [Vetus Latina; Heb. and NRSV, Jacob] said to his kinsfolk, "Gather stones," and they took stones, and made a heap; and they ate there by the heap.[62]

> [47]Laban called it Jegar-sahadutha: but Jacob called it Galeed.
>
> [48]Laban said, "This heap is a witness between you and me today." Therefore he called it Galeed, [49]and the pillar Mizpah, for he said, "The LORD watch between you and me, when we are absent one from the other."[63]

51 Then Laban said to Jacob, "See this heap and see the pillar, which I have set between you and me. [52]This heap is a witness, and the pillar is a witness, that I will not pass beyond this heap to you, and you will not pass beyond this heap and this pillar to me, for harm. [53a]May the God of Abraham and the God of Nahor"—the God of their father—"judge between us."

Jacob Prepares to Meet Esau

32:3 Jacob sent messengers before him to his brother Esau in the land of Seir, the country of Edom,[64] [4]instructing them, "Thus you shall say to my lord Esau: Thus says your servant Jacob, 'I have lived with Laban as an alien, and stayed until now; [5]and I have oxen, donkeys, flocks, male and female slaves; and I have sent to tell my lord, in order that I may find favor in your sight.' "

6 The messengers returned to Jacob, saying, "We came to your brother Esau, and he is coming to meet you, and four hundred men are with him." [7]Then Jacob was greatly afraid and distressed; and he divided the people that were with him, and the flocks and herds and camels, into two companies, [8]thinking, "If Esau comes to the one company and destroys it, then the company that is left will escape."

---

61. The reasons for assuming a gap here may be inferred from a consideration of the sequence in J. In Gen 31:27, 30a, and 31, before the gap, Laban asks why Jacob fled without a proper farewell, although he grants there were pious reasons for the sudden departure (v. 30a). Verses 36a and 38-40, after the gap, do not refer to these issues; instead, they portray an angry Jacob upbraiding Laban about the conditions of his former employment. The E story of Laban searching unsuccessfully for his household gods supplies a satisfactory transition. In the hypothesis of a continuous J narrative, something equivalent but less appealing may have fulfilled this function.

62. For Laban instead of Jacob, see Noth, *Pentateuchal Traditions*, 29 n. 95.

63. Verses 48-49 form a doublet with vv. 51-53a, both passages being concerned with the heap of stones erected by Laban (v. 46) and the pillar set up by Jacob (v. 45b). Noth follows Gunkel in attributing vv. 51-53a to J, with the references to the pillar in vv. 51 and 52 being secondary supplements based on v. 45b (Noth, *Pentateuchal Traditions*, 29 n. 96). Verses 51-53a are integral to the story line, more so than vv. 48-49. The heap is a witness that both parties have agreed not to enter each other's territory with malicious intent. Each swears by his own god in v. 53a, and their dispute is thereby resolved. The link with the story line is weaker in vv. 48-49. Verse 48 makes only a passing reference to the heap as a witness before moving on to its name, "Galeed." In v. 49, which is dependent on v. 48, the naming of the pillar is accompanied by a play on the name "Mizpah" and the Hebrew verb "to watch." For Noth, v. 47 is a still later addition which has the effect of attributing the name Galeed to Jacob instead of Laban, as in v. 48. By contrast, see Westermann, who regards vv. 51-53a as later (*Genesis 12–36*, 499).

64. This is Gen 32:4 in the Hebrew.

9 And Jacob said, "O God of my father Abraham and God of my father Isaac, O LORD who said to me, 'Return to your country and to your kindred, and I will do you good,' [10]I am not worthy of the least of all the steadfast love and all the faithfulness that you have shown to your servant, for with only my staff I crossed this Jordan; and now I have become two companies. [11]Deliver me, please, from the hand of my brother, from the hand of Esau, for I am afraid of him; he may come and kill us all, the mothers with the children. [12]Yet you have said, 'I will surely do you good, and make your offspring as the sand of the sea, which cannot be counted because of their number.' " [13a]So he spent that night there.

• • •[65]

Jacob Wrestles with God

22 The same night he got up and took his two wives, his two maids, and his eleven children, and crossed the ford of the Jabbok.[66] [23]He took them and sent them across the stream, and likewise everything that he had.[67] [24]Jacob was left alone; and a man wrestled with him until daybreak. [25]When the man saw that he did not prevail against Jacob, he struck him on the hip socket; and Jacob's hip was put out of joint as he wrestled with him. [26]Then he said, "Let me go,

for the day is breaking." But Jacob said, "I will not let you go, unless you bless me." [27]So he said to him, "What is your name?" And he said, "Jacob." [28]Then the man said, "You shall no longer be called Jacob, but Israel, for you have striven with God and with humans, and have prevailed." [29]Then Jacob asked him, "Please tell me your name." But he said, "Why is it that you ask my name?" And there he blessed him. [30]So Jacob called the place Peniel, saying, "For I have seen God face to face, and yet my life is preserved." [31]The sun rose upon him as he passed Penuel, limping because of his hip. [32]Therefore to this day the Israelites do not eat the thigh muscle that is on the hip socket, because he struck Jacob on the hip socket at the thigh muscle.[68]

Reconciliation between Jacob and Esau

33 Now Jacob looked up and saw Esau coming, and four hundred men with him. So he divided the children among Leah and Rachel and the two maids. [2]He put the maids with their children in front, then Leah with her children, and Rachel and Joseph last of all. [3]He himself went on ahead of them, bowing himself to the ground seven times, until he came near his brother. [6]Then the maids drew near, they and their children, and bowed down; [7]Leah likewise

---

65. According to Noth, after Gen 32:13a (Heb., v. 14a) an introduction and explanation of the name Mahanaim is expected, because this is the goal of vv. 3-13a (Heb., vv. 4-14a). In J, it seems, the actions of Jacob determined the name rather than the presence of angels. Mahanaim means "companies" or "camps/armies," and in v. 7 Jacob divides his people into two "companies." Moreover, v. 13a has Jacob lodge "there," which in the J text presumably referred to Mahanaim. The compiler suppressed the J introduction and explanation of the name in favor of the E variant in 32:1-2 (*Pentateuchal Traditions*, 29 n. 97).

66. This is Gen 32:23 in the Hebrew.

67. In Noth's view, the reference to Jacob's crossing the Jabbok (Gen 32:22b; Heb., v. 23b) is an

inappropriate addition, which he nevertheless leaves in his chapter and verse listing. It is repetitive and has Jacob himself cross, whereas v. 23a (Heb., v. 24a) states that he sent his family across, implying that he remained by himself on the other side. The first words of v. 23a ("He took them"—one word in Hebrew) take up the thread of the narrative after this addition (*Pentateuchal Traditions*, 29 n. 98). The addition identifies the place as the Jabbok Ford and portrays Jacob as leading the way.

68. Noth remarks that, although the story of Jacob wrestling with the angel has been put together from different motifs, it is not to be dissected source-critically (ibid.).

and her children drew near and bowed down; and finally Joseph and Rachel drew near, and they bowed down.

12 Then Esau said, "Let us journey on our way, and I will go alongside you." [13]But Jacob said to him, "My lord knows that the children are frail and that the flocks and herds, which are nursing, are a care to me; and if they are over-driven for one day, all the flocks will die. [14]Let my lord pass on ahead of his servant, and I will lead on slowly, according to the pace of the cattle that are before me and according to the pace of the children, until I come to my lord in Seir."

15 So Esau said, "Let me leave with you some of the people who are with me." But he said, "Why should my lord be so kind to me?" [16]So Esau returned that day on his way to Seir. [17]But Jacob journeyed to Succoth, and built himself a house, and made booths for his cattle; therefore the place is called Succoth.

• • •[69]

18b And he camped before the city.

Rape of Dinah

34 Now Dinah the daughter of Leah, whom she had borne to Jacob, went out to visit the women of the region.[70] [2]When Shechem son of Hamor the Hivite, prince of the region, saw her, he seized her and lay with her by force. [3]And his soul was drawn to Dinah daughter of Jacob; he loved the girl, and spoke tenderly to her.

[4]So Shechem spoke to his father Hamor, saying, "Get me this girl to be my wife."

5 Now Jacob heard that Shechem had defiled his daughter Dinah; but his sons were with his cattle in the field, so Jacob held his peace until they came.

[6]And Hamor the father of Shechem went out to Jacob to speak with him.

[7]And [Heb.; NRSV, just as] the sons of Jacob came in from the field when they heard of it. The men were indignant and very angry, because he had committed an outrage in Israel by lying with Jacob's daughter, for such a thing ought not to be done.

8 But Hamor spoke with them, saying, "The heart of my son Shechem longs for your daughter; please give her to him in marriage. [9]Make marriages with us; give your daughters to us, and take our daughters for yourselves. [10]You shall live with us; and the land shall be open to you; live and trade in it, and get property in it."

---

69. With Gen 33:18a attributed by Noth to P, there is a gap in the J text. The missing text presumably gave the reason for the move from Succoth to Shechem's city. If weight is given to the issue of settlement in v. 17 , the J narrative would have Jacob's journey end at Succoth (cf. Westermann, *Genesis 12–36*, 527). The move from Succoth would still remain unexplained. If the possibility were entertained that the Genesis 34 story was not originally part of the narrative here, then much of vv. 18-20 may have served to form a suitable context for it.

70. In Noth's view, Genesis 34 is not a unified text but one that has been expanded by observations derived from its own base, rather than by fragments of some variant narrative. The more extensive additions are concerned with the conditions for a marriage, introducing Shechem's father, Hamor, as the go-be-tween. They are vv. 4, 6, 8-10, 15-17, and 20-23, as well as the occurrence of Hamor in vv. 13a, 18, 24, and 26 (*Pentateuchal Traditions*, 30 n. 99). In the original story it was Shechem himself who initiated the marriage negotiations (v. 11). Verses 27 and 28 are also additions, their purpose being to involve all the sons of Jacob in the revenge for the rape of Dinah. In the original story revenge was exacted by Simeon and Levi (vv. 25-26, 29). Jacob's rebuke in v. 30 is addressed only to them.

In our judgment, however, Genesis 34 adds little or nothing to what may be perceived as the horizon of a Yahwist narrative. Such a judgment is obviously open to revision in the light of more insightful perception. In the meantime, it raises the question whether Genesis 34 has been appended here appropriately, perhaps to preserve a valuable tradition, perhaps by association with the Judah and Tamar story (Genesis 38). It leaves open the associated question whether, in this case, it was added by the Yahwist or some later redactor. In the absence of identifying characteristics of language or thought, such a question may have to remain unresolved. The implications of this suggestion for J's narrative thread are noted below, immediately before the Joseph story.

11 And Shechem [Heb.; NRSV, Shechem also] said to her father and to her brothers, "Let me find favor with you, and whatever you say to me I will give. [12]Put the marriage present and gift as high as you like, and I will give whatever you ask me; only give me the girl to be my wife." [13]The sons of Jacob answered Shechem *and his father Hamor* deceitfully, because he had defiled their sister Dinah. [14]They said to them, "We cannot do this thing, to give our sister to one who is uncircumcised, for that would be a disgrace to us."

[15]*"Only on this condition will we consent to you: that you will become as we are and every male among you be circumcised. [16]Then we will give our daughters to you, and we will take your daughters for ourselves, and we will live among you and become one people. [17]But if you will not listen to us and be circumcised, then we will take our daughter and be gone."*

18 Their words pleased *Hamor and* Hamor's son Shechem. [19]And the young man did not delay to do the thing, because he was delighted with Jacob's daughter. Now he was the most honored of all his family.

[20]*So Hamor and his son Shechem came to the gate of their city and spoke to the men of their city, saying,* [21]*"These people are friendly with us; let them live in the land and trade in it, for the land is large enough for them; let us take their daughters in marriage, and let us give them our daughters. [22]Only on this condition will they agree to live among us, to become one people: that every male among us be circumcised as they are circumcised. [23]Will not their livestock, their prop-erty, and all their animals be ours? Only let us agree with them, and they will live among us."*

[24]And all who went out of the city gate heeded *Hamor and his son* Shechem; and every male was circumcised, all who went out of the gate of his city.

25 On the third day, when they were still in pain, two of the sons of Jacob, Simeon and Levi, Dinah's brothers, took their swords and came against the city unawares, and killed all the males. [26]They killed *Hamor and his son* Shechem with the sword, and took Dinah out of Shechem's house, and went away.

[27]*And the other sons of Jacob came upon the slain, and plundered the city, because their sister had been defiled. [28]They took their flocks and their herds, their donkeys, and whatever was in the city and in the field.*

[29]All their wealth, all their little ones and their wives, all that was in the houses, they captured and made their prey. [30]Then Jacob said to Simeon and Levi, "You have brought trouble on me by making me odious to the inhabitants of the land, the Canaanites and the Perizzites; my numbers are few, and if they gather themselves against me and attack me, I shall be destroyed, both I and my household." [31]But they said, "Should our sister be treated like a whore?"

35:21 Israel journeyed on, and pitched his tent beyond the tower of Eder.

22a While Israel lived in that land, Reuben went and lay with Bilhah his father's concubine; and Israel heard of it.[71]

• • •[72]

---

71. The narrative is not continued beyond this introduction, but the two components of v. 22a—sexual transgression against a woman of Jacob/Israel's household and his hearing about it—parallel the opening scenes of Genesis 34. This parallel suggests that the remainder of the story told of a confrontation between Israel and Reuben and Reuben's punishment. A clue to the nature of this punishment may be found in Gen 49:3-4, namely, the loss of Reuben's pre-eminence as firstborn. It is difficult to explain why the story is missing (cf. Westermann, *Genesis 12–36*, 556). Because v. 22a serves as a reminder of such a story, without actually telling it, its purpose may have been to indicate that this is an appropriate point to tell this story, if desired, in conjunction with similar stories. It follows the Dinah story and is followed shortly by the story of Judah and Tamar.

72. At this juncture it may help to outline briefly four factors that we believe need to be taken into account in any treatment of the transition in J from

Joseph

37:3a Now Israel loved Joseph more than any other of his children, because he was the son of his old age. **4**But when his brothers saw that their father loved him more than all his brothers, they hated him, and could not speak peaceably to him.

5a Once Joseph had a dream, and [Heb.; NRSV, and when] he told it to his brothers. **6**He said to them, "Listen to this dream that I dreamed. **7**There we were, binding sheaves in the field. Suddenly my sheaf rose and stood upright; then your sheaves gathered around it, and bowed down to my sheaf." **8**His brothers said to him, "Are you indeed to reign over us? Are you indeed to have dominion over us?" So they hated him even more because of his dreams and his words.

9 He had another dream, and told it to his brothers, saying, "Look, I have had another dream: the sun, the moon, and eleven stars were bowing down to me." **10**But when he told it to his father and to his brothers, his father rebuked him, and said to him, "What kind of dream is this that you have had? Shall we indeed come, I and your mother and your brothers, and bow to the ground before you?" **11**So his brothers were jealous of him, but his father kept the matter in mind.

12 Now his brothers went to pasture their father's flock near Shechem. **13**And Israel said to Joseph, "Are not your brothers pasturing the flock at Shechem? Come, I will send you to them." He answered, "Here I am." **14**So he said to him, "Go now, see if it is well with your brothers and with the flock; and bring word back to me." So he sent him from the valley of Hebron.

He came to Shechem, **15**and a man found him wandering in the fields; the man asked him, "What are you seeking?" **16**"I am seeking my brothers," he said; "tell me, please, where they are pasturing the flock." **17**The man said, "They have gone away, for I heard them say, 'Let us go to Dothan.' " So Joseph went after his brothers, and found them at Dothan. **18**They saw him from a distance, and before he came near to them, they conspired to kill him. **19**They said to one another, "Here comes this dreamer. **20**Come now, let us kill him and throw him into one of the pits; then we shall say that a wild animal has devoured him, and we shall see what will become of his dreams." **21**But when Judah [Noth's emendation; Heb. and NRSV, Reuben] heard it, he

---

the Jacob–Esau story to the story of Joseph and his brothers. There is, first of all, the question raised above, whether Genesis 34 belongs within the horizon of the J narrative. Second, the fragments of itinerary on either side of Genesis 34 are problematic (33:18b; 35:21). The city in 33:18b is identified, if v. 18aα is included as J; in Noth's J, it is unnamed. The location of the tower of Eder in 35:21 is unknown (cf. Westermann, *Genesis 12–36*, 555). Third, 37:14 sets the Joseph story in the "valley of Hebron." Noth retains this as part of J, assuming an explanation in the now lost Reuben and Bilhah story (cf. 35:21–22a; *Pentateuchal Traditions*, 30 n. 100); others hold that it is an addition (cf. Westermann, *Genesis 37–50* [Minneapolis: Augsburg, 1986] 39–40). If it is an addition, J's Joseph story may have been located in the Succoth-Shechem area (37:12ff.), which would make the jour-

ney by the young Joseph in 37:14-17 more plausible. Furthermore, it improves the sequence of the Jacob–Esau and Joseph stories in the J narrative. Fourth, there are the differences between P and J. P has Jacob return to Hebron for the burial of Isaac (35:27-29). Although this is not totally incompatible with J's picture of the aged and near-to-death Isaac in 27:1-2, it sits most uncomfortably with it. The natural conclusion is that here J and P followed quite different trajectories. For J, the theft of the aged Isaac's blessing and Esau's murderous hatred (27:1-45) provided the stimulus for Jacob's flight to Haran; he eventually returned and, after reconciliation with Esau, settled in the Succoth-Shechem area (33:17, 18b). For P, in contrast, Canaanite wives were the issue (27:46—28:5), and Jacob returned to Isaac at Mamre (35:27).

delivered him out of their hands, saying, "Let us not take his life."[73]

25 Then they sat down to eat; and looking up they saw a caravan of Ishmaelites coming from Gilead, with their camels carrying gum, balm, and resin, on their way to carry it down to Egypt. [26]Then Judah said to his brothers, "What profit is it if we kill our brother and conceal his blood? [27]Come, let us sell him to the Ishmaelites, and not lay our hands on him, for he is our brother, our own flesh." And his brothers agreed, [28*]and sold Joseph [Heb.; NRSV, him] to the Ishmaelites for twenty pieces of silver. And they took Joseph to Egypt.

Judah and Tamar

38 It happened at that time that Judah went down from his brothers and settled near a certain Adullamite whose name was Hirah.[74] [2]There Judah saw the daughter of a certain Canaanite whose name was Shua; he married her and went in to her. [3]She conceived and bore a son; and he named him Er. [4]Again she conceived and bore a son whom she named Onan. [5]Yet again she bore a son, and she named him Shelah. She was in Chezib when she bore him. [6]Judah took a wife for Er his firstborn; her name was Tamar. [7]But Er, Judah's firstborn, was wicked in the sight of the LORD, and the LORD put him to death.

[8]Then Judah said to Onan, "Go in to your brother's wife and perform the duty of a brother-in-law to her; raise up offspring for your brother." [9]But since Onan knew that the offspring would not be his, he spilled his semen on the ground whenever he went in to his brother's wife, so that he would not give offspring to his brother. [10]What he did was displeasing in the sight of the LORD, and he put him to death also. [11]Then Judah said to his daughter-in-law Tamar, "Remain a widow in your father's house until my son Shelah grows up"—for he feared that he too would die, like his brothers. So Tamar went to live in her father's house.

12 In course of time the wife of Judah, Shua's daughter, died; when Judah's time of mourning was over, he went up to Timnah to his sheepshearers, he and his friend Hirah the Adullamite. [13]When Tamar was told, "Your father-in-law is going up to Timnah to shear his sheep," [14]she put off her widow's garments, put on a veil, wrapped herself up, and sat down at the entrance to Enaim, which is on the road to Timnah. She saw that Shelah was grown up, yet she had not been given to him in marriage. [15]When Judah saw her, he thought her to be a prostitute, for she had covered her face. [16]He went over to her at the road side, and said, "Come, let me come in to you," for he did not know that she

---

73. Noth's emendation is based on the identification of a doublet in vv. 21-22 (see Gunkel, *Genesis*, 401) and on his overall perception of how J and E were combined in this section of the story. Verse 22 repeats the introduction to Reuben's speech in v. 21, while the phrase "deliver him out of their hand" occurs in both verses (in v. 22, NRSV translates the verb as "rescue"). According to Noth, therefore, the J version describes how Judah "delivered him out of their hand" (v. 21) by temporarily staying his brothers' murderous intention. He subsequently persuaded them to sell Joseph to Ishmaelites, who chanced by while they were eating. The E version describes how Reuben persuaded his brothers to cast Joseph into a pit, so that later "he might rescue [deliver] him out of their hand" (v. 22). However passing Midianite traders

drew Joseph out of the pit and sold him in Egypt (vv. 28aα, 36). Reuben's discovery of the empty pit induced the brothers to deceive their father (vv. 31-35). In the combination of J and E, where Reuben's proposal is narrated before Judah's, it became necessary to change the subject of the verb in v. 21 from Judah to Reuben (*Pentateuchal Traditions*, 30 n. 100).

74. The comment made above on the relevance of Genesis 34 to the horizon of a Yahwist narrative could also be applied to Genesis 38. Valuable observations have been made by Robert Alter (*The Art of Biblical Narrative* [New York: Basic Books, 1981] 3–12) on its aptness in its present place and its subtle reflection of significant concerns of the Joseph story. Nevertheless, whether this points to inclusion by the Yahwist or a later hand is a matter not easily resolved.

was his daughter-in-law. She said, "What will you give me, that you may come in to me?" [17]He answered, "I will send you a kid from the flock." And she said, "Only if you give me a pledge, until you send it." [18]He said, "What pledge shall I give you?" She replied, "Your signet and your cord, and the staff that is in your hand." So he gave them to her, and went in to her, and she conceived by him. [19]Then she got up and went away, and taking off her veil she put on the garments of her widowhood.

20 When Judah sent the kid by his friend the Adullamite, to recover the pledge from the woman, he could not find her. [21]He asked the townspeople, "Where is the temple prostitute who was at Enaim by the wayside?" But they said, "No prostitute has been here." [22]So he returned to Judah, and said, "I have not found her; moreover the townspeople said, 'No prostitute has been here.'" [23]Judah replied, "Let her keep the things as her own, otherwise we will be laughed at; you see, I sent this kid, and you could not find her."

24 About three months later Judah was told, "Your daughter-in-law Tamar has played the whore; moreover she is pregnant as a result of whoredom." And Judah said, "Bring her out, and let her be burned." [25]As she was being brought out, she sent word to her father-in-law, "It was the owner of these who made me pregnant." And she said, "Take note, please, whose these are, the signet and the cord and the staff." [26]Then Judah acknowledged them and said, "She is more in the right than I, since I did not give her to my son Shelah." And he did not lie with her again.

27 When the time of her delivery came, there were twins in her womb. [28]While she was in labor, one put out a hand; and the midwife took and bound on his hand a crimson thread, saying, "This one came out first." [29]But just then he drew back his hand, and out came his brother; and she said, "What a breach you have made for yourself!" Therefore he was named Perez. [30]Afterward his brother came out with the crimson thread on his hand; and he was named Zerah.

Joseph in Egypt

39 Now Joseph was taken down to Egypt, and Potiphar, an officer of Pharaoh, the captain of the guard, an Egyptian, bought him from the Ishmaelites who had brought him down there.[75] [2]The LORD was with Joseph, and he became a successful man; he was in the house of his Egyptian master. [3]His master saw that the LORD was with him, and that the LORD caused all that he did to prosper in his hands. [4]So Joseph found favor in his sight and attended him; he made him overseer of his house and put him in charge of all that he had. [5]From the time that he made him overseer in his house and over all that he had, the LORD blessed the Egyptian's house for Joseph's sake; the blessing of the LORD was on all that he had, in house and field. [6]So he left all that he had in Joseph's charge; and, with him there, he had no concern for anything but the food that he ate.

Now Joseph was handsome and good-looking. [7]And after a time his master's wife cast her eyes on Joseph and said, "Lie with me." [8]But he refused and said to his master's wife, "Look, with me here, my master has no concern about anything in the house, and he has put everything that he has in my hand. [9]He is not greater in this

---

75. In his introductory discussion, Noth observes that the words "Potiphar, a eunuch of the Pharaoh, the captain of the guard" have obviously been taken from the E account in Gen 37:36 (*Pentateuchal Traditions*, 26 n. 77). The original J version referred simply to an unnamed Egyptian, who remains unnamed throughout Genesis 39. He is described variously as "his Egyptian master" (v. 2), "his master" (vv. 3, 7, 8, 16, 19), and "Joseph's master" (v. 20).

house than I am, nor has he kept back anything from me except yourself, because you are his wife. How then could I do this great wickedness, and sin against God?" [10]And although she spoke to Joseph day after day, he would not consent to lie beside her or to be with her. [11]One day, however, when he went into the house to do his work, and while no one else was in the house, [12]she caught hold of his garment, saying, "Lie with me!" But he left his garment in her hand, and fled and ran outside. [13]When she saw that he had left his garment in her hand and had fled outside, [14]she called out to the members of her household and said to them, "See, my husband has brought among us a Hebrew to insult us! He came in to me to lie with me, and I cried out with a loud voice; [15]and when he heard me raise my voice and cry out, he left his garment beside me, and fled outside." [16]Then she kept his garment by her until his master came home, [17]and she told him the same story, saying, "The Hebrew servant, whom you have brought among us, came in to me to insult me; [18]but as soon as I raised my voice and cried out, he left his garment beside me, and fled outside."

[19] When his master heard the words that his wife spoke to him, saying, "This is the way your servant treated me," he became enraged. [20]And Joseph's master took him and put him into the prison, the place where the king's prisoners were confined; he remained there in prison. [21]But the LORD was with Joseph and showed him steadfast love; he gave him favor in the sight of the chief jailer. [22]The chief jailer committed to Joseph's care all the prisoners who were in the prison, and whatever was done there, he was the one who did it. [23]The chief jailer paid no heed to anything that was in Joseph's care, because the LORD was with him; and whatever he did, the LORD made it prosper.

Joseph's Rise to Power in Egypt

40:1 Some time after this, the cupbearer of the king of Egypt and his baker offended their lord the king of Egypt.

• • •[76]

41:34a "Let Pharaoh proceed to appoint overseers over the land, [35b]and lay up grain under the authority of Pharaoh for food in the cities, and let them keep it."

41 And Pharaoh said to Joseph, "See, I have set you over all the land of Egypt." [42]Removing his signet ring from his hand, Pharaoh put it on Joseph's hand; he arrayed him in garments of fine linen, and put a gold chain around his neck. [43]He had him ride in the chariot of his second-in-command; and they cried out in front of him, "Bow the knee!" Thus he set him over all the land of Egypt. [44]Moreover Pharaoh said to Joseph, "I am Pharaoh, and without your consent no one shall lift up hand or foot in all the land of Egypt." [45]Pharaoh gave Joseph the name

---

76. According to Noth, the J version of Joseph's rise to power has been omitted in favor of E's graphic and detailed story of Joseph as the successful interpreter of dreams. This story comprises almost all of Genesis 40–41, a factor that suggests J did not know this tradition.

Noth's identification of J and E material here is based on a consideration of story line and differences in terminology (emphasized in what follows). In J's story, Joseph is thrown into *prison* by his *master* (39:20), an unnamed Egyptian. The Lord gives him favor in the eyes of the *keeper of the prison*, and he is placed in charge of prisoners (39:21-23). The J version breaks off with the report of an unspecified offense by the the *king of Egypt's butler* and *baker* (40:1). Presumably Joseph was put in charge of them and, in an account of which we have only fragments, rose to power (41:34a, 35b, 41-45a). In E's version, Joseph is a slave in the house of *Potiphar, the captain of the guard* (37:36). *Pharaoh* becomes angry with two of his *officers*, the *chief butler* and *chief baker*, and places them in *custody* (40:2-3aα). Joseph is assigned to wait on them (40:4). Then follows the story of the dreams and Joseph's rise to power in Egypt (*Pentateuchal Traditions*, 26 n. 77).

Zaphenath-paneah; and he gave him Asenath daughter of Potiphera, priest of On, as his wife. *Thus Joseph gained authority over the land of Egypt.*[77]

Onset of the Famine

46b And Joseph went out from the presence of Pharaoh, and went through all the land of Egypt. [49]So Joseph stored up grain in such abundance—like the sand of the sea—that he stopped measuring it; it was beyond measure.

55 When all the land of Egypt was famished, the people cried to Pharaoh for bread. Pharaoh said to all the Egyptians, "Go to Joseph; what he says to you, do."

[56]*And since the famine had spread over all the land*[78]
And [Heb; NRSV has no conjunction] Joseph opened all the storehouses, and sold to the Egyptians.

for the famine was severe in the land of Egypt.

[57]Moreover, all the world came to Joseph in Egypt to buy grain, because the famine became severe throughout the world.

Famine Affects Joseph's Family

42:1b And Jacob [Heb.; NRSV, he] said to his sons, "Why do you keep looking at one another?"[79]

• • •

Brothers' First Journey to Egypt

4 But Jacob did not send Joseph's brother Benjamin with his brothers, for he feared that harm might come to him.[80] [5]Thus the sons of Israel were among the other people who came to buy grain, for the famine had reached the land of Canaan.

• • •[81]

7* "Where do you come from?" he said. They said, "From the land of Canaan, to buy food." [8]Although Joseph had recognized his brothers,

---

77. Literally, "And Joseph went out over the land of Egypt." This statement recurs—in similar though slightly expanded form—in the next verse (Gen 41:46b). In Noth's view, v. 45b is an addition to J; it is missing from the Greek text. In the present text, v. 45b concludes the story of Joseph's rise to power, and the story of how he exercised that power begins with his age (v. 46a, P) and his administration (v. 46b, J).

78. Verses 56a and 56bβ are regarded by Noth as later embellishments of J, which intrude somewhat into the smooth narrative sequence. C. Westermann proposes bracketing v. 54b as a later insertion and transferring v. 56a to the end of v. 56 (*Genesis 37–50*, 98). Viewed as an example of narrative art, the triple reference to the famine in vv. 56-57, building on the initial "famished" in v. 55, may be seen as a technique to heighten the sense of the famine's impact and inescapability.

79. Genesis 42:1b forms a new introduction after v. 1a (E) and repeats the name "Jacob" (missing in the Greek). Noth understands v. 1b as evidence of a J sequence that has been omitted here in favor of E—hence the following ellipses. His perception that J favored the name "Israel" also leads him to suggest that "Jacob" may have replaced "Israel" in v. 1b, under

the influence of v. 1a (E). The name "Jacob" may also not have been present originally in v. 4 (*Pentateuchal Traditions*, 30 n. 101). However, the natural continuation of v. 1a is Jacob's request in v. 2 (E) rather than his question in v. 1b. Westermann identifies v. 1b as a fragment that would be more in place after v. 2 than before it (cf. Westermann, *Genesis 37–50*, 104–5).

80. Noth may well have given Gen 42:4 to J because of the concern over Benjamin, Joseph's brother. This concern is a prominent feature of the J narrative in Genesis 43–44; cf. esp. 43:3-10 and 44:27-28.

81. Noth's source analysis of Genesis 42 identifies a considerable number of gaps in J by comparison with the preceding chapters. The surviving J material is also quite fragmentary. Noth's identification of the text shows that, in his view, the situation in this chapter is different from Genesis 40–41 where the text is almost entirely from E. He concludes there was no parallel J version portraying Joseph as the successful interpreter of dreams (*Pentateuchal Traditions*, 27). In relation to Genesis 42, however, one must reckon with a J and E version of the brothers' encounter with Joseph in Egypt, his demand to see Benjamin, the brothers' return journey, and the discovery of money in their sacks. The evidence for this source division is

they did not recognize him. [9a]Joseph also remembered the dreams that he had dreamed about them.

• • •[82]

[9]* "You have come to see the nakedness of the land!" [10]They said to him, "No, my lord; your servants have come to buy food. [11a]We are all sons of one man." [12]But he said to them, "No, you have come to see the nakedness of the land!"

• • •

[27] When one of them opened his sack to give his donkey fodder at the lodging place, he saw his money at the top of the sack. [28a]He said to his brothers, "My money has been put back; here it is in my sack!"

• • •

[38] But he said, "My son shall not go down with you, for his brother is dead, and he alone is left. If harm should come to him on the journey that you are to make, you would bring down my gray hairs with sorrow to Sheol."

Brothers' Second Journey to Egypt

[43] Now the famine was severe in the land. [2]And when they had eaten up the grain that they had brought from Egypt, their father said to them, "Go again, buy us a little more food." [3]But Judah said to him, "The man solemnly warned us, saying, 'You shall not see my face unless your brother is with you.' [4]If you will send our brother with us, we will go down and buy you food; [5]but if you will not send him, we will not go down, for the man said to us, 'You shall

---

complex and debated, and attention is drawn here only to the main points.

Noth's distribution of the text between J and E points to a number of doublets in the initial encounter between Joseph and his brothers in the present text of 42:6-13. There are two reports of the brothers' arrival in Egypt (v. 5 and v. 6b), two reports of Joseph recognizing his brothers (v. 7a and v. 8a), two accusations against the brothers (of being spies and of coming to see the nakedness of the land), and two references by the brothers to being sons of the one man (v. 11a and v. 13a). In Noth's view, the E version of this encounter supplied the base, being enriched by elements from the parallel J version.

The background to Noth's postulating a parallel J version, both of Joseph's demand to see Benjamin and of the brothers' return journey, is probably provided by J. Wellhausen's reconstruction, based on J's report of events in Gen 43:3-7, 20-21, and 44:20-23. The E version of these events, 42:13-26, 29-37, was again used as the base in the present text, with most of J being left aside. For convenience's sake, it is worth reproducing Wellhausen's analysis with his reconstructed text in quotation marks; it is taken from *Die Composition des Hexateuchs und der Historischen Bücher des Alten Testaments*, 3d ed. (1899; reprint, Berlin: Walter de Gruyter, 1963) 56–57.

The brothers come before Joseph and buy grain, saying that they are from Canaan. "And Joseph asked them: Is your father still alive?

Have you another brother? And they said to him: We have a father, an old man, and a young brother, the child of his old age; and his brother is dead, and he alone is left of his mother's children; and his father loves him. And Joseph spoke: Bring him down to me, that I may set my eyes upon him. They said: No, sir. The lad cannot leave his father, for if he should leave his father, his father would die. But he gave them the solemn warning: Unless your youngest brother comes down with you, you shall see my face no more." (Cf. Gen 43:7; 44:20-23; 43:3.)

Then Joseph sent the brothers off together, including Simeon, with the grain, after he had had their money put back in the sacks. On the way home, they stayed overnight in a lodging place. "And as one of them opened his sack to give his donkey provender, he saw his money in the mouth of his sack; and he said to his brothers: My money has been put back; here it is in the mouth of my sack. Then the others opened their sacks and each saw his money lying in his sack, all their money in full weight. And they looked at each other frightened and said: What is this that God has done to us?" (Cf. 43:21-22; 42:27-28.)

82. The gap here is simply the omission of "He said to them, 'You are spies' "—see at Gen 42:9* in the Elohist, chap. 4, below.

not see my face, unless your brother is with you.' " [6]Israel said, "Why did you treat me so badly as to tell the man that you had another brother?" [7]They replied, "The man questioned us carefully about ourselves and our kindred, saying, 'Is your father still alive? Have you another brother?' What we told him was in answer to these questions. Could we in any way know that he would say, 'Bring your brother down'?" [8]Then Judah said to his father Israel, "Send the boy with me, and let us be on our way, so that we may live and not die—you and we and also our little ones. [9]I myself will be surety for him; you can hold me accountable for him. If I do not bring him back to you and set him before you, then let me bear the blame forever. [10]If we had not delayed, we would now have returned twice."

11 Then their father Israel said to them, "If it must be so, then do this: take some of the choice fruits of the land in your bags, and carry them down as a present to the man—a little balm and a little honey, gum, resin, pistachio nuts, and almonds. [12]Take double the money with you. Carry back with you the money that was returned in the top of your sacks; perhaps it was an oversight. [13]Take your brother also, and be on your way again to the man; [14]*may God Almighty grant you mercy before the man. As for me, if I am bereaved of my children, I am bereaved."[83] [15]So the men took the present, and they took double the money with them, as well as Benjamin. Then they went on their way down to Egypt, and stood before Joseph.

16 When Joseph saw Benjamin with them, he said to the steward of his house, "Bring the men into the house, and slaughter an animal and make ready, for the men are to dine with me at noon." [17]The man did as Joseph said, and brought the men to Joseph's house. [18]Now the men were afraid because they were brought to Joseph's house, and they said, "It is because of the money, replaced in our sacks the first time, that we have been brought in, so that he may have an opportunity to fall upon us, to make slaves of us and take our donkeys." [19]So they went up to the steward of Joseph's house and spoke with him at the entrance to the house. [20]They said, "Oh, my lord, we came down the first time to buy food; [21]and when we came to the lodging place we opened our sacks, and there was each one's money in the top of his sack, our money in full weight. So we have brought it back with us. [22]Moreover we have brought down with us additional money to buy food. We do not know who put our money in our sacks." [23a]He replied, "Rest assured, do not be afraid; your God and the God of your father must have put treasure in your sacks for you; I received your money." [24]When the steward had brought the men into Joseph's house, and given them water, and they had washed their feet, and when he had given their donkeys fodder, [25]they made the present ready for Joseph's coming at noon, for they had heard that they would dine there.

26 When Joseph came home, they brought him the present that they had carried into the house, and bowed to the ground before him. [27]He inquired about their welfare, and said, "Is your father well, the old man of whom you spoke? Is he still alive?" [28]They said, "Your servant our father is well; he is still alive." And they bowed their heads and did obeisance. [29]Then he looked up and saw his brother Benjamin, his mother's son, and said, "Is this your youngest brother, of whom you spoke to me? God be gracious to you, my son!" [30]With that, Joseph hurried out, because he was overcome with affection for his brother, and he was about to weep. So he went into a private room and wept

---

83. Genesis 43:14aβ and 43:23b, omitted here, are held by Noth to be redactional additions, linking the E episode of the imprisonment of Simeon to the J text (*Pentateuchal Traditions*, 30 n. 102).

there. [31]Then he washed his face and came out; and controlling himself he said, "Serve the meal." [32]They served him by himself, and them by themselves, and the Egyptians who ate with him by themselves, because the Egyptians could not eat with the Hebrews, for that is an abomination to the Egyptians. [33]When they were seated before him, the firstborn according to his birthright and the youngest according to his youth, the men looked at one another in amazement. [34]Portions were taken to them from Joseph's table, but Benjamin's portion was five times as much as any of theirs. So they drank and were merry with him.

Crisis over Benjamin

44 Then he commanded the steward of his house, "Fill the men's sacks with food, as much as they can carry.
and put each man's money in the top of his sack.
[2]Put my cup, the silver cup, in the top of the sack of the youngest."
with his money for the grain.[84]
And he did as Joseph told him. [3]As soon as the morning was light, the men were sent away with their donkeys. [4]When they had gone only a short distance from the city, Joseph said to his steward, "Go, follow after the men; and when you overtake them, say to them, 'Why have you returned evil for good? Why have you stolen my silver cup? [5]Is it not from this that my lord drinks? Does he not indeed use it for divination? You have done wrong in doing this.' "

[6] When he overtook them, he repeated these words to them. [7]They said to him, "Why does my lord speak such words as these? Far be it from your servants that they should do such a thing! [8]Look, the money that we found at the top of our sacks, we brought back to you from the land of Canaan; why then would we steal silver or gold from your lord's house? [9]Should it be found with any one of your servants, let him die; moreover the rest of us will become my lord's slaves." [10]He said, "Even so; in accordance with your words, let it be: he with whom it is found shall become my slave, but the rest of you shall go free." [11]Then each one quickly lowered his sack to the ground, and each opened his sack. [12]He searched, beginning with the eldest and ending with the youngest; and the cup was found in Benjamin's sack. [13]At this they tore their clothes. Then each one loaded his donkey, and they returned to the city.

[14] Judah and his brothers came to Joseph's house while he was still there; and they fell to the ground before him. [15]Joseph said to them, "What deed is this that you have done? Do you not know that one such as I can practice divination?" [16]And Judah said, "What can we say to my lord? What can we speak? How can we clear ourselves? God has found out the guilt of your servants; here we are then, my lord's slaves, both we and also the one in whose possession the cup has been found." [17]But he said, "Far be it from me that I should do so! Only the one in whose possession the cup was found shall be my slave; but as for you, go up in peace to your father."

[18] Then Judah stepped up to him and said, "O my lord, let your servant please speak a word in my lord's ears, and do not be angry with your servant; for you are like Pharaoh himself. [19]My lord asked his servants, saying, 'Have you a father or a brother?' [20]And we said to my lord, 'We have a father, an old man, and a young brother, the child of his old age. His brother is dead; he alone is left of his mother's children, and his father loves him.' [21]Then you said to your servants, 'Bring him down to me, so that I

---

84. The money described in 44:1b and 2aβ is not mentioned when the steward confronts the brothers in 44:6-12. Noth concludes therefore that vv. 1b and 2aβ were added to J to create a link with Joseph's earlier ruse, in which money was placed in the brothers' sacks (cf. 42:27-28a; 43:20-22).

may set my eyes on him.' [22]We said to my lord, 'The boy cannot leave his father, for if he should leave his father, his father would die.' [23]Then you said to your servants, 'Unless your youngest brother comes down with you, you shall see my face no more.' [24]When we went back to your servant my father we told him the words of my lord. [25]And when our father said, 'Go again, buy us a little food,' [26]we said, 'We cannot go down. Only if our youngest brother goes with us, will we go down; for we cannot see the man's face unless our youngest brother is with us.' [27]Then your servant my father said to us, 'You know that my wife bore me two sons; [28]one left me, and I said, Surely he has been torn to pieces; and I have never seen him since. [29]If you take this one also from me, and harm comes to him, you will bring down my gray hairs in sorrow to Sheol.' [30]Now therefore, when I come to your servant my father and the boy is not with us, then, as his life is bound up in the boy's life, [31]when he sees that the boy is not with us, he will die; and your servants will bring down the gray hairs of your servant our father with sorrow to Sheol. [32]For your servant became surety for the boy to my father, saying, 'If I do not bring him back to you, then I will bear the blame in the sight of my father all my life.' [33]Now therefore, please let your servant remain as a slave to my lord in place of the boy; and let the boy go back with his brothers. [34]For how can I go back to my father if the boy is not with me? I fear to see the suffering that would come upon my father."

Joseph Reveals Himself to His Brothers

45 Then Joseph could no longer control himself before all those who stood by him, and he cried out, "Send everyone away from me." So no one stayed with him when Joseph made himself known to his brothers.

4 Then Joseph said to his brothers, "Come closer to me." And they came closer. He said, "I am your brother, Joseph, whom you sold into Egypt. [5a]And now do not be distressed, or angry with yourselves, because you sold me here."

16 When the report was heard in Pharaoh's house, "Joseph's brothers have come," Pharaoh and his servants were pleased. [17]Pharaoh said to Joseph, "Say to your brothers, 'Do this: load your animals and go back to the land of Canaan. [18]Take your father and your households and come to me, so that I may give you the best of the land of Egypt, and you may enjoy the fat of the land.' [19]You are further charged to say, 'Do this: take wagons from the land of Egypt for your little ones and for your wives, and bring your father, and come. [20]Give no thought to your possessions, for the best of all the land of Egypt is yours.' "

21 The sons of Israel did so. Joseph gave them wagons according to the instruction of Pharaoh, and he gave them provisions for the journey. [22]To each one of them he gave a set of garments; but to Benjamin he gave three hundred pieces of silver and five sets of garments. [23]To his father he sent the following: ten donkeys loaded with the good things of Egypt, and ten female donkeys loaded with grain, bread, and provision for his father on the journey. [24]Then he sent his brothers on their way, and as they were leaving he said to them, "Do not quarrel along the way."

25 So they went up out of Egypt and came to their father Jacob in the land of Canaan. [26]And they told him, "Joseph is still alive! He is even ruler over all the land of Egypt." He was stunned; he could not believe them. [27]But when they told him all the words of Joseph that he had said to them, and when he saw the wagons that Joseph had sent to carry him, the spirit of their father Jacob revived. [28]Israel said, "Enough! My son Joseph is still alive. I must go and see him before I die."

Joseph Is Reunited with His Father

46:1* And [Heb.; NRSV, When] Israel set out on his journey with all that he had. 5bAnd the sons of Israel carried their father Jacob, their little ones, and their wives, in the wagons that Pharaoh had sent to carry him.

28 Israel sent Judah ahead to Joseph to lead the way before him into Goshen. When they came to the land of Goshen, 29Joseph made ready his chariot and went up to meet his father Israel in Goshen. He presented himself to him, fell on his neck, and wept on his neck a good while. 30Israel said to Joseph, "I can die now, having seen for myself that you are still alive." 31Joseph said to his brothers and to his father's household, "I will go up and tell Pharaoh, and will say to him, 'My brothers and my father's household, who were in the land of Canaan, have come to me. 32The men are shepherds, for they have been keepers of livestock; and they have brought their flocks, and their herds, and all that they have.' 33When Pharaoh calls you, and says, 'What is your occupation?' 34you shall say, 'Your servants have been keepers of livestock from our youth even until now, both we and our ancestors'—in order that you may settle in the land of Goshen, because all shepherds are abhorrent to the Egyptians."

Joseph's Family Is Given Land in Egypt

47 So Joseph went and told Pharaoh, "My father and my brothers, with their flocks and herds and all that they possess, have come from the land of Canaan; they are now in the land of Goshen." 2From among his brothers he took five men and presented them to Pharaoh. 3Pharaoh said to his brothers, "What is your occupation?" And they said to Pharaoh, "Your servants are shepherds, as our ancestors were." 4They said to Pharaoh, "We have come to reside as aliens in the land; for there is no pasture for your ser-

vants' flocks because the famine is severe in the land of Canaan. Now, we ask you, let your servants settle in the land of Goshen." 5aThen Pharaoh said to Joseph, 6b"Let them live in the land of Goshen; and if you know that there are capable men among them, put them in charge of my livestock."

The Egyptians Sell Their Land

13 Now there was no food in all the land, for the famine was very severe. The land of Egypt and the land of Canaan languished because of the famine. 14Joseph collected all the money to be found in the land of Egypt and in the land of Canaan, in exchange for the grain that they bought; and Joseph brought the money into Pharaoh's house. 15When the money from the land of Egypt and from the land of Canaan was spent, all the Egyptians came to Joseph, and said, "Give us food! Why should we die before your eyes? For our money is gone." 16And Joseph answered, "Give me your livestock, and I will give you food in exchange for your livestock, if your money is gone." 17So they brought their livestock to Joseph; and Joseph gave them food in exchange for the horses, the flocks, the herds, and the donkeys. That year he supplied them with food in exchange for all their livestock. 18When that year was ended, they came to him the following year, and said to him, "We can not hide from my lord that our money is all spent; and the herds of cattle are my lord's. There is nothing left in the sight of my lord but our bodies and our lands. 19Shall we die before your eyes, both we and our land? Buy us and our land in exchange for food. We with our land will become slaves to Pharaoh; just give us seed, so that we may live and not die, and that the land may not become desolate."

20 So Joseph bought all the land of Egypt for Pharaoh. All the Egyptians sold their fields, because the famine was severe upon them; and

the land became Pharaoh's. [21]As for the people, he made slaves of them from one end of Egypt to the other. [22]Only the land of the priests he did not buy; for the priests had a fixed allowance from Pharaoh, and lived on the allowance that Pharaoh gave them; therefore they did not sell their land. [23]Then Joseph said to the people, "Now that I have this day bought you and your land for Pharaoh, here is seed for you; sow the land. [24]And at the harvests you shall give one-fifth to Pharaoh, and four-fifths shall be your own, as seed for the field and as food for yourselves and your households, and as food for your little ones." [25]They said, "You have saved our lives; may it please my lord, we will be slaves to Pharaoh." [26]So Joseph made it a statute concerning the land of Egypt, and it stands to this day, that Pharaoh should have the fifth. The land of the priests alone did not become Pharaoh's.[85]

Death of Jacob/Israel

29 When the time of Israel's death drew near, he called his son Joseph and said to him, "If I have found favor with you, put your hand under my thigh and promise to deal loyally and truly with me. Do not bury me in Egypt. [30]When I lie down with my ancestors, carry me out of Egypt and bury me in their burial place." He answered, "I will do as you have said." [31]And he said,

"Swear to me"; and he swore to him. Then Israel bowed himself on the head of his bed.
• • •[86]

50 Then Joseph threw himself on his father's face and wept over him and kissed him. [2]Joseph commanded the physicians in his service to embalm his father. So the physicians embalmed Israel; [3]they spent forty days in doing this, for that is the time required for embalming. And the Egyptians wept for him seventy days.

4 When the days of weeping for him were past, Joseph addressed the household of Pharaoh, "If now I have found favor with you, please speak to Pharaoh as follows: [5]My father made me swear an oath; he said, 'I am about to die. In the tomb that I hewed out for myself in the land of Canaan, there you shall bury me.' Now therefore let me go up, so that I may bury my father; then I will return." [6]Pharaoh answered, "Go up, and bury your father, as he made you swear to do."

7 So Joseph went up to bury his father. With him went up all the servants of Pharaoh, the elders of his household, and all the elders of the land of Egypt, [8]as well as all the household of Joseph, his brothers, and his father's household. Only their children, their flocks, and their herds were left in the land of Goshen. [9]Both chariots and charioteers went up with him. It was a very great company. [10a]When they came to the

---

85. On these verses, see Westermann, *Genesis 37–50*, 173–77.

86. Following the dying patriarch's acknowledgment of Joseph's oath (cf. 1 Kings 1:47), the J narrative needs a report of his death before the scene in Gen 50:1-3.

In the present text, 47:29-31 is followed by Genesis 48, in which Joseph is informed that his father is ill. Joseph brings his two sons to Jacob, who blesses them and then announces to Joseph that he is about to die (v. 21). This material Noth attributes to E. In Gen 49:1-28, Jacob summons all his sons to receive his

final blessing; Noth does not attempt to attach the blessing (49:1b-28) to a source. Jacob's death is finally recorded in a section identified as P (49:29-33).

It may be presumed that, in line with Noth's principles, the deathbed scene from E has been included because of its account of the blessing of Joseph's sons, Manasseh and Ephraim (48:1-2, 7-14, 17-22). Finally the report of Jacob's death is given in the P version, favored because of Jacob's instructions for his burial alongside Abraham and Sarah, Isaac, Rebekah and Leah, in the field at Machpelah (49:1a, 29-33).

threshing floor of Atad, which is beyond the Jordan, they held there a very great and sorrowful lamentation.

• • •[87]

14 And [Heb.; NRSV reverses the order of this sentence] Joseph returned to Egypt with his brothers and all who had gone up with him to bury his father.

after he had buried his father.[88]

The Book of Exodus

ISRAEL IN EGYPT

Oppression of Israel

1:8 Now a new king arose over Egypt, who did not know Joseph.[89] [9]He said to his people, "Look, the Israelite people are more numerous and more powerful than we. [10]Come, let us deal shrewdly with them, or they will increase and, in the event of war, join our enemies and fight against us and escape from the land." [11]Therefore they set taskmasters over them to oppress them with forced labor. They built supply cities, Pithom and Rameses, for Pharaoh. [12]But the more they were oppressed, the more they multiplied and spread, so that they [Heb.; NRSV, the Egyptians] came to dread the Israelites.

[22]Then Pharaoh commanded all his people, "Every boy that is born to the Hebrews you shall throw into the Nile, but you shall let every girl live."

Birth of Moses

2 Now a man from the house of Levi went and married a Levite woman. [2]The woman conceived and bore a son; and when she saw that he was a fine baby, she hid him three months. [3]When she could hide him no longer she got a papyrus basket for him, and plastered it with bitumen and pitch; she put the child in it and placed it among the reeds on the bank of the river.

---

87. J's account of the burial of Jacob has been replaced by P, to bring it into line with P's version of his instructions in Gen 49:29-32.

88. The NRSV has reversed the order of the Hebrew here, locating v. 14b before v. 14a. Noth evidently regards v. 14b as an addition to J because of the way it repeats the report in v. 14a that Joseph buried his father. It is missing in the Greek text.

The analysis here represents Noth's position in *A History of Pentateuchal Traditions*. In the books of Exodus and Numbers we have the benefit of Noth's later commentaries, where not infrequently his earlier views are modified. This may reflect the balance of eagerness and caution in the younger and older scholar respectively, but it is a question of fine tuning within his overall source hypothesis rather than a matter that affects its essentials.

89. In Noth's J, the immediately preceding verse is Gen 50:14. There is continuity in the story line with the reference to Joseph and a new king, that is, the king who succeeded the one under whom Joseph served. But the verisimilitude of the narrative is strained by the impression that Israel grew from a family to a mighty nation within the course of these two reigns (Exod 1:9).

"King" is used in Exod 1:8 (and also in 2:23*), whereas vv. 11 and 22 have "Pharaoh." In Genesis 40–41 of the Joseph story, these terms alternate within J; elsewhere in J, "Pharaoh" predominates. Exodus 1:8 is needed to identify the subject of v. 9 as the king of Egypt and the subject of v. 11 as the Egyptians.

The J text has no report of Joseph's death; it has been replaced by Gen 50:26 (E) and Exod 1:6 (P).

*⁴His sister stood at a distance, to see what would happen to him.*⁹⁰

5 The daughter of Pharaoh came down to bathe at the river, while her attendants walked beside the river. She saw the basket among the reeds and sent her maid to bring it. ⁶When she opened it, she saw the child. He was crying, and she took pity on him, "This must be one of the Hebrews' children," she said.

⁷Then his sister said to Pharaoh's daughter, "Shall I go and get you a nurse from the Hebrew women to nurse the child for you?" ⁸Pharaoh's daughter said to her, "Yes." So the girl went and called the child's mother. ⁹Pharaoh's daughter said to her, "Take this child and nurse it for me, and I will give you your wages." So the woman took the child and nursed it. ¹⁰When the child grew up, she brought him to Pharaoh's daughter.

And she took him as her son. She named him Moses, "because," she said, "I drew him out of the water."

11 One day, after Moses had grown up, he went out to his people and saw their forced labor. He saw an Egyptian beating a Hebrew, one of his kinsfolk. ¹²He looked this way and that, and seeing no one he killed the Egyptian and hid him in the sand. ¹³When he went out the next day, he saw two Hebrews fighting; and he said to the one who was in the wrong, "Why do you strike your fellow Hebrew?" ¹⁴He answered, "Who made you a ruler and judge over us? Do you mean to kill me as you killed the Egyptian?" Then Moses was afraid and thought, "Surely the thing is known."

*¹⁵When Pharaoh heard of it, he sought to kill Moses.*⁹¹

And [Heb.; NRSV, But] Moses fled from Pharaoh. He settled in the land of Midian, and sat down by a well. ¹⁶The priest of Midian had seven daughters. They came to draw water, and filled the troughs to water their father's flock. ¹⁷But some shepherds came and drove them away. Moses got up and came to their defense and watered their flock. ¹⁸When they returned to their father Reuel, he said, "How is it that you have come back so soon today?" ¹⁹They said, "An Egyptian helped us against the shepherds; he even drew water for us and watered the flock." ²⁰He said to his daughters, "Where is he? Why did you leave the man? Invite him to break bread." ²¹Moses agreed to stay with the man, and he gave Moses his daughter Zipporah in marriage. ²²She bore a son, and he named him Gershom; for he said, "I have been an alien residing in a foreign land."

23* After a long time the king of Egypt died.

Call of Moses

*3 Moses was keeping the flock of his father-in-law Jethro, the priest of Midian; he led his flock beyond the wilderness, and came to Horeb, the mountain of God.*⁹² *²There the angel of the LORD*

---

90. Exodus 2:4 and 2:7-10aα, in which Moses' sister is obviously the older sibling, are in some tension with vv. 1-2 where Moses is the firstborn (cf. Noth, *Exodus* [OTL; Philadelphia: Westminster, 1962] 25). The naming of Moses in v. 10 occurs after the report of his growing up; this reverses the customary sequence in Hebrew narrative. There are also two references to Moses growing up (v. 10aα, and v. 11, with the identical verb in Hebrew). These additions may indicate a variant way of telling the story, showing Moses was raised as an Israelite before becoming a member of Pharaoh's household.

91. According to Noth, 2:15a looks to be a variant of 2:13-14 and is probably a secondary addition (*Exodus*, 36). A literary reading might disagree (cf. 4:19); the inclusion or omission of the verse does not alter the shape of J here.

92. In *A History of Pentateuchal Traditions*, Noth argues on two grounds that Exod. 3:1—4:19* is an addition in J: on the literary-critical basis that 2:23aα and 4:19-20a originally belonged together (30 n. 103); on traditio-historical grounds that 3:1—4:19 is secondary in its context (202-4). That is, the originally independent themes of the meeting with the Midian-

appeared to him in a flame of fire out of a bush; he looked, and the bush was blazing, yet it was not consumed. *3*Then Moses said, "I must turn aside and look at this great sight, and see why the bush is not burned up." *4a*And [Heb.; NRSV, When] the LORD saw that he had turned aside to see, *5*and [Heb.; NRSV, then] he said, "Come no closer! Remove the sandals from your feet, for the place on which you are standing is holy ground."

7 Then the LORD said, "I have observed the misery of my people who are in Egypt; I have heard their cry on account of their taskmasters. Indeed, I know their sufferings, *8*and I have come down to deliver them from the Egyptians, and to bring them up out of that land to a good and broad land.

to [Heb.; NRSV lacks "to"] a land flowing with milk and honey, to the country of the Canaanites, the Hittites, the Amorites, the Perizzites, the Hivites, and the Jebusites.*93*

16 Go and assemble the elders of Israel, and say to them, 'The LORD, the God of your ancestors, the God of Abraham, of Isaac, and of Jacob, has appeared to me, saying: I have given heed to you and to what has been done to you in Egypt. *17*I declare that I will bring you up out of the misery of Egypt.' "

to the land of the Canaanites, the Hittites, the Amorites, the Perizzites, the Hivites, and the Jebusites, a land flowing with milk and honey.'

*18*They will listen to your voice; and you and the elders of Israel shall go to the king of Egypt and say to him, 'The LORD, the God of the Hebrews, has met with us; let us now go a three days' journey into the wilderness, so that we may sacrifice to the LORD our God.' *19*I know, however, that the king of Egypt will not let you go unless compelled by a mighty hand. *20*So I will stretch out my hand and strike Egypt with all my wonders that I will perform in it; after that he will let you go. *21*I will bring this people into such favor with the Egyptians that, when you go, you will not go empty-handed; *22*each woman shall ask her neighbor and any woman living in the neighbor's house for jewelry of silver and of gold, and clothing, and you shall put them on your sons and on your daughters; and so you shall plunder the Egyptians."*94*

4 Then Moses answered, "But suppose they do not believe me or listen to me, but say, 'The LORD did not appear to you.' " *2*The LORD said to him, "What is that in your hand?" He said, "A staff." *3*And he said, "Throw it on the ground." So he threw the staff on the ground, and it became a snake; and Moses drew back from it. *4*Then the LORD said to Moses, "Reach out your hand, and seize it by the tail," so he reached out his hand and grasped it, and it became a staff in his hand. *5*"so that they may believe that the LORD, the

---

ites at the mountain of God, the guidance in the wilderness, and the revelation at Sinai are brought together and foreshadowed here.

In his later commentary, however, he accepts 3:1—4:19* as an integral part of J (*Exodus*, 33–34). For a discussion of these issues, see Childs, *Exodus* (OTL; London: SCM, 1974) 51–53.

93. The description of the land here is regarded by Noth in *Pentateuchal Traditions* as a later embellishment of the basic reference to "a good and broad land" (see also idem, *Exodus*, 41). In Exod 3:17, the same description is given in reverse order. The phrase "a land flowing with milk and honey" and the list of

nations occur in close association elsewhere in Exod 13:5; 33:2-3; Num 13:27-29.

94. The two major themes in Exod 3:17*-22—of the planned delegation to Pharaoh, with the opportunity it will provide for God to work wonders, and the despoliation of the Egyptians—are not addressed in 4:1, which refers directly back to 3:16-17aα. Furthermore, in 4:1 Moses contradicts the divine assertion that the elders will listen to him. Noth himself observes that 3:18-22 anticipates the plagues and their outcome, thus giving the divine proclamation a predictive element that it originally did not have (*Exodus*, 41).

God of their ancestors, the God of Abraham, the God of Isaac, and the God of Jacob, has appeared to you."[95]

6 *Again, the* LORD *said to him, "Put your hand inside your cloak." He put his hand into his cloak; and when he took it out, his hand was leprous, as white as snow.* [7]*Then he [Heb;* NRSV, *God] said, "Put your hand back into your cloak," so he put his hand back into his cloak, and when he took it out, it was restored like the rest of his body.*

[8]*"If they will not believe you or heed the first sign, they may believe the second sign.* [9]*If they will not believe even these two signs or heed you, you shall take some water from the Nile and pour it on the dry ground; and the water that you shall take from the Nile will become blood on the dry ground."*

10 *But Moses said to the* LORD, *"O my Lord, I have never been eloquent, neither in the past nor even now that you have spoken to your servant; but I am slow of speech and slow of tongue."* [11]*Then the* LORD *said to him, "Who gives speech to mortals? Who makes them mute or deaf, seeing or blind? Is it not I, the* LORD? [12]*Now go, and I will be with your mouth and teach you what you are to speak."*

[13]*But he said , "O my Lord, please send someone else."* [14]*Then the anger of the* LORD *was kindled against Moses and he said, "What of your brother Aaron, the Levite? I know that*

he can speak fluently; even now he is coming out to meet you, and when he sees you his heart will be glad. [15]*You shall speak to him and put the words in his mouth; and I will be with your mouth and with his mouth, and will teach you what you shall do.* [16]*He indeed shall speak for you to the people; he shall serve as a mouth for you, and you shall serve as God for him."*[96]

19 The LORD said to Moses in Midian, "Go back to Egypt; for all those who were seeking your life are dead." [20a]So Moses took his wife and his sons, put them on a donkey and went back to the land of Egypt.[97]

21 *And the* LORD *said to Moses, "When you go back to Egypt, see that you perform before Pharaoh all the wonders that I have put in your power; but I will harden his heart, so that he will not let the people go.* [22]*Then you shall say to Pharaoh, 'Thus says the* LORD: *Israel is my firstborn son.* [23]*I said to you, "Let my son go that he may worship me." But you refused to let him go; now I will kill your firstborn son.' "*[98]

24 On the way, at a place where they spent the night, the LORD met him and tried to kill him. [25]But Zipporah took a flint and cut off her son's foreskin, and touched Moses' feet with it, and said, "Truly you are a bridegroom of blood to me!" [26]So he let him alone. It was then she said, "A bridegroom of blood by circumcision."

---

95. The LORD's words resume abruptly after the narrative compliance of Exod 4:4b, without any introductory formula. Verses 8-9 continue the theme of belief through the signs and so are also identified as additions (Noth, *Exodus*, 47). In relation to v. 9, it is worth noting that the motif of the Nile being turned into blood occurs in the P plagues (Exod 7:19, 21b) but not in J.

96. Noth comments that the material on Aaron here and elsewhere has been inserted secondarily into J (*Pentateuchal Traditions*, 30 n. 104). The contours of these insertions are in places quite clear, as is the case here where the insertion was made by a skillful heightening of the repeated motif of Moses' objections. Another clear example is Exod 4:27-28. In other

places, e.g., 4:29-31, the addition has been worked into the J text in such a way that a precise distinction between the older J narrative and the "Aaron" material is no longer possible.

97. Note the potential continuity here with Exod 2:23*.

98. The wonders referred to here are those in Exod 4:1-4 and 6-7. According to these texts, they are meant for Israel rather than Pharaoh, as is the case in 4:21-22. Moreover, the subsequent J narrative does not report Moses working before Pharaoh the wonders of the staff turned snake or the leprous hand. Noth himself points out that 4:21-23 is similar to 3:18-22 in that it anticipates the plagues to come, in this case, the death of the firstborn (*Exodus*, 47).

27 The LORD said to Aaron, "Go into the wilderness to meet Moses." So he went; and he met him at the mountain of God and kissed him. 28Moses told Aaron all the words of the LORD with which he had sent him, and all the signs with which he had charged him.

29Then Moses and Aaron went and assembled all the elders of the Israelites.

30Aaron spoke all the words that the LORD had spoken to Moses, and performed the signs in the sight of the people. 31The people believed; and when they heard that the LORD had given heed to the Israelites and that he had seen their misery, they bowed down and worshiped.[99]

First Audience with Pharaoh

5 Afterward Moses and Aaron went to Pharaoh and said, "Thus says the LORD, the God of Israel, 'Let my people go, so that they may celebrate a festival to me in the wilderness.' " 2But Pharaoh said, "Who is the LORD, that I should heed him and let Israel go? I do not know the LORD, and I will not let Israel go." 3Then they said, "The God of the Hebrews has revealed himself to us; let us go a three days' journey into the wilderness to sacrifice to the LORD our God, or he will fall upon us with pestilence or sword."

4But the king of Egypt said to them, "Moses and Aaron, why are you taking the people away from their work? Get to your labors!"[100]

5And Pharaoh said [Heb.; NRSV, Pharaoh continued], "Now they are more numerous than the people of the land and yet you want them to stop working!" 6That same day Pharaoh commanded the taskmasters of the people, as well as their supervisors, 7"You shall no longer give the people straw to make bricks, as before; let them go and gather straw for themselves. 8But you shall require of them the same quantity of bricks as they have made previously; do not diminish it, for they are lazy; that is why they cry, 'Let us go and offer sacrifice to our God.' 9Let heavier work be laid on them; then they will labor at it and pay no attention to deceptive words."

10 So the taskmasters and the supervisors of the people went out and said to the people, "Thus says Pharaoh, 'I will not give you straw. 11Go and get straw yourselves, wherever you can find it; but your work will not be lessened in the least.' " 12So the people scattered throughout the land of Egypt, to gather stubble for straw. 13The taskmasters were urgent, saying, "Complete your work, the same daily assignment as when you were given straw." 14And the supervisors of the Israelites, whom Pharaoh's taskmasters had set over them, were beaten, and were asked, "Why did you not finish the required quantity of bricks yesterday and today, as you did before?"

15 Then the Israelite supervisors came to Pharaoh and cried, "Why do you treat your servants like this? 16No straw is given to your servants, yet they say to us, 'Make bricks!' Look how your servants are beaten! You are unjust to your own people." 17He said, "You are lazy, lazy; that is why you say, 'Let us go and sacrifice to the LORD.' 18Go now, and work; for no straw shall be given you, but you shall still deliver the same number of bricks." 19The Israelite supervisors saw that they were in trouble when they were told, "You shall not lessen your daily number of bricks." 20As they left Pharaoh, they came upon Moses and Aaron who were waiting to

---

99. Exodus 4:30-31 is treated by Noth as of a piece with 3:1—4:19, where it is also one of the additions involving Aaron (*Pentateuchal Traditions*, 30 nn. 103–4).

100. Noth bases his identification of 5:4 as an addition on his reading of 5:5. He holds that v. 5a should be read as referring to a thought by Pharaoh. In support of this, he turns to the Samaritan Pentateuch, where it is rendered as "And Pharaoh thought, 'They are now more numerous than the (native) people of the land' "(*Exodus*, 53). Verse 4 is therefore not really appropriate before v. 5, because it anticipates Pharaoh's instructions in vv. 6-9, which are given on the basis of his reflection in v. 5.

meet them. [21]They said to them, "The LORD look upon you and judge! You have brought us into bad odor with Pharaoh and his officials, and have put a sword in their hand to kill us."

22 Then Moses turned again to the LORD and said, "O LORD, why have you mistreated this people? Why did you ever send me? [23]Since I first came to Pharaoh to speak in your name, he has mistreated this people, and you have done nothing at all to deliver your people."

6:1 Then the LORD said to Moses, "Now you shall see what I will do to Pharaoh: Indeed, by a mighty hand he will let them go; by a mighty hand he will drive them out of his land."

Plagues against Egypt

Polluting of the Nile

7:14 Then the LORD said to Moses, "Pharaoh's heart is hardened; he refuses to let the people go. [15]Go to Pharaoh in the morning, as he is going out to the water; stand by at the river bank to meet him, and take in your hand the staff that was turned into a snake.[101] [16]Say to him, 'The LORD, the God of the Hebrews, sent me to you to say, "Let my people go, so that they may worship me in the wilderness." But until now you have not listened.' [17*]Thus says the LORD, "By this you shall know that I am the LORD." See, with the staff that is in my hand I will strike the water that is in the Nile.[102] [18]The fish in the river shall die, the river itself shall stink, and the Egyptians shall be unable to drink water from the Nile.' "

20* In the sight of Pharaoh and of his officials he lifted up the staff and struck the water in the river, [21a]and the fish in the river died. The river stank so that the Egyptians could not drink its water. [23]Pharaoh turned and went into his house, and he did not take even this to heart. [24]And all the Egyptians had to dig along the Nile for water to drink, for they could not drink the water of the river.

Frogs

25 Seven days passed after the LORD had struck the Nile.

8 Then the LORD said to Moses, "Go to Pharaoh and say to him, 'Thus says the LORD: Let my people go, so that they may worship me. [2]If you refuse to let them go, I will plague your whole country with frogs. [3]The river shall swarm with frogs; they shall come up into your palace, into your bedchamber and your bed, and into the houses of your officials and of your people, and into your ovens and your kneading bowls. [4]The frogs shall come up on you and on your people and on all your officials.' "[103]
• • •[104]

---

101. Noth originally included in J the references to Moses' staff in Exod 7:15, 17, 20; 9:22-23; 10:12-13, 21-22. In his later commentary, the first three are identified as additions to J and both 9:22-23 and 10:12-13, 21-22 attributed to P (*Exodus*, 70). Childs distributes the passages between E and P (*Exodus*, 131).

102. The last phrase of v. 17 ("and it shall be turned to blood"), as well as v. 20b, are considered by Noth to be redactional bracketings with the P variant (*Pentateuchal Traditions*, 30 n. 105). The J source refers only to the Nile in this and the following plague of frogs. In contrast, P refers to rivers, canals, and pools (7:19; 8:1 [NRSV 8:5]).

103. Exodus 8:1-4 is numbered 7:26-29 in the Hebrew.

104. According to Noth, the J version of the onset of the plague of frogs has been suppressed in favor of P. The J and P versions of the plagues are distinguished principally by their narrative patterns.

The pattern discernible in J is: Moses is commanded to request Israel's release from Pharaoh, with the threat of plague if the request is denied. The threat is carried out and the plague strikes. Pharaoh then summons Moses and a dialogue takes place. Moses intercedes and the plague is removed, but Pharaoh's heart remains hardened.

In P, by contrast, as we have noted earlier, Moses

8 Then Pharaoh called Moses and Aaron, and said, "Pray to the LORD to take away the frogs from me and my people, and I will let the people go to sacrifice to the LORD." [9]Moses said to Pharaoh, "Kindly tell me when I am to pray for you and for your officials and for your people, that the frogs may be removed from you and your houses."

and be left only in the Nile."[105]

[10]And he said, "Tomorrow." Moses said, "As you say! So that you may know that there is no one like the LORD our God, [11]the frogs shall leave you and your houses and your officials and your people; they shall be left only in the Nile." [12]Then Moses and Aaron went out from Pharaoh; and Moses cried out to the LORD concerning the frogs that he had brought upon Pharaoh. [13]And the LORD did as Moses requested: the frogs died in the houses, the courtyards, and the fields. [14]And they gathered them together in heaps, and the land stank. [15*]But when Pharaoh saw that there was a respite, he hardened his heart.[106]

Flies

20 Then the LORD said to Moses, "Rise early in the morning and present yourself before Pharaoh, as he goes out to the water, and say to him, 'Thus says the LORD: Let my people go, so that they may worship me. [21]For if you will not let my people go, I will send swarms of flies on you, your officials, and your people, and into your houses; and the houses of the Egyptians shall be filled with swarms of flies; so also the land where they live. [22]But on that day I will set apart the land of Goshen, where my people live, so that no swarms of flies shall be there, that you may know that I the LORD am in this land. [23]Thus I will make a distinction between my people and your people. This sign shall appear tomorrow.' " [24]The LORD did so, and great swarms of flies came into the house of Pharaoh and into his officials' houses; in all of Egypt the land was ruined because of the flies.[107]

25 Then Pharaoh summoned Moses and Aaron, and said,[108]

"Go, sacrifice to your God within the land." [26]But Moses said, "It would not be right to do so; for the sacrifices that we offer to the LORD our God are offensive to the Egyptians. If we offer in the sight of the Egyptians sacrifices that are offensive to them, will they not stone us? [27]We must go a three days' journey into the wilderness and sacrifice to the LORD our God as he commands us."

---

and Aaron are instructed to perform certain actions that normally involve the staff. This is followed by their execution of the instruction and the onset of the plague. The magicians of Egypt then attempt to match their display of power and the account of the plague ends with a report of Pharaoh's hardness of heart (cf. Exod 7:8-13; 8:1-3 [NRSV 8:5-7], 16-19 [NRSV 11:15]; 9:8-12). The different patterns are discussed briefly in Noth, *Exodus*, 69–70; more fully in Childs, *Exodus*, 133–41.

105. Noth leaves us to speculate why he should have relegated this harmless half-verse to secondary addition status, both here and in his commentary. Perhaps alerted by its absence from the Syriac, he

sought to lighten Moses' style by making the repetition progressive (from v. 9a to v. 11). The redactor then would have wanted the two statements to correspond. In Noth's version, Moses' first assurance corresponds closely with Pharaoh's request: take the frogs away!

106. Exodus 8:8-15 is numbered 8:4-11 in the Hebrew.

107. Exodus 8:20-24 is numbered 8:16-20 in the Hebrew.

108. Although the verb "and said" strictly belongs in v. 25b, it seems clear from Noth's interpretation that he meant to retain it in the original narrative.

28So Pharaoh said, "I will let you go to sacrifice to the LORD your God in the wilderness, provided you do not go very far away."[109] "Pray for me." [29]Then Moses said, "As soon as I leave you, I will pray to the LORD that the swarms of flies may depart tomorrow from Pharaoh, from his officials, and from his people; only do not let Pharaoh again deal falsely by not letting the people go to sacrifice to the LORD."

30 So Moses went out from Pharaoh and prayed to the LORD. [31]And the LORD did as Moses asked: he removed the swarms of flies from Pharaoh, from his officials, and from his people; not one remained. [32]But Pharaoh hardened his heart this time also, and would not let the people go.[110]

Death of the Livestock

9 Then the LORD said to Moses, "Go to Pharaoh, and say to him, 'Thus says the LORD, the God of the Hebrews: Let my people go, so that they may worship me. [2]For if you refuse to let them go and still hold them, [3]the hand of the LORD will strike with a deadly pestilence your livestock in the field: the horses, the donkeys, the camels, the herds, and the flocks. [4]But the LORD will make a distinction between the livestock of Israel and the livestock of Egypt, so that nothing shall die of all that belongs to the Israelites.' " [5]The LORD set a time, saying,

"Tomorrow the LORD will do this thing in the land." [6]And on the next day the LORD did so; all the livestock of the Egyptians died, but of the livestock of the Israelites not one died. [7]Pharaoh inquired and found that not one of the livestock of the Israelites was dead. But the heart of Pharaoh was hardened, and he would not let the people go.[111]

Hail

13 Then the LORD said to Moses, "Rise up early in the morning and present yourself before Pharaoh, and say to him, 'Thus says the LORD, the God of the Hebrews: Let my people go, so that they may worship me.

14For this time I will send all my plagues upon you yourself, and upon your officials, and upon your people, so that you may know that there is no one like me in all the earth. 15For by now I could have stretched out my hand and struck you and your people with pestilence, and you would have been cut off from the earth. 16But this is why I have let you live: to show you my power, and to make my name resound through all the earth.[112] [17]You are still exalting yourself against my people, and will not let them go. [18]Tomorrow at this time I will cause the heaviest hail to fall that has ever fallen in Egypt from the day it was founded until now. [19]Send, therefore, and have your livestock and everything that you have in

109. Noth does not comment on the identification of 8:25b-28a as an addition to J. It may be inferred from remarks in the later commentary on Exodus that he regarded v. 28b ("Pray for me") as the beginning of negotiations, on the analogy of 8:8; so vv. 25b-28a became an addition. In the commentary, despite this formal discrepancy between 8:8-11 and 8:25-28, he considers that the progressive heightening of the theme of negotiations throughout the J version of the plagues argues in favor of 8:25b-28a as an integral part of J (*Exodus*, 77).
110. Exodus 8:25-32 is numbered 8:21-28 in the Hebrew.
111. In his commentary, Noth sees Exod 9:1-7 as a

secondary addition to J, because of variations from the J pattern elsewhere (*Exodus*, 79).
112. The J plagues so far have all begun with the demand that Israel should be released to serve the Lord, and this is the thrust of 9:13. As Noth points out in his commentary, 9:14-16 introduces another theme, that of the Lord's power and renown. Pharaoh and the Egyptians have been allowed to live so that they might see the Lord's power. This display of power will bring renown for the divine name. Noth believes that such a reflection would be more appropriate immediately before the decisive final plague of the firstborn, so he omits it as secondary (*Exodus*, 80). This, of course, leaves its presence in the text unexplained.

the open field brought to a secure place; every human or animal that is in the open field and is not brought under shelter will die when the hail comes down upon them.' " [20]Those officials of Pharaoh who feared the word of the LORD hurried their slaves and livestock off to a secure place. [21]Those who did not regard the word of the LORD left their slaves and livestock in the open field.

22 The LORD said to Moses, "Stretch out your hand toward heaven so that hail may fall on the whole land of Egypt."

on humans and animals and all the plants of the field in the land of Egypt."[113]

[23]Then Moses stretched out his staff toward heaven, and the LORD sent thunder and hail, and fire came down on the earth. And the LORD rained hail on the land of Egypt; [24]there was hail, *with fire flashing continually in the midst of it,* such heavy hail as had never fallen in all the land of Egypt since it became a nation. [25]The hail struck down everything that was in the open field throughout all the land of Egypt, *both human and animal;*[114] the hail also struck down all the plants of the field, and shattered every tree in the field. [26]Only in the land of Goshen, where the Israelites were, there was no hail.

27 Then Pharaoh summoned Moses and Aaron, and said to them, "This time I have sinned; the LORD is in the right, and I and my people are in the wrong. [28]Pray to the LORD! Enough of God's thunder and hail! I will let you go; you need stay no longer." [29]Moses said to him, "As soon as I have gone out of the city, I will stretch out my hands to the LORD; the thunder will cease, and there will be no more hail, so that you may know that the earth is the LORD's. [30]But as for you and your officials, I know that you do not yet fear the LORD God."

[31]Now the flax and the barley were ruined, for the barley was in the ear and the flax was in bud. [32]But the wheat and the spelt were not ruined, for they are late in coming up.[115]

[33]So Moses left Pharaoh, went out of the city, and stretched out his hands to the LORD; then the thunder and the hail ceased, and the rain no longer poured down on the earth. [34]But when Pharaoh saw that the rain and the hail and the thunder had ceased, he sinned once more and hardened his heart, he and his officials.

[35]So the heart of Pharaoh was hardened, and he would not let the Israelites go, just as the LORD had spoken through Moses.[116]

---

113. Although Noth does not spell out in his *History of Pentateuchal Traditions* why he identifies v. 22b as an addition, a consideration of the preceding verses in J may point to his reason. A distinctive feature of this account is that the announcement of the plague of hail is followed by the advice that Pharaoh's officials should seek shelter for every human and animal that was in the field (v. 19). According to v. 20, a number of those who feared the word of the Lord did so. According to v. 21, others left their slaves and livestock in the field. The point about v. 22b may be that it disregards this distinction and does not identify the humans and animals destined for destruction as the ones that were left in the field. Whether seen as an addition or as original, it emphasizes the mighty power of God manifested in the plague, unfolding its impact on the "whole land of Egypt."

In his commentary Noth resolves the difficulty differently, assigning v. 22 to P, along with v. 23aα and v. 35 (*Exodus*, 80).

114. These additions are minor and clearly Noth regarded them as intrusive. A better case can be made for this in v. 24 than in v. 25 (cf. *Exodus*, 65). In v. 24, the phrase breaks up the three Hebrew words for "the heaviest hail" of v. 18; the NRSV reflects this in its resumptive repetition, "hail . . . such heavy hail."

115. In his commentary, Noth remarks that these verses are located in a somewhat unsuitable position, because the destruction wrought by the plague of hail is described in Exod 9:25. He also observes that v. 32 was added with an eye to the following plague of locusts (*Exodus*, 81).

116. Verse 35 is a doublet of v. 34, and the final phrase occurs elsewhere in the P version of the plagues.

Locusts

10 Then the LORD said to Moses, "Go to Pharaoh."

"For I have hardened his heart and the heart of his officials, in order that I may show these signs of mine among them, ²and that you may tell your children and grandchildren how I have made fools of the Egyptians and what signs I have done among them—so that you may know that I am the LORD."[117]

3 So Moses and Aaron went to Pharaoh, and said to him, "Thus says the LORD, the God of the Hebrews, 'How long will you refuse to humble yourself before me? Let my people go, so that they may worship me. ⁴For if you refuse to let my people go, tomorrow I will bring locusts into your country. ⁵They shall cover the surface of the land, so that no one will be able to see the land. They shall devour the last remnant left you after the hail, and they shall devour every tree of yours that grows in the field. ⁶They shall fill your houses, and the houses of all your officials and of all the Egyptians—something that neither your parents nor your grandparents have seen, from the day they came on earth to this day.' " Then he turned and went out from Pharaoh.

7 Pharaoh's officials said to him, "How long shall this fellow be a snare to us? Let the people go, so that they may worship the LORD their God; do you not yet understand that Egypt is ruined?" ⁸So Moses and Aaron were brought back to Pharaoh, and he said to them, "Go, worship the LORD your God! But which ones are to go?" ⁹Moses said, "We will go with our young and our old; we will go with our sons and daughters and with our flocks and herds, because we

have the LORD's festival to celebrate." ¹⁰He said to them, "The LORD indeed will be with you, if ever I let your little ones go with you! Plainly, you have some evil purpose in mind. ¹¹No, never! Your men may go and worship the LORD, for that is what you are asking." And they were driven out from Pharaoh's presence.

12 Then the LORD said to Moses, "Stretch out your hand over the land of Egypt, so that the locusts may come upon it and eat every plant in the land, all that the hail has left." ¹³So Moses stretched out his staff over the land of Egypt, and the LORD brought an east wind upon the land all that day and all that night; when morning came, the east wind had brought the locusts. ¹⁴The locusts came upon all the land of Egypt and settled on the whole country of Egypt, such a dense swarm of locusts as had never been before, nor ever shall be again. ¹⁵They covered the surface of the whole land, so that the land was black; and they ate all the plants in the land and all the fruit of the trees that the hail had left; nothing green was left, no tree, no plant in the field, in all the land of Egypt. ¹⁶Pharaoh hurriedly summoned Moses and Aaron and said, "I have sinned against the LORD your God, and against you. ¹⁷Do forgive my sin just this once, and pray to the LORD your God that at the least he remove this deadly thing from me." ¹⁸So he went out from Pharaoh and prayed to the LORD. ¹⁹The LORD changed the wind into a very strong west wind, which lifted the locusts and drove them into the Red Sea; not a single locust was left in all the country of Egypt.

²⁰But the LORD hardened Pharaoh's heart, and he would not let the Israelites go.[118]

---

117. The theme of the manifestation of divine power recalls Exod 9:14-16, which Noth identified as an addition to J. Nevertheless, in his commentary vv. 1b-2 are treated as part of the original (*Exodus*, 66).

118. Two features distinguish Exod 10:20 from parallel texts elsewhere in J: (1) the statement that it

was the Lord who hardened Pharaoh's heart, and (2) the use of the verb *ḥāzaq*. This verb also occurs in 9:35, which Noth identified as an addition to J.

The parallel texts in J state that Pharaoh's heart was hardened (7:14; 9:7—literally "was heavy") or that he himself hardened his heart (8:15*, 32; 9:34), and all

Darkness

21 Then the LORD said to Moses, "Stretch out your hand toward heaven so that there may be darkness over the land of Egypt, a darkness that can be felt." 22So Moses stretched out his hand toward heaven, and there was dense darkness in all the land of Egypt for three days. 23People could not see one another, and for three days they could not move from where they were; but all the Israelites had light where they lived. 24Then Pharaoh summoned Moses, and said, "Go, worship the LORD. Only your flocks and your herds shall remain behind. Even your children may go with you." 25But Moses said, "You must also let us have sacrifices and burnt offerings to sacrifice to the LORD our God. 26Our livestock also must go with us; not a hoof shall be left behind, for we must choose some of them for the worship of the LORD our God, and we will not know what to use to worship the LORD until we arrive there." 27But the LORD hardened Pharaoh's heart, and he was unwilling to let them go.[119]

28Then Pharaoh said to him, "Get away from me! Take care that you do not see my face again, for on the day you see my face you shall die." 29Moses said, "Just as you say! I will never see your face again.[120]

Death of the Firstborn

11 The LORD said to Moses, "I will bring one more plague upon Pharaoh and upon Egypt; afterwards he will let you go from here; indeed, when he lets you go, he will drive you away. 2Tell the people that every man is to ask his neighbor and every woman is to ask her neighbor for objects of silver and gold." 3The LORD gave the people favor in the sight of the Egyptians. Moreover, Moses himself was a man of great importance in the land of Egypt, in the sight of Pharaoh's officials and in the sight of the people. 4Moses said,[121]

Thus says the LORD: About midnight I will go out through Egypt. 5Every firstborn in the land of Egypt shall die, from the firstborn of Pharaoh

---

use the verb *kābed*. (This verb also occurs in 10:1b, which Noth identified as an addition to J.)

Both in 9:35 and here in 10:20, the type of formulation is in fact closer to that found in parallel texts in the P version of the plagues (7:3, 13, 22; 8:19; 9:12). In his later commentary, Noth assigns 9:35 and 10:20 to P (*Exodus*, 82).

119. The plague of darkness lacks a number of elements that are present in the preceding plague stories in J: the request for release, the threat of plague if the request is refused, Pharaoh's entreaty that the plague be removed, and a report of the end of the plague. If 10:21-27 is an addition, then the original J source narrated six plagues up to this point, with the death of the firstborn making the seventh. The six initial plagues form two series of three. The first three plagues are disruptive of everyday life (foul water, frogs, flies), whereas the second three are life-threatening (death of the livestock, crop-destroying hail, and locusts). In his commentary Noth accepts there was a J version of the plague of darkness, but its amalgamation with elements from P means that its original form can no longer be recovered (*Exodus*, 83). Childs distributes 10:21-27 between J and E (*Exodus*, 131).

120. Earlier commentators (e.g., Holzinger) saw

the conclusion of an E passage in 10:27, with the J conclusion in vv. 28-29. In his Exodus commentary, Noth includes vv. 28-29 in the secondary passage, probably under the influence of his desire for a continuous text where possible. As they stand here, 10:19 and 10:28-29 do not provide a satisfactory sequence. See also the discussion in Childs, *Exodus*, 130–33.

121. The introduction to the final plague, the death of the firstborn, differs from the preceding plague stories in J. It begins, in the present text, with the LORD telling Moses that there is one more plague to come; but instead of informing him about the nature of this plague, as in the preceding accounts, the LORD gives instructions for Israel's despoiling of the Egyptians. The report in Exod 11:3 implies that the despoliation was successfully carried out, and this is confirmed by 12:35-36. The nature of the final plague is then described in vv. 4-8.

In *Pentateuchal Traditions*, Noth identifies 11:1-3 as an addition to J, with v. 4aα included in this addition presumably because it is a resumptive repetition of the same phrase in 10:29. Reversing himself in his later commentary, he judges that, despite these variations, all of 11:1-4 should be included in the original J narrative (*Exodus*, 92–93).

who sits on his throne to the firstborn of the female slave who is behind the handmill, and all the firstborn of the livestock. [6]Then there will be a loud cry throughout the whole land of Egypt, such as has never been or will ever be again. [7]But not a dog shall growl at any of the Israelites—not at people, not at animals—so that you may know that the LORD makes a distinction between Egypt and Israel. [8]Then all these officials of yours shall come down to me, and bow low to me, saying, 'Leave us, you and all the people who follow you.' After that I will leave." And in hot anger he left Pharaoh.

Exodus from Egypt

The Passover

12:21 Then Moses called all the elders of Israel and said to them, "Go, select lambs for your families, and slaughter the passover lamb. [22]Take a bunch of hyssop, dip it in the blood that is in the basin, and touch the lintel and the two doorposts with the blood in the basin. None of you shall go outside the door of your house until morning. [23]For the LORD will pass through to strike down the Egyptians; when he sees the blood on the lintel and on the two doorposts, the LORD will pass over that door and will not allow the destroyer to enter your houses to strike you down." [27b]And the people bowed down and worshiped.[122]

29 At midnight the LORD struck down all the firstborn in the land of Egypt, from the firstborn of Pharaoh who sat on his throne to the firstborn of the prisoner who was in the dun-geon, and all the firstborn of the livestock. [30]Pharaoh arose in the night, he and all his officials and all the Egyptians; and there was a loud cry in Egypt, for there was not a house without someone dead. [31]Then he summoned Moses and Aaron in the night, and said, "Rise up, go away from my people, both you and the Israelites! Go, worship the LORD, as you said. [32]Take your flocks and your herds, as you said, and be gone. And bring a blessing on me too!"

Departure from Egypt

33 The Egyptians urged the people to hasten their departure from the land, for they said, "We shall all be dead." [34]So the people took their dough before it was leavened, with their kneading bowls wrapped up in their cloaks on their shoulders.

[35]The Israelites had done as Moses told them; they had asked the Egyptians for jewelry of silver and gold, and for clothing, [36]and the LORD had given the people favor in the sight of the Egyptians, so that they let them have what they asked. And so they plundered the Egyptians.[123]

37 The Israelites journeyed from Rameses to Succoth, about six hundred thousand men on foot, besides children. [38]A mixed crowd also went up with them, and livestock in great numbers, both flocks and herds. [39]They baked unleavened cakes of the dough that they had brought out of Egypt; it was not leavened, because they were driven out of Egypt and could not wait, nor had they prepared any provisions for themselves.

---

122. Noth regards the account of the Passover with the killing of the firstborn as a separate tradition from the plagues; he nevertheless considers it an integral and necessary part of the J source. Without it, the story of the plagues in J ends in Exod 10:28-29 with Israel still enslaved and Moses announcing his final departure from Pharaoh (*Exodus*, 68).

123. As has already been pointed out, in *Pentateuchal Traditions* Noth regarded the material in Exod 11:1-3 and 12:35-36, which deals with the despoliation of the Egyptians, as an addition to J, a position he subsequently revised in his Exodus commentary.

ISRAEL'S JOURNEY TOWARD THE LAND

Through the Wilderness to Sinai

13:20 They set out from Succoth, and camped at Etham, on the edge of the wilderness. [21]The LORD went in front of them in a pillar of cloud by day, to lead them along the way, and in a pillar of fire by night, to give them light, so that they might travel by day and by night. [22]Neither the pillar of cloud by day nor the pillar of fire by night left its place in front of the people.

Deliverance at the Sea

14:5b And the [Heb.; NRSV, The] minds of Pharaoh and his officials were changed toward the people, and they said, "What have we done, letting Israel leave our service?" [6]So he had his chariot made ready, and took his army with him. [9*]The Egyptians pursued them. [10*]And the [Heb.; NRSV, The] Israelites looked back, and there were the Egyptians advancing on them, and they were in great fear.[124] [13]But Moses said to the people, "Do not be afraid, stand firm, and see the deliverance that the LORD will accomplish for you today; for the Egyptians whom you see today you shall never see again. [14]The LORD will fight for you, and you have only to keep still."[125]

[19b] And the pillar of cloud moved from in front of them and took its place behind them. [20]It came between the army of Egypt and the army of Israel. And so the cloud was there with the darkness, and it lit up the night; one did not come near the other all night.

[21*] The LORD drove the sea back by a strong east wind all night, and turned the sea into dry land. [24]At the morning watch the LORD in the pillar of fire and cloud looked down upon the Egyptian army, and threw the Egyptian army into panic. [25b]The Egyptians said, "Let us flee from the Israelites, for the LORD is fighting for them against Egypt." [27*]And at dawn the sea returned to its normal depth. As the Egyptians fled before it, the LORD tossed the Egyptians into the sea.

[30] Thus the LORD saved Israel that day from the Egyptians; and Israel saw the Egyptians dead on the seashore. [31]Israel saw the great work that the LORD did against the Egyptians. So the people feared the LORD and believed in the LORD and in his servant Moses.

15:20 Then the prophet Miriam, Aaron's sister, took a tambourine in her hand; and all the women went out after her with tambourines and with dancing. [21]And Miriam sang to them:

"Sing to the LORD, for he has triumphed gloriously; horse and rider he has thrown into the sea."[126]

---

124. The clause "and they were in great fear" is taken from the RSV in order to mirror the Hebrew more closely. The Hebrew has two finite verbs, fear and cry, which the NRSV translates idiomatically, "In great fear the Israelites cried out." This is a fully legitimate rendering of the present text. A more literal translation is needed to represent the division into sources.

125. In J's portrayal, Israel's role is to stand firm, keep still, and see the deliverance that the Lord will accomplish for them. The Lord goes between them and the Egyptians in the pillar of cloud, drives the sea back by an east wind through the night, and in the

early morning discomfits the Egyptians so that they attempt to flee across the area of dry land exposed during the night. They are overwhelmed as the sea returns to its bed. For the discussion of P and E, see chap. 6, below.

126. Noth comments that 15:20-21 shows no clear literary relationship to its context; the attribution to J cannot be proved. In Noth's view, 15:22* connects better with 14:31 than with 15:21, and he therefore regards vv. 20-21 as a secondary insertion in J. He considers the hymn in 15:1-19 to be so isolated that it cannot be assigned to any source (*Pentateuchal Traditions*, 30 n. 107).

Sweetening of the Waters
at Marah

22* And they went into the wilderness of Shur. They went three days in the wilderness and found no water. [23]When they came to Marah, they could not drink the water of Marah because it was bitter. That is why it was called Marah. [24]And the people complained against Moses, saying, "What shall we drink?" [25a]He cried out to the LORD; and the LORD showed him a piece of wood; he threw it into the water, and the water became sweet.

Provision of Manna

• • •[127]

16:4* Then the LORD said to Moses, "I am going to rain bread from heaven for you, and each day the people shall go out and gather enough for that day. [5]On the sixth day, when they prepare what they bring in, it will be twice as much as they gather on other days.

• • •

[29]See! The LORD has given you the sabbath, therefore on the sixth day he gives you food for two days; each of you stay where you are; do not leave your place on the seventh day." [30]So the people rested on the seventh day.

31 The house of Israel called it manna; it was like coriander seed, white, and the taste of it was like wafers made with honey.

• • •

[35b]They ate manna, until they came to the border of the land of Canaan. [36]An omer is a tenth of an ephah.

Provision of Water at
Massah-Meribah

• • •[128]

17:1* And [Heb.; NRSV, But] there was no water for the people to drink. [2]The people quarreled with Moses, and said, "Give us water to drink." Moses said to them, "Why do you quarrel with me? Why do you test the LORD?" [4]So Moses cried out to the LORD, "What shall I do with this people? They are almost ready to stone me." [5]The LORD said to Moses, "Go on ahead of the people, and take some of the elders of Israel with you; take in your hand the staff with which you struck the Nile, and go. [6]I will be standing there in front of you on the rock at Horeb. Strike the rock, and water will come out of it, so that the people may drink." Moses did so, in the sight of the elders of Israel. [7]He called the place Massah and Meribah, because the Israelites quarreled and tested the LORD, saying, "Is the LORD among us or not?"[129]

War with Amalek

8 Then Amalek came and fought with Israel at Rephidim. [9]Moses said to Joshua, "Choose some men for us and go out, fight with Amalek. Tomorrow I will stand on the top of the hill with

---

127. The present text of Exodus 16 tells the story of the provision of manna and quails in the wilderness. Noth assigns the bulk of this chapter to P, with some J elements that, as can be seen, are all associated with the provision of manna. The three gaps in Exodus 16 reflect Noth's tentative suggestion that a J manna story was originally located in the context of Numbers 11 and the theme there of the provision of food in the wilderness (*Pentateuchal Traditions*, 31 n. 110). In this hypothesis, the fragments of the manna story we have here are J material, originally from Numbers 11, which have been incorporated into the P story in Exodus 16. See also Noth, *Exodus*, 131–32; and idem, *Numbers* (OTL; Philadelphia: Westminster, 1968) 85–86.

128. The older J itinerary linking the wilderness journey stories has been replaced by the P itinerary (cf. Exod 15:22aα, 27; 16:1; 17:1abα; 19:1-2a).

129. While leaving the text intact, Noth comments that the references to Massah (along with Meribah) in this section and the allusions in the verbs to test (for Massah) and to quarrel (for Meribah) are secondary deuteronomistic insertions (*Pentateuchal Traditions*, 31 n. 111). He bases this identification on his observation that the juxtaposition of Meribah and Massah occurs elsewhere only in Deut 33:8; Ps 95:8. Massah alone occurs also in Deut 6:16; 9:22.

the staff of God in my hand." [10]So Joshua did as Moses told him, and fought with Amalek, while Moses, Aaron, and Hur went up to the top of the hill. [11]Whenever Moses held up his hand, Israel prevailed; and whenever he lowered his hand, Amalek prevailed. [12]But Moses' hands grew weary; so they took a stone and put it under him, and he sat on it. Aaron and Hur held up his hands, one on one side, and the other on the other side; so his hands were steady until the sun set. [13]And Joshua defeated Amalek and his people with the sword.

[14]Then the LORD said to Moses, "Write this as a reminder in a book and recite it in the hearing of Joshua: I will utterly blot out the remembrance of Amalek from under heaven." [15]And Moses built an altar and called it, The LORD is my banner. [16]He said, "A hand upon the banner of the LORD! The LORD will have war with Amalek from generation to generation."

Covenant at Sinai

• • •[130]

Preparations

19:2b Israel camped there in front of the mountain.[131] [10]The LORD said to Moses: "Go to the people and consecrate them today and tomorrow. Have them wash their clothes [11]and prepare for the third day, because on the third day the LORD will come down upon Mount Sinai in the sight of all the people. [12]You shall set limits for the people all around, saying, 'Be careful not to go up the mountain or to touch the edge of it.' "

Any who touch the mountain shall be put to death. [13a]No hand shall touch them, but they shall be stoned or shot with arrows; whether animal or human being, they shall not live.[132]

[14] So Moses went down from the mountain to the people. He consecrated the people, and they washed their clothes. [15]And he said to the people, "Prepare for the third day." *Do not go near a woman.*[133] [16*]And it happened on [Heb.; NRSV, On] the morning of the third day [18]that [literal Heb. "and"; NRSV, Now] Mount Sinai was wrapped in smoke, because the LORD had descended upon it in fire; the smoke went up like the smoke of a kiln, while the whole mountain shook violently.

[20]When the LORD descended upon Mount Sinai, to the top of the mountain, the LORD summoned Moses to the top of the mountain, and Moses went up. [21]Then the LORD said to Moses, "Go down and warn the people not to break through to the LORD to look; otherwise many of them will perish. [22]Even the priests who approach the LORD must consecrate themselves or the LORD will break out against them." [23]Moses said to the LORD, "The people are not permitted to come up to Mount Sinai; for you yourself warned us, saying, 'Set limits around the mountain and keep it holy.' " [24]The LORD said to him, "Go down, and come up bringing Aaron with you; but do not let either the priests or the people break through to come up to

---

130. The J itinerary has been replaced here by the P version, as occurred earlier in Exod 15:22aα, 27; 16:1; 17:1abα.

131. Noth remarks that, because of the importance of Sinai, it is quite likely that the narrative in Exodus 19–24 and 32–34 underwent considerable development within the old pentateuchal tradition. This makes it difficult to carry out a successful literary-critical analysis. His assignation of texts to sources or

redaction is therefore tentative. In particular, however, he does regard the golden calf episode (in 24:12—32:35*) as secondary (see below; *Pentateuchal Traditions*, 31 n. 115).

132. In the later commentary, despite some unevenness in the text, Noth includes these verses in J (*Exodus*, 158).

133. This prohibition does not form part of the LORD's instructions in Exod 19:10-11.

the LORD; otherwise he will break out against them." ²⁵So Moses went down to the people and told them.¹³⁴

24:12 The LORD said to Moses, "Come up to me on the mountain, and wait there; and I will give you the tablets of stone, with the law and the commandments, which I have written for their instruction." ¹³So Moses set out with his assistant Joshua.

and Moses went up into the mountain of God.

¹⁴To the elders he had said, "Wait here for us, until we come to you again; for Aaron and Hur are with you; whoever has a dispute may go to them."

15a And [Heb.; NRSV, Then] Moses went up on the mountain.¹³⁵

Golden Calf

32:1a And [Heb.; NRSV, When] the people saw that Moses delayed to come down from the mountain.¹³⁶

• • •¹³⁷

4bAnd they said, "These are your gods, O Israel, who brought you up out of the land of Egypt!" ⁵When Aaron saw this, he built an altar before it; and Aaron made proclamation and said, "Tomorrow shall be a festival to the LORD." ⁶They rose early the next day, and offered burnt offerings and brought sacrifices of well-being; and the people sat down to eat and drink, and rose up to revel.¹³⁸

15 Then Moses turned and went down from the mountain, carrying the two tablets of the covenant in his hands, tablets that were written on both sides, written on the front and on the back. ¹⁶The tablets were the work of God, and the writing was the writing of God, engraved upon the tablets. ¹⁷When Joshua heard the noise of the people as they shouted, he said to Moses, "There is a noise of war in the camp." ¹⁸But he said,

"It is not the sound made by victors,
or the sound made by losers;
it is the sound of revelers that I hear."

¹⁹As soon as he came near the camp and saw the calf and the dancing, Moses' anger burned hot, and he threw the tablets from his hands

---

134. Noth regards Exod 19:20-25 as a series of additions to J that expand on the concern, expressed in vv. 12-13a, that the people must not approach the holy mountain (cf. Noth, *Exodus*, 160). For a fuller discussion of these verses and their function within the narrative, see Childs, *Exodus*, 361–64, 369–70.

135. This section, 24:12-15a, is regarded by Noth as the introduction to the story of the golden calf; see n. 136, below.

136. In agreement with W. Rudolph (*Der "Elohist" von Exodus bis Josua* [BZAW 68; Berlin: Walter de Gruyter, 1938] 48), Noth judges that the story of the golden calf—with its introduction in Exod 24:12-15a—is a secondary element in J (*Pentateuchal Traditions*, 31 n. 115). Literary-critical considerations indicate that the tablets of stone occurred originally only in Exodus 34 and that their presence in 24 and 32 is a later expansion. Attention will be drawn to the literary-critical evidence in n. 143, below. Traditio-historical considerations lead Noth to link the story of the golden calf with Jeroboam's setting up of two golden calves in Bethel and Dan after the schism in the kingdom (cf. 1 Kings 12:28-30). This would mean either

that J is to be dated in the postschism era or that Exodus 32 is a later addition to a J narrative of the Solomonic era. Noth's overall assessment of J leads him to assign it to the Solomonic era and so to favor the second position (cf. *Exodus*, 246).

137. Noth initially listed Exod 32:1b-4a (Aaron's fashioning of a golden calf) and 32:21-24 (his report of this to Moses) under E but italicized to indicate there was insufficient evidence to assign them positively to E (cf. *Pentateuchal Traditions*, 35 n. 129 and 36; see the Elohist in chap. 4 below). Further reflection in his commentary led Noth to conclude these verses derived from circles hostile to the Aaronide priesthood but probably before P, when Aaron had assumed the position of ancestor of the sole legitimate priesthood. In support of this, Noth observes how the first part of v. 5 implies that Aaron had nothing to do with what is described in vv. 1b-4a, a fact that points to an older account in which the people themselves fashioned the calf (*Exodus*, 244–45).

138. Noth comments that Exod 32:7-14 is commonly and correctly regarded as a deuteronomistic addition.

and broke them at the foot of the mountain. *20He took the calf that they had made, burned it with fire, ground it to powder, scattered it on the water, and made the Israelites drink it.*

25 When Moses saw that the people were running wild (for Aaron had let them run wild, to the derision of their enemies), 26then Moses stood in the gate of the camp, and said, "Who is on the LORD's side? Come to me!" And all the sons of Levi gathered around him. 27He said to them, "Thus says the LORD, the God of Israel, 'Put your sword on your side, each of you! Go back and forth from gate to gate throughout the camp, and each of you kill your brother, your friend, and your neighbor.' " 28The sons of Levi did as Moses commanded, and about three thousand of the people fell on that day. 29Moses said, "Today you have ordained yourselves for the service of the LORD, each one at the cost of a son or a brother, and so have brought a blessing on yourselves this day."139

30 On the next day Moses said to the people, "You have sinned a great sin. But now I will go up to the LORD; perhaps I can make atonement for your sin." 31So Moses returned to the LORD and said, "Alas, this people has sinned a great sin; they have made for themselves gods of gold. 32But now, if you will only forgive their sin—but if not, blot me out of the book that you have written." 33But the LORD said to Moses, "Whoever has sinned against me I will blot out of my book. 34But now go, lead the people to the place about which I have spoken to you.

See, my angel shall go in front of you. Nevertheless, when the day comes for punishment, I will punish them for their sin."

35 Then the LORD sent a plague on the people, because they made the calf—the one that Aaron made.[140]

• • •[141]

Making of the Covenant

34 The LORD said to Moses, "Cut two tablets of stone.[142]

like the former ones. And I will write on the tablets the words that were on the former tablets, which you broke.[143]
²Be ready in the morning, and come up in the

---

139. Exodus 32:25-29 is a variant of the punishment theme in v. 20, which involves the destruction of the calf and so is an integral part of the story. Noth observes in his commentary that, although the punishment theme provides the occasion for the addition, its real function, as expressed in v. 29, is to legitimate the entrusting of the priestly office to the Levites (*Exodus*, 245).

140. This report of the people's punishment by plague is in conflict with the preceding vv. 30-34, which describe the postponement of punishment; hence Noth's view in *Pentateuchal Traditions* of v. 35 as a later addition. In his commentary he substantially revises this position (*Exodus*, 251).

141. Noth comments that a literary-critical analysis of Exodus 33 is probably impossible; hence the gap left here. It is a gap in the analysis rather than in the narrative. In his view, the chapter is a conglomeration of secondary accretions connected with the command "But now go, lead the people to the place about which I have spoken to you" (v. 34*). They may have been added to J while it was still independent.

142. The LORD's speech here follows directly on Exod 19:18, in Noth's view of the original J narrative.

143. The mention of the "former tablets" here, as well as the phrase "like the former ones" in Exod 34:1a and 34:4, clearly refers to the tablets that the LORD had personally inscribed in 24:12 and that Moses in his anger smashed in 32:19. The LORD proposes to inscribe the new tablets with the same words. What is reported later on in Exodus 34, however, is that the LORD makes a covenant and proclaims a set of commands (vv. 10-26) and then instructs Moses to write them down (vv. 27-28).

According to Noth, these discrepancies show that v. 1b and the phrases "like the former ones" in vv. 1a and 4 are later additions to the chapter (*Pentateuchal Traditions*, 31 n. 116). The effect of these additions is to transform J's account of the inauguration of the covenant in Exodus 34 into an account of covenant renewal after the episode of the golden calf in Exodus 32. Noth's analysis here is based on the earlier work of Wellhausen (for a discussion, see Childs, *Exodus*, 605–10).

morning to Mount Sinai and present yourself there to me, on the top of the mountain. ³No one shall come up with you, and do not let anyone be seen throughout all the mountain; and do not let flocks or herds graze in front of that mountain." ⁴So Moses cut two tablets of stone *like the former ones;* and he rose early in the morning and went up on Mount Sinai, as the LORD had commanded him, and took in his hand the two tablets of stone. ⁵The LORD descended in the cloud and stood with him there, and proclaimed the name, "The LORD." ⁶The LORD passed before him.

> *and proclaimed,*
> *"The LORD, the LORD,*
> *a God merciful and gracious,*
> *slow to anger,*
> *and abounding in steadfast love and faithfulness,*
> ⁷*keeping steadfast love for the thousandth*
> *generation,*
> *forgiving iniquity and transgression and sin,*
> *yet by no means clearing the guilty,*
> *but visiting the iniquity of the parents*
> *upon the children*
> *and the children's children,*
> *to the third and the fourth generation."*¹⁴⁴

⁸And Moses quickly bowed his head toward the earth, and worshiped.

> ⁹*He said, "If now I have found favor in your sight, O LORD, I pray, let the LORD go with us. Although this is a stiff-necked people, pardon our iniquity and our sin, and take us for your inheritance."*¹⁴⁵

¹⁰He said: I hereby make a covenant.¹⁴⁶

> *Before all your people I will perform marvels, such as have not been performed in all the earth or in any nation; and all the people among whom you live shall see the work of the LORD; for it is an awesome thing that I will do with you.*

¹¹Observe what I command you today,

> *See, I will drive out before you the Amorites, the Canaanites, the Hittites, the Perizzites, the Hivites, and the Jebusites.* ¹²*Take care not to make a covenant with the inhabitants of the land to which you are going, or it will become a snare among you.*
>
> ¹³*You shall tear down their altars, break their pillars, and cut down their sacred poles.*

¹⁴for you shall worship no other god, because the LORD, whose name is Jealous, is a jealous God.

> ¹⁵*Lest you [Heb.; NRSV, You shall not] make a covenant with the inhabitants of the land.*
> *for when they prostitute themselves to their gods and sacrifice to their gods, someone among them will invite you, and you will eat of the sacrifice.*
>
> ¹⁶*and you [Heb.; NRSV, And you will] take wives from among their daughters for your sons, and their daughters who prostitute themselves to their gods will make your sons also prostitute themselves to their gods.*¹⁴⁷

---

144. In Noth's opinion, this speech contains a number of "customary, stereotyped phrases" and intrudes between the theophany and Moses' reaction (*Exodus,* 261).

145. This verse anticipates the departure for the land after the conclusion of the covenant (Noth, *Exodus,* 261). Moreover, the reference to a stiff-necked people and their need for pardon recalls the apostasy of Exodus 32.

146. For Noth, the original announcement of the covenant was followed immediately by the proclamation of its stipulations. This sequence is now interrupted by the promise of v. 10aβb. Noth goes on to assert that the stipulations were originally formulated in concise, apodictic style, as in the decalogue (Exod 20:2-17). The additions are identifiable by their more expansive style and by the way they elaborate on the basic stipulations (cf. *Exodus,* 261–65).

147. The NRSV renders the final text well. But when Exod 34:15b is separated as secondary, it introduces complications for the understanding of v. 16. The more literal RSV has been used in v. 15a.

¹⁷You shall not make cast idols.

¹⁸You shall keep the festival of unleavened bread. Seven days you shall eat unleavened bread, as I commanded you, at the time appointed in the month of Abib; for in the month of Abib you came out from Egypt.

¹⁹All that first opens the womb is mine.

All your male livestock, the firstborn of cow and sheep. ²⁰The firstborn of a donkey you shall redeem with a lamb, or if you will not redeem it you shall break its neck. All the firstborn of your sons you shall redeem.

No one shall appear before me empty-handed.

²¹Six days you shall work, but on the seventh day you shall rest.

Even in plowing time and in harvest time you shall rest. ²²You shall observe the festival of weeks, the first fruits of wheat harvest, and the festival of ingathering at the turn of the year.

²³Three times in the year all your males shall appear before the LORD God, the God of Israel.

²⁴For I will cast out nations before you, and enlarge your borders; no one shall covet your land when you go up to appear before the LORD your God three times in the year.

²⁵You shall not offer the blood of my sacrifice with leaven, and the sacrifice of the festival of the passover shall not be left until the morning. ²⁶The best of the first fruits of your ground you shall bring to the house of the LORD your God. You shall not boil a kid in its mother's milk.

²⁷ The LORD said to Moses: Write these words; in accordance with these words I have made a covenant with you and with Israel. ²⁸He was there with the LORD forty days and forty nights; he neither ate bread nor drank water. And he wrote on the tablets the words of the covenant.

the ten commandments.

²⁹ Moses came down from Mount Sinai with the two tablets of the covenant in his hand.¹⁴⁸ *As he came down from the mountain, Moses did not know that the skin of his face shone because he had been talking with God. ³⁰When Aaron and all the Israelites saw Moses, the skin of his face was shining, and they were afraid to come near him. ³¹But Moses called to them;*

and Aaron and all the leaders of the congregation returned to him, and Moses spoke with them. ³²Afterward all the Israelites came near,

and he gave them in commandment all that the LORD had spoken with him on Mount Sinai.

³³When Moses had finished speaking with them, he put a veil on his face; ³⁴but whenever Moses went in before the LORD to speak with him, he would take the veil off, until he came out; and when he came out, and told the Israelites what he had been commanded, ³⁵the Israelites would see the face of Moses, that the skin of his face was shining; and Moses would put the veil on his face again, until he went in to speak with him.

● ● ●¹⁴⁹

---

148. The order of the NRSV has been altered here to reflect the Hebrew more closely (cf. RSV).

On what follows (Exod 34:29-35), Noth comments that "if one agrees with Hugo Gressmann . . . in distinguishing within Ex. 34:29-35 between basic material which clearly tells about a unique event and secondary literary expansions which speak about a continuous custom of Moses, then there is no reason to think of P here as most scholars do. Instead, the basic material could be attributed to J and the expan-

sions—of which only v. 31aβ shows characteristics of P style—could be regarded as having been gradually added" (*Pentateuchal Traditions*, 31 n. 118). In his commentary he reduces the amount of material attributed to J to v. 29aα and v. 32b (*Exodus*, 267).

149. A gap in the J narrative is presumed by Noth, between the completion of the covenant at Sinai in Exodus 34 and Moses' invitation to Hobab son of Reuel in Num 10:29-33 to join Israel in the journey to the promised land.

The Book of Numbers

From Sinai through the Wilderness

Departure from Sinai

10:29 Moses said to Hobab son of Reuel the Midianite, Moses' father-in-law, "We are setting out for the place of which the LORD said, 'I will give it to you'; come with us, and we will treat you well; for the LORD has promised good to Israel."[150] [30]But he said to him, "I will not go, but I will go back to my own land and to my kindred." [31]He said, "Do not leave us, for you know where we should camp in the wilderness, and you will serve as eyes for us. [32]Moreover, if you go with us, whatever good the LORD does for us, the same we will do for you."

33 So they set out from the mount of the LORD three days' journey with the ark of the covenant of the LORD going before them three days' journey, to seek out a resting place for them.

[34]the cloud of the LORD being over them by day when they set out from the camp.[151]

[35]Whenever the ark set out, Moses would say,
"Arise, O LORD, let your enemies
　　be scattered,
and your foes flee before you."[152]
[36]And whenever it came to rest, he would say,
"Return, O LORD of the ten thousand
　　thousands of Israel."

Rebellion in the Wilderness

11 Now when the people complained in the hearing of the LORD about their misfortunes, the LORD heard it and his anger was kindled. Then the fire of the LORD burned against them, and consumed some outlying parts of the camp.[153] [2]But the people cried out to Moses; and Moses prayed to the LORD, and the fire abated. [3]So that place was called Taberah, because the fire of the LORD burned against them.

4 The rabble among them had a strong craving; and the Israelites also wept again, and said, "If only we had meat to eat! [5]We remember the fish we used to eat in Egypt for nothing, the cucumbers, the melons, the leeks, the onions,

---

150. Noth observes in his commentary that the description given here of Hobab is a harmonization within J of two originally independent traditions about the identity of Moses' father-in-law. One tradition is preserved in Exod 2:16-21, which tells of Moses' marriage into the family of the priest of Midian. This priest was subsequently, according to Noth, given the name Reuel (cf. v. 18). The other tradition is preserved in Judg 4:11, where Hobab is described as Moses' father-in-law. The harmonization effected in Num 10:29 is to make Hobab the son of Reuel (Noth, *Numbers*, 77). The E story in Exodus 18, which describes the visit of Jethro, the father-in-law of Moses, preserves a third tradition (cf. Exod 3:1, seen as supplementary in J).

151. This verse is identified as an addition by Noth because the role of guiding Israel in the wilderness has already been assigned in J to the ark. The cloud does, however, serve as Israel's guide in P (cf. Num

9:15-23; 10:11-12). Noth concludes that a later hand has sought to resolve the tension between J and P by including a reference to the cloud here (*Numbers*, 79).

152. Noth does not have Num 10:35 in J (*Pentateuchal Traditions*, 32), but neither is it listed in his P or E texts. It is required here and would appear to be an omission (cf. *Numbers*, 79-80).

153. Noth's view in *Pentateuchal Traditions* was that the unity of Numbers 11 is not a literary-critical but a traditio-historical problem (32 n. 119). Different materials have merged here into an indissoluble unity, in which only the land promised on oath at the end of v. 12 is an addition and the only foreign material is the description of the manna in vv. 6*, 7-9. In his subsequent commentary he asserts that a basic J narrative can be identified in vv. 1-3, 4-6, 10-13 (omitting the end of v. 12), 18-24a, 31-34. A later hand inserted traditions relating to the spirit, vv. 14-17 and 24b-30 (*Numbers*, 83, 86-87).

and the garlic; [6]but now our strength is dried up, and there is nothing at all but this manna to look at."[154]

7 Now the manna was like coriander seed, and its color was like the color of gum resin. [8]The people went around and gathered it, ground it in mills or beat it in mortars, then boiled it in pots and made cakes of it; and the taste of it was like the taste of cakes baked with oil. [9]When the dew fell on the camp in the night, the manna would fall with it.

10 Moses heard the people weeping throughout their families, all at the entrances of their tents. Then the LORD became very angry, and Moses was displeased. [11]So Moses said to the LORD, "Why have you treated your servant so badly? Why have I not found favor in your sight, that you lay the burden of all this people on me? [12]Did I conceive all this people? Did I give birth to them, that you should say to me, 'Carry them in your bosom, as a nurse carries a sucking child,' to the land that you promised on oath to their ancestors? [13]Where am I to get meat to give to all this people? For they come weeping to me and say, 'Give us meat to eat!' [14]I am not able to carry all this people alone, for they are too heavy for me. [15]If this is the way you are going to treat me, put me to death at once—if I have found favor in your sight—and do not let me see my misery."

16 So the LORD said to Moses, "Gather for me seventy of the elders of Israel, whom you know to be the elders of the people and officers over them; bring them to the tent of meeting, and have them take their place there with you. [17]I will come down and talk with you there; and I will take some of the spirit that is on you and put it on them; and they shall bear the burden of the people along with you so that you will not bear it all by yourself. [18]And say to the people: Consecrate yourselves for tomorrow, and you shall eat meat; for you have wailed in the hearing of the LORD, saying, 'If only we had meat to eat! Surely it was better for us in Egypt.' Therefore the LORD will give you meat, and you shall eat. [19]You shall eat not only one day, or two days, or five days, or ten days, or twenty days, [20]but for a whole month—until it comes out of your nostrils and becomes loathsome to you—because you have rejected the LORD who is among you, and have wailed before him, saying, 'Why did we ever leave Egypt?' " [21]But Moses said, "The people I am with number six hundred thousand on foot; and you say, 'I will give them meat, that they may eat for a whole month'! [22]Are there enough flocks and herds to slaughter for them? Are there enough fish in the sea to catch for them?" [23]The LORD said to Moses, "Is the LORD's power limited? Now you shall see whether my word will come true for you or not."

24 So Moses went out and told the people the words of the LORD; and he gathered seventy elders of the people, and placed them all around the tent. [25]Then the LORD came down in the cloud and spoke to him, and took some of the spirit that was on him and put it on the seventy elders; and when the spirit rested upon them, they prophesied. But they did not do so again.

26 Two men remained in the camp, one named Eldad, and the other named Medad, and the spirit rested on them; they were among those registered, but they had not gone out to the tent, and so they prophesied in the camp. [27]And a young man ran and told Moses, "Eldad and Medad are prophesying in the camp." [28]And Joshua son of Nun, the assistant of Moses, one of his chosen men, said, "My lord Moses, stop them!" [29]But Moses said to him, "Are you

154. For Noth's analysis of the relationship in J between the reference to manna here and in Exodus 16, see n. 127, above.

jealous for my sake? Would that all the LORD's people were prophets, and that the LORD would put his spirit on them!" [30]And Moses and the elders of Israel returned to the camp.

31 Then a wind went out from the LORD, and it brought quails from the sea and let them fall beside the camp, about a day's journey on this side and a day's journey on the other side, all around the camp, about two cubits deep on the ground. [32]So the people worked all that day and night and all the next day, gathering the quails; the least anyone gathered was ten homers; and they spread them out for themselves all around the camp. [33]But while the meat was still between their teeth, before it was consumed, the anger of the LORD was kindled against the people, and the LORD struck the people with a very great plague. [34]So that place was called Kibroth-hattaavah, because there they buried the people who had the craving. [35]From Kibroth-hattaavah the people journeyed to Hazeroth.

Miriam and Aaron against Moses

12 While they were at Hazeroth, Miriam and Aaron spoke against Moses because of the Cushite woman whom he had married (for he had indeed married a Cushite woman);[155] [2]and they said, "Has the LORD spoken only through Moses? Has he not spoken through us also?" And the LORD heard it. [3]Now the man Moses was very humble, more so than anyone else on the face of the earth. [4]Suddenly the LORD said to Moses, Aaron, and Miriam, "Come out, you three, to the tent of meeting." So the three of them came out. [5]Then the LORD came down in a pillar of cloud, and stood at the entrance of the tent, and called Aaron and Miriam; and they both came forward. [6]And he said, "Hear my words:

When there are prophets among you,
    I the LORD make myself known to them
      in visions;
    I speak to them in dreams.
[7]Not so with my servant Moses;
    he is entrusted with all my house.
[8]With him I speak face to face—clearly,
    not in riddles;
    and he beholds the form of the LORD.

Why then were you not afraid to speak against my servant Moses?" [9]And the anger of the LORD was kindled against them, and he departed.

10 When the cloud went away from over the tent, Miriam had become leprous, as white as snow. And Aaron turned towards Miriam and saw that she was leprous. [11]Then Aaron said to Moses, "Oh, my lord, do not punish us for a sin that we have so foolishly committed. [12]Do not let her be like one stillborn, whose flesh is half consumed when it comes out of its mother's womb." [13]And Moses cried to the LORD, "O God, please heal her." [14]But the LORD said to Moses, "If her father had but spit in her face, would she not bear her shame for seven days? Let her be shut out of the camp for seven days, and after that she may be brought in again." [15]So Miriam was shut out of the camp for seven days; and the people did not set out on the march until Miriam had been brought in again. [16]After that the people set out from Hazeroth, and camped in the wilderness of Paran.

---

155. In Noth's opinion, this chapter is too broken for source analysis to be feasible; it has been altered and added to, as well as suffering a number of losses. He initially thought that the presence of the divine name "LORD" throughout could be a sign that its basic material was J (*Pentateuchal Traditions*, 32 n. 120). Subsequent reflection in the commentary persuaded him that it was more likely an addition to J, because of its thematic similarity to the additions in Num 11:14-17 and 24b-30 (*Numbers*, 92–93).

At Kadesh, on the Edge of the Land

Story of the Spies

• • •[156]

13:17b And he [Heb.; NRSV, And] said to them, "Go up there into the Negeb, and go up into the hill country, [18]and see what the land is like, and whether the people who live in it are strong or weak, whether they are few or many, [19]and whether the land they live in is good or bad, and whether the towns that they live in are unwalled or fortified, [20]and whether the land is rich or poor, and whether there are trees in it or not. Be bold, and bring some of the fruit of the land." Now it was the season of the first ripe grapes.[157]

22 They went up into the Negeb, and came to Hebron; and Ahiman, Sheshai, and Talmai, the Anakites, were there. (Hebron was built seven years before Zoan in Egypt.) [23]And they came to the Wadi Eshcol, and cut down from there a branch with a single cluster of grapes, and they carried it on a pole between two of them. They also brought some pomegranates and figs. [24]That place was called the Wadi Eshcol, because of the cluster that the Israelites cut down from there.

• • •[158]

26*at Kadesh.

• • •

[27]And they told him, "We came to the land to which you sent us; *it flows with milk and honey,* and this is its fruit. [28]Yet the people who live in the land are strong, and the towns are fortified and very large; and besides, we saw the descendants of Anak there."

[29]*The Amalekites live in the land of the Negeb; the Hittites, the Jebusites, and the Amorites live in the hill country; and the Canaanites live by the sea, and along the Jordan."*[159]

30 But Caleb quieted the people before Moses, and said, "Let us go up at once and occupy it, for we are well able to overcome it." [31]Then the men who had gone up with him said, "We are not able to go up against this people, for they are stronger than we."[160]

Crisis in Israel

14:1b And the people wept that night. [4]So they said to one another, "Let us choose a captain, and go back to Egypt."

---

156. The beginning of the story of the spies in J has been omitted in favor of P. In his commentary, Noth proposes that the contents of the omitted J text may be reconstructed from Deut 1:19b-45, granted that this version of the spies episode depends on J. The verses on which he bases his reconstruction are Deut 1:19b-23. In these Moses describes how the Israelites arrived at Kadesh-barnea, where he charged them to take possession of the promised land. They requested that some men be sent to spy out the land beforehand. Moses complied with the request and selected twelve of them. Noth assumes that the extant J text in Num 13:17b-20 describes Moses giving this group their commission (*Numbers*, 104).

157. Noth comments that, although Num 13:17b-20 is overfull, the attempt to isolate two narrative variants does not succeed. It is best to assume that a basic narrative underwent secondary expansion (*Pentateuchal Traditions*, 32 n. 121).

158. J's report of the return of the spies has been replaced here by P. According to Noth, the phrase "at Kadesh" in Num 13:26 is a fragment from J. It has been inserted into the P account by a later editor because it appeared factually significant, even though this creates tension with P's statement "in the wilderness of Paran" (*Numbers*, 106). Noth believes that the identification of Kadesh as J's setting for the story of the spies is supported by Deut 1:19b and 46 (cf. n. 156, above).

159. The description of the land flowing with milk and honey and the list of nations in v. 29 occur also in Exod 3:8; 13:5; and 33:2-3. Noth regards all of these texts as later additions to J (see n. 93, above).

160. In the J narrative, Caleb stands firm against the disquiet of the Israelites and his fellow spies. In the P text of Num 14:6-9, this role is attributed to Caleb and Joshua.

[11]And the LORD said to Moses, "How long will this people despise me?

And how long will they refuse to believe in me, in spite of all the signs that I have done among them? [12]*I will strike them with pestilence and disinherit them, and I will make of you a nation greater and mightier than they."*

13 But Moses said to the LORD, "Then the Egyptians will hear of it, for in your might you brought up this people from among them, [14]and they will tell the inhabitants of this land. They have heard that you, O LORD, are in the midst of this people; for you, O LORD, are seen face to face, and your cloud stands over them and you go in front of them, in a pillar of cloud by day and in a pillar of fire by night. [15]Now if you kill this people all at one time, then the nations who have heard about you will say, [16]'It is because the LORD was not able to bring this people into the land he swore to give them that he has slaughtered them in the wilderness.' [17]And now, therefore, let the power of the LORD be great in the way that you promised when you spoke, saying,

[18]*'The LORD is slow to anger,
and abounding in steadfast love,
forgiving iniquity and transgression,
but by no means clearing the guilty,
visiting the iniquity of the parents
upon the children
to the third and the fourth generation.'*

[19]*Forgive the iniquity of this people according to the greatness of your steadfast love, just as you have pardoned this people, from Egypt even until now."*

20 Then the LORD said, "I do forgive, just as

you have asked; [21]nevertheless—as I live, and as all the earth shall be filled with the glory of the LORD—[22]none of the people who have seen my glory and the signs that I did in Egypt and in the wilderness, and yet have tested me these ten times and have not obeyed my voice, [23a]shall see the land that I swore to give to their ancestors[161]

• • •[162]

[23b]None of those who despised me shall see it. [24]But my servant Caleb, because he has a different spirit and has followed me wholeheartedly, I will bring into the land into which he went, and his descendants shall possess it.

[25]*Now, since the Amalekites and the Canaanites live in the valleys*

Turn tomorrow and set out for the wilderness by the way to the Red Sea."

*Israel's Attempt to Enter
the Land Fails*

39 When Moses told these words to all the Israelites, the people mourned greatly. [40]They rose early in the morning and went up to the heights of the hill country, saying, "Here we are. We will go up to the place that the LORD has promised, for we have sinned." [41]But Moses said, "Why do you continue to transgress the command of the LORD? That will not succeed. [42]Do not go up, for the LORD is not with you; do not let yourselves be struck down before your enemies. [43]For the Amalekites and the Canaanites will confront you there, and you shall fall by the sword; because you have turned back from following the LORD, the LORD will not be with you." [44]But they presumed to go up to the

---

161. Noth holds that Num 14:11b-23a is a later addition to J on two counts: (1) the passage is permeated throughout by deuteronomistic thought and terminology; and (2) v. 23b has the same verb, "to despise," as in v. 11a, but this verb does not occur in vv. 11b-23a (*Numbers*, 108–10). The passage's portrayal of Moses as intercessor on behalf of a sinful

Israel recalls Exod 32:7-14, which Noth also identifies as a deuteronomistic addition.

162. According to Noth, a sentence in the original J narrative was suppressed here in favor of Num 14:11b-23a (the addition above). This sentence referred to the promised land which, according to v. 23b ("it"), none of those who despised the LORD would see (*Numbers*, 109).

heights of the hill country, even though the ark of the covenant of the LORD, and Moses, had not left the camp. ⁴⁵Then the Amalekites and the Canaanites who lived in that hill country came down and defeated them, pursuing them as far as Hormah.

Dathan and Abiram against Moses

• • •¹⁶³

16:1* And [Heb.; NRSV, along with] Dathan and Abiram, sons of Eliab,
and On son of Peleth—descendants of Reuben
2*and they confronted Moses.¹⁶⁴

• • •¹⁶⁵

12 Moses sent for Dathan and Abiram sons of Eliab; but they said, "We will not come! ¹³Is it too little that you have brought us up out of a land flowing with milk and honey to kill us in the wilderness, that you must also lord it over us? ¹⁴It is clear you have not brought us into a land flowing with milk and honey, or given us an inheritance of fields and vineyards. Would you put out the eyes of these men? We will not come!"

15 Moses was very angry and said to the LORD, "Pay no attention to their offering. I have not taken one donkey from them, and I have not harmed any one of them."

• • •¹⁶⁶

25 So Moses got up and went to Dathan and Abiram; the elders of Israel followed him. ²⁶He said to the congregation, "Turn away from the tents of these wicked men, and touch nothing of theirs, or you will be swept away for all their sins." ²⁷ᵇAnd Dathan and Abiram came out and stood at the entrance of their tents, together with their wives, their children, and their little ones. ²⁸And Moses said, "This is how you shall know that the LORD has sent me to do all these works; it has not been of my own accord: ²⁹If these people die a natural death, or if a natural fate comes on them, then the LORD has not sent me. ³⁰But if the LORD creates something new, and the ground opens its mouth and swallows them up, with all that belongs to them, and they go down alive into Sheol, then you shall know that these men have despised the LORD."

31 As soon as he finished speaking all these words, the ground under them was split apart. ³²ᵃThe earth opened its mouth and swallowed them up, along with their households.
everyone who belonged to Korah and all their goods.

---

163. Noth does not comment on the gap here, but it may be taken as a reference to the beginning of J's story of Dathan and Abiram. Part of this was suppressed when, in the combined text, J was worked into the story of the rebellion of Korah, which for Noth is an addition to P. The mention of Dathan and Abiram in Num 16:1* was presumably accompanied by a plural verb, of which they were the subject. The Hebrew now has a singular verb at the beginning of the sentence, with Korah as its subject; it is translated as "took" in the NRSV and placed at the end of the verse. What is identified as J here is evidently fragmentary.

164. Although this clause occurs at the end of v. 2 in the NRSV, it is in fact Num 16:2aα; the NRSV has been obliged to alter the order of the Hebrew. In his commentary Noth regards only "and On son of Peleth" as secondary, which he emends to "he was the son of Pallu" and correlates with Num 26:5, 8 (*Numbers*, 118, 122).

165. In his commentary, Noth observes how the report in Num 16:12 that Moses sent for Dathan and Abiram implies that they did not address their complaint to him directly but spread it among the people. Apart from the brief remark in v. 2, however, there is in the surviving J text no description of this spreading disaffection or of Moses learning about it. The original J narrative presumably supplied such a description, but it has been suppressed in favor of the confrontation between Moses and Korah in vv. 3-11 (cf. Noth, *Numbers*, 125).

166. Noth initially posited a gap in the J narrative here; in his later commentary he revised this position, proposing that Num 16:25 connects directly with 16:15 (*Numbers*, 127).

[33]So they with all that belonged to them went down alive into Sheol; the earth closed over them.

and they perished from the midst of the assembly.
[34]All Israel around them fled at their outcry, for they said, "The earth will swallow us too!"
20:1*And the people stayed in Kadesh.[167]

Edom Refuses Israel Passage

• • •[168]

19 The Israelites said to him, "We will stay on the highway; and if we drink of your water, we and our livestock, then we will pay for it. It is only a small matter; just let us pass through on foot." [20]But he said, "You shall not pass through." And Edom came out against them with a large force, heavily armed.

• • •[169]

From Kadesh toward the Land

Israel Sets Out from Kadesh

22a They set out from Kadesh,

21 When the Canaanite, the king of Arad, who lived in the Negeb, heard that Israel was coming by the way of Atharim, he fought against Israel and took some of them captive.

[2]*Then Israel made a vow to the LORD and said, "If you will indeed give this people into our hands, then we will utterly destroy their towns."* [3]*The LORD listened to the voice of Israel, and handed over the Canaanites; and they utterly destroyed them and their towns; so the place was called Hormah*[170]

[4]*by the way to the Red Sea, to go around the land of Edom.

The Bronze Serpent

But the people became impatient on the way.
[5]*The people spoke against God and against Moses, "Why have you brought us up out of Egypt to die in the wilderness? For there is no food and no water, and we detest this miserable food."*
[6]*Then the LORD sent poisonous serpents among the people, and they bit the people, so that many Israelites died.* [7]*The people came to Moses and said, "We have sinned by speaking against the LORD and against you; pray to the LORD to take away the serpents from us." So Moses prayed for the people.* [8]*And the LORD said to Moses, "Make a poisonous serpent, and set it on a pole; and everyone who is bitten shall look at it and live." [9]So Moses made a serpent of bronze, and put it upon a*

---

167. This report in J implies that Israel had not moved from Kadesh after the disastrous invasion attempt described in Num 14:39-45. The departure from Kadesh in 20:22a, after the breakdown of negotiations with Edom, marks the renewal of Israel's journey toward the promised land (cf. Noth, *Numbers*, 151).

168. According to Noth, only Num 20:19-20 remains of J's version of the negotiations with Edom; it has been replaced by E's version, which is the first appearance of this source in the book of Numbers (*Numbers*, 149). The negotiations with Edom in Num 20:14-21 provide a good example of a source division being based on the presence of doublets in the text; in this case, Noth identifies doublets in vv. 17-18 and 19-20.

169. Noth does not comment on this gap in J, but presumably it reported how Israel retired to Kadesh

in the face of Edomite hostility. The statement in Num 20:21, that Israel turned away from Edom, is assigned by Noth to E. The J narrative resumes in v. 22a and 21:4* with the report that Israel set out from Kadesh to go around the land of Edom.

170. Noth considers that Num 21:1-3 might have been an original element in J, but for a story set in the Negeb, its present location in the context of Israel's journey around the land of Edom is incongruous. Along with the P passage 20:22b-29, it disturbs the probably original connection between 20:22a and 21:4*. Noth proposes that the pentateuchal redactor could not make use of the story in its original place—which unfortunately can no longer be determined with any certainty (according to Noth)—and therefore transposed it to the present location (*Pentateuchal Traditions*, 32 n. 122).

pole; and whenever a serpent bit someone, that person would look at the serpent of bronze and live.[171]

● ● ●[172]

Balaam Is Summoned to Curse Israel

22:[3b]Moab was overcome with fear of the people of Israel. [4]And Moab said to the elders of Midian, "This horde will now lick up all that is around us, as an ox licks up the grass of the field." Now Balak son of Zippor was king of Moab at that time. [5]He sent messengers to Balaam son of Beor at Pethor, which is on the Euphrates, in the land of Amaw, to summon him, saying, "A people has come out of Egypt; they have spread over the face of the earth, and they have settled next to me. [6]Come now, curse this people for me, since they are stronger than I; perhaps I shall be able to defeat them and drive them from the land; for I know that whomever you bless is blessed, and whomever you curse is cursed."

[7] So the elders of Moab and the elders of Midian departed with the fees for divination in their hand; and they came to Balaam, and gave him Balak's message. [8]He said to them, "Stay here tonight, and I will bring back word to you, just as the LORD speaks to me"; so the officials of Moab stayed with Balaam. [13]So Balaam rose in the morning, and said to the officials of Balak, "Go to your own land, for the LORD has refused to let me go with you." [14]So the officials of Moab rose and went to Balak, and said, "Balaam refuses to come with us."

[15] Once again Balak sent officials, more numerous and more distinguished than these. [16]They came to Balaam and said to him, "Thus says Balak son of Zippor: 'Do not let anything hinder you from coming to me; [17]for I will surely do you great honor, and whatever you say to me I will do; come, curse this people for me.' " [18]But Balaam replied to the servants of Balak, "Although Balak were to give me his house full of silver and gold, I could not go beyond the command of the LORD my God, to do less or more. [19]You remain here, as the others did, so that I may learn what more the LORD may say to me." [21]But [Heb.; NRSV, So] Balaam got up in the morning, saddled his donkey, and went with the officials of Moab.[173]

[22] God's anger was kindled because he was going, and the angel of the LORD took his stand in the road as his adversary. Now he was riding on the donkey, and his two servants were with him. [23]The donkey saw the angel of the LORD standing in the road, with a drawn sword in his hand; so the donkey turned off the road, and went into the field; and Balaam struck the donkey, to turn it back onto the road. [24]Then the angel of the LORD stood in a narrow path between the vineyards, with a wall on either side. [25]When the donkey saw the angel of the LORD, it scraped against the wall, and scraped Balaam's

---

171. According to Noth, the story of the bronze serpent is probably a later addition to J because it is a wilderness story located immediately before the theme of occupation of the land. He is doubtful whether it belongs to any source (*Pentateuchal Traditions*, 32 n. 123).

172. The postulated gap in the J narrative here presumably refers to a report of Israel arriving at the borders of Moab and camping there; this is the context of the message conveyed to Balaam in Num 22:5. J's itinerary has been replaced by P in 22:1b, with v. 1a regarded by Noth as an editorial, transitional passage (*Numbers*, 171).

173. Numbers 22:20, giving Balaam permission to go, belongs to E (or another version of the story). The story of the donkey (vv. 22-35) presents Balaam's departure as a disobedient or at least unauthorized act. Noth does not indicate a gap, presumably accepting the present J text as satisfactory. In this case, the silence of the text is taken to mean that there was no authorizing communication from God. Verse 34 supports this understanding of the text; there is no awareness expressed on Balaam's part of having gone against God's will.

foot against the wall; so he struck it again. [26]Then the angel of the LORD went ahead, and stood in a narrow place, where there was no way to turn either to the right or to the left. [27]When the donkey saw the angel of the LORD, it lay down under Balaam; and Balaam's anger was kindled, and he struck the donkey with his staff. [28]Then the LORD opened the mouth of the donkey, and it said to Balaam, "What have I done to you, that you have struck me these three times?" [29]Balaam said to the donkey, "Because you have made a fool of me! I wish I had a sword in my hand! I would kill you right now!" [30]But the donkey said to Balaam, "Am I not your donkey, which you have ridden all your life to this day? Have I been in the habit of treating you this way?" And he said, "No."

31 Then the LORD opened the eyes of Balaam, and he saw the angel of the LORD standing in the road, with his drawn sword in his hand; and he bowed down, falling on his face. [32]The angel of the LORD said to him, "Why have you struck your donkey these three times? I have come out as an adversary, because your way is perverse before me. [33]The donkey saw me, and turned away from me these three times. If it had not turned away from me, surely just now I would have killed you and let it live." [34]Then Balaam said to the angel of the LORD, "I have sinned, for I did not know that you were standing in the road to oppose me. Now therefore, if it is displeasing to you, I will return home." [35]The angel of the LORD said to Balaam, "Go with the men; but speak only what I tell you to speak." So Balaam went on with the officials of Balak.

36 When Balak heard that Balaam had come, he went out to meet him at Ir-moab, on the boundary formed by the Arnon, at the farthest point of the boundary. [37]Balak said to Balaam,

"Did I not send to summon you? Why did you not come to me? Am I not able to honor you?" [38]*Balaam said to Balak, "I have come to you." [39]Then Balaam went with Balak, and they came to Kiriath-huzoth. [40]Balak sacrificed oxen and sheep, and sent them to Balaam and to the officials who were with him.

23:28 So Balak took Balaam to the top of Peor, which overlooks the wasteland.

Balaam Is Moved to Bless Israel

24 Now Balaam saw that it pleased the LORD to bless Israel,
> so he did not go, as at other times, to look for omens[174]

and he [Heb.; NRSV, but] set his face toward the wilderness. [2]Balaam looked up and saw Israel camping tribe by tribe. Then the spirit of God came upon him, [3]and he uttered his oracle, saying:
> "The oracle of Balaam son of Beor,
>   the oracle of the man whose eye is clear,
> [4] the oracle of one who hears the words
>   of God,
>   who sees the vision of the Almighty,
>   who falls down, but with eyes uncovered:
> [5]how fair are your tents, O Jacob,
>   your encampments, O Israel!
> [6]Like palm groves that stretch far away,
>   like gardens beside a river,
> like aloes that the LORD has planted,
>   like cedar trees beside the waters.
> [7]Water shall flow from his buckets,
>   and his seed shall have abundant water,
> his king shall be higher than Agag,
>   and his kingdom shall be exalted.
> [8]God who brings him out of Egypt,
>   is like the horns of a wild ox for him;
> he shall devour the nations that are his foes

---

174. Noth regards this as an editorial remark, with a derogatory comment on omens (*Numbers*, 188).

and break their bones.
He shall strike with his arrows.
⁹He crouched, he lay down like a lion,
and like a lioness; who will rouse him up?
Blessed is everyone who blesses you,
and cursed is everyone who curses you."

10 Then Balak's anger was kindled against Balaam, and he struck his hands together. Balak said to Balaam, "I summoned you to curse my enemies, but instead you have blessed them *these three times.*[175] ¹¹Now be off with you! Go home! I said, 'I will reward you richly,' but the LORD has denied you any reward." ¹²And Balaam said to Balak, "Did I not tell your messengers whom you sent to me, ¹³'If Balak should give me his house full of silver and gold, I would not be able to go beyond the word of the LORD, to do either good or bad of my own will; what the LORD says, that is what I will say'? ¹⁴So now, I am going to my people; let me advise you what this people will do to your people in days to come."

15 So he uttered his oracle, saying:
"The oracle of Balaam son of Beor,
the oracle of the man whose eye is clear,
¹⁶the oracle of one who hears the
words of God,
and knows the knowledge of the
Most High,
who sees the vision of the Almighty,
who falls down, but with his eyes
uncovered:
¹⁷I see him, but not now;
I behold him, but not near—
a star shall come out of Jacob,
and a scepter shall rise out of Israel;

it shall crush the borderlands of Moab,
and the territory of all the Shethites.
¹⁸Edom will become a possession,
Seir a possession of its enemies,
while Israel does valiantly.
¹⁹One out of Jacob shall rule,
and destroy the survivors of Ir."
20 Then he looked on Amalek, and uttered his oracle, saying:
"First among the nations was Amalek,
but its end is to perish forever."
21 Then he looked on the Kenite, and uttered his oracle, saying:
"Enduring is your dwelling place,
and your nest is set in the rock;
²²yet Kain is destined for burning.
How long shall Asshur take you away
captive?"
23 Again he uttered his oracle, saying:
"Alas, who shall live when God does this?
²⁴But ships shall come from Kittim
and shall afflict Asshur and Eber;
and he also shall perish forever."[176]

25 Then Balaam got up and went back to his place, and Balak also went his way.

Israel Follows the
Baal of Peor

25 While Israel was staying at Shittim[177]
The people began to have sexual relations with the women of Moab. ²These invited the people to the sacrifices of their gods, and the people ate and bowed down to their gods. ³Thus Israel yoked itself to the Baal of Peor, and the LORD's anger was kindled against Israel. ⁴The LORD said

---

175. The comment derives from the combined JE text.

176. Numbers 24:20-24 is regarded by Noth as a series of additional oracles that have been appended to the J narrative. Each oracle has its own introduction (cf. vv. 20, 21, 23). For further details, see Noth, *Numbers*, 193–94.

177. For Noth, it is at least questionable whether Num 25:1a, because of its mention of Shittim, was not added later with a view to Josh 2:1; 3:1. The following story does not take place at Shittim in the valley of Jordan but on the highlands at the sanctuary of Baal Peor (*Pentateuchal Traditions*, 32 n. 125).

to Moses, "Take all the chiefs of the people, and impale them in the sun before the LORD, in order that the fierce anger of the LORD may turn away from Israel." [5]And Moses said to the judges of Israel, "Each of you shall kill any of your people who have yoked themselves to the Baal of Peor."

• • •[178]

Conquest of East Jordan

32:1 Now the Reubenites and the Gadites owned a very great number of cattle. And [Heb.; NRSV, When] they saw that the land of Jazer and the land of Gilead was a good place for cattle.

[16]Then they came up to him and said, "We will build sheepfolds here for our flocks, and towns for our little ones."[179]

• • •[180]

[39]The descendants of Machir son of Manasseh went to Gilead, captured it,

and dispossessed the Amorites who were there; [40]*so Moses gave Gilead to Machir son of Manasseh*

and he settled there. [41]Jair son of Manasseh went and captured their villages, and renamed them Havvoth-jair. [42]And Nobah went and captured Kenath and its villages, and renamed it Nobah after himself.[181]

• • •[182]

---

178. According to Noth, it is very difficult to say anything certain about the original form of the penta-teuchal material in this area because of a variety of additions made in various literary stages and the results of the literary combination of the Pentateuch with the Deuteronomistic History.

He does, however, consider the possibility that there was an account of the death of Moses in J between Numbers 25 and 32. Two factors point to this: (1) Moses does not appear at all in the basic J material of chap. 32; and (2) the position of Num 27:12-23, a P passage in which the Lord informs Moses that he is to die outside the land. Noth asks whether the pentateuchal redactor could have been motivated to locate this P passage before chap. 32 by the fact that the death of Moses had been related in J between chaps. 25 and 32.

According to Noth, this would mean that the account of the death of Moses occurred in J before the transition to the theme of the occupation of the land, indeed, even before the theme of the occupation of East Jordan. In relation to this last point, Noth observes that there is no evidence for the division of the occupation into two stages—an East Jordan stage under Moses and a West Jordan stage under Joshua—until the deuteronomistic construction of this history (*Pentateuchal Traditions*, 32 n. 126).

179. "In actual fact, vv. 16-19 contain old source-material, although this has been reworked to a certain

extent" (Noth, *Numbers*, 238). This probably explains Noth's retention of Num 32:16 for J, although the reference "to him," implying Moses, clashes with his basic view of the original J in this chapter.

180. Noth does not comment on this gap explic-itly, but its presence can be explained from his reflec-tions on where J narrated the death of Moses, as these were outlined in n. 178, above. He considers it is quite possible that J related Moses' death before Numbers 32, in which case Moses did not figure in the original J version of this chapter. In the present text, however, Moses distributes land to the Reubenites and Gadites, as well as the half-tribe of Manasseh, in v. 33. Presum-ably, for Noth, this verse has replaced the J account of how the Reubenites and Gadites acquired land in East Jordan.

181. In his commentary, Noth regards Num 32:39-42 as an appendix, unconnected to any of the narra-tive sources. "Its origin is unknown, as is the date of its insertion at the present point" (*Numbers*, 240).

182. Noth states that the J account of the occupa-tion of West Jordan came after Numbers 32 and was suppressed in the compilation of the Pentateuch. He believes that it cannot be demonstrated from a liter-ary-critical point of view that parts of this discarded account are still preserved in Judges 1, which for Noth is a very secondary addition to the Deuteronomistic History (*Pentateuchal Traditions*, 33 n. 127).

CHAPTER 4

The Elohist Texts

The fundamental issue to be faced in studies of the so-called Elohist traditions in the Pentateuch is not whether they constituted an original and continuous source but how they function within the text now. The question whether the Elohist was ever a complete source reaches back into a past that no longer exists; too little is left. There is widespread agreement that, if ever it had been a source, the Elohist is the least well preserved of the pentateuchal sources. The primary questions are, therefore: What is the nature of these Elohist texts that are now preserved in the Pentateuch? How do they function? and What are the implications of this for our understanding of Israelite literature and the history of thought and theology in ancient Israel?

Within Genesis, the E traditions preserved relate principally to the Jacob–Esau cycle and to the Joseph story. Roughly half the E material in Genesis is in the Joseph story and another quarter in the Jacob–Esau cycle. Within Exodus, the only relatively self-contained traditions are the story of Jethro and the meeting with God on Sinai. In Numbers, there are two stories of the Transjordan conquest and a variant of the Balaam tradition. When all these traditions are put together, the Jacob–Esau cycle and the Joseph story still account for a little more than half of the extant text.

These observations point to the existence of two major story cycles (Jacob–Esau and Joseph) being represented in E, as well as a limited number of other independent stories for which significant text is preserved.

Beyond an awareness of the extent and concentration of the E traditions, it is important also to recognize the contribution they make to our knowledge of matters pentateuchal. Little of the material is new in relation to the J narrative. The exceptions are the sacrifice of Abraham (Genesis 22*); the blessing of Ephraim and Manasseh (Genesis 48*); the Jethro story (Exodus 18*); and the account of the victory over Sihon, king of the Amorites (Numbers 21*). There are shorter traditions without parallels in J, such as the return to Bethel and the birth of Benjamin (Gen 35:1-8, 16-20), Jacob's theophany at Beer-sheba (Gen 46:1-5*), or Joseph's final reconciliation with his brothers (Gen 50:15-21) and the testament of Joseph (Gen 50:22-26), but the first four above are the substantial passages. They constitute about one-sixth of the total E material. The rest is made up of variant expressions of traditions similar to those in J, or traditions complementary to those in J, or variant traditions contrasting with those in J.

The significance of this is that some five-sixths of the E tradition offers variants of known episodes. Only about one-sixth can be considered new traditions about otherwise unknown episodes in the life of Israel.

The distribution of these E traditions is worth noting. The Abraham traditions are grouped at the end of J's Abraham cycle (cf. Genesis 20–22). Apart from the variant view contributed within the Jacob–Esau cycle, further Jacob traditions are gathered at the end of this cycle (cf. Genesis 33 and 35). Again, there is an E variant view contributed within the Joseph story, with further Joseph traditions gathered toward the end (cf. particularly Genesis 48 and 50). The specifically E material in Exodus touches on the call of Moses, a variant version of the deliverance at the sea, the story of Moses and Jethro, and, finally, the variant version of the encounter with God at the mountain. In Numbers, there are the two traditions concerning Edom and Sihon and the variant version of the Balaam story.

The clustering suggests E traditions have been added at the end of the ancestral cycles, within both the Jacob–Esau cycle and the Joseph story, and at relatively few points elsewhere. Although this is consistent with a number of conceptions of enrichment, it leaves little evidence of an underlying narrative unity and continuity.

To paint the picture with a broad brush, the overall impression is of the addition of variant aspects of Israel's tradition at nodal points in the Yahwist narrative, with some extensive variants expressed in the Jacob–Esau cycle and the Joseph story. Within the context of a source hypothesis, the enrichment of the Yahwist from the riches of the storehouse of Israel's storytelling and tradition seems highly likely.

This enrichment is primarily in terms of vari-ant traditions. Variant expressions of similar traditions are to be found, for example, in the promise to Abraham (Genesis 15*), the ancestress-in-danger story (Genesis 20*), the story of Hagar and Ishmael (Genesis 21*), the Jacob–Esau cycle as a whole (Genesis 28–35*), the Joseph story (Genesis 37–50*), the deliverance at the sea (Exodus 13–14*), and the Balaam story (Numbers 22–23*). Among the complementary traditions are Abraham's conflict with Abimelech over wells (Genesis 21*), complementing the Isaac and Abimelech traditions (J in Genesis 26*); the birth of Jacob's children (Genesis 30*); the call of Moses (Exodus 3–4*); the encounter with God at Sinai (Exodus 19–24*); and the conflict with Edom (Numbers 20*). Variant traditions include the little note of Jacob's purchase of land from Shechem (Gen 34:19-20) and Pharaoh's initiative in settling Jacob's family in Egypt (Genesis 47*).[1]

What the Elohist material provides, then, are traditions that go beyond J in one way or another. Where there is no parallel in J, at the least these traditions provide new information not otherwise available. Where some comparable tradition does exist, the complementary or variant material in E may provide further information or further insight.

For example, E's version of the Jacob–Esau cycle has a passive Jacob, the victim of Laban's disfavor, rather than a cunningly active Jacob accumulating wealth and envy (Genesis 30–31*). On Jacob's return, E's Esau is actively welcoming and accepting (Gen 33:4-5, 8-11), in contrast with the suspicious and grudging Esau of J (Gen 33:12-16). Is this no more than further information about how the story might be told? Or is it a further insight into how matters may unfold between brothers involved in near-to-fratricidal conflict over a period of years? In the

---

1. These classifications are provisional and might be changed in a number of cases, depending on how a text is read and related to comparable traditions.

Joseph story, by contrast, while J's concern is with reconciliation within the family, E is more concerned with God's care to keep peoples alive. Along with a variant way of telling the story, are we given a theological insight into the understanding of providence?

From another standpoint, these differing traditions offer the storyteller or performer a new way of telling the stories, and they offer the reader another way of perceiving the text. The storyteller presumably told only one version of a story at any one time; the listeners heard only one. The reader is offered variant versions and may choose which one to attend to or whether to attend to several. Sometimes what is offered is new information, sometimes new insight, and often both.

The "Elohist" text does not now constitute even a substantially continuous source. It is just too fragmentary. There are elements of continuity across the episodes in Noth's text. For example, Rachel's death at the birth of Benjamin is noted in Gen 35:16-20 and referred to in the context of the blessing of Ephraim and Manasseh (Gen 48:7); Ephraim and Manasseh are again referred to in Gen 50:23. Joseph requests that his bones be taken up to Canaan (Gen 50:25); the fulfillment of this is noted in Exod 13:19. But such traces are scarcely enough to mount a case for a continuous source. Rather, they are quite consistent with the notion of story cycles.[2]

Whatever there may have been once, what now remains is a collection of alternative traditions which differ in various ways from the J narrative.

This is not the place to undertake a full-scale study of the Elohist source, its independence, and its integrity; nor is it our intention to do so. It would seem appropriate, however, to reconsider the arguments alleged by Martin Noth for regarding E as a separate source. At this distance they seem to have been more directly a response to Paul Volz and Wilhelm Rudolph than a reflective evaluation of the evidence overall and the possibilities it raised.

Recognition must be given, first, to Noth's broad agreement with Volz on the question of the value of linguistic criteria for source analysis and, second, to his acknowledgment that Volz and Rudolph have "wrested from customary literary criticism the literary unity of many a beautiful story." Nevertheless, Noth remained adamantly opposed to their elimination of the Elohist as a documentary source.[3] Noth was a careful and cautious scholar, but where the Elohist is concerned, the reasons he adduced hardly seem adequate to motivate the strength of the conviction he expressed. Perhaps the reasons are concealed deep in his experience of the biblical text. Perhaps they lie elsewhere.

One of Noth's strongly held convictions is that criticism of the source hypothesis is frequently misplaced. It is not the JE hypothesis which is flawed but "the conception of the way in which these two old sources were combined, a conception which is not necessarily inherent in the source hypothesis but is almost always connected with it in principle."[4] Noth evidently felt himself a pioneer in this regard. The existence of the Elohist as a source appears to have been firmly associated with this new procedure

---

2. The reverse position, arguing against a cycle of stories and for a continuous coherent text in the case of the Prophetic Record, is defended by A. F. Campbell (*Of Prophets and Kings: A Late Ninth-Century Document [1 Samuel 1–2 Kings 10]* [CBQMS 17; Washington, D.C.: Catholic Biblical Association of America, 1986] 64–65).

3. See Martin Noth, *A History of Pentateuchal Traditions*, trans. B. W. Anderson (Englewood Cliffs, N.J.: Prentice-Hall, 1972; reprint, Chico, Calif.: Scholars Press, 1981) 21 and 24, respectively.

4. Ibid., 24.

in Noth's advocacy. The association is less evident today.

Another pioneering conviction expressed by Noth sounds remarkably modern and deserves celebration in literary circles even now. He wrote in 1948: "It must remain, or rather become once again, a principle of any sound criticism of the Pentateuch not to assume literary disunity unless the occurrence of variants, of obvious seams and secondary connections, and the like, *compels* such an assumption."[5] Readers of this volume will recognize that Noth was not always free to be faithful to his own principle here.

The first argument Noth brings against Volz and Rudolph is double-barreled. He takes aim at the idea that E is to be understood as a series of secondary accretions to a literary and unified Yahwist narrative. He argues that the occurrence of E material is too regular to be simply secondary accretions; moreover, the E material is different from the usual run of secondary accretions. In his own words:

> To assume that there were secondary accretions upon a narrative that originally was a literary unity [as does Rudolph] does not do justice to it; for this recurrence is found too regularly, and furthermore secondary accretions usually add *new* materials, not the same material in new versions.[6]

It is difficult to see what the issue of regularity has to do with it. It is surely possible for a unified J narrative to be regularly enriched from the wide range of Israel's storytelling, without the need to postulate that these stories were themselves organized into a similar narrative unity. When the irregularity of the E enrich-

ment is taken into account, the argument has even less force. Given Noth's vast experience of the biblical text, one hesitates to challenge his view that secondary additions bring new materials rather than new versions of existing traditions; but it is not immediately evident that this is so. Even if it were so in fact, there is no reason for arguing that it must always be so in theory.

The second argument is directed against Volz. Particularly in connection with O. Eissfeldt's *Hexateuch-Synopse* (see chapter 1, p. 7), Volz argues against any special approaches being used to explain the pentateuchal text that were not in use for other biblical texts. Therefore, minor interventions in the pentateuchal text were to be explained, there as elsewhere, by glosses. Second, in Volz's view, great storytellers and collectors such as the Yahwist were not afraid to include variant stories and a variety of ideas in their stories and their narrative collections. Finally, there are sections in the great narratives where, then and now, people have found grounds for objection. The narratives were wanted for teaching and liturgy; so a new edition was produced with additions and parallel recensions so that the new could replace the old in instruction and liturgical reading. Its editor was "a clergyman or educator, a scrupulous man, more spiritual than the great narrator of the past."[7] The person responsible for this new edition was none other than the Elohist. And the Elohist was none other than that: an editor, not a storyteller. In fact, Volz goes on, the Elohist hardly seems necessary, because the deuteronomistic school did a thorough job of editing the Pentateuch later on.[8]

---

5. Ibid.

6. Ibid., 23–24.

7. P. Volz in P. Volz and W. Rudolph, *Der Elohist als Erzähler: Ein Irrweg der Pentateuchkritik?* (Giessen: Töpelmann, 1933) 21–23. "Ein Geistlicher oder ein Pädagog war dieser Mann, ängstlicher, spiritueller als jener große Erzähler der Vergangenheit" (23).

8. Ibid., 24. Perhaps Noth was particularly infuri-

ated by Volz's description of E's activity: "In the whole of Genesis, there is not a single independent story which comes from him. He had absolutely no material of his own. In a few cases where he appears to be a narrator, he models himself on existing material. Beyond that, here and there he painted over a little, added a little, toned down, eliminated the offensive, etc." (24).

Noth moves in on the obvious flaw in Volz's position. No bowdlerizing editor leaves the objectionable material in the new edition; there is little point in combining the expurgated with the unexpurgated. Noth writes:

> To assume that an older narrative work was later issued under a new edition with the intention of replacing older versions with new ones at various places [as does Volz] is an equally inadequate explanation, for it leaves unexplained why the older versions were preserved along with the new ones.[9]

Noth is perfectly correct on this point, but once other reasons are brought into play to explain the presence of variant materials, Noth's argument loses its force. If the new additions exist to preserve valued traditions, to offer variant versions of familiar stories, to provide new perspectives on old traditions, and so on, then there is no difficulty in preserving both old and new side by side. It is surprising that Noth totally ignored such possibilities.

Noth continues: "The only possible explanation of the matter is that in the old Pentateuchal tradition several originally independent parallel strands of narrative were later connected with one another. This leads us basically to the well-known documentary hypothesis which has proved to be sound."[10] Today the matter does not look quite so clear. Noth's arguments lack force. If there are other, more convincing grounds for the existence of an independent, continuous E source, they have yet to be given appropriate expression.[11]

Noth has expressed the view that "on the whole E represents rather an earlier stage in the history of tradition than J."[12] If J, as a source, drew together into a single narrative a cross section of the stories of Israel, the scenario in which other viewpoints and perspectives from some of the tradition were incorporated into the J text fits well with the nature of the E material and its distribution in the J narrative.

In the E texts there is little difference in the use of the divine name, *Elohim*, before and after the revelation to Moses of YHWH as the name of God (see pp. 184–85, n. 51). It is possible, therefore, that the use of *Elohim* in conjunction with J (and before the existence of P) was a heuristic device to allow traditions to be combined while retaining the marks of their separate origins. It is tempting to ask whether, possibly, the compositional and redactional techniques necessary were first developed in Israel for the combination of the E traditions with the J narrative.[13]

The question begs to be asked: What was the purpose of such an interweaving of traditions? The question that can be properly answered is probably: What can we see as the meaning of such interweaving? As we have seen, what it offers us is new information, alternative traditions, and varying points of view and perspectives. Whether to us as retellers of traditions and their stories or as listeners, readers, and theological thinkers, this process of skillful interweaving offers a constant variety of options in the way stories are told and heard. Beyond variant options and perspectives, the process of

---

9. Noth, *Pentateuchal Traditions*, 22.

10. Ibid. Because almost all the recurrences are duplications, it is very probable from the outset that there were two sources in the old pentateuchal traditions.

11. This despite studies such as H. W. Wolff, "The Elohistic Fragments in the Pentateuch," in *The Vitality of Old Testament Traditions*, ed. W. Brueggemann and H. W. Wolff, 2d ed. (Atlanta: John Knox, 1982); or Alan W. Jenks, *The Elohist and North Israelite Traditions*

(SBLMS 22; Missoula, Mont.: Scholars Press, 1977). See now R. B. Coote, *In Defense of Revolution: The Elohist History* (Minneapolis: Fortress, 1991).

12. Noth, *Pentateuchal Traditions*, 38 n. 143. An early (tenth century) date is shared by Jenks, *Elohist and North Israelite Traditions*, 1, 101–6.

13. On the evidence for such procedures in the ancient world, see Jeffrey H. Tigay, ed., *Empirical Models for Biblical Criticism* (Philadelphia: University of Pennsylvania Press, 1985).

skilled interweaving can enhance storytelling in a variety of ways, heightening interest, adding complexity and depth, opening up manifold new vistas. Some of these are explored in chapter 6.

The upshot of these observations is that the definitive description of the Elohist texts is yet to be drawn up. As we have been working with these texts, our impression tends to favor the application of a supplementary hypothesis to the combination of J and E. By this we mean that the so-called Elohist material was used to supplement and enrich the Yahwist narrative. It need not itself have ever formed a continuous narrative; it may have been drawn from across the range of Israel's storytelling and tradition. This view of E was anathema to Noth. Ironically, the procedures that he outlined and implemented may allow a supplementary hypothesis

to be the most convincing explanation of the nonpriestly pentateuchal texts.

Where P and J are concerned, Noth's source analysis stands on far surer ground. The source hypothesis as envisaged by Noth, with the analysis of the sources that he proposes, offers two reasonably intact and reasonably independent documents worthy of serious consideration as an explanation of the signals in the pentateuchal text.

It is our hope that the presentation here of Noth's Elohist texts in easily accessible form will advance their study and bring greater clarity to bear on their origins, combination, and meaning. Basically, however, it is not "what was" that matters but how "what is" functions and gives meaning. The fragmentary Elohist texts we have are part of what is.

The Book of Genesis

• • •

God's Promise to Abram

15:1* "Do not be afraid, Abram, I am your shield."[14] [3a]And Abram said, "You have given me no offspring." [5]He brought him outside

and said, "Look toward heaven and count the stars, if you are able to count them." Then he said to him, "So shall your descendants be."
• • •
[13]And he said (Heb.; NRSV, Then the LORD said)[15] to Abram, "Know this for certain, that

---

14. In the Elohist texts, Noth distinguishes two subsets of tradition. He places in italics material that stands out clearly from the J context as narrative variants but that offers no clues to identify it with the Elohist (e.g., in Genesis 15, Exodus 1, and Exodus 32). He puts parentheses around the chapters and verses that he believes to be secondary in the E context. Because elsewhere in this volume we have used indented italics to identify secondary material, we continue to do so here. The narrative variants that cannot be clearly attributed to E, as here in Genesis 15, are indented. Secondary additions within these narrative variants will be treated as the others, i.e., italicized and further indented.

The material designated as narrative variants in Genesis 15 contributes an emphasis on Abram's

numerous descendants in v. 5 and a brief foreshadowing of Israel's history to come in vv. 13-16 (Noth, *Pentateuchal Traditions*, 33).

15. The NRSV margin notes that "the LORD" here replaces a simple "he"; the Hebrew has "And he said." In the context of v. 12, this "he" would have to be Abram, the result being that the sentence reading "And he said to Abram" would be absurd. The translator needed to introduce a name for God, and the only one appropriate in the context is YHWH (see A. F. Campbell, *The Study Companion to Old Testament Literature: An Approach to the Writings of Pre-Exilic and Exilic Israel* [A Michael Glazier Book; Old Testament Studies 2; Collegeville, Minn.: Liturgical Press, 1989/1992], 118–19).

your offspring shall be aliens in a land that is not theirs, and shall be slaves there, and they shall be oppressed,

for four hundred years

[14]but I will bring judgment on the nation that they serve, and afterward they shall come out.

with great possessions

[15]As for yourself, you shall go to your ancestors in peace; you shall be buried in a good old age. [16]And they shall come back here in the fourth generation; for the iniquity of the Amorites is not yet complete."

• • •

Abraham and Sarah at Gerar

20:1b While residing in Gerar as an alien, [2]Abraham said of his wife Sarah, "She is my sister." And King Abimelech of Gerar sent and took Sarah. [3]But God came to Abimelech in a dream by night, and said to him, "You are about to die because of the woman whom you have taken; for she is a married woman." [4]Now Abimelech had not approached her; so he said, "Lord, will you destroy an innocent people? [5]Did he not himself say to me, 'She is my sister'? And she herself said, 'He is my brother.' I did this in the integrity of my heart and the innocence of my hands." [6]Then God said to him in the dream, "Yes, I know that you did this in the integrity of your heart; furthermore it was I who kept you from sinning against me. Therefore I did not let you touch her. [7]Now then, return the man's wife; for he is a prophet, and he will pray for you and you shall live. But if you do not restore her, know that you shall surely die, you and all that are yours."

8 So Abimelech rose early in the morning, and called all his servants and told them all these things; and the men were very much afraid. [9]Then Abimelech called Abraham, and said to him, "What have you done to us? How have I sinned against you, that you have brought such great guilt on me and my kingdom? You have done things to me that ought not to be done." [10]And Abimelech said to Abraham, "What were you thinking of, that you did this thing?" [11]Abraham said, "I did it because I thought, There is no fear of God at all in this place, and they will kill me because of my wife. [12]Besides, she is indeed my sister, the daughter of my father but not the daughter of my mother; and she became my wife. [13]And when God caused me to wander from my father's house, I said to her, 'This is the kindness you must do me: at every place to which we come, say of me, He is my brother.' " [14]Then Abimelech took sheep and oxen, and male and female slaves, and gave them to Abraham, and restored his wife Sarah to him. [15]Abimelech said, "My land is before you; settle where it pleases you." [16]To Sarah he said, "Look, I have given your brother a thousand pieces of silver; it is your exoneration before all who are with you; you are completely vindicated." [17]Then Abraham prayed to God; and God healed Abimelech, and also healed his wife and female slaves so that they bore children.[16]

[18]For the LORD had closed fast all the wombs of the house of Abimelech because of Sarah, Abraham's wife.

• • •

---

16. This is one of the three well-known versions of the "ancestress in danger" story, the others being in Gen 12:10-20 and 26:1-11*. Its particular fascination is with the issues of guilt and truth, which are not dealt with in the other versions. According to John Van Seters, Genesis 20 is not an originally independent narrative but a theological reflection based on Gen 12:10-20 (*Abraham in History and Tradition* [New Haven: Yale University Press, 1975] 167–91), a view that finds favor with C. Westermann (*Genesis 12–36* [Minneapolis: Augsburg, 1985] 318–19). As such, it indicates another and theologically more reflective way of telling the "ancestress in danger" story.

Hagar and Ishmael

21:6 Now Sarah said, "God has brought laughter for me; everyone who hears will laugh with me."[17]

8 And the [Heb.; NRSV, The] child grew, and was weaned; and Abraham made a great feast on the day that Isaac was weaned. [9]But Sarah saw the son of Hagar the Egyptian, whom she had borne to Abraham, playing with her son Isaac. [10]So she said to Abraham, "Cast out this slave woman with her son; for the son of this slave woman shall not inherit along with my son Isaac." [11]The matter was very distressing to Abraham on account of his son. [12]But God said to Abraham, "Do not be distressed because of the boy and because of your slave woman; whatever Sarah says to you, do as she tells you, for it is through Isaac that offspring shall be named for you. [13]As for the son of the slave woman, I will make a nation of him also, because he is your offspring." [14]So Abraham rose early in the morning, and took bread and a skin of water, and gave it to Hagar, putting it on her shoulder, along with the child, and sent her away. And she departed, and wandered about in the wilderness of Beer-sheba.

15 When the water in the skin was gone, she cast the child under one of the bushes. [16]Then she went and sat down opposite him a good way off, about the distance of a bowshot; for she said, "Do not let me look on the death of the child." And as she sat opposite him, she lifted up her voice and wept. [17]And God heard the voice of the boy; and the angel of God called to Hagar from heaven, and said to her, "What troubles you, Hagar? Do not be afraid; for God has heard the voice of the boy where he is. [18]Come, lift up the boy and hold him fast with your hand, for I will make a great nation of him." [19]Then God opened her eyes and she saw a well of water. She went, and filled the skin with water, and gave the boy a drink.

20 God was with the boy, and he grew up; he lived in the wilderness, and became an expert with the bow.

[21]He lived in the wilderness of Paran And his mother got a wife for him from the land of Egypt.[18]

Abraham and Abimelech

22 At that time Abimelech, with Phicol the commander of his army, said to Abraham, "God

---

17. Views on Gen 21:6 differ; some place v. 6b after v. 7, giving both to J and attributing only v. 6a to E (so, e.g., Hermann Gunkel, *Genesis*, 8th ed. [Göttingen: Vandenhoeck & Ruprecht, 1969] 227, and J. Skinner, *Genesis*, 2d ed. [ICC; Edinburgh: T. & T. Clark, 1930] 321). The verse may be seen as preserving etymologies for Isaac, duplicating aspects of vv. 3 and 7, and using the name *Elohim* for God. Against any source-critical significance in the name here, see Westermann, *Genesis 12–36*, 333.

18. Genesis 21:8-21 is a similar story to that of Genesis 16. The jealousy, Sarah's initiative, the expulsion, the intervention by the angel are all fundamentally the same. Noth attributes 16:9 to the redactor who combined the texts (*Pentateuchal Traditions*, 28 n. 86). The difference is between a story of the expulsion of a mother shortly before childbirth (J) and the expulsion of a mother and her young child (E). In the

present text, the episodes are harmonized; the pregnant Hagar of the J tradition is told to return and bear her son (16:9-10), and then here, in the E version, she and her young child are banished by Abraham, and by God called to an independent existence. As a story of the conception and birth of Ishmael, the J version naturally belongs earlier in the combined text.

The present location of the E version, in which Ishmael is "sacrificed" for the sake of Isaac, prepares the way for the sacrifice of Isaac story in Genesis 22. Practically speaking, Sarah does to Abraham, and Abraham in turn does to Hagar, what God will do to Abraham in Genesis 22. We may note that a similar dynamic occurs in the Joseph story, where Joseph basically does to his brothers what they did to him—and in this process, insight breaks through and reconciliation between Joseph and his brothers is achieved.

is with you in all that you do; [23] now therefore swear to me here by God that you will not deal falsely with me or with my offspring or with my posterity, but as I have dealt loyally with you, you will deal with me and with the land where you have resided as an alien." [24] And Abraham said, "I swear it."

25 When Abraham complained to Abimelech about a well of water that Abimelech's servants had seized, [26] Abimelech said, "I do not know who has done this; you did not tell me, and I have not heard of it until today." [27] So Abraham took sheep and oxen and gave them to Abimelech.

and the two men made a covenant

[28] Abraham set apart seven ewe lambs of the flock. [29] And Abimelech said to Abraham, "What is the meaning of these seven ewe lambs that you have set apart?" [30] He said, "These seven ewe lambs you shall accept from my hand, in order that you may be a witness for me that I dug this well." [31] Therefore that place was called Beer-sheba; because there both of them swore an oath.

[32] When they had made a covenant at Beer-sheba, Abimelech, with Phicol the commander of his army, left and returned to the land of the Philistines.

[33] Abraham planted a tamarisk tree in Beer-sheba, and called there on the name of the LORD, the Everlasting God.[19]

[34] And Abraham resided as an alien many days in the land of the Philistines.

Sacrifice of Isaac

22 After these things God tested Abraham. He said to him, "Abraham!" And he said, "Here I am." [2] He said, "Take your son, your only son Isaac, whom you love, and go to the land of Moriah, and offer him there as a burnt offering on one of the mountains that I shall show you." [3] So Abraham rose early in the morning, saddled his donkey, and took two of his young men with him, and his son Isaac; he cut the wood for the burnt offering, and set out and went to the place in the distance that God had shown him. [4] On the third day Abraham looked up and saw the place far away. [5] Then Abraham said to his young men, "Stay here with the donkey; the boy and I will go over there; we will worship, and then we will come back to you." [6] Abraham took the wood of the burnt offering and laid it on his son Isaac, and he himself carried the fire and the knife. So the two of them walked on together. [7] Isaac said to his father Abraham, "Father!" And he said, "Here I am, my son." He said, "The fire and the wood are here, but where is the lamb for a burnt offering?" [8] Abraham said, "God himself will provide the lamb for a burnt offering, my son." So the two of them walked on together.

9 When they came to the place that God had shown him, Abraham built an altar there and laid the wood in order. He bound his son Isaac, and laid him on the altar, on top of the wood. [10] Then Abraham reached out his hand and took the knife to kill his son. [11] But the angel of the LORD called to him from heaven, and said, "Abraham, Abraham!" And he said, "Here I am." [12] He said, "Do not lay your hand on the boy or do anything to him; for now I know that you fear God, since you have not withheld your son, your only son, from me." [13] And Abraham looked up and saw a ram, caught in a thicket by its horns. Abraham went and took the ram and

---

19. The dispute between Abraham and Abimelech over a well and its resolution by an oath foreshadows the more involved dispute between Isaac and Abimelech in J's narrative in Genesis 26 and its resolution through the covenant forged in 26:28-31. The successful resolution of disputes means peace for the inhabitants of the land: the digging of wells ensures that the land itself will be fertile.

The material deemed to be secondary additions transforms the dispute into a covenant-making, in line with Genesis 26, and identifies Abimelech and the territory as Philistine, again in line with chap. 26.

offered it up as a burnt offering instead of his son. ¹⁴So Abraham called that place "The LORD will provide"; as it is said to this day, "On the mount of the LORD it shall be provided."

15 The angel of the LORD called to Abraham a second time from heaven, ¹⁶and said, "By myself I have sworn, says the LORD: Because you have done this, and have not withheld your son, your only son, ¹⁷I will indeed bless you, and I will make your offspring as numerous as the stars of heaven and as the sand that is on the seashore. And your offspring shall possess the gate of their enemies, ¹⁸and by your offspring shall all the nations of the earth gain blessing for themselves, because you have obeyed my voice."

¹⁹So Abraham returned to his young men, and they arose and went together to Beer-sheba; and Abraham lived at Beer-sheba.²⁰

• • •

Jacob

Jacob's Dream at Bethel

28:11* Taking one of the stones of the place, he put it under his head and lay down in that

place. ¹²And he dreamed that there was a ladder set up on the earth, the top of it reaching to heaven; and the angels of God were ascending and descending on it. ¹⁷And he was afraid, and said, "How awesome is this place! This is none other than the house of God, and this is the gate of heaven."

18 So Jacob rose early in the morning, and he took the stone that he had put under his head and set it up for a pillar and poured oil on the top of it. ²⁰Then Jacob made a vow, saying, "If God will be with me, and will keep me in this way that I go, and will give me bread to eat and clothing to wear, ²¹so that I come again to my father's house in peace,

then the LORD shall be my God²¹

²²then [Heb.; NRSV, and] this stone, which I have set up for a pillar, shall be God's house; and of all that you give me I will surely give one tenth to you."²²

• • •

Jacob's Children

30:1* And Rachel [Heb.; NRSV, She] envied her sister; and she said to Jacob, "Give me chil-

---

20. The sacrifice of Isaac in Genesis 22 is one of the few major stories in E without parallels in J. The attribution of Genesis 22 to E has been a commonplace of source criticism, but characteristic E features are difficult to pin down in demonstrable fashion. The expected E term for God, *Elohim*, is not used throughout: angel of YHWH occurs in v. 11 and YHWH in v. 14. Noth comments that the divine name in v. 14 is an exceptional case involving the explanation of a place name, and that this may have led to an original *Elohim* in v. 11 being replaced by YHWH. Westermann attributes the variation to the author of the story, who is not wedded to any particular term for God and is simply employing formulaic terminology in vv. 11 and 14 (*Genesis 12–36*, 360–63).

In the present text, the location of this chapter in which Abraham passes the supreme test of faith makes it a fitting climax to the whole Abraham cycle. At the same time, the tension generated in the story is not entirely released at its end, for v. 19 contains no report of Isaac returning with his father. It is not said; in the

context, it is inappropriate to presume it. We are left to ponder the potential significance of this for the story of Abraham. In the present text, there is no contact until Isaac with Ishmael buries Abraham (Gen 25:9, P).

Verses 15-18, which Noth identifies as an addition, are also strategically located. After the crisis of the apparent threat to Isaac's life and as the Abraham cycle draws to a close, a reaffirmation of the promises is appropriate. The addition reiterates, in different terminology, the promise of blessing in Gen 12:1-3, portrayed as a reward for fidelity in v. 16 and for obedience in v. 18; v. 17 also reiterates in different terminology the promise of numerous offspring in 13:14-17.

21. This is regarded by Noth as superfluous and therefore probably secondary, as the use of YHWH indicates (*Pentateuchal Traditions*, 35 n. 133).

22. The text attributed to E is here interwoven with the J variant. It contributes the element of the ladder linking heaven and earth, the dedication of the

dren, or I shall die!" [2]Jacob became very angry with Rachel and said, "Am I in the place of God, who has withheld from you the fruit of the womb?" [3*]Then she said, "Here is my maid Bilhah; go in to her, that she may bear upon my knees."

• • •

[6]Then Rachel said, "God has judged me, and has also heard my voice and given me a son"; therefore she named him Dan.

• • •

[17]And God heeded Leah, and she conceived and bore Jacob a fifth son. [18]Leah said, "God has given me my hire,"

because I gave my maid to my husband

so she named him Issachar. [19]And Leah conceived again, and she bore Jacob a sixth son. [20*]Then Leah said, "God has endowed me with a good dowry."

• • •

22 Then God remembered Rachel, and God heeded her and opened her womb. [23]She conceived and bore a son, and said, "God has taken away my reproach."[23]

• • •

Jacob and Laban

31:2 And Jacob saw that Laban did not regard him as favorably as he did before. [4]So Jacob sent and called Rachel and Leah into the field where his flock was, [5]and said to them, "I see that your father does not regard me as favorably as he did before. But the God of my father has been with me. [6]You know that I have served your father with all my strength; [7]yet your father has cheated me and changed my wages ten times, but God did not permit him to harm me. [8]If he said, 'The speckled shall be your wages,' then all the flock bore speckled; and if he said, 'The striped shall be your wages,' then all the flock bore striped. [9]Thus God has taken away the livestock of your father, and given them to me.

10 During the mating of the flock I once had a dream in which I looked up and saw that the male goats that leaped upon the flock were striped, speckled, and mottled. [11]Then the angel of God said to me in the dream, 'Jacob,' and I said, 'Here I am!' [12]And he said, 'Look up and see that all the goats that leap on the flock are striped, speckled, and mottled; for I have seen all that Laban is doing to you. [13]I am the God of Bethel, where you anointed a pillar and made a

---

sanctuary at Bethel, Jacob's vow, and his promise of a tithe. The dedication of the site legitimates it as a sanctuary where vows can be made and tithes paid. For E, it is then an appropriate place to which—at God's command—Jacob returns in Genesis 35 after his adventures with Laban and his meeting with Esau. Jacob's invocation of divine protection in v. 20 also prepares the way for Genesis 31, where God protects Jacob during his conflict with Laban (cf. vv. 5, 24, 29, 42); for Genesis 33 and the conflict with Esau (cf. v. 11); and for the final note of gratitude in Gen 35:3.

Although the E text in the Jacob–Esau cycle is fragmentary, it witnesses to another set of emphases that may be brought into play in telling these stories.

23. The fragmentary nature of these verses in Genesis 30 makes it difficult to determine their provenance with any certainty (see Westermann, who rejects two sources for J and a revision, *Genesis 12–36*, 471–76). The births in vv. 6, 17-20, and 22-23 are

attributed to E as the result of the explicit role given *Elohim*. E.g., God has judged me (v. 6), God has given me (v. 18), God has endowed me (v. 20), and God has taken away (v. 20).

Note that, for three of these names, two independent etymologies are offered in the tradition, divided here between J and E. J's etymology for Issachar is in 30:16; for Zebulun, J's etymology with the name is in 30:20*, while E's etymology alone is here at the beginning of 30:20; similarly for Joseph, the J etymology and the name are in 30:24, while E's etymology alone is in 30:23.

This is one of the passages in which appeal was made to difference in terminology, because J's word for the maid was *šipḥâ* and E's word was *'āmâ*. What has since been recognized is that although this distinction is valid in this particular context, it cannot necessarily be claimed for all other uses of these terms.

vow to me. Now leave this land at once and return to the land of your birth.' " [14]Then Rachel and Leah answered him, "Is there any portion or inheritance left to us in our father's house? [15]Are we not regarded by him as foreigners? For he has sold us, and he has been using up the money given for us. [16]All the property that God has taken away from our father belongs to us and to our children; now then, do whatever God has said to you."[24]

• • •

19b And Rachel stole her father's household gods. [21]*And he started out and [Heb.; NRSV, starting out he] crossed the Euphrates. [24]And [Heb.; NRSV, But] God came to Laban the Aramean in a dream by night, and said to him, "Take heed that you say not a word to Jacob, either good or bad."

• • •

[25a]Laban overtook Jacob.

• • •

[26]* "What have you done? You have deceived me, and carried away my daughters like captives of the sword? [28]And why did you not permit me to kiss my sons and my daughters farewell? What you have done is foolish. [29]It is in my power to do you harm; but the God of your father spoke to me last night, saying, 'Take heed that you speak to Jacob neither good nor bad.' "

• • •

[30b]"Why did you steal my gods?"

• • •

[32]"But anyone with whom you find your gods shall not live. In the presence of our kinsfolk,

point out what I have that is yours, and take it." Now Jacob did not know that Rachel had stolen the gods.

33 So Laban went into Jacob's tent, and into Leah's tent, and into the tent of the two maids, but he did not find them. And he went out of Leah's tent, and entered Rachel's. [34]Now Rachel had taken the household gods and put them in the camel's saddle, and sat on them. Laban felt all about in the tent, but did not find them. [35]And she said to her father, "Let not my lord be angry that I cannot rise before you, for the way of women is upon me." So he searched, but did not find the household gods.

36b Jacob said to Laban, "What is my offense? What is my sin, that you have hotly pursued me? [37]Although you have felt about through all my goods, what have you found of all your household goods? Set it here before my kinsfolk and your kinsfolk, so that they may decide between us two. [41]These twenty years I have been in your house; I served you fourteen years for your two daughters, and six years for your flock, and you have changed my wages ten times. [42]If the God of my father, the God of Abraham and the Fear of Isaac, had not been on my side, surely now you would have sent me away empty-handed. God saw my affliction and the labor of my hands, and rebuked you last night."

43 Then Laban answered and said to Jacob, "The daughters are my daughters, the children are my children, the flocks are my flocks, and all that you see is mine. But what can I do today

---

24. This is a variant of the J episode of Jacob's wages in Gen 30:25-43. In the J account, the initiative is given to Jacob, who outwits Laban through selective breeding. Here, to the contrary, Jacob's wealth is explained as the result of God's intervention, protecting Jacob from Laban's cheating him of his wages (31:7-9). It offers another way of telling the story of how Jacob acquired wealth at Laban's expense.

The passage is introduced at a pivotal point in the larger narrative. In relation to the preceding J material, it emphasizes that God protected Jacob throughout in his dealings with Laban. In relation to what follows, it explains why Jacob left Laban and why his wives Rachel and Leah left with him willingly.

about these daughters of mine, or about their children whom they have borne? ⁴⁴Come now, let us make a covenant, you and I."

and let it be a witness between you and me
⁴⁵So Jacob took a stone, and set it up as a pillar. ⁵⁰"If you ill-treat my daughters, or if you take wives in addition to my daughters, though no one else is with us, remember that God is witness between you and me." ^{53b}So Jacob swore by the Fear of his father Isaac, ⁵⁴and Jacob offered a sacrifice on the height and called his kinsfolk to eat bread; and they ate bread and tarried all night in the hill country.[25]

⁵⁵ Early in the morning Laban rose up, and kissed his grandchildren and his daughters and blessed them; then he departed and returned home.[26]

Jacob and Esau

32 Jacob went on his way and the angels of God met him; ²and when Jacob saw them he said, "This is God's camp!" So he called that place Mahanaim.[27]

• • •

13b And from what he had with him he took a present for his brother Esau, ¹⁴two hundred female goats and twenty male goats, two hundred ewes and twenty rams, ¹⁵thirty milch camels and their colts, forty cows and ten bulls, twenty female donkeys and ten male donkeys. ¹⁶These he delivered into the hand of his servants, every drove by itself, and said to his servants, "Pass on ahead of me, and put a space between drove and drove." ¹⁷He instructed the foremost, "When Esau my brother meets you, and asks you, 'To whom do you belong? Where are you going? And whose are these ahead of you?' ¹⁸then you shall say, 'They belong to your servant Jacob; they are a present sent to my lord Esau; and moreover he is behind us.' " ¹⁹He likewise instructed the second and the third and all who followed the droves, "You shall say the same thing to Esau when you meet him, ²⁰and you shall say, 'Moreover your servant Jacob is behind us.' " For he thought, "I may appease him with the present that goes ahead of me, and afterwards I shall see his face; perhaps he will accept me." ²¹So the present passed on

---

25. A recurring motif in the material attributed to E between Gen 31:19b and 31:54 is God's protection of Jacob (cf. vv. 24, 29, 42). This points to a thematic link with the preceding E passage (31:2-16), where Jacob acknowledged God's protection in his dealings with Laban, and with 28:20-21, where Jacob had prayed for divine protection when making his vow. By contrast, the powerlessness of Laban's household gods against the protection afforded by the God of Jacob is shown in vv. 32-35, where Laban searches fruitlessly for the gods Rachel has stolen (on this, see W. Brueggemann, *Genesis* [Interpretation; Atlanta: John Knox, 1982] 259; and Westermann, *Genesis 12–36*, 495).

There are thematic links here backward to Gen 31:2-16 and 28:20-21 and forward to Genesis 35. It is worth noting that these particular links within the E material all fall within the Jacob–Esau cycle. They are part of the variant version of the story offered by E.

The E version of the covenant between Jacob and Laban in vv. 43-54 is quite broken. The report of Jacob's actions in vv. 45 and 53b-54 does not contain any reference to Laban. There is no introduction to

Laban's speech in v. 50. This speech appears to invoke Jacob's God; Jacob himself is reported in v. 53b as swearing by the "Fear of his father Isaac." The broken nature of the text makes it difficult to decide whether the verses are fragments of an E version or discrete additions. Despite these difficulties, the overall effect of the combined text is the resolution of the conflict between Jacob and Laban.

26. This is Gen 32:1 in the numbering of the Hebrew.

27. According to Noth, Gen 32:1-2 (Heb., vv. 2-3) was inserted by the compiler instead of J's reference to Mahanaim ("camps" or "armies") at the end of 32:3-13a (Heb., vv. 4-14a). In this account, Jacob divides his people into two camps or companies in preparation for meeting his brother Esau (see the parallel comment on p. 117 n. 65).

Genesis 32:1-2 is located at a significant point in the narrative. The appearance of the angels of God recalls Jacob's dream in 28:12. Hence, as Jacob encountered angels when he fled from Esau (cf. 35:1), so he encounters them again on his return, just before his meeting with Esau.

ahead of him; and he himself spent that night in the camp.[28]

• • •

33:4 But Esau ran to meet him, and embraced him, and fell on his neck and kissed him, and they wept. [5]When Esau looked up and saw the women and children, he said, "Who are these with you?" Jacob said, "The children whom God has graciously given your servant." [8]Esau said, "What do you mean by all this company that I met?" Jacob answered, "To find favor with my lord." [9]But Esau said, "I have enough, my brother; keep what you have for yourself." [10]Jacob said, "No, please; if I find favor with you, then accept my present from my hand; for truly to see your face is like seeing the face of God—since you have received me with such favor. [11]Please accept my gift that is brought to you, because God has dealt graciously with me, and because I have everything I want." So he urged him, and he took it.[29]

• • •

Jacob's Purchase of Land

[19]And from the sons of Hamor, Shechem's father, he bought for one hundred pieces of money the plot of land on which he had pitched his tent. [20]There he erected an altar and called it El-Elohe-Israel.[30]

Jacob at Bethel

35 God said to Jacob, "Arise, go up to Bethel, and settle there. Make an altar there to the God who appeared to you when you fled from your brother Esau." [2]So Jacob said to his household and to all who were with him, "Put away the foreign gods that are among you, and purify yourselves, and change your clothes; [3]then come, let us go up to Bethel, that I may make an altar there to the God who answered me in the day of my distress and has been with me wherever I have gone." [4]So they gave to Jacob all the foreign gods that they had, and the rings that were in their ears; and Jacob hid them under the oak that was near Shechem.

5 As they journeyed, a terror from God fell upon the cities all around them, so that no one pursued them.

7 And there he built an altar and called the place El-bethel, because it was there that God had revealed himself to him when he fled from his brother. [8]And Deborah, Rebekah's nurse, died, and she was buried under an oak below Bethel. So it was called Allon-bacuth.

---

28. The E text in Gen 32:13b-21 (Heb., vv. 14b-22) is a variant of J's preparations to meet Esau in vv. 3-13a (Heb., vv. 4-14a). The difference is that in E the livestock is a present to win over Esau, whereas in J a fearful Jacob hopes that, if necessary, it will serve as a precautionary tactic so that he can escape. In the combined text the more positive and hopeful E version is located appropriately after Jacob has prayed to God (cf. vv. 9-12 [Heb., vv. 10-13]).

29. In the meeting of the brothers the element of reconciliation is more to the fore in E than in J. Also in the E version, it is Esau who initiates the reconciliation (Gen 33:4) and who then receives Jacob's gift (vv. 8-11). By contrast, in the J version Jacob is very much a supplicant as he approaches his brother. In the combined text it is this attitude of Jacob that prompts Esau's gesture of reconciliation. The portrait of Jacob as supplicant forms a remarkable ending to a story that began with him as a dominant figure, acquiring Esau's birthright and stealing his blessing.

Jacob's acknowledgment in v. 11 that God has dealt graciously with him recalls the theme of divine protection that recurs throughout the E version of the Jacob story.

30. As Westermann notes, this verse portrays Jacob as a tent-dweller, in rather uncomfortable juxtaposition with Jacob as sedentary house-builder of 33:17. The purchase of land has echoes of Genesis 23 (cf. Westermann, *Genesis 12–36*, 528–29).

14 Jacob set up a pillar in the place where he had spoken with him, a pillar of stone; and he poured out a drink offering on it, and poured oil on it.[31]

Birth of Benjamin

16 Then they journeyed from Bethel; and when they were still some distance from Ephrath, Rachel was in childbirth, and she had hard labor. [17]When she was in her hard labor, the midwife said to her, "Do not be afraid; for now you will have another son." [18]As her soul was departing (for she died), she named him Benoni; but his father called him Benjamin. [19]So Rachel died, and she was buried on the way to Ephrath (that is, Bethlehem), [20]and Jacob set up a pillar at her grave; it is the pillar of Rachel's tomb, which is there to this day.[32]

• • •

Joseph

37:3b And he had made him a long robe with sleeves.

• • •

22 Reuben said to them, "Shed no blood; throw him into this pit here in the wilderness, but lay no hand on him"—that he might rescue him out of their hand and restore him to his father. [23]So when Joseph came to his brothers, they stripped him of his robe, the long robe with sleeves that he wore; [24]and they took him and threw him into a pit. The pit was empty; there was no water in it.

28* And [Heb.; NRSV, When] some Midianite traders passed by, and they [Heb.; NRSV, they] drew Joseph up, lifting him out of the pit.

29 When Reuben returned to the pit and saw that Joseph was not in the pit, he tore his clothes. [30]He returned to his brothers, and said, "The boy is gone; and I, where can I turn?" [31]Then they took Joseph's robe, slaughtered a goat, and dipped the robe in the blood.

[32]*And they sent the long robe with sleeves* [33] And they [Heb.; RSV, and] brought it to their

---

31. This passage complements E in Genesis 28. Jacob is commanded to return and build an altar at Bethel, where he first encountered God on his journey. The theme of divine protection recurs here, in Jacob's acknowledgment of it in v. 3 and in the narrative report of it in v. 5. Jacob's disposal of foreign gods (*'ĕlōhê hannekār*) may refer to the ones stolen by Rachel in Gen 31:30-35*, although there they are described as household gods (*tĕrāpîm*).

There is no report of God speaking to Jacob in the E version of Genesis 28; this element is assigned entirely to J. It is also worth noting that Jacob's erection of a pillar (v. 14) has already been described in 28:18 (E). The possibility arises that the passage in Genesis 35 is a later addition that borrowed elements from J (God's speech to Jacob) and E (the pillar) in Genesis 28. Westermann, who rules against an E source, identifies 35:1-7 as an independent construction of the pentateuchal redactor, with vv. 8 and 14 as possible J elements (*Genesis 12–36*, 549–50).

32. The account of the death of Rachel during the birth of Benjamin lacks the distinctive features that are normally appealed to for the identification of sources. It contains no mention of God and has no parallel in J or P. The journey beyond Bethel also places it outside the narrative arc of the E story of Jacob, in which Jacob sets out from Bethel after his encounter with God and returns to settle there at God's command (35:1). Associations with the setting up of a pillar (Gen 28:18, 22; 35:14) and the reference in Gen 48:7 to the death of Rachel were influential in the attribution to E. For a different view, see Westermann, *Genesis 12–36*, 549.

At the end of this Jacob–Esau cycle, it is interesting to note the variant traditions. For J, the ending is at Succoth or Shechem's city; for E, at Bethel; and for P, at Mamre (Kiriath-arba/Hebron).

33. There is tension here between "they sent" and "they brought"; see n. 34, below. For a discussion of the possibilities, see Westermann, *Genesis 37–50* (Minneapolis: Augsburg, 1986) 43.

father,[34] and they said, "This we have found; see now whether it is your son's robe or not." [33]He recognized it, and said, "It is my son's robe! A wild animal has devoured him; Joseph is without doubt torn to pieces." [34]Then Jacob tore his garments, and put sackcloth on his loins, and mourned for his son many days. [35]All his sons and all his daughters sought to comfort him; but he refused to be comforted, and said, "No, I shall go down to Sheol to my son, mourning." Thus his father bewailed him. [36]Meanwhile the Midianites had sold him in Egypt to Potiphar, one of Pharaoh's officials, the captain of the guard.[35]

Joseph in Egypt: Interpreter of Dreams

40:2 Pharaoh was angry with his two officers, the chief cupbearer and the chief baker,[36] [3*]and he put them in custody in the house of the captain of the guard. [4]The captain of the guard charged Joseph with them, and he waited on them; and they continued for some time in custody. [5a]One night they both dreamed, each his own dream, and each dream with its own meaning. [6]When Joseph came to them in the morning, he saw that they were troubled. [7]So he asked Pharaoh's officers, who were with him in custody in his master's house, "Why are your faces downcast today?" [8]They said to him, "We have had dreams, and there is no one to interpret them." And Joseph said to them, "Do not interpretations belong to God? Please tell them to me."

9 So the chief cupbearer told his dream to Joseph, and said to him, "In my dream there was a vine before me, [10]and on the vine there were three branches. As soon as it budded, its blossoms came out and the clusters ripened into grapes. [11]Pharaoh's cup was in my hand; and I took the grapes and pressed them into Pharaoh's cup, and placed the cup in Pharaoh's hand." [12]Then Joseph said to him, "This is its interpretation: the three branches are three days;

---

34. For the sake of a clearer representation of the Hebrew text, the RSV has been used here in Gen 37:32a. The NRSV's "They had the long robe with sleeves taken to their father" is one possible solution to the tension between "send" and "bring"; it does not resolve the tension of using a messenger to take the robe and being present to address their father.

35. The E version of the Joseph story here focuses on the role of Reuben and the Midianites, whereas the parallel J version focuses on Judah and the Ishmaelites. For a discussion of these versions and the artful way in which they have been combined, see chap. 6.

36. Genesis 40–42 is the one area in Genesis where, according to Noth, the normal practice of combining J and E was reversed, with E being used as a base and enriched by J. Noth's evidence for two versions of Joseph's rise to power in Genesis 40–41 and of his encounter with his brothers in 42 is outlined in chap. 3 (pp. 123 n. 76, 124 n. 79, 124–25 n. 81, on the parallel J texts).

The E material contributes a fine account of how Joseph came to power in Egypt, matching the quality of the surrounding J material, principally in Genesis 39 and 43–44.

In addition to providing an engaging and rich story of Joseph's rise to power in Egypt, the text identified here as E contributes the important motif of God's presence in the unfolding of events. This is affirmed by Joseph in his interpretation of dreams (cf. Gen 40:8; 41:16, 25, 28, 32) and by Pharaoh in his recognition that God has revealed to Joseph the meaning of his dreams (cf. Gen 41:38, 39). It should be noted that the term for God throughout is *Elohim*, occurring with the definite article in 41:25, 28, and 32. These occurrences may be translated as "God," or "the God," or "the gods," usage particularly appropriate for the Hebrew–Egyptian context. The divine guidance of events is a motif that runs throughout the remainder of the E version of the story of Joseph.

Westermann believes the plan of the Joseph story would be destroyed by division into sources. He proposes that an old family story underwent "two expansions, chs. 39–41 and 42–45, in accordance with the principle of doubling that governs the narrative." Genesis 39–41 is a political narrative with royal motifs; Genesis 42–45 combines the family and political motifs (Westermann, *Genesis 37–50*, 24).

[13]within three days Pharaoh will lift up your head and restore you to your office; and you shall place Pharaoh's cup in his hand, just as you used to do when you were his cupbearer. [14]But remember me when it is well with you; please do me the kindness to make mention of me to Pharaoh, and so get me out of this place. [15a]For in fact I was stolen out of the land of the Hebrews."

16 When the chief baker saw that the interpretation was favorable, he said to Joseph, "I also had a dream: there were three cake baskets on my head, [17]and in the uppermost basket there were all sorts of baked food for Pharaoh, but the birds were eating it out of the basket on my head." [18]And Joseph answered, "This is its interpretation: the three baskets are three days; [19]within three days Pharaoh will lift up your head—from you!—and hang you on a pole; and the birds will eat the flesh from you."

20 On the third day, which was Pharaoh's birthday, he made a feast for all his servants, and lifted up the head of the chief cupbearer and the head of the chief baker among his servants. [21]He restored the chief cupbearer to his cupbearing, and he placed the cup in Pharaoh's hand; [22]but the chief baker he hanged, just as Joseph had interpreted to them. [23]Yet the chief cupbearer did not remember Joseph, but forgot him.

Interpreter
of Pharaoh's Dreams

41 After two whole years, Pharaoh dreamed that he was standing by the Nile, [2]and there came up out of the Nile seven sleek and fat cows, and they grazed in the reed grass. [3]Then seven other cows, ugly and thin, came up out of the Nile after them, and stood by the other cows on the bank of the Nile. [4]The ugly and thin cows ate up the seven sleek and fat cows. And Pharaoh awoke. [5]Then he fell asleep and dreamed a second time; seven ears of grain, plump and good, were growing on one stalk. [6]Then seven ears,

thin and blighted by the east wind, sprouted after them. [7]The thin ears swallowed up the seven plump and full ears. Pharaoh awoke, and it was a dream. [8]In the morning his spirit was troubled; so he sent and called for all the magicians of Egypt and all its wise men. Pharaoh told them his dreams, but there was no one who could interpret them to Pharaoh.

9 Then the chief cupbearer said to Pharaoh, "I remember my faults today. [10]Once Pharaoh was angry with his servants, and put me and the chief baker in custody in the house of the captain of the guard. [11]We dreamed on the same night, he and I, each having a dream with its own meaning. [12]A young Hebrew was there with us, a servant of the captain of the guard. When we told him, he interpreted our dreams to us, giving an interpretation to each according to his dream. [13]As he interpreted to us, so it turned out; I was restored to my office, and the baker was hanged."

[14]* Then Pharaoh sent for Joseph. When he had shaved himself and changed his clothes, he came in before Pharaoh. [15]And Pharaoh said to Joseph, "I have had a dream, and there is no one who can interpret it. I have heard it said of you that when you hear a dream you can interpret it." [16]Joseph answered Pharaoh, "It is not I; God will give Pharaoh a favorable answer." [17]Then Pharaoh said to Joseph, "In my dream I was standing on the banks of the Nile; [18]and seven cows, fat and sleek, came up out of the Nile and fed in the reed grass. [19]Then seven other cows came up after them, poor, very ugly, and thin. Never had I seen such ugly ones in all the land of Egypt. [20]The thin and ugly cows ate up the first seven fat cows, [21]but when they had eaten them no one would have known that they had done so, for they were still as ugly as before. Then I awoke. [22]I fell asleep a second time and I saw in my dream seven ears of grain, full and good, growing on one stalk, [23]and seven ears, withered, thin, and blighted by the east wind,

sprouting after them; [24]and the thin ears swallowed up the seven good ears. But when I told it to the magicians, there was no one who could explain it to me."

25 Then Joseph said to Pharaoh, "Pharaoh's dreams are one and the same; God has revealed to Pharaoh what he is about to do. [26]The seven good cows are seven years, and the seven good ears are seven years; the dreams are one. [27]The seven lean and ugly cows that came up after them are seven years, as are the seven empty ears blighted by the east wind. They are seven years of famine. [28]It is as I told Pharaoh; God has shown to Pharaoh what he is about to do. [29]There will come seven years of great plenty throughout all the land of Egypt. [30]After them there will arise seven years of famine, and all the plenty will be forgotten in the land of Egypt; the famine will consume the land. [31]The plenty will no longer be known in the land because of the famine that will follow, for it will be very grievous. [32]And the doubling of Pharaoh's dream means that the thing is fixed by God, and God will shortly bring it about. [33]Now therefore let Pharaoh select a man who is discerning and wise, and set him over the land of Egypt, [34b]and take one-fifth of the produce of the land of Egypt during the seven plenteous years. [35a]Let them gather all the food of these good years that are coming. [36]That food shall be a reserve for the land against the seven years of famine that are to befall the land of Egypt, so that the land may not perish through the famine."

Joseph's Rise to Power
in Egypt

37 The proposal pleased Pharaoh and all his servants. [38]Pharaoh said to his servants, "Can we find anyone else like this—one in whom is

the spirit of God?" [39]So Pharaoh said to Joseph, "Since God has shown you all this, there is no one so discerning and wise as you. [40]You shall be over my house, and all my people shall order themselves as you command; only with regard to the throne will I be greater than you."

47 During the seven plenteous years the earth produced abundantly. [48]He gathered up all the food of the seven years when there was plenty in the land of Egypt, and stored up food in the cities; he stored up in every city the food from the fields around it.

50 Before the years of famine came, Joseph had two sons, [whom Asenath daughter of Potiphera, priest of On, bore to him]. [51]Joseph named the firstborn Manasseh, "For," he said, "God has made me forget all my hardship and all my father's house." [52]The second he named Ephraim, "For God has made me fruitful in the land of my misfortunes."[37]

Onset of the Famine

53 The seven years of plenty that prevailed in the land of Egypt came to an end; [54]and the seven years of famine began to come, just as Joseph had said. There was famine in every country, but throughout the land of Egypt there was bread.

Brothers' First Journey
to Egypt

42:1a And [Heb.; NRSV, When] Jacob learned that there was grain in Egypt. [2]"I have heard," he said, "that there is grain in Egypt; go down and buy grain for us there, that we may live and not die." [3]So ten of Joseph's brothers went down to buy grain in Egypt.

6 Now Joseph was governor over the land; it was he who sold to all the people of the land.

---

37. Noth presumably regarded this information on Joseph's family as a later addition to E because it interrupts the account of Joseph's preparations for the famine. Within the larger horizon of the combined text, the account of the birth of Joseph's sons prepares the way for their blessing in Genesis 48 (E).

And Joseph's brothers came and bowed themselves before him with their faces to the ground. 7*When Joseph saw his brothers, he recognized them, but he treated them like strangers and spoke harshly to them. 9* He said to them, "You are spies."

•••38

Crisis over Benjamin

11b "We are honest men; your servants have never been spies." 13They said, "We, your servants, are twelve brothers, the sons of a certain man in the land of Canaan; the youngest, however, is now with our father, and one is no more." 14But Joseph said to them, "It is just as I have said to you; you are spies! 15Here is how you shall be tested: as Pharaoh lives, you shall not leave this place unless your youngest brother comes here! 16Let one of you go and bring your brother, while the rest of you remain in prison, in order that your words may be tested, whether there is truth in you; or else, as Pharaoh lives, surely you are spies." 17And he put them all together in prison for three days.

18 On the third day Joseph said to them, "Do this and you will live, for I fear God: 19if you are honest men, let one of your brothers stay here where you are imprisoned. The rest of you shall go and carry grain for the famine of your households, 20and bring your youngest brother to me. Thus your words will be verified, and you shall not die." And they agreed to do so. 21They said to one another, "Alas, we are paying the penalty for what we did to our brother; we saw his anguish when he pleaded with us, but we would not listen. That is why this anguish has come upon us." 22Then Reuben answered them, "Did

I not tell you not to wrong the boy? But you would not listen. So now there comes a reckoning for his blood." 23They did not know that Joseph understood them, since he spoke with them through an interpreter. 24He turned away from them and wept; then he returned and spoke to them. And he picked out Simeon and had him bound before their eyes. 25Joseph then gave orders to fill their bags with grain, to return every man's money to his sack, and to give them provisions for their journey. This was done for them. 26And they [Heb.; NRSV, They] loaded their donkeys with their grain, and departed.

29 When they came to their father Jacob in the land of Canaan, they told him all that had happened to them, saying, 30"The man, the lord of the land, spoke harshly to us, and charged us with spying on the land. 31But we said to him, 'We are honest men, we are not spies. 32We are twelve brothers, sons of our father; one is no more, and the youngest is now with our father in the land of Canaan.' 33Then the man, the lord of the land, said to us, 'By this I shall know that you are honest men: leave one of your brothers with me, take grain for the famine of your households, and go your way. 34Bring your youngest brother to me, and I shall know that you are not spies but honest men. Then I will release your brother to you, and you may trade in the land.' "

35 As they were emptying their sacks, there in each one's sack was his bag of money. When they and their father saw their bundles of money, they were dismayed. 28bAt this they lost heart and turned trembling to one another, saying, "What is this that God has done to us?"39 36And their father Jacob said to them, "I am the one

---

38. This is the sort of text where a division is hardly necessary. In the hypothesis of sources, there is a degree of duplication; compare the parallel passage in J (pp. 124–25). It is a matter of intuitive preference rather than evidential judgment.

39. According to Noth, v. 28b originally belonged here in E; in the combination of sources it was attached to J's version of the discovery of money in the sacks (vv. 27–28a; see Noth, *Pentateuchal Traditions*, 36 n. 135).

you have bereaved of children: Joseph is no more, and Simeon is no more, and now you would take Benjamin. All this has happened to me!" [37]Then Reuben said to his father, "You may kill my two sons if I do not bring him back to you. Put him in my hands, and I will bring him back to you."[40]

• • •

Joseph Reveals Himself to His Brothers

45:2 And he wept so loudly that the Egyptians heard it, and the household of Pharaoh heard it. [3]Joseph said to his brothers, "I am Joseph. Is my father still alive?" But his brothers could not answer him, so dismayed were they at his presence.[41]

• • •

5b "For God sent me before you to preserve life. [6]For the famine has been in the land these two years; and there are five more years in which there will be neither plowing nor harvest. [7]God

sent me before you to preserve for you a remnant on earth, and to keep alive for you many survivors. [8]So it was not you who sent me here, but God; he has made me a father to Pharaoh, and lord of all his house and ruler over all the land of Egypt. [9]Hurry and go up to my father and say to him, 'Thus says your son Joseph, God has made me lord of all Egypt; come down to me, do not delay. [10]You shall settle in the land of Goshen, and you shall be near me, you and your children and your children's children, as well as your flocks, your herds, and all that you have. [11]I will provide for you there—since there are five more years of famine to come—so that you and your household, and all that you have, will not come to poverty.' [12]And now your eyes and the eyes of my brother Benjamin see that it is my own mouth that speaks to you. [13]You must tell my father how greatly I am honored in Egypt, and all that you have seen. Hurry and bring my father down here." [14]Then he fell upon his brother Benjamin's neck and wept,

---

40. The account here of the brothers' journey to Egypt and the resulting crisis over Benjamin gives a prominent role to Reuben in Gen 42:22 and 42:37. This is in accord with the material in Genesis 37 that Noth assigns to E. The passage also uses the term *Elohim* in v. 18 (with the article) and v. 28b. In the texts assigned to J, there is a parallel version of the discovery of money in the sacks (vv. 27-28a) and of Jacob's response to the crisis over Benjamin (v. 38).

In the combination of sources in Genesis 40–42, Noth judges that E was used as the base and enriched by J, a reversal of the normal procedure, coupled with the probable absence of a dream story in J (*Pentateuchal Traditions*, 27). The predominant E passage contributes the episode of Simeon as a hostage in vv. 19-24, which Noth believes was not present in J; the references to Simeon in 43:14aβ and 23b are redactional additions linking this E episode to J (ibid., 30 n. 102). The E passage also continues the motif of God's presence in the unfolding of events, to which attention was drawn in n. 36, above. In Genesis 42 it is

present implicitly in Joseph's statement in v. 18 and explicitly in the brothers' question in v. 28b.

41. The identification of E and J versions of Joseph's revelation of his identity to his brothers is based on the perception of a doublet in v. 3 (E) and v. 4 (J). There has been considerable debate over whether this signals the presence of sources or a narrator achieving dramatic effect (cf. Westermann's report of the debate in *Genesis 37–50*, 141–42, and R. Alter's comment in *The Art of Biblical Narrative* [New York: Basic Books, 1981] 175).

This is a good example of a case where, in the hypothesis of two sources, the classification of vv. 3 and 4 as a doublet and their division between these sources is reasonable. In the hypothesis of skillful redactional composition, the sequence of the present text is repetitive but effective and progressive. Were there no evidence elsewhere for sources, the alleged doublet in vv. 3-4 would be explained in terms of literary emphasis.

while Benjamin wept upon his neck. [15]And he kissed all his brothers and wept upon them; and after that his brothers talked with him.[42]

• • •

Joseph Is Reunited with His Father

46:1*And he [Heb.; NRSV, and] came to Beer-sheba, and he [Heb.; NRSV, he] offered sacrifices to the God of his father Isaac. [2]God spoke to Israel in visions of the night, and said, "Jacob, Jacob." And he said, "Here I am." [3]Then he said, "I am God, the God of your father; do not be afraid to go down to Egypt, for I will make of you a great nation there. [4]I myself will go down with you to Egypt, and I will also bring you up again; and Joseph's own hand shall close your eyes." [5a]Then Jacob set out from Beer-sheba.[43]

• • •

47:5*And Jacob and his sons came to Egypt to Joseph, and Pharaoh king of Egypt heard and Pharaoh spoke to Joseph saying,[44] [5b]"Your father and your brothers have come to you. [6a]The land of Egypt is before you; settle your father and your brothers in the best part of the land."

[7] Then Joseph brought in his father Jacob, and presented him before Pharaoh, and Jacob blessed Pharaoh. [8]Pharaoh said to Jacob, "How many are the years of your life?" [9]Jacob said to Pharaoh, "The years of my earthly sojourn are one hundred thirty; few and hard have been the years of my life. They do not compare with the years of the life of my ancestors during their long sojourn." [10]Then Jacob blessed Pharaoh, and went out from the presence of Pharaoh. [11]Joseph settled his father and his brothers, and granted them a holding in the land of Egypt, in the best part of the land, in the land of Rameses, as Pharaoh had instructed. [12]And Joseph provided his father, his brothers, and all his father's household with food, according to the number of their dependents.[45]

Blessing of Ephraim and Manasseh

48 After this Joseph was told, "Your father is ill." So he took with him his two sons, Manasseh and Ephraim. [2]When Jacob was told, "Your son Joseph has come to you," Israel (Heb.; NRSV, he) summoned his strength and sat up in bed. [7]"For when I came from Paddan, Rachel, alas, died in the land of Canaan on the way, while there was

---

42. This passage is identified as E because of the occurrence of the term *Elohim* for God. Also, in concert with the preceding E passages it provides a theological interpretation of the events in the story. All that happened between Joseph and his brothers and all that happened to Joseph in Egypt were part of God's initiative to preserve life in the crippling famine. Joseph then urges his brothers to bring their father and their families to Egypt, where he can provide for them all in the famine.

Here the theme of God's preservation of life in the famine has taken over from that of reconciliation between Joseph and his brothers. This accounts for its position after the reconciliation.

43. In the E passage in Gen 45:5b-15, Joseph assured his brothers that the events that had taken place were according to God's plan. In 46:1-4 God is portrayed as giving a similar assurance to Jacob for events that are to come. This interpretative movement, which began in E's story of how Joseph rose to power in Egypt and is continued in the story of the brothers' encounter with Joseph in Egypt, culminates in Gen 50:20.

44. Noth's emended text, following the Septuagint.

45. This passage is identified by Noth as the E version of the presentation of Joseph's family to Pharaoh, the parallel J version being Gen 47:1-5a, 6b. The E version describes Jacob's blessing of Pharaoh (vv. 7 and 10) and the fulfillment of Joseph's promise, made in Genesis 45, that he would provide for his father and his family. The location of this version in the combined text gives prominence to the blessing and to the grant of land that the family received in Egypt.

still some distance to go to Ephrath; and I buried her there on the way to Ephrath" (that is, Bethlehem).[46]

8 When Israel saw Joseph's sons, he said, "Who are these?" [9]Joseph said to his father, "They are my sons, whom God has given me here." And he said, "Bring them to me, please, that I may bless them." [10]Now the eyes of Israel were dim with age, and he could not see well. So Joseph brought them near him; and he kissed them and embraced them. [11]Israel said to Joseph, "I did not expect to see your face; and here God has let me see your children also." [12]Then Joseph removed them from his father's knees, and he bowed himself with his face to the earth. [13]Joseph took them both, Ephraim in his right hand toward Israel's left, and Manasseh in his left hand toward Israel's right, and brought them near him. [14]But Israel stretched out his right hand and laid it on the head of Ephraim, who was the younger, and his left hand on the head of Manasseh, crossing his hands, for Manasseh was the firstborn.

[15]*He blessed Joseph, and said,*
"The God before whom my ancestors
Abraham and Isaac walked,
the God who has been my shepherd all my life
to this day,
[16]*the angel who has redeemed me from all*
harm, bless the boys;

and in them let my name be perpetuated, and
the name of my ancestors
Abraham and Isaac;
and let them grow into a multitude
on the earth."

17 When Joseph saw that his father laid his right hand on the head of Ephraim, it displeased him; so he took his father's hand, to remove it from Ephraim's head to Manasseh's head. [18]Joseph said to his father, "Not so, my father! Since this one is the firstborn, put your right hand on his head." [19]But his father refused, and said, "I know, my son, I know; he also shall become a people, and he also shall be great. Nevertheless his younger brother shall be greater than he, and his offspring shall become a multitude of nations." [20]So he blessed them that day, saying,

"By you Israel will invoke blessings, saying,
'God make you like Ephraim and like
    Manasseh.' "

So he put Ephraim ahead of Manasseh. [21]Then Israel said to Joseph, "I am about to die, but God will be with you and will bring you again to the land of your ancestors. [22]I now give to you one portion more than to your brothers, the portion that I took from the hand of the Amorites with my sword and with my bow."[47]

• • •

---

46. Noth identifies a gap between v. 7 and v. 8, which he does not mark in the listing of his text (*Pentateuchal Traditions*, 36 n. 136). Another gap, which surprisingly he does not comment on, obviously occurs between v. 2 and v. 7. Noth presumably included v. 7 because of his earlier assignation of the death of Rachel in Gen 35:16-20 to E. Westermann eliminates the problem by regarding v. 7 as an appendage to the P text in vv. 3-6 (*Genesis 37–50*, 182).

47. According to Noth, the pre-priestly material in Genesis 48 is "very broken and no longer in its original form" (*Pentateuchal Traditions*, 36 n. 136). He believes its literary complexity is explained more satisfactorily by additions to a basic E text than by separation into sources. Thus the blessing for Joseph in vv.

15-16 is an insertion into the account of the blessing of Joseph's sons. The name "Israel" is regularly attributed to J in the source division. Noth proposes that its occurrence in v. 2b is an addition, because the name "Jacob" occurs in v. 2a. Its occurrence in the account of the blessing of Joseph's sons is due, in Noth's view, to this being a special tradition about tribal history. Hence the name Israel was retained when the tradition was incorporated into the E source.

Despite the literary-critical difficulties in Genesis 48, its function within the story of Joseph is clear enough. As Joseph provided a future for his father and family, so now his father provides a future for Joseph's family by blessing the two sons who were born to him in Egypt.

Mourning for Jacob

50:10b And he observed a time of mourning for his father seven days. [11]When the Canaanite inhabitants of the land saw the mourning on the threshing floor of Atad, they said, "This is a grievous mourning on the part of the Egyptians." Therefore the place was named Abel-mizraim; it is beyond the Jordan.

• • •

Final Reconciliation with His Brothers

15 Realizing that their father was dead, Joseph's brothers said, "What if Joseph still bears a grudge against us and pays us back in full for all the wrong that we did to him?" [16]So they approached Joseph, saying, "Your father gave this instruction before he died, [17]'Say to Joseph: I beg you, forgive the crime of your brothers and the wrong they did in harming you.' Now therefore please forgive the crime of the servants of the God of your father." Joseph wept when they spoke to him. [18]Then his brothers also wept, fell down before him, and said, "We are here as your slaves." [19]But Joseph said to

them, "Do not be afraid! Am I in the place of God? [20]Even though you intended to do harm to me, God intended it for good, in order to preserve a numerous people, as he is doing today. [21]So have no fear; I myself will provide for you and your little ones." In this way he reassured them, speaking kindly to them.[48]

Testament of Joseph

22 So Joseph remained in Egypt, he and his father's household; and Joseph lived one hundred ten years. [23]Joseph saw Ephraim's children of the third generation; the children of Machir son of Manasseh were also born on Joseph's knees.

24 Then Joseph said to his brothers, "I am about to die; but God will surely come to you, and bring you up out of this land to the land that he swore to Abraham, to Isaac, and to Jacob." [25]So Joseph made the Israelites swear, saying, "When God comes to you, you shall carry up my bones from here." [26]And Joseph died, being one hundred ten years old; he was embalmed and placed in a coffin in Egypt.[49]

The Book of Exodus

Israel's Oppression in Egypt

• • •

1:15 The king of Egypt said to the Hebrew midwives, one of whom was named Shiphrah and the other Puah, [16]"When you

act as midwives to the Hebrew women, and see them on the birthstool, if it is a boy, kill him; but if it is a girl, she shall live." [17]But the midwives feared God; they did not do as the king of Egypt commanded them, but they

---

48. This passage continues the theme of Genesis 45—that God turned the brothers' evil action to good, to preserve life—and it reaffirms Joseph's commitment to provide for the family.

It also contributes the motif of the brothers' confession of guilt to Joseph and plea for pardon, albeit motivated by fear of what might happen to them now that their father is dead. The passage reveals Joseph's brothers as lacking trust in Joseph and still prepared

to lie to achieve their security. This too is in continuity with Genesis 45, where the theme of reconciliation is less central than in J.

49. This passage is typical of the testamentary activity of the patriarchs, as they set their affairs in order before they die. It uses the name *Elohim* and accords with interest shown in E's Genesis 48 in the future of Joseph's sons. See the compliance with Joseph's request in Exod 13:19.

let the boys live. [18]So the king of Egypt summoned the midwives and said to them, "Why have you done this, and allowed the boys to live?" [19]The midwives said to Pharaoh, "Because the Hebrew women are not like the Egyptian women; for they are vigorous and give birth before the midwife comes to them." [20]So God dealt well with the midwives; and the people multiplied and became very strong.[50]

[21]*And because the midwives feared God, he gave them families.*

• • •

Call of Moses

3:4b God called to him out of the bush, "Moses, Moses!" And he said, "Here I am." [6]He said further, "I am the God of your father, the God of Abraham, the God of Isaac, and the God

of Jacob." And Moses hid his face, for he was afraid to look at God. [9]"The cry of the Israelites has now come to me; I have also seen how the Egyptians oppress them. [10]So come, I will send you to Pharaoh to bring my people, the Israelites, out of Egypt." [11]But Moses said to God, "Who am I that I should go to Pharaoh, and bring the Israelites out of Egypt?" [12]He said, "I will be with you; and this shall be the sign for you that it is I who sent you: when you have brought the people out of Egypt, you shall worship God on this mountain."

13 But Moses said to God, "If I come to the Israelites and say to them, 'The God of your ancestors has sent me to you,' and they ask me, 'What is his name?' what shall I say to them?" [14]God said to Moses, "I am who I am." He said further, "Thus you shall say to the Israelites, 'I am has sent me to you.' "[51]

---

50. In Exod 1:15-21, Pharaoh is referred to as "the king of Egypt" (except in v. 19, where "to Pharaoh" may be an addition; see Noth, *Exodus* [OTL; Philadelphia: Westminster, 1962] 23) and the name "God" is used throughout; v. 22 refers to "Pharaoh" and follows smoothly on v. 12. Therefore vv. 15-21 and v. 22 are divided between two strata of the text. Verse 22 is J. In *Pentateuchal Traditions*, Noth puts vv. 15-21 in the category of "those passages which stand out clearly as elements of a variant narrative in the J context but for which there are not positive clues to identify them as belonging originally to the E narrative" (35 n. 129). In his Exodus commentary, Noth refers to the passage as E (*Exodus*, 23). It preserves a view of Israel as small enough in numbers to be cared for by two midwives alone. Their "fear of God" empowers them to disobey the king of Egypt and so save their people from premature destruction.

Verse 21 is regarded as secondary because it comes after the concluding sentence (v. 20) and simply adds detail to the broad "God dealt well with the midwives."

In the present text the passage provides a suitable lead-up to the story of the birth of Moses. Pharaoh, frustrated by the shrewd and God-fearing midwives, turns to his own people to control the Israelite male population. Ironically, it is his own daughter who ends up preserving the life of Israel's deliverer.

51. There is no narrative continuity here with the preceding E passage. The beginning as it stands ("God called to him") needs a reference point both for the person (Moses) and the place (mountain of God). In his Exodus commentary, Noth attributes the end of Exod 3:1 (v. 1bβ) to E, which still leaves the start of the passage in fragmentary condition. The passage doubles the J account in Exod 3:1-4a, 5, 7, 8*, 16, 17*. Noth comments on the "strikingly abrupt changes between the divine name Yahweh and the word 'God,' " as well as the doublets between vv. 7-8 and 9-10 (*Exodus*, 34). These differences are noteworthy. An introduction to the divine speech is clearly lacking in v. 9, after the interruption of the comment about Moses (cf. Noth, *Exodus*, 41).

In the J material, the angel of the LORD is involved; the LORD has already "come down" and will deliver Israel. In E, God calls to Moses, who hides his face as in the presence of a theophany; instead of God delivering Israel, God sends Moses to deliver Israel (sent: cf. vv. 10, 12, 13, 14). "Of course this is an insignificant difference. . . . But the difference is none the less there" (Noth, *Exodus*, 40–41).

The sign in v. 12 is unhelpful in its present context; in Noth's judgment, "v. 12 has obviously been transmitted in a fragmentary state" (*Exodus*, 42). The complexity of vv. 14-15 is notorious. In his commentary Noth reverses the position taken here: "If then

15God also said to Moses, "Thus you shall say to the Israelites, 'The LORD, the God of your ancestors, the God of Abraham, the God of Isaac, and the God of Jacob, has sent me to you':

> *This is my name forever,*
> *and this my title for all generations."*

• • •

4:17 "Take in your hand this staff, with which you shall perform the signs."

18 Moses went back to his father-in-law Jethro and said to him, "Please let me go back to my kindred in Egypt and see whether they are still living." And Jethro said to Moses, "Go in peace."

• • •

20bAnd Moses carried the staff of God in his hand.[52]

• • •

Deliverance at the Sea

13:17 When Pharaoh let the people go, God did not lead them by way of the land of the Philistines, although that was nearer; for God thought, "If the people face war, they may change their minds and return to Egypt." 18So God led the people by the roundabout way of the wilderness toward the Red Sea. The Israelites went up out of the land of Egypt prepared for battle. 19And Moses took with him the bones of Joseph who had required a solemn oath of the Israelites, saying, "God will surely take notice of you, and then you must carry my bones with you from here."

14:5a When the king of Egypt was told that the people had fled, 7he took six hundred picked chariots and all the other chariots of Egypt with officers over all of them.[53]

• • •

---

we have both primary and secondary material in these verses, we must hold the simpler expression to be the original and thus should not understand v. 15 to be a secondary expansion of v. 14 . . . especially as v. 14 could hardly have been in need of such express interpretation. Instead we should regard the simple giving of the name in v. 15 as an original answer to the question at the end of v. 13" (*Exodus*, 43; for a fuller discussion, see ibid., 42–45; for vv. 12-15, see B. S. Childs, *Exodus* [OTL; London: SCM, 1974] 56–77).

It is worth noting that after this revelation there is little change within the E material in the use of the divine name. YHWH is used extremely rarely in E, both before and after Exodus 3. For original E texts after Exodus 3, there are eight occurrences of YHWH in the exceptional Numbers 23 (Balaam) and some nineteen occurrences in secondary additions to E (including Exod 24:1a); for the sake of comparison, before Exodus 3 there are some four occurrences in original E texts and four in secondary material. It is therefore unlikely that Exod 3:14-15 is to be regarded in E as an epochal revelation, in contrast to its function in P. Rather, there may well be at the core of this E tradition the recognition that Moses, who has been brought up at the Egyptian court, must be given the name of the god of the Israelites to whom he is now sent. Note the use of "your," not "our," in vv. 13 and 15: "The God of *your* ancestors" (for other views, see

Childs, *Exodus*, 66–70). As a legitimation of Moses' role and authority, the question has no value unless the Israelites themselves know and can verify the answer.

Against this background, the avoidance of YHWH throughout the E material may have nothing to do with the revelation or nonrevelation of the divine name but may be simply a heuristic device to distinguish the variant material from the original. Alternatively, these variant traditions were preserved in a context that preferred to use the name "God" alone.

The sources have been skillfully combined in such a way that J's announcement in v. 8 *that* YHWH has come to deliver Israel is followed by E's text, which announces *how* this deliverance will be effected—through the agency of Moses. Each stage of this announcement is prefaced by a statement of God's awareness of Israel's dire predicament (vv. 7 and 9).

52. In Exod 4:17, the staff reappears suddenly, in a different role from 4:1-5. Verse 18 is a doublet of vv. 19-20a; v. 20b refers to the staff as in v. 17 (cf. Noth, *Exodus*, 47). Therefore this material is given to E. Note the tension between 4:20a (J) and 18:2-6* (E).

53. The term "king of Egypt" for the Pharaoh is used across the sources. In J: Exod 1:8; 2:23 (3:18-19; 5:4); in P: Exod 6:11 (13, 27, 29); 14:8—all as "Pharaoh, king of Egypt"; in E: Exod 14:5a; in nonsource material: Exod 1:15, 17, 18.

[11]They said to Moses, "Was it because there were no graves in Egypt that you have taken us away to die in the wilderness? What have you done to us, bringing us out of Egypt? [12]Is this not the very thing we told you in Egypt, 'Let us alone and let us serve the Egyptians'? For it would have been better for us to serve the Egyptians than to die in the wilderness."

• • •

19a The angel of God who was going before the Israelite army moved and went behind them.

• • •

[25a]He clogged their chariot wheels so that they turned with difficulty.[54]

• • •

17:3 But the people thirsted there for water; and the people complained against Moses and said, "Why did you bring us out of Egypt, to kill us and our children and livestock with thirst?"[55]

• • •

Moses and
Jethro, the Priest of Midian

18 Jethro, the priest of Midian, Moses' father-in-law, heard of all that God had done for Moses and for his people Israel.

how the LORD *had brought Israel out of Egypt.*
[2]And [Heb.; RSV, Now][56] Jethro, Moses' father-in-law, had taken Zipporah, Moses' wife,
after he had sent her away
[3]along with her two sons.
The name of the one was Gershom for he said, "I have been an alien in a foreign land," [4]and the name of the other, Eliezer for he said, "The God of my father was my help, and delivered me from the sword of Pharaoh."
[5]Jethro, Moses' father-in-law, came into the wilderness where Moses was encamped at the mountain of God, bringing Moses' sons and wife to him. [6]He sent word to Moses, "I, your father-in-law Jethro, am coming to you, with your wife and her two sons." [7]Moses went out to meet his father-in-law; he bowed down and kissed him; each asked after the other's welfare, and they went into the tent. [8]Then Moses told his father-in-law
all that the LORD *had done to Pharaoh and to the Egyptians for Israel's sake*
all the hardship that had beset them on the way.
and how the LORD *had delivered them. [9]Jethro rejoiced for all the good that the* LORD *had done to Israel, in delivering them from the Egyptians.*
10 Jethro said, "Blessed be the LORD, *who has*

---

54. Again, there is no narrative continuity between this deliverance at the sea in E and the preceding. Exodus 13:17-19 uses "God" for the divine name, and vv. 17-18 are a doublet of v. 20. Verse 19 refers to the concern of the E passage, Gen 50:25. Therefore this material is attributed to E.

Exodus 14:5 contains tensions. "Flight" suggests an unauthorized departure (v. 5a); "letting Israel leave" suggests an authorized departure (v. 5b). Moreover, vv. 6 and 7 are doublets. Because J in this context uses the term "Pharaoh," Noth in *Pentateuchal Traditions* attributes vv. 5a and 7 to E (in his commentary he is emphatic both that vv. 6 and 7 constitute a doublet and that either one may be attributed to J or E [*Exodus*, 106]).

Exodus 14:11-12 is not prepared for in any way in the preceding text and is not picked up directly in Moses' response; it may well come from E (contrary view in Childs, *Exodus*, 220). Verse 19a is a clear doublet of v. 19b and is to be attributed to E. Verse 25a stands out in its context and in the language used for chariots; there are no indications of its source, but it may be E (for these, see Noth, *Exodus*, 105–6; see also below, chap. 6).

55. Noth sees the verse as a doublet of vv. 1b-2a* and possibly to be attributed to E. It appears to be "a fragment of a narrative variant," but its inclusion here is not easily explained (cf. Noth, *Pentateuchal Traditions*, 36 n. 137). In his commentary, "only v. 3 remains as quite certainly Elohistic" (*Exodus*, 139).

56. For the sake of a clearer representation of the Hebrew text, the RSV has been used here in Exod 18:2.

delivered you from the Egyptians and from Pha- raoh. [11]*Now I know that the* LORD *is greater than all gods, because he delivered the people from the Egyptians, when they dealt arrogantly with them."*

[12]And Jethro, Moses' father-in-law, brought a burnt offering and sacrifices to God; and Aaron came with all the elders of Israel to eat bread with Moses' father-in-law in the presence of God.

13 The next day Moses sat as judge for the people, while the people stood around him from morning until evening. [14]When Moses' father-in-law saw all that he was doing for the people, he said, "What is this that you are doing for the people? Why do you sit alone, while all the people stand around you from morning until evening?" [15]Moses said to his father-in-law, "Because the people come to me to inquire of God. [16]When they have a dispute, they come to me and I decide between one person and another, and I make known to them the statutes and instructions of God." [17]Moses' father-in-law said to him, "What you are doing is not good. [18]You will surely wear yourself out, both you and these people with you. For the task is too heavy for you; you cannot do it alone. [19]Now listen to me. I will give you counsel, and God be with you! You should represent the people before God, and you should bring their cases before God; [20]teach them the statutes and instructions and make known to them the way they are to go and the things they are to do. [21]You should also look for able men among all the people, men who fear God, are trustworthy, and hate dishonest gain; set such men over them as officers over thousands, hundreds, fifties and tens. [22]Let them sit as judges for the people at all times; let them bring every important case to you, but decide every minor case themselves. So it will be easier for you, and they will bear the burden with you. [23]If you do this, and God so commands you, then you will be able to endure, and all these people will go to their home in peace."

24 So Moses listened to his father-in-law and did all that he had said. [25]Moses chose able men from all Israel and appointed them as heads over the people, as officers over thousands, hundreds, fifties, and tens. [26]And they judged the people at all times; hard cases they brought to Moses, but any minor case they decided themselves. [27]Then Moses let his father-in-law depart, and he went off to his own country.[57]

• • •

Encounter with God at the Mountain

19:3a Then Moses went up to God

• • •

[13*]When the trumpet sounds a long blast

[16*] There was thunder and lightning, as well as a thick cloud on the mountain, and a blast of a trumpet so loud that all the people who were in the camp trembled. [17]Moses brought the people out of the camp to meet God. They took their stand at the foot of the mountain. [19]As the blast of the trumpet grew louder and louder, Moses

---

57. Exodus 18 is another of the principal stories that are unique to the material identified as E. The rest of E. is comprised of variants of J material. The use of the name "God" in Exodus 18, especially at key points, underpins its attribution to E.

Exodus 18 falls into two parts, vv. 1-12 and 13-27.

There are "striking discrepancies and repetitions" in vv. 1-12, suggesting secondary J expansions of the E material (cf. Noth, *Exodus*, 145–46). Thus this chapter is one of those rare occasions in the Pentateuch where the E text has been maintained substantially intact, enriched by J expansions.

would speak and God would answer him in thunder.[58]

Decalogue

20 *Then God spoke all these words:*

2 I am the LORD *your God, who brought you out of the land of Egypt, out of the house of slavery; ³you shall have no other gods before me.*

4 You shall not make for yourself an idol, whether in the form of anything that is in heaven above, or that is on the earth beneath, or that is in the water under the earth. ⁵You shall not bow down to them or worship them; for I the LORD *your God am a jealous God, punishing children for the iniquity of parents, to the third and the fourth generation of those who reject me, ⁶but showing steadfast love to the thousandth generation of those who love me and keep my commandments.*

7 You shall not make wrongful use of the name of the LORD *your God, for the* LORD *will not acquit anyone who misuses his name.*

8 Remember the sabbath day, and keep it holy. ⁹Six days you shall labor and do all your work. ¹⁰But the seventh day is a sabbath to the LORD *your God; you shall not do any work—you, your son or your daughter, your male or female slave, your livestock, or the alien resident in your towns. ¹¹For in six days the* LORD *made heaven and earth, the sea, and all that is in them, but rested the seventh day; therefore the* LORD *blessed the sabbath day and consecrated it.*

12 Honor your father and your mother, so that your days may be long in the land that the LORD *your God is giving you.*

13 You shall not murder.

14 You shall not commit adultery.

15 You shall not steal.

16 You shall not bear false witness against your neighbor.

17 You shall not covet your neighbor's house; you shall not covet your neighbor's wife, or male or female slave, or ox, or donkey, or anything that belongs to your neighbor.[59]

---

58. It is perhaps helpful to introduce this Sinai section with Noth's comment on its difficulty: "Of course it is no longer possible to make a smooth and satisfactory division of the whole between the two older sources. This is not surprising, as it is easily understandable that the important central section of the tradition of the theophany on Sinai should frequently have been worked over and provided with expansions" (*Exodus*, 154).

The division between J and E in this material is controlled by the use of the divine names and also by the recognition that, in E, awesome signs of divine presence occur as soon as the people arrive at the mountain, so that in terror they keep their distance and insist that Moses mediate between them and God; in J, by contrast, the people have to be warned against coming too near the mountain (Noth, *Exodus*, 154).

Exodus 19:3b-9a is omitted as a later addition, because it anticipates both the theophany and the covenant that is yet to be concluded.

Verse 13b, omitted here, is difficult to interpret without any context. It appears to refer to an unnamed group who will ascend the mountain when summoned by the trumpet. "We therefore have in this passage a fragment from a narrative sequence no longer extant,

which appears to have some factual connection with Ex. 24.1 f., 9-11, where a clearly defined group of people are said to ascend the mountain" (Noth, *Exodus*, 158). Although the trumpet (*šōpār*) is referred to in vv. 16 and 19, the word used in v. 13b is different (*yōbēl*).

59. The decalogue (Ten Commandments) is loosely tied into its context. Exodus 20:1 is general; vv. 18-21 relate back to Exod 19:16b, 17, and 19. Any attribution to J or E is without sound foundation. Noth is, as usual, cautious: "The Decalogue is thus so loosely inserted into the narrative that we are led to the conclusion that from a literary aspect it is a secondary passage in the account of the theophany on Sinai. . . . We can thus only come to the negative conclusion that the Decalogue did not originally stand in any of the old narratives of the theophany on Sinai, but was only inserted into them during the course of time" (*Exodus*, 154–55). As Noth is careful to insist, this says nothing about the age or origin of the decalogue, which had a tradition history all of its own.

Without the commandments, the E portrayal of Sinai might be characterized as a meeting with God and the sharing of a sacred meal on the mountain of God.

18 When all the people witnessed the thunder and lightning, the sound of the trumpet, *and the mountain smoking, they were afraid and trembled* and stood at a distance, [19]and said to Moses, "You speak to us, and we will listen; but do not let God speak to us, or we will die." [20]Moses said to the people, "Do not be afraid; for God has come only to test you and to put the fear of him upon you so that you do not sin." [21]Then the people stood at a distance, while Moses drew near to the thick darkness where God was.[60]

• • •[61]

24 Then he said to Moses, "Come up to the LORD, you and Aaron, Nadab, and Abihu, and seventy of the elders of Israel."
and worship at a distance.

[2]*Moses alone shall come near the* LORD; *but the others shall not come near, and the people shall not come up with him.*

9 Then Moses and Aaron, Nadab, and Abihu, and seventy of the elders of Israel went up, [10]and they saw the God of Israel. Under his feet there was something like a pavement of sapphire stone, like the very heaven for clearness. [11]God did not lay his hand on the chief men of the people of Israel; also they beheld God, and they ate and drank.[62]

• • •

Anti-Aaronide Traditions

32:1b The people gathered around Aaron, and said to him, "Come, make gods for us, who shall go before us; as for this Moses, the

---

60. These verses have the E theme of the people instinctively keeping their distance from the sacred mountain.

61. Because of the word order, Noth postulates a gap before Exod 24:1a (*Pentateuchal Traditions*, 36, 139). It is not to be filled by the Book of the Covenant (Exod 20:22—23:33). Noth comments, "It is probable that this collection once formed an independent book of law which has been inserted into the Pentateuchal narrative as an already self-contained entity. . . . No clear relationship to any one of the Pentateuchal narrative 'sources' is recognizable" (*Exodus*, 173).

62. Exodus 24:1-2* and 24:9-11 are one account of a covenant meal on the sacred mountain. The reference to God, in particular in v. 11, suggests attribution to E.

For Noth, the introduction (vv. 1-2) "obviously no longer presents its original wording" (*Exodus*, 196). The Hebrew is unusually formulated and the use of YHWH in "Come up to the LORD" would point to a third person issuing the order. Noth opts for regarding the whole passage as secondary (*Exodus*, 197). This does not explain how it came to be inappropriately formulated and why it was later inserted here. The latter part (vv. 1b-2) is an apparent correction, since in vv. 9-11 no distinctions are made within the group who see and eat with God.

A hypothetical reconstruction of E's account of Sinai would have to include the arrival at the mountain and Moses' going up it to receive instructions for the theophany (19:3a); the people's "meeting" with God at the foot of the mountain and Moses' exchange with God (19:16*, 17, 19); Moses' being asked to mediate while the people keep their distance (20:19-21); presumably, instructions for the deputation who are to ascend the mountain; the ascent and the covenant meal on the mountain (24:1*, 9-11; see Noth, *Exodus*, 197).

The meaning of the covenant meal is sensitively expressed by Dennis J. McCarthy: "The significance of the meal as seal of the alliance seems to stem from Bedouin culture. It is a sign that the weaker is taken into the family of the stronger, a reassuring gesture on the part of the superior toward the inferior and not a pledge by the latter. This rite with its echo of nomad life reinforces the impression of antiquity which the style and atmosphere of these verses give. This is an authentic gesture of covenant making, and it is ancient, but it is not in the character of the treaties. The ratification of alliance by rite rather than by oath, and the gesture of superior to inferior rather than vice versa, these things are uncharacteristic of the treaty tradition" (*Treaty and Covenant* [AnBib 21a; new edition completely rewritten; Rome: Biblical Institute, 1978] 254).

Noth remarks delicately that "only the appearance 'under his feet' is described and it is thus intimated that the deputation did not dare to raise their eyes to the 'God of Israel' himself" (*Exodus*, 195).

man who brought us up out of the land of Egypt, we do not know what has become of him." ²Aaron said to them, "Take off the gold rings that are on the ears of your wives, your sons, and your daughters, and bring them to me." ³So all the people took off the gold rings from their ears, and brought them to Aaron. ⁴ᵃHe took the gold from them, formed it in a mold, and cast an image of a calf.

• • •

21 Moses said to Aaron, "What did this

people do to you that you have brought so great a sin upon them?" ²²And Aaron said, "Do not let the anger of my lord burn hot; you know the people, that they are bent on evil. ²³They said to me, 'Make us gods, who shall go before us; as for this Moses, the man who brought us up out of the land of Egypt, we do not know what has become of him.' ²⁴So I said to them, 'Whoever has gold, take it off '; so they gave it to me, and I threw it into the fire, and out came this calf!"⁶³

• • •

The Book of Numbers

*Refusal of Passage
through Edom*

20:14 Moses sent messengers from Kadesh to the king of Edom, "Thus says your brother Israel: You know all the adversity that has befallen us:

¹⁵*how our ancestors went down to Egypt, and we lived in Egypt a long time; and the Egyptians oppressed us and our ancestors; ¹⁶and when we cried to the LORD, he heard our voice, and sent an angel and brought us out of Egypt;*

and here we are in Kadesh, a town on the edge

of your territory. ¹⁷Now let us pass through your land. We will not pass through field or vineyard, or drink water from any well; we will go along the King's Highway, not turning aside to the right hand or to the left until we have passed through your territory."

18 But Edom said to him, "You shall not pass through, or we will come out with the sword against you." ²¹Thus Edom refused to give Israel passage through their territory; so Israel turned away from them.⁶⁴

---

63. Exodus 32:21-24 is seen as secondary by Noth because it is out of sequence in relation to what is reported of Moses in 32:19-20 (*Exodus*, 244). Whereas in Hebrew narrative action is often followed by the accompanying words, here the reference to "this calf" (v. 24) suggests that it has not yet been burned, ground to powder, and drunk (v. 20).

Aaron refers to what is reported of him in vv. 1b-4a, with some difference in the level of responsibility depicted in vv. 4a and 24. In his commentary, Noth regards Aaron's presence in the text here as secondary. It is possible both passages are later. "Unfortunately we can no longer ascertain the time or the circumstances of the addition of these passages" (Noth, *Exodus*, 245).

In Noth's *History of Pentateuchal Traditions*, these two passages belong in the same category as material

in Genesis 15 and Exodus 1. They are considered to stand out clearly as elements of a variant narrative that is not J, without there being positive clues to identify them as belonging originally to E.

64. Two sources have been worked together in Num 20:14-21, and there is no trace of P; so this has to be the first demonstrable appearance of E tradition in the book of Numbers. Numbers 20:17-18 is a doublet of vv. 19-20; there are several other inconsistencies (Noth, *Numbers* [OTL; Philadelphia: Westminster Press, 1968] 149). Noth insists on the extreme difficulty of identifying and separating the sources in this passage. Hard evidence is lacking. The arguments we have "lead no further than the assertion that in this section we have a composite text of J and E in front of us and that the two sources both seem to have contained very similar narratives" (Noth, *Numbers*, 149–50).

Victory over
Sihon of the Amorites

21:21 Then Israel sent messengers to King Sihon of the Amorites, saying, ²²"Let me pass through your land; we will not turn aside into field or vineyard; we will not drink the water of any well; we will go by the King's Highway until we have passed through your territory." ²³But Sihon would not allow Israel to pass through his territory. Sihon gathered all his people together, and went out against Israel to the wilderness; he came to Jahaz, and fought against Israel. ²⁴Israel put him to the sword, and took possession of his land from the Arnon to the Jabbok, as far as to the Ammonites; for the boundary of the Ammonites was strong. ²⁵Israel took all these towns, and Israel settled in all the towns of the Amorites, in Heshbon, and in all its villages. ²⁶For Heshbon was the city of King Sihon of the Amorites, who had fought against the former king of Moab and captured all his land as far as the Arnon. ²⁷Therefore the ballad singers say,

"Come to Heshbon, let it be built;
let the city of Sihon be established.
²⁸For fire came out from Heshbon,
flame from the city of Sihon.
It devoured Ar of Moab,
and swallowed up the heights of the
Arnon.

²⁹Woe to you, O Moab!
You are undone, O people of Chemosh!
He has made his sons fugitives,
and his daughters captives,
to an Amorite king, Sihon.
³⁰So their posterity perished
from Heshbon to Dibon,
and we laid waste until fire spread
to Medeba."

31 Thus Israel settled in the land of the Amorites.[65]

³²Moses sent to spy out Jazer; and they captured its villages, and dispossessed the Amorites who were there.

33 Then they turned and went up the road to Bashan; and King Og of Bashan came out against them, he and all his people, to battle at Edrei. ³⁴But the LORD said to Moses, "Do not be afraid of him; for I have given him into your hand, with all his people, and all his land. You shall do to him as you did to King Sihon of the Amorites, who ruled in Heshbon." ³⁵So they killed him, his sons, and all his people, until there was no survivor left; and they took possession of his land.

Israel Is Blessed by Balaam

22:2 Now Balak son of Zippor saw all that Israel had done to the Amorites. ³ᵃMoab was in great dread of the people, because they were so numerous.[66]

---

65. The literary unity of this passage need not be doubted. The references to the Amorites point to E as the source, because J tends to prefer the term Canaanites. The song in Num 21:27-30 is an older tradition, inserted into the narrative.

Verse 32, coming after the conclusion in v. 31, has Moses as its subject rather than Israel. In Noth's view, it is an ill-fitting note, added with reference to 32:1. Verses 33-35a are an almost verbatim repetition of Deut 3:1-3, expanding the Sihon story here with the Og story, which is peculiar to the deuteronomistic literature (Noth, *Numbers*, 161-62).

66. According to Noth, it is generally agreed that P has only the itinerary note in Num 22:1b and

that the alternation of the divine names and the presence of clear doublets points to the presence of two sources, J and E. The detailed analysis is highly problematic. Numbers 22:41—23:26 forms an obvious doublet with 23:28—24:19; the former is assigned to E, taking the designation for God into account. Numbers 23:27, 29, and 30 are considered "secondary editorial material" linking the major variant passages. The episode with the donkey (22:21-35) goes to J. Noth comments, "The remainder of the chapter . . . can no longer be divided up with any certainty; one can only point to doublets and variants and make the general assertion that this is a combination of J and E" (*Numbers*, 171-72).

• • •

⁹God came to Balaam and said, "Who are these men with you?" ¹⁰Balaam said to God, "King Balak son of Zippor of Moab, has sent me this message: ¹¹'A people has come out of Egypt and has spread over the face of the earth; now come, curse them for me; perhaps I shall be able to fight against them and drive them out.' " ¹²God said to Balaam, "You shall not go with them; you shall not curse the people, for they are blessed."

• • •

²⁰That night God came to Balaam and said to him, "If the men have come to summon you, get up and go with them; but do only what I tell you to do."

• • •

38*"Have I now any power at all to speak anything?⁶⁷ The word God puts in my mouth, that is what I must say."

41 On the next day Balak took Balaam and brought him up to Bamoth-baal; and from there he could see part of the people of Israel.

23 Then Balaam said to Balak, "Build me seven altars here, and prepare seven bulls and seven rams for me." ²Balak did as Balaam had said; and Balak and Balaam offered a bull and a ram on each altar. ³Then Balaam said to Balak, "Stay here beside your burnt offerings while I go aside. Perhaps the LORD will come to meet me. Whatever he shows me I will tell you." And he went to a bare height.⁶⁸

4 Then God met Balaam; and Balaam said to him, "I have arranged the seven altars, and have offered a bull and a ram on each altar." ⁵The LORD put a word in Balaam's mouth, and said, "Return to Balak, and this is what you must say." ⁶So he returned to Balak, who was standing beside his burnt offerings with all the officials of Moab. ⁷Then Balaam uttered his oracle, saying:

"Balak has brought me from Aram,
  the king of Moab from the eastern
  mountains:
'Come, curse Jacob for me;
  Come, denounce Israel!'
⁸How can I curse whom God has not cursed?
How can I denounce those
  whom the LORD has not denounced?
⁹For from the top of the crags I see him,
  from the hills I behold him;
Here is a people living alone,
  and not reckoning itself among the
  nations!
¹⁰Who can count the dust of Jacob,
  or number the dust-cloud of Israel?
Let me die the death of the upright,
  and let my end be like his!"

11 Then Balak said to Balaam, "What have you done to me? I brought you to curse my enemies, but now you have done nothing but bless them." ¹²He answered, "Must I not take care to say what the LORD puts into my mouth?"

13 So Balak said to him, "Come with me to another place from which you may see them; you shall see only part of them, and shall not see them all; then curse them for me from there." ¹⁴So he took him to the field of Zophim, to the top of Pisgah. He built seven altars, and offered a bull and a ram on each altar. ¹⁵Balaam said to Balak, "Stand here beside your burnt offerings, while I meet the LORD over there." ¹⁶The LORD met Balaam, put a word into his mouth, and said, "Return to Balak, and this is what you shall say." ¹⁷When he came to him, he was standing beside his burnt offerings with the officials of Moab.

---

67. For a clearer representation of the Hebrew text, the RSV is used in Num 22:38*.

68. For Noth, the occurrences of YHWH here and in vv. 5, 12, and 16 are probably to be changed back into an original *Elohim* in accordance with the Septuagint and other textual witnesses (*Pentateuchal Traditions*, 36 n. 141).

Balak said to him, "What has the LORD said?"
[18]Then Balaam uttered his oracle, saying:
"Rise, Balak, and hear;
    listen to me, O son of Zippor:
[19]God is not a human being, that he
    should lie,
    or a mortal, that he should change
    his mind.
Has he promised, and will he not do it?
    Has he spoken, and will he not fulfill it?
[20]See, I received a command to bless;
    he has blessed, and I cannot revoke it.
[21]He has not beheld misfortune in Jacob;
    nor has he seen trouble in Israel.
The LORD their God is with them,
    acclaimed as a king among them.
[22]God, who brings them out of Egypt,
    is like the horns of a wild ox for them.
[23]Surely there is no enchantment against
    Jacob,

    no divination against Israel;
now it shall be said of Jacob and Israel,
    'See what God has done!'
[24]Look, a people rising up like a lioness,
    and rousing itself like a lion!
It does not lie down until it has eaten the prey
    and drunk the blood of the slain."
[25]Then Balak said to Balaam, "Do not curse them at all, and do not bless them at all." [26]But Balaam answered Balak, "Did I not tell you, 'Whatever the LORD says, that is what I must do'?"[69]

[27]So Balak said to Balaam, "Come now, I will take you to another place; perhaps it will please God that you may curse them for me from there." [29]Balaam said to Balak, "Build me seven altars here, and prepare seven bulls and seven rams for me." [30]So Balak did as Balaam had said, and offered a bull and a ram on each altar.

• • •

---

69. In Noth's view, the Balaam story is entirely from the old pentateuchal material, but it is "obviously not a unified whole." The changes in the divine name are otherwise unmotivated. There is agreement that it consists of J and E, but the detailed division of the sources is much more problematic, with the difficulty increased by uncertainty in the transmission of the text. Numbers 22:41—23:26 constitutes the main part of the E version, forming a doublet with the J text, 23:28—24:19 (*Numbers*, 171). Numbers 23:27-30 is considered an editorial link between the E and J versions (*Numbers*, 187).
    For Noth, an Elohist conquest account has been sacrificed in the integration with P. He conjectures that an E account of Moses' death could have been situated between Num 20:14 (subject: Moses) and 21:21 (subject: Israel), therefore before any account of the conquest and also before the Balaam stories (*Pentateuchal Traditions*, 36 n. 142).
    The last word on Balaam may be given to Noth: "However much the Balaam story may have been elaborated in the course of time, the nucleus of it must have been formed by the appearance, in Israel's early period, of a 'man of God' by the name of Balaam, who had come from afar to one of the sanctuaries of southern Transjordan . . . and of whom it would be reported that he had uttered words of blessing on neighbouring Israel" (*Numbers*, 175).

CHAPTER 5

Nonsource Texts:
Material Other than P, J, and E

Texts exist, from small fragments to large blocks, which Noth sees as additions to either a completed source (P, J, or E) or the combined sources. Tensions between a text and the source where it is found may suggest that the text was not originally part of the source. When a text reflects the combination of the sources, it cannot have belonged to one alone. We refer to these texts, therefore, as nonsource texts; they have been incorporated subsequently into either a completed source or the combined sources.

Some examples may help.

1. Genesis 7:3a echoes both J and P (n. 3, below). Noth sees it as an addition to the combined text. See too Gen 7:8-9.
2. Genesis 4:25 seeks to smooth out a tension within J, but uses *Elohim* and *Adam* in ways uncharacteristic of J. Noth sees it as an addition to the completed J source, not a harmonization within J.
3. Genesis 6:1-4 is so isolated a passage that its origin is quite uncertain. Noth remarks that it could be part of J, a supplement to J, or an addition to the completed Pentateuch. Noth does not include the passage in his list of J material, so we locate it here—without prejudice to other possibilities. See too Genesis 14; 25:1-4.

4. The great collections of priestly law have been inserted at appropriate places into the Priestly narrative of Sinai. The collection of laws in Exod 20:22—23:33 cannot be identified with either P, J, or E, and Noth sees the collection as an independent unit inserted into the pentateuchal narrative.
5. Noth considers deuteronomistic expansions later than J and E and quite different from and independent of P (e.g., Exod 12:24-27a; 13:1-16; 15:25b-26). They derive from circles associated with the Book of Deuteronomy and the Deuteronomistic History.
6. The cultic calendar in Numbers 28–29 presupposes a wide variety of texts. Noth sees it as a very late addition to the Pentateuch.
7. The list of camping sites in Numbers 33 not only draws on the combined pentateuchal text but reflects the combination of the Pentateuch with the Deuteronomistic History.

It is one thing to identify texts as additions; it is another to interpret such additions in the context to which they have been added. Ideally, as much attention needs to be given to appreciating and explaining an addition as was invested in the first place to identify the text as additional. In this chapter, we provide brief notes pointing to reasons why these texts are considered subsequent additions; it is not possible to pursue systematically the task of their interpretation.

The Book of Genesis

4:25 Adam knew his wife again, and she bore a son and named him Seth, for she said, "God has appointed for me another child instead of Abel, because Cain killed him." [26]To Seth also a son was born, and he named him Enosh. At that time people began to invoke the name of the LORD.[1]

6 When people began to multiply on the face of the ground, and daughters were born to them, [2]the sons of God saw that they were fair; and they took wives for themselves of all that they chose. [3]Then the LORD said, "My spirit shall not abide in mortals forever, for they are flesh; their days shall be one hundred twenty years." [4]The Nephilim were on the earth in those days—and also afterward—when the sons of God went in to the daughters of humans, who bore children to them. These were the heroes that were of old, warriors of renown.[2]

7:3a and seven pairs of the birds of the air also, male and female[3]

7* with his sons and his wife and his sons' wives[4]

8 Of clean animals, and of animals that are not clean, and of birds, and of everything that creeps on the ground, [9]two and two, male and female, went into the ark with Noah, as God had commanded Noah.[5]

17a The flood continued forty days on the earth[6]

23* they were blotted out from the earth[7]

14:1-24 •The Melchizedek story[8]

15:2b and the heir of my house is Eliezer of Damascus[9]

16:9 The angel of the LORD said to her, "Return to your mistress, and submit to her." [10]The angel of the LORD also said to her, "I will

---

1. See p. 95 n. 3, on Gen 4:24.

2. See p. 95 n. 6, before Gen 6:5.

3. "Seven pairs" echoes J, and "male and female" echoes P, suggesting an addition to the combined text (i.e., J and P).

4. See p. 96 n. 12, on Gen 7:7.

5. Genesis 7:8-9, like 7:3a, is a later addition to the combined text, blending elements from J and P. The distinction between clean and unclean animals is from J; the phrase "male and female" and the use of "God" instead of "LORD" are drawn from P. See the discussion of this text on pp. 217–19.

6. Opinions differ over this half-verse, due to the complications of combining contrasting chronologies. Similarities with v. 6b suggest a P origin; the forty days suggests J. Noth has opted for an addition to the combined text. See p. 26 n. 10, on Gen 7:16a.

7. The little phrase is similar to J statements in Gen 6:7 and 7:4, and particularly the beginning of

7:23 here, which it reduplicates. In contrast to these J texts, which have *'ădāmâ* (ground), v. 17a uses *'ereṣ* (earth); the NRSV's "earth" in 6:7 does not maintain this distinction (cf. RSV).

8. Martin Noth comments that "the question of the source to which Gen. 14 belongs is as completely obscure today as it has been in the past" (*A History of Pentateuchal Traditions*, trans. B. W. Anderson [Englewood Cliffs, N.J.: Prentice-Hall, 1972; reprint, Chico, Calif.: Scholars Press, 1981] 28).

9. Noth here is in line with common exegetical opinion that Gen 15:2b is a later gloss; the Hebrew is obscure, making accurate translation difficult. On the name Eliezer, C. Westermann remarks that "a well known trait of the history of the narratives is that minor characters acquire names in the course of tradition" (*Genesis 12–36* [Minneapolis: Augsburg, 1985] 220).

so greatly multiply your offspring that they cannot be counted for multitude."[10]

25 Abraham took another wife, whose name was Keturah. [2]She bore him Zimran, Jokshan, Medan, Midian, Ishbak, and Shuah. [3]Jokshan was the father of Sheba and Dedan. The sons of Dedan were Asshurim, Letushim, and Leummim. [4]The sons of Midian were Ephah, Epher, Hanoch, Abida, and Eldaah. All these were the children of Keturah.[11]

18 They settled from Havilah to Shur, which is opposite Egypt in the direction of Assyria; he settled down alongside of all his people.[12]

26:1* besides the former famine that had occurred in the days of Abraham[13]

35:13b at the place where he had spoken with him[14]

36:15-43   •The descendants of Esau[15]

37:2* he was a helper to the sons of Bilhah and Zilpah, his father's wives[16]

5b they hated him even more[17]

40:3* in the prison where Joseph was confined[18]

5b—the cupbearer and the baker of the king of Egypt, who were confined in the prison—[19]

15b and here also I have done nothing that they should have put me into the dungeon[20]

41:14* and he was hurriedly brought out of the dungeon[21]

43:14* so that he may send back your other brother and Benjamin[22]

---

10. See p. 101 n. 29, on Gen 16:8.

11. See p. 108 n. 45, on Gen 25:5.

12. According to Noth, "25:18 is probably a gloss—maybe a very late one—whose first part is to be compared with 1 Sam 15:7 and also 1 Sam 27:8, while the second part obviously is derived from Gen. 16:12b" (*Pentateuchal Traditions*, 17). Gunkel regarded it as the original ending of J's story of Hagar in Genesis 16. Westermann sees it, along with 25:13-16, as a tradition taken over by P (*Genesis 12–36*, 399). So Gen 25:18 is attributed variously to J, P, and a later gloss; within the overall source hypothesis, these would be regarded as minor variations.

13. This is regarded as a redactional addition to draw attention to links with the ancestress-in-danger story in Gen 12:10-20 (see Hermann Gunkel, *Genesis*, 8th ed. [Göttingen: Vandenhoeck & Ruprecht, 1969] 300). Westermann, who follows Van Seters here, notes that the term translated as "besides" occurs especially in deuteronomic and P passages (*Genesis 12–36*, 422).

14. Oddly placed in the Hebrew, repetitive of vv. 14 (E, specifying the location of the pillar) and 15 (P, specifying the location of Bethel), and lacking in the Vulgate, Gen 35:13b is commonly regarded as an addition. For reasons it might be appropriate in the combined text, see Westermann, *Genesis 12–36*, 553.

15. See p. 34 n. 30, on Gen 36:14.

16. Noth believes that the literary origins and concrete meaning of this statement in Gen 37:2 are obscure (*Pentateuchal Traditions*, 18). Gunkel, von Rad, Skinner, and Westermann all include it in P.

17. Missing from the Greek and repeated in v. 8, this clause has been regarded as additional (so Gunkel and Skinner, who omit both occurrences as redactional). With an eye to literary art, this might well be seen as a careful envelope structure; however, the plural "dreams" in v. 8 militates against this, because the second dream is outside the envelope (cf. C. Westermann, *Genesis 37–50* [Minneapolis: Augsburg, 1986] 39). See the discussion of this passage on pp. 227-31.

18. Genesis 40:3* is regarded by Noth as a later redactional addition that reflects the combination of the J and E stories of Joseph in Egypt. It seeks to identify the "house of the captain of the guard" in the E version (v. 3aα) with the "prison" in the J version (cf. 39:20, 22).

19. Genesis 40:5b is seen as a later addition for the same reason as v. 3*. It identifies E's "chief cupbearer" and "chief baker" with the "cupbearer" and "baker" of the J version (40:1), and their place of custody as the prison of 39:20, 22.

20. In the E context of Genesis 40, Joseph's insistence on his innocence, evoking an episode in J, suggests that Gen 40:15b is an addition to the combined text. The only point of reference in the text is the J account of the charges laid against Joseph in 39:14-18 by the wife of his Egyptian master.

21. The presence of the same word, "dungeon," as in Gen 40:15b suggests that this element was added to the narrative by the same redactional hand. These two occurrences are the only use of the word in the Joseph story outside Genesis 37, where it is used for the pit.

22. See p. 126 n. 83, on Gen 43:14.

23b Then he brought Simeon out to them[23]

47:27a Thus Israel settled in the land of Egypt, in the region of Goshen[24]

49:1b-28   •The blessing of Jacob[25]

The Book of Exodus

7:17* and it shall be turned to blood[26]

20b and all the water in the river was turned into blood[27]

12:24 You shall observe this rite as a perpetual ordinance for you and your children. [25]When you come to the land that the LORD will give you, as he has promised, you shall keep this observance. [26]And when your children ask you, 'What do you mean by this observance?' [27a]you shall say, 'It is the passover sacrifice to the LORD, for he passed over the houses of the Israelites in Egypt, when he struck down the Egyptians but spared our houses.' "[28]

13:1-16   •Instruction on the firstborn and unleavened bread[29]

15:1-19   •The song of Miriam[30]

25b There the LORD made for them a statute and an ordinance and there he put them to the test. [26]He said, "If you will listen carefully to the voice of the LORD your God, and do what is right in his sight, and give heed to his commandments and keep all his statutes, I will not bring

upon you any of the diseases that I brought upon the Egyptians; for I am the LORD who heals you."[31]

16:4* In that way I will test them, whether they will follow my instruction or not[32]

28 The LORD said to Moses, "How long will you refuse to keep my commandments and instructions?"[33]

19:3b The LORD called to him from the mountain, saying, "Thus you shall say to the house of Jacob, and tell the Israelites: [4]You have seen what I did to the Egyptians, and how I bore you on eagles' wings and brought you to myself. [5]Now therefore, if you obey my voice and keep my covenant, you shall be my treasured possession out of all the peoples. Indeed, the whole earth is mine, [6]but you shall be for me a priestly kingdom and a holy nation. These are the words that you shall speak to the Israelites."

7 So Moses came, summoned the elders of the people, and set before them all these words that the LORD had commanded him. [8]The peo-

---

23. See p. 126 n. 83, on Gen 43:14.

24. Gunkel regards "in the land of Egypt" as P and gives the rest of v. 23 to J; and Skinner regards "in the region of Goshen" as a gloss and gives the verse to P. The plural subject for the P text in v. 27b was originally supplied by Gen 46:7. "Israel," with the following plural here, suggests a reference to the nation (cf. Gen 48:20), and v. 27a could be a transitional clause necessary for the combined text. Noth sees it as non-source. For Westermann, v. 27a is the end of the Joseph story and v. 27b (with 47:7-10, 11*) provides a link to the end of the Jacob story—and 47:13-26 is an appendage (*Genesis 37-50*, 167).

25. See p. 130 n. 86, before Gen 50:1.

26. See p. 136 n. 102, on Exod 7:17.

27. See p. 136 n. 102, on Exod 7:17.

28. Exodus 12:24-27a is considered a deuterono-

mistic expansion (cf. Martin Noth, *Exodus* [OTL; Philadelphia: Westminster, 1962] 97–98).

29. Exodus 13:1-16 is also a deuteronomistic expansion, built up from a series of gradual additions (Noth, *Exodus*, 101–2).

30. See p. 143 n. 126, on Exod 15:21.

31. Exodus 15:25b-26 is a deuteronomistic addition, only loosely connected to the preceding (Noth, *Exodus*, 129).

32. This little motivational clause is couched in deuteronomistic language. It is attached to a fragment of J (see p. 144 n. 127, before Exod 16:4).

33. Exodus 16:28 is a deuteronomistic addition, prefacing a fragment of the J story that may be the oldest reference to the sabbath in the Old Testament (Noth, *Exodus*, 135-36).

ple all answered as one: "Everything that the LORD has spoken we will do." Moses reported the words of the people to the LORD. [9]Then the LORD said to Moses, "I am going to come to you in a dense cloud, in order that the people may hear when I speak with you and so trust you ever after."

When Moses had told the words of the people to the LORD[34]

13* they may go up on the mountain[35]

20:22—23:33 •A legal collection: the Book of the Covenant[36]

24:3 Moses came and told the people all the words of the LORD and all the ordinances; and all the people answered with one voice, and said, "All the words that the LORD has spoken we will do." [4]And Moses wrote down all the words of the LORD. He rose early in the morning, and built an altar at the foot of the mountain, and set up twelve pillars, corresponding to the twelve tribes of Israel. [5]He sent young men of the people of Israel, who offered burnt offerings and sacrificed oxen as offerings of well-being to the LORD. [6]Moses took half of the blood and put it in basins, and half of the blood he dashed against the altar. [7]Then he took the book of the covenant, and read it in the hearing of the people; and they said, "All that the LORD has spoken we will do, and we will be obedient." [8]Moses took the blood and dashed it on the people, and said, "See the blood of the covenant that the LORD has made with you in accordance with all these words."[37]

32:7 The LORD said to Moses, "Go down at once! Your people, whom you brought up out of the land of Egypt, have acted perversely; [8]they have been quick to turn aside from the way that I commanded them; they have cast for themselves an image of a calf, and have worshiped it and sacrificed to it, and said, 'These are your gods, O Israel, who brought you up out of the land of Egypt!' " [9]The LORD said to Moses, "I have seen this people, how stiff-necked they are. [10]Now let me alone, so that my wrath may burn hot against them and I may consume them; and of you I will make a great nation."

11 But Moses implored the LORD his God, and said, "O LORD, why does your wrath burn hot against your people, whom you brought out of the land of Egypt with great power and with a mighty hand? [12]Why should the Egyptians say, 'It was with evil intent that he brought them out to kill them in the mountains, and to consume them from the face of the earth'? Turn from your fierce wrath; change your mind and do not bring disaster on your people. [13]Remember Abraham, Isaac, and Israel, your servants, how you swore to them by your own self, saying to them, 'I will multiply your descendants like the stars of heaven, and all this land that I have promised I will give to your descendants, and they shall inherit it forever.' " [14]And the LORD changed his mind about the disaster that he planned to bring on his people.[38]

33:1-23 •A collection on the theme of the presence of God.[39]

---

34. See p. 188 n. 58, on Exod 19:19. Verse 9b is transitional, modulating into a new divine speech in Exod 19:10 (Noth, *Exodus*, 158).

35. See p. 188 n. 58, on Exod 19:19.

36. See p. 189 n. 61, before Exod 24:1.

37. In Exod 24:1-2 and 9-11, the covenant is made on the mountain; here, in vv. 3-8, it takes place at the foot of the mountain. It is not easy to determine the origin of this version of the covenant. Noth suggests that it may have been the covenant narrative closing the Book of the Covenant at quite an early period (*Exodus*, 197–99).

38. In his commentary Noth says: "It is certain that because of their style vv. 9-14 must be regarded as a deuteronomistic addition which explains the sparing of Israel . . . after their apostasy" (*Exodus*, 244). In Noth's earlier *History of Pentateuchal Traditions*, the whole of Exod 32:7-14 is considered deuteronomistic (31 n. 113).

39. Noth comments that "a literary-critical analysis of Ex. 33 is probably impossible." He sees it as "a conglomeration of secondary accretions" attached to the first clause of Exod 32:34, "But now go, lead the people to the place about which I have spoken to you" (*Pentateuchal Traditions*, 31 n. 114).

The Book of Leviticus

1–7   •A collection of laws on sacrifice[40]

11–15   •A collection of laws on clean and unclean[41]

17–27   •A collection of laws: the Holiness Code[42]

The Book of Numbers

5–6   •A collection of various laws[43]

8 The LORD spoke to Moses, saying: [2]Speak to Aaron and say to him: When you set up the lamps, the seven lamps shall give light in front of the lampstand. [3]Aaron did so; he set up its lamps to give light in front of the lampstand, as the LORD had commanded Moses. [4]Now this was how the lampstand was made, out of hammered work of gold. From its base to its flowers, it was hammered work; according to the pattern that the LORD had shown Moses, so he made the lampstand.[44]

15:1-41   •A collection of laws for cult and ritual[45]

16:24* from the dwellings of Korah, Dathan, and Abiram[46]

27a* the dwellings of . . . , Dathan, and Abiram[47]

19:1-22   •Instructions concerning the water of purification[48]

21:10 The Israelites set out, and camped in Oboth. [11]They set out from Oboth, and camped at Iye-abarim, in the wilderness bordering Moab toward the sunrise. [12]From there they set out, and camped in the Wadi Zered. [13]From there they set out, and camped on the other side of the Arnon, in the wilderness that extends from the boundary of the Amorites; for the Arnon is the boundary of Moab, between Moab and the Amorites. [14]Wherefore it is said in the Book of the Wars of the LORD,

"Waheb in Suphah and the wadis.
The Arnon [15]and the slopes of the wadis
that extend to the seat of Ar,
and lie along the border of Moab."

[16] From there they continued to Beer; that is the well of which the LORD said to Moses, "Gather the people together, and I will give them water." [17]Then Israel sang this song:

"Spring up, O well!—Sing to it!—
[18]the well that the leaders sank,
that the nobles of the people dug,
with the scepter, with the staff."

From the wilderness to Mattanah, [19]from Mattanah to Nahaliel, from Nahaliel to Bamoth, [20]and from Bamoth to the valley lying in the

---

40. See p. 61 n. 76, on Lev 8:1.

41. See p. 61 n. 76.

42. See p. 61 n. 76.

43. See p. 74 n. 89, on Num 4:49.

44. Numbers 8:1-4 is thought by Noth to function as an appendix to Exod 25:31-40. It amplifies Exod 25:37b, without adding any new information. Verse 4 summarizes Exod 25:31-34, with particular emphasis on the hammered work (see Martin Noth, *Numbers,* [OTL; Philadelphia: Westminster, 1968] 65–66).

45. Numbers 15:1-41 is considered by Noth a "rather unsystematically arranged collection of various cultic-ritual ordinances." Why the collection is added at this point is not particularly clear. In Noth's view, overall it "ought to be considered one of the very latest sections of the Pentateuch"; there are no definite features for dating either the whole or its parts (Noth, *Numbers,* 114).

46. See p. 83 n. 100, on Num 16:27a*.

47. See p. 83 n. 100.

48. See final paragraph of n. 103, pp. 85–86, on Num 18:32.

region of Moab by the top of Pisgah that overlooks the wasteland.[49]

22:1a The Israelites set out[50]

25:6—27:11 •Phinehas, a census, and a
legal case[51]

28-30 •A cultic calendar and women's
vows[52]

32:2-15, 17-38 •The case of Gadites and
Reubenites[53]

33-36 •A diversity of traditions: the sta-
tions on the route of Israel's wandering; the land
west of the Jordan; levitical cities and cities of
refuge; daughters' rights of inheritance[54]

---

49. In Noth's view, Num 21:10-20 contains no
material that was part of a source, only fragments of
the most secondary kind (*Pentateuchal Traditions*, 32 n.
124; for more details, see idem, *Numbers*, 158–60).

50. See p. 157 n. 172, on the gap before Num
22:3b.

51. The Phinehas episode comes from "a late
period in which there was an 'Aaronite' high-priest-
hood with an 'Aaronite' succession" (Noth, *Numbers*,
195). In Numbers 26 we have a clan list, which Noth
regards as "ancient and certainly reliable," and the
results of a census; the two documents may have combined "in Israel's early period." The redactional additions in vv. 1-4a, 52–56, and 62b-64 suggest that the
chapter was added here at the late stage when
the Pentateuch was being revised for combination
with the Deuteronomistic History (ibid., 202–4). The
legal case is considered to be "certainly a later addition" (ibid., 211).

52. The great cultic calendar in Numbers 28–29 is
an appendix to the pentateuchal narrative that presupposes a wide variety of texts, including Leviticus 1–7,
the Holiness Code, and Num 15:1-16. "This must,
therefore, be one of the latest sections of the Pentateuch, although the period of its composition cannot be determined even approximately" (ibid., 219).
Numbers 30 is a passage that stands on its own.
"Without having any connection with what precedes
or with what follows, it has been included in the series
of final instructions which Moses, at Yahweh's command, gives to the Israelites" (ibid., 224).

53. Noth comments that the basic form of Numbers 32 is neither deuteronomistic nor Priestly, but "it
is . . . generally and correctly accepted that the basic
form of the narrative goes back to the 'old Penta-

teuchal sources.'" There has been so much revision
and addition, however, that he regards any convincing
analysis as impossible (ibid., 235). Numbers 32:2-4 is
not the continuation of 32:1, although its opening and
close might go back to old tradition. Numbers 32:5-
15 is late, presupposing the Numbers 13–14 spy story
in its final combined form, about the time that the
Pentateuch and the Deuteronomistic History were
combined (ibid., 237–38). In his commentary, Noth
envisages the possibility that vv. 16-19 may have been
directly linked to v. 1. Verses 20-33 are considered a
"later addition in the deuteronomistic-priestly style"
(ibid., 238). The list of towns in vv. 34-38 spells out
what was intended in 32:16 (ibid., 239).

54. The list of camping sites (Numbers 33) draws
on the combined pentateuchal text and is thus a late
secondary element (ibid., 242). The description of the
territory west of the Jordan (Numbers 34) is closely
related to the similar descriptions in Joshua 14–19.
The whole section presupposes the Pentateuch and
the Deuteronomistic History and derives from the
time of their combination (ibid., 248). The material in
Numbers 35 on the levitical cities and the cities of
refuge is dependent on Joshua 20–21; it follows Numbers 34, just as Joshua 20–21 follows Joshua 14–19.
"The present passage, then, also belongs to the redactional unification of Pentateuchal narrative and deuteronomistic historical work" (ibid., 253). Of Numbers 36, Noth remarks: "This is an appendix to
27.1-11, which has been included at the very end of
the book of Numbers." As in Numbers 27, the family
of Zelophehad (Num 26:33) is used as a legal precedent for establishing the rights of daughters to inherit,
here limited to marriages within the tribe.

CHAPTER 6

Studies
in Composite Texts

Introductory Reflections

One result of the most welcome entry of serious literary study to the field of modern biblical scholarship is the commitment of considerable scholarly energy to demonstrating that apparently composite texts are or can be read as coherent literary unities.[1] This raises a serious, if ironic, question: Are we in such cases unconsciously imposing a modern Western convention on ancient texts? In this chapter, which looks at some of the implications for interpretation of a final text comprising preexisting sources, such an issue is critical. It is important to have some sense of what we can know about the conventions governing Israel's biblical literature.[2]

The only basic route to discovery of literary conventions is study of the literature itself. Conclusions about literature will be affected by assumptions concerning its use. The conditions of use for ancient literature are likely to be very different from the conditions surrounding the use of literature today. It is worthwhile looking at what we know in this area.

1. The royal court, whether in Samaria or Jerusalem, would be an evident source for administrative and legal documents and historical records, as well as narratives for both entertainment and the education of courtiers.
2. The temple in Jerusalem is another major source of administrative documents, literature, and law related to liturgy (cult), as well as apparently legal documents (Josiah: the law code); sacred legends, stories, and literature (ark narrative, priestly docu-

---

1. E.g., the attitude evinced by Meir Sternberg: "Moreover, traditional speculations about documents and sources and twice-told tales have now piled up so high on the altar of genesis as to obscure the one remarkable fact in sight, which bears on poetics. Granting the profusion of variants that went into the making of the Bible, the fact remains that the finished discourse never introduces them *as* variants but rather strings them together into continuous action" (*The Poetics of Biblical Narrative: Ideological Literature and the Drama of Reading* [Bloomington: Indiana University Press, 1985] 127). It is legitimate to ask whether Sternberg is demanding introductions in the form of subheads and footnotes in the finished discourse of the biblical manuscripts, or whether something more subtle might do.

2. On the concepts of competence and convention, see John Barton, *Reading the Old Testament: Method in Biblical Study* (London: Darton, Longman & Todd, 1984) 11–16, 26–29.

ment); and prayers and psalms. Similarly, major sanctuaries outside Jerusalem, such as Bethel and Dan or Gibeon and Gilgal, would have kept cultic legends and liturgical texts.

3. Private collections should not be overlooked; for example, much of the Ugaritic mythic and legendary literature found at Ras Shamra was recovered from a private house, and the scribal house of Shaphan was evidently influential in Jerusalem.

4. We would also need to take account of the prophetic schools, responsible for the written records of the sayings and doings of the prophets (cf. Isa 8:16ff. and the whole concept of the transmission of prophetic books). If the story of the Baruch scroll in Jeremiah 36 has any verisimilitude, it reflects a view of the commission of the prophetic sayings to writing and their preservation for public use. There is also the substantial body of literature associated with Elijah and the Elisha school.

5. While we have very little direct evidence for the existence of guilds of storytellers, there is a widespread assumption that there must have been something of the kind, although we do not know in what settings and circumstances. Possible settings would include the court and courtiers, town squares, family hearths, sanctuaries, and temples.

6. Theological thought was evidently highly developed in ancient Israel. We are aware of its outcome and the texts it generated. We are not able to be specific about where it went on and under what circumstances.

7. The whole area of wisdom and the generation of the wisdom literature also must be considered. Proverbs were formulated,

collected, and written down. Again, we have little in the way of specific information on these literary and sociological processes.

When this wide diversity is surveyed, it is hard to avoid the admission that we are comparatively ignorant about the whole industry of literature in ancient Israel. We know remarkably little about the conditions under which texts were produced, how they were distributed and who read them, or how and where they were preserved and made available. Qumran provides some valuable glimpses, but it comes late in the piece.

Where biblical narrative and story is concerned, at least it is certain that stories were told and put down in writing. But few, if any, texts in the Bible are likely to be verbatim transcripts of the telling of a story. It is uncertain just what proportion of the biblical texts should be seen as finished works of written literary art, to be read and enjoyed as such. We can be certain that our post-Gutenberg concept of texts written for distribution to a wide readership was not the case in ancient times. Once we have accepted that texts were not written for widespread reading, it then takes an imaginative leap to envisage the variety of purposes these written texts served in ancient times, purposes that differed widely according to the literary genres of the texts. When stories or traditions became part of works such as the Pentateuch, the Deuteronomistic History, and the prophetic books, they were on their way toward sacred status, for consultation and public proclamation (cf. 2 Kings 23:1-3; Neh 8:1-8)—but that was at a relatively late stage in the literature's development.

We do not know, for example, whether stories were always recorded in full or sometimes simply as outlines of what the story was about, with significant details noted or particular literary artifices recorded. We do not know the details of how traditions were preserved. We assume there was a process by which prophetic traditions were collected and organized into the prophetic books. We assume that something similar happened in the pentateuchal narratives and the major sources of the Deuteronomistic History. But again, we do not know the details of the process.

A case can be made out for the existence in the Bible of what might be called "reported stories":

> A reported story—the outcome of reporting what a story is about—would provide the basic elements from which the full narrative of a story can be developed but would fall short of actually telling the story. The basic elements include characters and plot, key details which impart color or significance and memorable lines or exchanges. In the telling of a story, all these must be introduced and unfolded in the appropriate sequence demanded by the plot. In the report of a story, the sequence is less significant; the obvious or the ordinary can be left out, since they can be supplied easily from the storyteller's imagination.[3]

The need for such reported stories or "plot summaries" might have been as an aid to storytellers' memories or as a means of reducing to writing, in a composition of many stories such as the Story of David's Rise, stories and traditions that would have been far more extensive when told in full. The purpose of a reported story is to communicate the gist of a story, along with its best literary gems, so that it can be recalled or retold. This is quite different from telling or writing a story for edification, education, or entertainment.[4]

In addition to the aid-to-memory function, there would be the possibility of noting variant ways in which a story was traditionally told. There are cases in the biblical text of where variant versions of a particular story have been preserved separately.[5] There are also a number of cases where it seems highly likely that a narrative text contains indications of variant versions of basically the same story. "While these apparent expansions might be considered as simple contamination from the other versions, in the hypothesis of a reported story they make eminent sense as reminders of other themes which can be introduced or of other ways in which a story can be told."[6]

One such possibility is the well-known presence of the tree-of-life motif at the beginning and end of the Yahwist's story of creation and sin (Gen 2:9 and 3:22-23). In our present context, Westermann's comment is illuminating:

> The introduction of the tree of life in 2:9 is to be explained from 3:22-24. The person who attached the motif of the tree of life to the end of the narrative and at the same time set it in the introduction, 2:9, intended it to be part of the overarching span of the narrative. He wanted to say that a similar event was linked with the tree of life as with the tree of the narrative. If we presume a variety of narratives about the primeval event from which one type was chosen, then this procedure of allowing the narrative of the tree of life to speak through that of the tree of knowledge—a second voice as it were together with the melody—is an ingenious

---

3. Antony F. Campbell, "The Reported Story: Midway between Oral Performance and Literary Art," *Semeia* 46 (1989) 78.
   4. Ibid., 80.
   5. The best known are the "ancestress in danger" stories in Genesis 12, 20, and 26; an example from the Davidic traditions is the sparing of Saul's life (1 Samuel 24 and 26).
   6. Campbell, "Reported Story," 80–82.

and intelligent resolution. We can take it that we are not dealing with a secondary addition; the whole has been deliberately shaped by J himself so that the final product appears as a unified composition.[7]

Genesis 2:4b—3:24 is not a reported story. Although it might be given a much fuller form in oral performance, our written version is a fully crafted literary piece. The inclusion of the tree of life at two points, however, may have served as a reminder of the variant version, a pointer to another traditional way of telling this story.[8]

As traditions began to be collected in written documents, both preservation and recovery of what had been written would have become important. When a story is to be preserved, which scroll should it be written down in, and which scroll would naturally be consulted to recover it? Stories and traditions about the classical prophets appear to have been preserved among the collections of their sayings (cf. particularly Jeremiah). Something similar seems to have been the case for the kings (cf., for example, 2 Sam 21–24, a discrete collection appropriately located before David's death and Solomon's accession). Without the convenience of modern libraries' subject and author catalogs, the recording of traditions in association with other traditions on the same subject appears to have been an appropriate aid to their easy recovery. In this case, we may have to revise modern notions about the suitable level of coherence and unity required for a narrative text.

The "redactor factor" as a semiautomatic and self-justifying explanation for tensions in a text—by implicit appeal to the fact that "those inept redactors got their damned hands on it"[9]—is outmoded, although still present more discreetly in much modern interpretation. The basic challenge is to invest at least as much scholarly energy in appreciating and accounting for a redactional change to a text as was invested in identifying the change in the first place. The question we need to ask now is whether the intelligence of the biblical compilers and redactors is appropriately valued by seeking out a sometimes unnaturally forced unity in their texts. When we find that unity in a biblical text has been sought but that duality has not been suppressed, we must ask the meaning of this. Similarly, when a biblical text has duality present at the price of unity, we must ask what this means and how this text is to be interpreted.[10]

Only a careful and open-minded study of the varieties of biblical texts will reveal further to us the conventions applicable in their composition and initiate us into the competence necessary for their interpretation.

Exegetes or the practitioners of biblical interpretation, as we are, often relate to literary theory rather as swimmers to ocean surf. Sometimes a wave catches you perfectly and the ride is effortless and energizing. Sometimes the sea is flat calm and the effortless perfection is of a totally different order. Sometimes, however, there is a confluence of currents, it is very difficult to hold your footing, and the foam may sweep over you, obscure your vision and your sense of direction, and seem to stifle you and deprive you of breath.

---

7. C. Westermann, *Genesis 1–11* (Minneapolis: Augsburg, 1984) 212–13 (translation slightly modified).

8. This understanding of pointers to variant ways of telling stories or narrating traditions is a refinement of a position advocated by Paul Volz (Paul Volz and Wilhelm Rudolph, *Der Elohist als Erzähler: Ein Irrweg der Pentateuchkritik?* [Giessen: Töpelmann, 1933] 22–24).

9. The phrase is from Robert Polzin, *A Literary Study of the Deuteronomic History*, part 2, *Samuel and the Deuteronomist* (San Francisco: Harper & Row, 1989) 2.

10. See A. F. Campbell, "Past History and Present Text: The Clash of Classical and Post-Critical Approaches to Biblical Text," *AusBR* 39 (1991) 1–18.

We came on the scene at a time of relative calm, when the wave of New Criticism was nearing the beach and the waters in its wake were quiet. It was a time when focus on the text in its autonomy was emphasized. Freedom from the historicism of the nineteenth century was a valuable gain. In due course, structuralism swirled around us in many forms from many sources. As the foam settled and the direction of the water steadied, a strong sense of the importance of the whole and the need to be aware of the role of parts within a total system and the correlation of these parts with overall meaning remained as part of the interpretative task. In the vast literary landscape of Pentateuch and narrative books, that too was an important gain. Deconstruction must have caught us out of breath and looking the other way; it swept on toward the beach, leaving us unsure that it had passed. Reception theory and reader-response criticism are on us now, with particular interest in the aspect that focuses on the signals that the text sends to its reader for guidance in the art of reading it.

Terry Eagleton quotes an acute observation from John Maynard Keynes, "that those economists who disliked theory, or claimed to get along better without it, were simply in the grip of an older theory." As Eagleton adds, this is just as true of literary students and critics.[11] Regular dips in the waters of theory provide new energy for present practice or fresh surges toward possibilities for new directions.

Our concern is closely related to the principal areas in which we have worked, namely, the Pentateuch and Joshua–Kings. There a fundamental task today seems to be the reconciliation of what might be called critical and postcritical approaches to the biblical text. The critical approach has held sway since the Enlightenment, bringing an awareness of the manifold origins of much of the biblical text, the different times it represents, and the different theologies it expresses.[12] It can be crudely summed up in the quip "mosaic rather than Mosaic." The postcritical approach is struggling to establish itself, without losing the gains of centuries of critical study. Recognition that, for the most part at least, the present text has been shaped by people of great intelligence, great patience, and great skill has led to emphasis on the need to interpret adequately the text they have created.[13]

It may be that much of the difficulty lies in the past's silent dismissal of compilers and redactors. The emphasis on the primacy of the text should not downplay the significance and responsibility of authors or compilers for their texts. As Paul Ricoeur comments, "For my part, I could not conceive what a text would be with-

---

11. Terry Eagleton, *Literary Theory: An Introduction* (Oxford: Basil Blackwell, 1983) vii.

12. "Scholarly study has changed attitudes to the Old Testament. No longer can its writing be attributed to the great and inspired figures of a distant past: Moses, Joshua, Samuel, David, Solomon, and the prophets——figures of religious genius, who communed in intimacy with God. Rather than a book of the inspired few, the Old Testament has come to be seen as a book of the living community. What was once simply taken as straightforward history, recorded by those close to the events, is now known to be often carefully structured narrative, frequently based on traditions celebrated in liturgy or preserved in story, concerned much more with theological interest than with historical record" (A. F. Campbell, *The Study Companion to Old Testament Literature: An Approach to the Writings of Pre-exilic and Exilic Israel* [A Michael Glazier Book; Old Testament Studies 2; Collegeville, Minn.: Liturgical Press, 1989/1992] 488).

13. Structuralist, canonical, and literary endeavors have pressed in this direction. A valuable project is Robert Polzin, *A Literary Study of the Deuteronomic History*, because it takes seriously the critical as well as the literary realities (part 1, *Moses and the Deuteronomist* [New York: Seabury, 1980]; part 2, *Samuel and the Deuteronomist*). At the other end of the spectrum, there is reason to be cautious of neoconservatives who masquerade in the lambskin of literary theory.

out an author, a text which nobody had written."[14] Many texts have sources of some form or other, all texts have authors, and composite texts have compilers; and all texts are conceived in some way for an audience. Nevertheless, it is the text that tells us about its sources, its author or compiler, and its audience. Our task is always to interpret the text. In nineteenth-century higher criticism, an underlying assumption was often that the critic's task was to ascertain the author's intention. Today that task is more accurately defined as interpreting the meaning of the text.

The primary task is that of reading sensitively the "signals which give a wide variety of directives to the reader as to how to actualize the text."[15] The conviction manifest in most literary approaches is that these composite texts have been so combined as to constitute unified literary works—one might hazard the label "grand unified text" theory. In our reading of the signals—what we tend to call the "phenomena of the text"—this does not do adequate justice to the outcome of the labors of those who produced these composite texts. In our judgment, it

is by no means clear that the signals in the text always direct us toward an unblinking vision of unity. To the contrary, aspects of disunity are present in the text in sometimes thoroughly disconcerting fashion. They constitute signals and their direction has to be read and their texts actualized.

In our understanding so far, unity and disunity in composite texts can generate a variety of possible meanings. Significant for us is the question of whether all our biblical texts are the final product of literary output or whether some of them are intended as the starting point from which literary output is produced. For example, are some of our texts reported stories rather than either performed or polished stories?[16] Similarly, do some of our composite texts offer clear indications of variant ways of telling the main story which is outlined in the body of the text rather than tell but a single story in a single version? Or does the juxtaposition of conflicting views within one and the same text direct the reader toward reflection on matters under serious debate?[17]

Two traditions may be composed in a single

---

14. Paul Ricoeur, "Esquisse de Conclusion," in Roland Barthes, et al., *Exégèse et herméneutique* (Paris: Editions du Seuil, 1971) 292–93. We have already referred to S. Talmon's reflections on the continuity existing between author, editor, transmitter, scribe, and copyist, to whom we may add compiler and redactor ("The Textual Study of the Bible—A New Outlook," in *Qumran and the History of the Biblical Text*, ed. F. M. Cross and S. Talmon [Cambridge: Harvard University Press, 1975] 321–400).

15. The phrase is taken from Bernard C. Lategan, "Introduction: Coming to Grips with the Reader," *Semeia* 48 (1989) 9.

16. See Campbell, "Reported Story."

17. Lyle M. Eslinger skates too lightly over this issue: "When, on the other hand, we are faced with a text that holds the two contrary views in a state of narrative tension, and we read unencumbered by the theoretical predisposition to regard such tension as *prima facie* evidence of a composite text, the possibility that a neutral perspective—the study of a debated problem—is being voiced cannot be overlooked. In fact, the tables can be turned. The existence of a text

containing contradictory views should be assumed to present an examination of a controversy. Only if such an assumption proves unfruitful should genetic explanations be considered as a last resort" (*Kingship of God in Crisis: A Close Reading of 1 Samuel 1–12* [Bible and Literature Series 10; Sheffield: Almond Press, 1985] 38).

If, unencumbered, we approach a text that expresses contrary views, it is legitimate to ask about the origin of these contrary views—authored or quoted. If the text is such as to sustain a hypothesis of single authorship, the origin of the views is a traditio-historical question. In what circles are they likely to have been handed down until they have been expressed by this one author in this one text? If the text is such as to sustain a hypothesis of multiple authorship, with perhaps a single compiler, the origin of the views may be a source-critical question and the answer may be genetic. Explanations of "last resort" have nothing to do with it. Composite texts do not fall together all of a piece; they imply skillful composition of traditions of varying genetic origin to form a text, a process that can take place in a number of ways. The text's reading is then a work of interpretative art.

text to give witness to a single faith, a single theology. Traditions may be composed in a single text to give expression to different views and different theologies. Traditions may be composed in a single text to enrich a narrative, heighten its complexity, and intensify its capacity to give enjoyment. Traditions may be composed in a single text to remind storytellers of variant ways in which a particular story may be told. Traditions may be composed in a single text to keep them in a community's memory and recall that the reality of the past can be interpreted in a variety of ways. The list could be extended further, but surely the point is clear.[18] The universal conviction of a "grand unified text," with its emphasis on literary unity, is suspect. Often the signals in the text seem to be set against it. These signals cannot be safely ignored.

An aspect of reader-response theory is the emphasis that can be placed on the interpretative community within which the reader is situated.[19] This understanding has potential for easing the often-felt but seldom-voiced complaint that the scholars have stolen the Bible from the people of God. Biblical scholarship has brought so much impressive knowledge to bear on the biblical text that all too often the ordinary practitioners of its interpretation—whether in pulpit, pew, or prayerstool—feel cast out into the darkness of unfathomable doubt, where there is weeping and gnashing of teeth. After dipping into biblical texts in theological schools, they feel powerless before the immensity of the knowledge they do not have, and they cling to the relatively few texts where they have been given some security.

It is liberating for such readers to recognize that they have usually imbibed a critical attitude in their studies. They are more familiar with "mosaic" than "Mosaic." They are unlikely to fall back into precritical attitudes. They are likely to be aware that most texts are less concerned with ascertaining the historicity of a tradition than with expressing and proclaiming the faith that is engendered by that tradition. They can trust themselves to a postcritical reading without fear of precritical folly or undue fear of gross critical error. As a matrix within which interpretation is elaborated, the interpretative community—understood broadly rather than restrictively—is a source of security liberating those who are not themselves scholars. With the added security of adverting to the difference between meaning and significance—the meaning of the text as critically established and the meaning of the text for me—the biblical text can be safely repossessed by its original readers, the believing community.[20] Text and community have a long and noble lineage together as primary pillars in the interpretative tradition.[21]

18. In similar vein, redactors can add material to confirm a text, to subvert a text, to update a text, or simply to keep an associated tradition alive and remembered. There are as many possibilities as there was ingenuity and intelligence in the past.

19. It is the fifth element, e.g., in Stanley Porter's delineation of reader-response criticism ("Why Hasn't Reader-Response Criticism Caught On in New Testament Studies?" *Journal of Literature and Theology* 4 [1990] 278–92, see esp. 279). Note Porter's cautious comment, "reader-response is many things to many people" (280), and the valuable discussion of historical concerns and reading strategies (283–89).

20. The confusion of verbal meaning with significance is vigorously attacked by E. D. Hirsch, *Validity*

in Interpretation (New Haven: Yale University Press, 1967). The distinction is important, whether or not one agrees fully with the use Hirsch makes of it. Note that Hirsch's understanding of verbal meaning has to be placed in the context of his Husserlian understanding of horizon (cf. 209–24)

21. For early Jewish theology, see Harold Fisch, who gives the community's role to the oral Torah: "The biblical text as a whole is founded in relationality. It demands an audience, actively participating not merely in understanding but even in constituting the text. This is of course classical Jewish doctrine. The written law, *tôrâ šebhiktāb*, cannot stand alone; it is validated by the *tôrâ šebbĕ 'al-peh*, i.e., the oral Torah, or continuing tradition of interpretation" (*Poetry*

In this chapter devoted to selected studies of composite texts, we treat aspects of the interpretation of three such texts: the flood, the beginning of the Joseph story, and the deliverance at the sea. We are not entering the realm of recent literary theory and its application. Instead, we are concerned with what should be a basic task in Old Testament studies: To give appropriate attention and interpretation to the final text when it is clearly a combination of disparate elements.

It is not possible within the space available to give a full exegetical treatment of the selected texts, with all the levels of reflection desirable: the present text at surface and at depth; the texts that went before it; the traces, consequences, skills, and techniques of compilation; and the meaning expressed in all these moments. But it is important to look practically at some of the impact of recent approaches to the text on those approaches that have long been held as classical.

The composite or combined texts have been printed out at the start of each section, with the relevant sources distinguished by different typefaces for ease of identification. The danger exists that too rapid an identification of the component sources in this way may obscure the fine qualities of the present text or lead to solutions being embraced without enough awareness of the problems they seek to resolve. To guard against this, readers may well be advised to consult the present text in their Bibles while reading the discussions below of the unity and duality in these selections.

The three texts studied here are not equally typical of composite texts in the Pentateuch. In the story of the deliverance at the sea, it is likely that both P and J have been preserved in their entirety, with some enrichment from E. In the story of the flood, P is complete, and, despite gaps, the J story is largely complete. In the beginning of the Joseph story, only the J story is complete, with significant enrichment from E and some enrichment from P. The beginning of the Joseph story is closer to the usual pattern of pentateuchal composition. In the other two, the substantial preservation of both sources and the tight interweaving of the sources is atypical.

In Noth's understanding of pentateuchal composition, the close interweaving of both sources in their relative entirety is the exception not the rule. Normally, the compilers did not attempt to preserve intact the substance of both sources. According to Noth, as we have seen, their approach was to choose one source as a base and, in the process of compilation, enrich it with what was special from the other. Noth singles out the flood story as a prime example of the sort of combination that happens "quite rarely" (*ziemlich selten*) in the Pentateuch. He laments the fact that, because of a faulty understanding of the process of compilation, combined texts such as the flood story are often viewed as the very frequent or even normal way of combining sources. Not so; instead: "usually a smaller or larger narrative section or a compact narrative was inserted into the context of another." Noth adds that this is a thoroughly appropriate procedure for compilation, since the individual sources themselves grew in similar ways, bringing together traditions of various kinds and styles without achieving perfect harmony.[22]

---

with a Purpose: Biblical Poetics and Interpretation [Bloomington: Indiana University Press, 1988] 48). For more recent Christian theology, see David H. Kelsey's related comment: "If a theologian does use the results of historical and literary studies of biblical texts to help determine how he will construe and use scripture, his decision to do so is itself determined by a logically prior imaginative judgment. . . . And for that prior decision the only 'explanation' that can be given is genetic: It is shaped by the concrete particularities of the way scripture functions in the common life of the Christian community as he has experienced it" (*The Uses of Scripture in Recent Theology* [Philadelphia: Fortress, 1975] 183).

22. Noth, *Pentateuchal Traditions*, 249–50.

The basic methodological issue explored here is the same for any composite text: how does the interpretation find meaning in the aspects of source and discourse, diachrony and synchrony, plurality and unity, history of growth and reality of present text, all of which are embedded in the text through the process of its composition. These aspects are among the signals guiding the reader in the actualization of a composite text. They have to be respected; they should generate meaning.

Interpretation of the Flood Story

KEY: **Yahwist**/Priestly/<u>additions</u>
(Source division according to Martin Noth)

GENESIS 6:5 The LORD saw that the wickedness of humankind was great in the earth, and that every inclination of the thoughts of their hearts was only evil continually. 6And the LORD was sorry that he had made humankind on the earth, and it grieved him to his heart. 7So the LORD said, "I will blot out from the earth the human beings I have created—people together with animals and creeping things and birds of the air, for I am sorry that I have made them." 8But Noah found favor in the sight of the LORD.

9 These are the descendants of Noah. Noah was a righteous man, blameless in his generation; Noah walked with God. 10And Noah had three sons, Shem, Ham, and Japheth.

11 Now the earth was corrupt in God's sight, and the earth was filled with violence. 12And God saw that the earth was corrupt; for all flesh had corrupted its ways upon the earth. 13And God said to Noah, "I have determined to make an end of all flesh, for the earth is filled with violence because of them; now I am going to destroy them along with the earth. 14Make yourself an ark of cypress wood; make rooms in the ark, and cover it inside and out with pitch. 15This is how you are to make it: the length of the ark three hundred cubits, its width fifty cubits, and its height thirty cubits. 16Make a roof for the ark, and finish it to a cubit above; and put the door of the ark in its side; make it with lower, second, and third decks. 17For my part, I am going to bring a flood of waters on the earth, to destroy from under heaven all flesh in which is the breath of life; everything that is on the earth shall die. 18But I will establish my covenant with you; and you shall come into the ark, you, your sons, your wife, and your sons' wives with you. 19And of every living thing, of all flesh, you shall bring two of every kind into the ark, to keep them alive with you; they shall be male and female. 20Of the birds according to their kinds, and of the animals according to their kinds, of every creeping thing of the ground according to its kind, two of every kind shall come in to you, to keep them alive. 21Also take with you every kind of food that is eaten, and store it up; and it shall serve as food for you and for them." 22Noah did this; he did all that God commanded him.

7 Then the LORD said to Noah, "Go into the ark, you and all your household, for I have seen that you alone are righteous before me in this generation. 2Take with you seven pairs of all clean animals, the male and its mate; and a pair of the animals that are not clean, the male and its mate; 3and seven pairs <u>of the birds of the air also, male and female,</u> to keep their kind alive on the face of all the

earth. **⁴For in seven days I will send rain on the earth for forty days and forty nights; and every living thing that I have made I will blot out from the face of the ground." ⁵And Noah did all that the LORD had commanded him.**

6 Noah was six hundred years old when the flood of waters came on the earth. **⁷And Noah** <u>with his sons and his wife and his sons' wives</u> **went into the ark to escape the waters of the flood.** ⁸<u>Of clean animals, and of animals that are not clean, and of birds, and of everything that creeps on the ground, ⁹two and two, male and female, went into the ark with Noah, as God had commanded Noah.</u> **¹⁰And after seven days the waters of the flood came on the earth.**

11 In the six hundredth year of Noah's life, in the second month, on the seventeenth day of the month, on that day all the fountains of the great deep burst forth, and the windows of the heavens were opened. **¹²The rain fell on the earth forty days and forty nights.** ¹³On the very same day Noah with his sons, Shem and Ham and Japheth, and Noah's wife and the three wives of his sons entered the ark, ¹⁴they and every wild animal of every kind, and all domestic animals of every kind, and every creeping thing that creeps on the earth, and every bird of every kind—every bird, every winged creature. ¹⁵They went into the ark with Noah, two and two of all flesh in which there was the breath of life. ¹⁶And those that entered, male and female of all flesh, went in as God had commanded him; **and the LORD shut him in.**

17 <u>The flood continued forty days on the earth;</u> **and the waters increased, and bore up the ark, and it rose high above the earth.** ¹⁸The waters swelled and increased greatly on the earth; and the ark floated on the face of the waters. ¹⁹The waters swelled so mightily on the earth that all the high mountains under the whole heaven were covered; ²⁰the waters swelled above the mountains, covering them fifteen cubits deep. ²¹And all flesh died that moved on the earth, birds, domestic animals, wild animals, all swarming creatures that swarm on the earth, and all human beings; **²²everything on dry land in whose nostrils was the breath of life died.** **²³He blotted out every living thing that was on the face of the ground, human beings and animals and creeping things and birds of the air;** <u>they were blotted out from the earth.</u> **Only Noah was left, and those that were with him in the ark.** ²⁴And the waters swelled on the earth for one hundred fifty days.

8 But God remembered Noah and all the wild animals and all the domestic animals that were with him in the ark. And God made a wind blow over the earth, and the waters subsided; ²the fountains of the deep and the windows of the heavens were closed, **the rain from the heavens was restrained, ³and the waters gradually receded from the earth.** At the end of one hundred fifty days the waters had abated; ⁴and in the seventh month, on the seventeenth day of the month, the ark came to rest on the mountains of Ararat. ⁵The waters continued to abate until the tenth month; in the tenth month, on the first day of the month, the tops of the mountains appeared.

6 **At the end of forty days Noah opened the window of the ark that he had made** ⁷and sent out the raven; and it went to and fro until the waters were dried up from the earth. **⁸Then he sent out the dove from him, to see if the waters had subsided from the face of the ground;** ⁹but the dove found no place to set its foot, and it returned to him to the ark, for the waters were still on the face of the whole earth. So he put out his hand and took it and brought it into the ark with him. **¹⁰He waited another seven days, and again he sent out the dove from the ark; ¹¹and the dove came back to him in the evening, and there in its beak was a freshly plucked olive leaf; so Noah knew that the waters had subsided from the earth. ¹²Then he waited another seven days,**

and sent out the dove; and it did not return to him any more.

13 In the six hundred first year, in the first month, the first day of the month, the waters were dried up from the earth; **and Noah removed the covering of the ark, and looked, and saw that the face of the ground was drying.** [14]In the second month, on the twenty-seventh day of the month, the earth was dry. [15]Then God said to Noah, [16]"Go out of the ark, you and your wife, and your sons and your sons' wives with you. [17]Bring out with you every living thing that is with you of all flesh—birds and animals and every creeping thing that creeps on the earth—so that they may abound on the earth, and be fruitful and multiply on the earth." [18]So Noah went out with his sons and his wife and his sons' wives. [19]And every animal, every creeping thing, and every bird, everything that moves on the earth, went out of the ark by families.

20 **Then Noah built an altar to the LORD, and took of every clean animal and of every clean bird, and offered burnt offerings on the altar.** [21]**And when the LORD smelled the pleasing odor, the LORD said in his heart, "I will never again curse the ground because of humankind, for the inclination of the human heart is evil from youth; nor will I ever again destroy every living creature as I have done.**
[22]**As long as the earth endures,**
  seedtime and harvest, cold and heat,
  summer and winter, day and night,
    shall not cease."

9 God blessed Noah and his sons, and said to them, "Be fruitful and multiply, and fill the earth. [2]The fear and dread of you shall rest on every animal of the earth, and on every bird of the air, on everything that creeps on the ground, and on all the fish of the sea; into your hand they are delivered. [3]Every moving thing that lives shall be food for you; and just as I gave you the green plants, I give you everything. [4]Only,

you shall not eat flesh with its life, that is, its blood. [5]For your own lifeblood I will surely require a reckoning: from every animal I will require it and from human beings, each one for the blood of another, I will require a reckoning for human life.
[6]Whoever sheds the blood of a human,
  by a human shall that person's blood be shed;
  for in his own image
  God made humankind.
[7]And you, be fruitful and multiply, abound on the earth and multiply in it."

8 Then God said to Noah and to his sons with him, [9]"As for me, I am establishing my covenant with you and your descendants after you, [10]and with every living creature that is with you, the birds, the domestic animals, and every animal of the earth with you, as many as came out of the ark. [11]I establish my covenant with you, that never again shall all flesh be cut off by the waters of a flood, and never again shall there be a flood to destroy the earth." [12]God said, "This is the sign of the covenant that I make between me and you and every living creature that is with you, for all future generations: [13]I have set my bow in the clouds, and it shall be a sign of the covenant between me and the earth. [14]When I bring clouds over the earth and the bow is seen in the clouds, [15]I will remember my covenant that is between me and you and every living creature of all flesh; and the waters shall never again become a flood to destroy all flesh. [16]When the bow is in the clouds, I will see it and remember the everlasting covenant between God and every living creature of all flesh that is on the earth." [17]God said to Noah, "This is the sign of the covenant that I have established between me and all flesh that is on the earth."

Interpretation

After reading closely a composite text such as the flood narrative, one thing is startlingly obvious yet seldom said: there is evidence of both duality and unity in the text, and both must have their place in its meaning. To begin to correlate with the text's features, the meaning of the text will have to encompass both its unity and its duality (or plurality). It is worth emphasizing the danger of discussing such matters in terms of events behind the text—authors, compilers, and their intentions. It is necessary to work at the level of the text itself and to think in terms of the "meaning of the text" rather than the less helpful "intention of the text" or the positively unhelpful "intention of the author."

The meaning of the text must encompass both unity and duality. The structure of the flood narrative is quite different from that of creation in Gen 1:1—2:4a and Gen 2:4b-25. There duality has been placed in juxtaposed sequence to form a quite different unity. In Genesis 6–9, however, the duality has been interwoven within the single narrative. The duality might easily have been eliminated in favor of unity; the unity might have been subordinated by juxtaposing the dual texts. But neither has happened. The interweaving of threads within the fabric of a passage creates a different outcome from the joining of pieces of fabric to form a larger entity. The meaning of the text must therefore embrace both unity and duality.[23]

The unity of the text can be seen by foregrounding the structure of the plot; most ordinary reading does this automatically.[24] The story begins with the great wickedness of humankind and God's decision to blot out life. Noah is then introduced, the ark is built and boarded, the flood comes and then subsides, and the survivors leave the ark. The story ends with God's guarantee of continued life on earth. The duality of the text is seen by foregrounding the detail of the narrative: there is a dual chronology for the flood, a dual set of prescriptions about the animals to survive, a dual set of conceptions about the nature of the flood, a dual set of terms for God, and there is a dual account of most of the elements of the narrative.[25]

Foregrounding Unity

Foregrounding the unity of the text has been made possible by the remarkable skill exercised in its compilation. The text begins with God's perception of human wickedness, the decision to blot out life, and the note that Noah found favor (Gen 6:5-8). This is followed by the more formal introduction of Noah, his own blamelessness, and the names of his sons. God's instructions to Noah to build the ark are prefaced by a short recall of the earth's corruption and a communication to Noah of God's decision

23. Among recent literature, B. W. Anderson argues for F. M. Cross's view that "the Flood story has been completely rewritten by P," emphasizing the text's structural and functional unity ("From Analysis to Synthesis: The Interpretation of Genesis 1–11," *JBL* 97 [1978] 23–39); and J. A. Emerton painstakingly examines five attempts to defend the unity of the flood narrative and finds none of them convincing ("An Examination of Some Attempts to Defend the Unity of the Flood Narrative in Genesis," part 1, *VT* 27 [1987] 401–20; part 2, *VT* 28 [1988] 1–21).

24. Note Richard Nelson's comment on such ordinary reading: "The willing suspension of a critical attitude is part of the unstated contract between text and reader" (review of *Into the Hands of the Living God*, by Lyle M. Eslinger, *JBL* 110 [1991] 142).

25. Details narrated twice:

	J	P
The corruption of humanity	Gen. 6:5	Gen. 6:11-12
The decision to destroy	6:7	6:13
Commission to enter the ark	7:1-3	6:18-21
Entering of the ark	7:7	7:13
Coming of the flood	7:10	7:11
Death of all creatures	7:22-23	7:20-21
End of the flood	8:2b-3a	8:3b-5
Promise that the flood will not recur	8:21b-22	9:1-17

See Westermann, *Genesis 1–11*, 397–98.

to make an end of all flesh. Then Noah is given instructions on the building of the ark, its purpose, and how it is to be used. Finally, Noah's compliance with these instructions is noted very briefly (6:22).

This note of compliance has to serve as notice that the ark has been built and provisioned. The text moves directly to a new stage in the narrative with God's instructions to Noah to enter the ark (7:1-5). There is a reinsistence on Noah's righteousness (v. 1), a change in the numbers of pairs of animals (vv. 2-3), and fresh details on the nature of the flood (v. 4), and again a note of Noah's compliance (v. 5). Within this new stage of the narrative, the repetitions are easy to accept as further specifications or new details as the instructions unfold.

With the ark complete and provisioned and Noah duly instructed, the narrative moves toward the flood itself. Noah's age is noted and the entry into the ark is narrated: Noah and his family; clean and unclean animals, birds, and everything that creeps. The waters of the flood arrived just seven days later.

On the very day the flood began, the exact day being noted and the exact nature of the flood being specified, intense activity is described. On that very day, Noah and his family entered the ark, and with them entered every animal, wild and domestic, everything that creeps, and every bird (vv. 13-14). When all had entered, the LORD shut them in and the ark is set on its course for survival.

The flood waters are described as they continue for forty days, covering even the high mountains, and all life is blotted out except for the survivors in the ark. A final note gives the full length of this stage of the flood as one hundred and fifty days (7:17-24).

With all life blotted out, the flood has done its deadly work. God remembers Noah and the animals in the ark, and the narrative has reached its turning point. The closing off of the inrushing waters is noted and their gradual receding chronicled. Through the raven and the dove, Noah is portrayed monitoring the receding waters until it is safe to remove the ark's cover. On the New Year's Day of Noah's seventh century, Noah was once again able to look out at the world and see that the ground was drying. Almost two months later, Noah and his family and the animals in the ark moved out in orderly fashion (8:1-19).

There are two stages to the ending of the story. In the first, Noah's sacrifice is followed by God's decision never again to destroy life because of human evil. What was intolerable before the flood (6:5) is now tolerated. While there is no reflection offered on this, the place of Gen 6:5 and 8:21b-22 in the same narrative can only imply that God has had a radical change of heart.

In the second stage, much the same is said in different language. The world is blessed again, as at the start of creation. But it is a less-than-perfect world, a world in which there is to be fear and bloodshed. Yet God makes a covenant never again to destroy this world by flood, a covenant to which no condition is attached.

Foregrounding Duality

Once aware of the presence of duality in the text, it may be instructive to reread the text with an alert but gentle eye, giving due attention to the detail and thus foregrounding the duality. There is duality in the reporting of God's decision, but with a divine soliloquy (presumably in heaven) and a divine speech to Noah on earth it reinforces the solemnity and significance of what is to come. In the midst of this destruction there will be human survivors, and two of every kind of living thing will survive.

The first strong mark of duality occurs when Noah is told by God to enter the ark with seven pairs of clean animals and only one pair of those that are unclean (7:2-3). The change in number is puzzling, but with the flood only seven days away, the narrative has an urgency that does not invite us to ponder the change. Duality returns when, in reporting Noah's compliance with God's command to enter the ark, the number entering the ark is given as two again (vv. 8-9). This is particularly puzzling because the distinction of clean and unclean is also repeated. The number two is again reinforced with the entry of the animals on the actual day the flood began (vv. 13-16). We might be tempted to read this simply as "in pairs" without the actual count being specified, but it seems unlikely.

Duality is present here in a different form. Beyond the question of the number of animals involved, it suddenly becomes clear here that they are all entering the ark together at two quite different times. They all entered the ark seven days before the rains of the flood began to fall (7:1-5). Later they all entered the ark again on the actual day when the flood and the rains began (vv. 13-16).

Another aspect of duality emerges in this context. The flood had been spoken of as "rain on the earth for forty days and forty nights." Alongside that there is a different concept, in which the flood appears as a veritable reversal of the creative process of separating the waters below from the waters above (Gen 1:6-7). Now the narrative has: "on that day all the fountains of the great deep burst forth, and the windows of the heavens were opened" (v. 11). The forty days of rain are still in sight (v. 12), but the two cataclysms seem to be of a quite different nature. The temptation to brush this aside as a minor aberration is repulsed when exactly the same difference is encountered at the end of the flood: "the fountains of the deep and the windows of the heavens were closed, the rain from the heavens was restrained" (8:2). So the duality is there.

Duality seems present again as the narrative continues with a flood spoken of in terms of "forty days and forty nights" (7:4, 12, 17; also 8:6) and then suddenly in terms of one hundred and fifty days (7:24; also 8:3). The temptation is to see the forty days as a briefer period within the longer duration of the flood. A lingering sense remains—heightened by the dates given in months and days—that the numbers do not entirely add up and that this, too, is best understood as a further example of duality in the narrative.[26]

Duality returns at the end of the narrative. As at the beginning, God's decisions are reported twice. But, equally as at the beginning, one of these is set in heaven, being placed in the heart of God (8:20-22), and the other is set on earth, where God's decisions are communicated to Noah and his sons (9:1-17). As at the beginning, this duality reinforces the solemnity and significance of the decisions taken, of God's unconditional commitment to humankind.

Art of Combination

What we have seen in chapters 2 and 3 as two separate and different accounts have been successfully combined to form one narrative. How has this been achieved?

The narrative opens with the J account of God's decision to blot out life. It is brief and sparse; it ends with a reference to Noah's favor with God (6:5-8). Instead of the J instructions for building the ark, we find the P account of Noah, his righteousness, and his sons. Thus a continuity is established. A section of J is sacrificed, but building instructions are hardly cen-

---

26. In fact, plurality would be more accurate, as there are probably three chronologies present in the text. For a concise account of the chronological data, see J. Skinner, *Genesis*, 2d ed. (ICC; Edinburgh: T. & T. Clark, 1930) 167–69; and S. E. McEvenue, *The Narrative Style of the Priestly Writer* (AnBib 50; Rome: Biblical Institute, 1971) 54–59.

tral to J's story. The P account goes on with the decision to blot out life (6:11-13), not narrated as God's reaching that decision (J) but rather as God's communication of it to Noah. The difference in language used complements the brevity and sparsity of the earlier remarks. This is followed by P's account of the instructions for building the ark, filling it, and provisioning it. The account ends with a note of Noah's compliance (6:22). Thus the two introductory sections are preserved intact, with both their agreement on what is to come and their different emphases in its presentation.[27]

Noah has complied with his instructions; the ark is complete. The order is given to enter it, taken from the J account. Here there is a reminder that duality is not sacrificed to unity. Unity is important, but its importance is not wholly overriding. The larger number of animals is required for the sacrifice; the numbers forty and seven are significant throughout the J account. Both features need to be maintained. If v. 3a is taken as an addition, the "seven pairs" occurs only once. P's "male and female" and J's "male and its mate" create resonances that may help in the foregrounding of unity.

The report of the entry into the ark creates real difficulties for elucidating the meaning of the present text as a unity, because the entry is reported twice, seven days apart. The primary difficulty lies in 7:6-10. If we leave this section out of consideration for the moment, it is possible to see a reasonable unity in the remaining text. Consideration of vv. 6-10 may then reveal a skillful redactional exercise.

An understanding that foregrounds unity would be as follows. God's command to Noah to enter the ark (vv. 1-4) included a warning that the flood was close, beginning in just seven days. The note of compliance (v. 5) is simply a general statement requiring, as so often in Hebrew narrative, to be filled out by a more detailed account. The more detailed account, then, is given in vv. 13-16. The flood did indeed begin (vv. 11-12); the entry into the ark took place that very same day. In this way, unity would be clearly foregrounded and the aspect of duality would be greatly diminished.

To achieve this unified reading of the text, vv. 6-10 must be omitted and the command to Noah in J (7:1-4) must be understood as fulfilled in the P account of the entry into the ark (vv. 11-16). In 7:1-4, Noah is commanded to enter the ark, for in seven days the flood will begin. Verse 5 asserts that "Noah did all that the LORD had commanded him," allowing Noah's obedience to be emphasized and the section to be brought to closure. The details of this compliance are held in abeyance until vv. 13-16. Prescinding from vv. 6-10, there can now be a focus on the beginning of the flood (vv. 11-12). Not only do the fountains of the great deep burst forth, but the windows of the heavens were opened so that the rain might fall. Then Noah's compliance with the command to enter the ark may be unfolded, with the report that "on the very same day" (v. 13) Noah entered the ark. For P, Noah did not need a specific command to enter the ark; that had already been given in 6:18-20.

This understanding is supported by the presence in v. 16b of the little note, "and the LORD shut him in." Both the language (LORD) and the content (anthropomorphism) point to its being from J; but it is placed at the end of the P account of the entry into the ark. The natural conclusion is that the P account is meant to narrate the entry begun in J and here concluded with the final phrase of J's account. The original place for the phrase would have been at the end of v. 5, followed then by v. 12.[28] The sequence in J becomes:

---

27. Cf. Westermann, *Genesis 1–11*, 424–25.

28. This, of course, differs from Noth's analysis in the treatment of Gen 7:6-10. It also avoids the transposition of vv. 7* and 10.

⁵And Noah did all that the LORD had commanded him. ¹⁶ᵇAnd the LORD shut him in. ¹²The rain fell on the earth forty days and forty nights; ¹⁷ᵇand the waters increased, and bore up the ark, and it rose high above the earth.

As a sequence this is satisfactory, if a trace terse. All it omits is an explicit statement of entry and the note of fulfillment to indicate that what the LORD had said would happen did (v. 10), both matters that could be readily presumed. J's own narration of the entry into the ark is then simply understood as expressed in the report of Noah's compliance with God's command (v. 5). This is no different from the P narrative having the building of the ark implicit in the report of Noah's compliance with God's orders (6:22).

It is extremely difficult to give an account of the meaning of 7:6-10 in the context of a coherent sequence in the present text. Understandably, it is usual to allot vv. 7* and 10 to J, filling out J's narrative sequence. Verses 8-9 have then been attributed to later redaction, without throwing much light on the meaning of such a redactional addition.²⁹

It is worth noting that, when attention is given to the literary coherence of the present text, it makes particularly good sense to attribute 7:6-10 in its entirety to a redactor. On the one hand, when vv. 6-10 are omitted, the remaining text is considerably closer to a coherent unity. On the other hand, vv. 6-10, taken together, can be given meaning as a significant redactional insertion.³⁰

The basic reality of the text is that either vv. 8-9 on their own or vv. 6-10 as a whole portray an entry into the ark before the entry narrated in vv. 13-16. On this point, duality has uncompromisingly taken over from unity. To win meaning from the text in this situation, it seems reasonable to appeal to the concept of noting variant versions, discussed earlier in the introduction to this chapter.

The P account has Noah and his extended family and two of every kind of wild animal, domestic animal, creeping thing, and bird enter the ark on the very same day that the fountains of the great deep burst forth and the windows of the heavens were opened and the rain started to fall (vv. 11-16). It would not be helpful to calculate whether, in the knowledge of P's time about the number of species involved, such an entry procession would have been envisaged as quite manageable and orderly or whether it might have been crassly imagined as an undignified stampede. Storytelling is about verisimilitude and imagination rather than brute facts. For Westermann, this "entrance into the ark is portrayed with a fulness of detail and a studied solemnity of tone."³¹ The phrase used for "on this very day" (v. 13) is used only in priestly writing and clearly carries special weight and significance.³² So understood, the narrative portrayal is strongly symbolic and is not to be demeaned and diminished by materialist calculations of space, time, and animal numbers.

However, 7:6-10 (or vv. 8-9) gives us a description of the entry into the ark that, although not narrated with such solemnity, occurs within the more leisurely space of seven days advance warning. Whether this is offered because of dissatisfaction with a one-day entry scheme or because it was traditional, we cannot know. All the text gives us is the alternative, not the reason for it.

---

29. Westermann suggests that the addition gives a dominating role to the entry into the ark (*Genesis 1–11*, 431). It is not particularly helpful; it still fails to explain the entry's occurring twice.

30. There is little to be gained here by pursuing these issues through the history of the exegesis of these verses. The classical position is clearly presented by Skinner, *Genesis*, 153–54; see also Westermann, *Genesis 1–11*, 430–32.

31. Westermann, *Genesis 1–11*, 436.

32. "On this day of condemnation, on this same very day a festive salvation by entry" (McEvenue, *Narrative Style*, 61–62; cf. Westermann, *Genesis 1–11*, 436–37.

If we are unable to perceive meaning in the two entries into the ark narrated sequentially, the presence of the dual entry in the text obliges us to look for its meaning not in sequence but, as it were, in parallel, as presenting alternative ways of telling this part of the story.

It is well known that 7:8-9 contains a mixture of the features usually distributed between J and P; therefore it is generally attributed to someone working with the combined text.[33] If we are content to regard the J report of Noah's entry into the ark as implicit in the statement of Noah's compliance with God's command (7:5), then 7:6-10 can be treated independently. With both vv. 6 and 10 attributed to the redaction, the passage becomes a skilled example of the redactor's art. The reference to Noah's age in v. 6 picks up and anticipates v. 11; the reference to the seven days in v. 10 echoes v. 4, noting the fulfillment of what was predicted there by God. Between these two redactional seams, the desired presentation of the entry into the ark is reported. In this way, a well-rounded presentation of an alternative portrayal of the entry into the ark has been skillfully inserted into the text.

With the insertion of 7:6-10, duality has uncompromisingly taken over from unity. But meaning is not sacrificed if we recognize that vv. 6-10 are not part of the sequential plot but offer an alternative version of this part of the flood narrative. Rather than coherent sequence, parallel alternatives appear to be the most meaningful reading of these verses.

Before moving on, it is worth noting the total simplicity of the blending of the two presentations of the flood. For J it was a forty-day rainstorm (7:4); for P it was the inrushing of the waters separated at creation. By the simple expedient of placing P before J, so that the "windows of the heavens" were opened before the rain fell (7:11-12) and closed before the rain stopped (8:2), a perfectly coherent text emerges. The bursting forth of all of "the fountains of the great deep" cannot, of course, be correlated with the rains; for the foregrounding of unity, it does not have to be.

Sequential unity is taken up again easily in what follows. J text is used as an envelope around the P material. Verse 17b speaks of the waters increasing and the ark rising high above the earth; vv. 18-20 continue this picture until the waters are fifteen cubits above the mountains. The death of all flesh follows in v. 21; vv. 22-23 follow on smoothly, a general statement (v. 21) apparently being followed by details complementing the picture in different language (vv. 22-23). The sequence from forty days (7:17a) to one hundred and fifty days (7:24) presents no problem, unless the detail is foregrounded.[34]

Unity continues to hold easy sway through the abating of the waters and the sending out of the birds and the departure from the ark.

God's reaction at the end of the flood is reported first of all as a decision within God's heart (8:21-22). It is then communicated to Noah and expressed in the solemn form of a covenant (9:1-17). Thus both conclusions are preserved, with both expressing in their different ways God's unconditional commitment to creation, flawed and fragile though it may be.[35]

Reflection

The narrative of the flood opened with a striking and devastating statement. A radical

---

33. McEvenue, to the contrary, regards 7:7-8 as J, providing the source for seven out of the eight elements in the four P lists of those saved (*Narrative Style*, 25).

34. McEvenue's comment is valuable: "However difficult it is for the modern mind to discover mystery or metaphysics in numbers, since man and his machines now use mathematics as a docile tool to con-

trol or change nature, this effort must be made if the power of many ancient texts is not to escape us entirely" (*Narrative Style*, 57–58 n. 50).

35. In Noth's analysis, 7:3a, 7*, 8-9, 17a, and 23aβ are considered as additions to the combined text. Further discussion of the possible reasons for these decisions would take us too far beyond the present scope.

change has taken place in God's perception of the human world. The opening account of creation ended with God's perception of all God had made as "very good" (1:31); the account of the flood has now opened with God's perception that "the wickedness of humankind was great" (6:5). This general affirmation is taken a step further in the more colorful and detailed statement that "every inclination of the thoughts of their hearts was only evil continually" (6:5). The picture of humankind has radically changed since Genesis 1 and 2. Sin has indeed been "lurking at the door" of the human heart and, instead of being mastered, it has established its mastery (cf. Gen 4:7).

The focus is on God who saw and was sorry and was grieved. The devastating statement is God's decision: "I will blot out from the earth the human beings I have created" (6:7). Those given into human power and responsibility at creation—birds, beasts, and creeping things (1:26)—are now to be destroyed in the destruction of the human race. They too have fallen from favor (6:7). Familiarity can leave us untroubled by such a sentence. If we allow ourselves the suspense of disbelief and enter imaginatively into the power of the narrative, this total divine condemnation of all life is so massively threatening that even the fear of nuclear holocaust is but a bad dream beside it. There is the tiniest glimmer of light: "Noah found favor in the sight of the Lord" (6:8).

The towering significance of this story bears in its own way on the nature of the composite text in which it is now recorded. While the discussion above on unity and duality hardly touches the depths of the flood narrative, it reveals certain phenomena present in the text. In the combination of sources, unity almost always has priority over duality. In one instance only has duality stubbornly refused to bow to unity's yoke (i.e., the issue of dual entry into the

ark, 7:6-16). Yet duality has consistently been maintained; although not in the foreground, it has seldom been eliminated.

The principal conclusion to be drawn from this must be that although unity is the principal concern of the combined text, the duality is also of sufficient significance to be preserved.

The need for unity is simply explained. The flood is evidently a once-and-for-all event; it can scarcely be recounted twice. Although the rationale for this is rooted deeply within the function of the flood narrative as myth, it can be justified very simply from the narrative. Both the J and P versions end with God's determination never again to destroy the world. Were these versions juxtaposed, as the creation accounts are, the first would end with a guarantee never again to destroy the world only to be followed immediately by the second version of divine destruction. The two stories would subvert each other.

However, when the two accounts are blended into a unity such as we have seen, the duality, far from being mutually subverting, becomes a strong source of confirmation and reinforcement. So, above all, the divine decision triggering the flood is narrated twice, once in heaven and once on earth. Similarly, the divine decision never again to destroy is narrated twice, once in heaven and once on earth. Confronted with the massive theological and human significance of these decisions, any inconvenient duality in the remaining text pales into insignificance.

To those acutely aware of human fragility and sin and equally aware of the utterly transcendent holiness of God, nothing could be more important than the divine promise that God would never again destroy every living creature, despite the inevitably evil inclination of the human heart (8:21). The expression of this in the Noah covenant is a theological claim of the highest order.[36]

At this point, the duality becomes more easily

---

36. It is worth reiterating that the concepts of favor and righteousness do not feature here in either J or P. This is in contrast to the start of the story, when Noah was singled out for deliverance.

intelligible. In the biblical flood narrative, the primary theological–mythological communication being made concerns the relationship of Creator and creation. Despite all that is manifestly wrong and unholy in creation, it is the unchangeable decision of the Creator that creation will endure until the end of time.

It is one of the Yahwist's great achievements to have given this clear expression. The J text opening the story with the reason for the flood—**every inclination of the thoughts of their hearts was only evil continually**—is explicitly matched by the J text concluding the flood story with the reason why God will never bring such a calamity again—**for the inclination of the human heart is evil from youth.** The paradox is blindingly evident. Within the Creator-creation relationship there has been a marked change, amounting to a total reversal, from annihilation to preservation. There has been no change in humankind. Therefore, the change must have been in the creator God.

Gerhard von Rad attributes this insight to the Yahwist, claiming that the Yahwist "certainly found no precedent in the tradition for what he gives as Yahweh's word."[37] His development of the insight is worth quoting extensively.

This saying of Yahweh [8:21-22] without doubt designates a profound turning point in the Yahwistic primeval history, in so far as it expresses with surprising directness a will for salvation directed towards the whole of Noachite humanity, "although" (the Hebrew particle can be translated in this way) "the imagination of man's heart is evil from his youth." . . . In its hard paradox this v. 21 is one of the most remarkable theological statements in the Old Testament: it shows the pointed and concentrated way in which

the Yahwist can express himself at decisive points. The same condition which in the prologue is the basis for God's judgment in the epilogue reveals God's grace and providence. The contrast between God's punishing anger and his supporting grace, which pervades the whole Bible, is here presented almost inappropriately, almost as indulgence, an adjustment by God towards man's sinfulness.[38]

The same perception is developed sensitively by Walter Brueggemann.[39] "The narrative is centered in the grief of God, whose heart knows about our hearts."[40] Brueggemann expresses clearly the relational dynamics that are at stake:

Humankind is hopeless. Creation has not changed. It is deeply set against God's purposes. The imagination of the heart first recognized as evil in 6:5 is still imagination of the heart which is evil in 8:21. All the terror of the waters has not changed that. Hope for the future is not premised on possibility thinking or human actualization. Hope will depend on a move from God.[41]

The "move from God" is then spelled out thoroughly by Brueggemann.

The flood has effected no change in humankind. But it has effected an irreversible change in God, who now will approach his creation with an unlimited patience and forebearance. To be sure, God has been committed to his creation from the beginning. But this narrative traces a new decision on the part of God. Now the commitment is intensified. For the first time, it is marked by grief, the hurt of betrayal. It is now clear that such a commitment on God's part is costly. The God-world relation is not simply that of strong God and needy world. Now it is a

37. Gerhard von Rad, *Genesis* (OTL; Philadelphia: Westminster, 1972) 122.
38. Ibid., 122–23.
39. Walter Brueggemann, *Genesis* (Interpretation; Atlanta: John Knox, 1982) 77–82.
40. Ibid., 78.
41. Ibid., 80–81.

tortured relation between a grieved God and a resistant world. And of the two, the real changes are in God. This is a key insight of the gospel against every notion that God stands outside of the hurt as a judge.[42]

Here a conviction is expressed that runs strongly through the Pentateuch and the scriptures of Israel: God's commitment is enduring.

The covenant may be broken; the relationship [with God] is not. Time and again in the desert Israel disobeys; time and again God is portrayed as furious. Always Israel remains God's people. . . . God may be portrayed as angry, fulminating, and threatening; but God is never portrayed as giving up. The presence of the All-Holy in the midst of Israel is both source of life and strength and a danger to their existence; but the danger can be circumscribed and overcome. . . . The Pentateuch portrays a God who is capable of threatening and dangerous anger, but a God whose love is stronger than anger, whose commitment endures.[43]

As the prophecies of salvation witness strongly, so it is with Israel's faith throughout its history.

Once this theological affirmation of faith has been recognized, it is remarkable to find it reaffirmed in the P text and most understandable that the Priestly writer, believing it, should have wanted to express it strongly. In the turbulence and upset around the time of exile, a faith in God's enduring commitment was an affirmation that needed to be heard. It ran against the grain of all that one might have regarded as obvious. As Ezekiel quotes the exiles saying, "Our bones are dried up, and our hope is lost; we are cut off completely" (Ezek 37:11). The word given to Ezekiel expresses the same faith as the Priestly writer: " 'I will put my spirit within you, and you shall live, and I will place you on your own soil;

then you shall know that I, the LORD, have spoken and will act' says the LORD" (Ezek 37:14).

The Priestly writer cannot resort to a prophetic saying. As narrative theologian, P must work in other terms. This may be why the flood narrative is so important within the text of P. The world is set in place at creation, majestically ordered, culminating in God's observance of the sabbath observed by Israel alone. Without narrating the stories of sin, P took on board the tradition's annihilation of that world. After the flood, P depicts an imperfect world, with "fear and dread" upon the animal kingdom and murder and bloodshed foreseen within the human realm (Gen 9:2-6). It is with this world that P has God make an unconditional covenant with Noah never ever to destroy it again.

As for me, I am establishing my covenant with you and your descendants after you, and with every living creature that is with you, . . . I establish my covenant with you, that never again shall all flesh be cut off by the waters of a flood, and never again shall there be a flood to destroy the earth. (Gen 9:9-11)

For the Priestly writer, this is the understanding of God that underpins the enduring relationship between God and our world. It is against this understanding of God that P can portray the enduring relationship that exists between God and Israel, especially exiled Israel.

That is P's message to his people. Just as God has set the world in order, ordained toward sabbath, so too God has set Israel on the road toward Canaan, the promised land. God, the creator, has the power to achieve it. Israel's unbelief can delay the accomplishment of God's will; it cannot deflect God from it. God's love for Israel is unconditional; it will not bow to rejection. God's presence is set in Israel's midst; it will not be

---

42. Ibid., 81.

43. Campbell, *Study Companion*, 59–60.

withdrawn. . . . In all of this, the fragility of Israel can only delay God's purpose; human fragility cannot cancel out the divine will. Whether or not P portrayed Israel's taking possession of the land, there can hardly be any justifiable doubt that for P the everlasting possession of the land lay in the future, at the end of a stately march which had as its driving force the unswerving will of God.

There is in the Priestly Document a boldness of theological genius which can unfold the majestic holiness of God and, at the same time, assert the unshakable commitment of this all-holy God to a creation and a nation that had so deeply experienced its weakness and its failure.[44]

With this understanding expressed in P, it is not surprising to find it echoed and reaffirmed in Second Isaiah, explicitly with reference to Noah and God's decision after the flood.

This is like the days of Noah to me:
  Just as I swore that the waters of Noah
    would never again go over the earth,
so I have sworn that I will not be angry with you
    and will not rebuke you.

For the mountains may depart
  and the hills be removed,
but my steadfast love shall not depart from you,
  and my covenant of peace shall not be removed,
  says the LORD, who has compassion on
    you. (Isa 54:9-10)

Against all of this background, the need for the unity and duality of the flood account in its final form becomes transparently clear. In depicting a fundamental decision in the being of God with regard to the continued existence of earth, the unity of the narrative was essential for expressing a once-and-for-all decision with its implications for all time.[45] Given the importance and theological significance of this understanding of faith, it needed to be expressed with all of the available weight of tradition, therefore of J and of P. In the combination of both, two voices have joined in the singing of one song, and the song is the more powerful for their harmony. Two witnesses give testimony to the faith of Israel; in such a matter of life and death, at least two witnesses are required. The compiler of our composite final text has done marvelously well.

Interpretation of the Beginning of the Joseph Story

KEY: **Yahwist**/Priestly/*Elohist*/<u>additions</u>
(Source division according to Martin Noth)

GENESIS 37 Jacob settled in the land where his father had lived as an alien, the land of Canaan. [2]This is the story of the family of Jacob.

Joseph, being seventeen years old, was shepherding the flock with his brothers; <u>he was a helper to the sons of Bilhah and Zilpah, his father's wives;</u> and Joseph brought a bad report

---

44. Ibid., 82–83, 85–86.

45. Against Westermann (*Genesis 1–11*, 456), it is dubious whether justice is done to this decision by equating it with the New Testament saying that God "makes his sun rise on the evil and on the good, and sends rain on the righteous and on the unrighteous" (Matt 5:45). After the trauma of the flood narrative, God's commitment has the potential for far more positive evaluation.

of them to their father. ³Now Israel loved Joseph more than any other of his children, because he was the son of his old age; *and he had made him a long robe with sleeves.* ⁴But when his brothers saw that their father loved him more than all his brothers, they hated him, and could not speak peaceably to him.

5 Once Joseph had a dream, and [Heb.; NRSV, and when] he told it to his brothers, they hated him even more. ⁶He said to them, "Listen to this dream that I dreamed. ⁷There we were, binding sheaves in the field. Suddenly my sheaf rose and stood upright; then your sheaves gathered around it, and bowed down to my sheaf." ⁸His brothers said to him, "Are you indeed to reign over us? Are you indeed to have dominion over us?" So they hated him even more because of his dreams and his words.

9 He had another dream, and told it to his brothers, saying, "Look, I have had another dream: the sun, the moon, and eleven stars were bowing down to me." ¹⁰But when he told it to his father and to his brothers, his father rebuked him, and said to him, "What kind of dream is this that you have had? Shall we indeed come, I and your mother and your brothers, and bow to the ground before you?" ¹¹So his brothers were jealous of him, but his father kept the matter in mind.

12 Now his brothers went to pasture their father's flock near Shechem. ¹³And Israel said to Joseph, "Are not your brothers pasturing the flock at Shechem? Come, I will send you to them." He answered, "Here I am." ¹⁴So he said to him, "Go now, see if it is well with your brothers and with the flock; and bring word back to me." So he sent him from the valley of Hebron.

He came to Shechem, ¹⁵and a man found him wandering in the fields; the man asked him, "What are you seeking?" ¹⁶"I am seeking my brothers," he said; "tell me, please,

where they are pasturing the flock." ¹⁷The man said, "They have gone away, for I heard them say, 'Let us go to Dothan.' " So Joseph went after his brothers, and found them at Dothan. ¹⁸They saw him from a distance, and before he came near to them, they conspired to kill him. ¹⁹They said to one another, "Here comes this dreamer. ²⁰Come now, let us kill him and throw him into one of the pits; then we shall say that a wild animal has devoured him, and we shall see what will become of his dreams." ²¹But when Reuben heard it, he delivered him out of their hands, saying, "Let us not take his life." *²²Reuben said to them, "Shed no blood; throw him into this pit here in the wilderness, but lay no hand on him"—that he might rescue him out of their hand and restore him to his father. ²³So when Joseph came to his brothers, they stripped him of his robe, the long robe with sleeves that he wore; ²⁴and they took him and threw him into a pit. The pit was empty; there was no water in it.*

25 Then they sat down to eat; and looking up they saw a caravan of Ishmaelites coming from Gilead, with their camels carrying gum, balm, and resin, on their way to carry it down to Egypt. ²⁶Then Judah said to his brothers, "What profit is it if we kill our brother and conceal his blood? ²⁷Come, let us sell him to the Ishmaelites, and not lay our hands on him, for he is our brother, our own flesh." And his brothers agreed. *²⁸When some Midianite traders passed by, they drew Joseph up, lifting him out of the pit,* and sold him to the Ishmaelites for twenty pieces of silver. And they took Joseph to Egypt.

29 When Reuben returned to the pit and saw that Joseph was not in the pit, he tore his clothes. ³⁰He returned to his brothers, and said, "The boy is gone; and I, where can I turn?" ³¹Then they took Joseph's robe, slaughtered a goat, and dipped the robe in the blood. ³²They had the long robe with sleeves taken to their father, and they said, "This we have *found; see now whether it is your son's robe or not." *[33]*He recognized it, and said, "It is my son's robe! A wild animal has devoured him; Joseph is without doubt torn to pieces." *[34]*Then Jacob tore his garments, and put sackcloth on his loins, and mourned for his son many days. *[35]*All his sons and all his daughters sought to comfort him; but he refused to be comforted, and said, "No, I shall go down to Sheol to my son, mourning." Thus his father bewailed him. *[36]*Meanwhile the Midianites had sold him in Egypt to Potiphar, one of Pharaoh's officials, the captain of the guard.*

Interpretation

There is perhaps no other area of the Pentateuch where the issue of the relationship between the duality of a text—as identified by source analysis—and the unity of that text is more pressing than this story. The growing appreciation of the literary qualities of Old Testament narrative has led to the realization that the story of Joseph is a remarkably unified and finely crafted example. Indeed, there is no other narrative in the Pentateuch that displays these literary qualities to the same degree or sustains them to the same extent. Whether the Joseph story is regarded as embracing Genesis 37 and 39–45 or extending to include Genesis 46–50, it is an impressive piece of work. How is the duality that traditional source analysis claims to have uncovered in the Joseph story integrated with the evidence of unity and sophisticated narrative art highlighted in more recent literary analysis?

This is not the place to embark on a full-scale study of the Joseph story. Nevertheless, the issue of duality and unity in the story is important enough to warrant some treatment here. Genesis 37 is a manageable section of the story which provides plenty of scope for exploring the issue of duality and its relationship to unity. It is also a key chapter in the story. According to Noth's source division, Genesis 37 contains material from each of the sources P, J, and E. From his point of view, therefore, the chapter is very much a composite. Yet given that the Joseph story is widely regarded as a highly unified narrative, one would also expect to find solid evidence for this unity in Genesis 37. This is the opening chapter of the story; it describes the conflict between Joseph and his brothers over power, and it is this conflict that gives the rest of the narrative its impetus and cohesion. The overall unity of the Joseph story is in a real sense dependent on the unity of Genesis 37.

Our analysis of Genesis 37 is not meant to be a defense of Noth's source division. Rather, Noth's analysis of the text provides a useful basis for our purpose, which is to examine how the sort of duality that the source hypothesis identifies functions in relation to the unity of the text and its overall meaning. In carrying out this analysis a particular concern, as in the analysis of the flood story, is to give due weight to the evidence for duality. The search for unity and meaning in a text should resist gliding over problem areas to settle for some vague unity; forcing the text to conform to a preconceived notion of unity is just as undesirable.

Foregrounding Unity

The modern reader may be struck by an abruptness at points in Genesis 37. Nowhere is this abruptness more striking than in v. 36, as we shall see. Modern readers may also be troubled by aspects of the story that are dealt with in rather summary fashion and that they would like to see fleshed out. With due regard for the fact that we are dealing with literature from another age and culture, however, and with a measure of imagination, we can follow this first chapter of the story of Joseph through and gain a good appreciation of its prevailing unity.

The story begins with a sketch of the main characters and their situation, with the relationships between Joseph, his father, and his brothers to the fore. The critical element that dominates the chapter and, indeed, powers the whole of the Joseph story is signaled: there is conflict in the family. At the outset it takes the form of conflict between Joseph and his brothers. Although some abruptness is present in the way this conflict is introduced in v. 2, it forms the first stage in a developing conflict that reaches a critical point in vv. 5-11, where Joseph tells his brothers about his dreams of power. Their reaction is predictable. They hate Joseph and are jealous of him. The tension generated by this conflict needs to be released, and the hatred and jealousy that consume the brothers—they could not speak peaceably to him and hated him even more—suggest that its release may be violent.

Their father creates a dangerous situation by sending Joseph on an errand to his brothers, who are away shepherding their flocks. He seems unaware of the hostility the brothers harbor toward Joseph. The sense of impending danger, of Joseph leaving his father's protective love for his brothers' hatred, is heightened by the scene with the man in the fields (vv. 15-17). His directions take Joseph even farther from his father.[46]

The narrative reaches a critical phase as Joseph, alone and unprotected, approaches his brothers. The dramatic development of the story is intensified by a series of three scenes, in each of which Joseph's fate hangs in the balance. In the first scene the sight of the approaching Joseph prompts the brothers to plot his murder (vv. 18-20). Their murderous intention is deflected, for the moment, by the intervention of Reuben in vv. 21-24. In these verses there is a second scene in which Joseph's fate hangs in the balance. Reuben successfully persuades his brothers to throw Joseph into a nearby pit.

Although the narrative tells us that Reuben intervenes in this way because he intends to restore Joseph to his father, we do not know what the other brothers intend to do. Throwing Joseph into a pit can hardly rank as a satisfactory substitute for their initial plot to murder him. Joseph's fate still hangs in the balance.

The third scene, in which again Joseph's fate will hang in the balance, is delayed as the brothers take a meal. The pause allows for thought. A passing Ishmaelite caravan gives Judah the idea of selling Joseph to them, a plan to which the brothers agree (vv. 25-27). In this way they can have the satisfaction of deciding Joseph's fate without incurring bloodguilt for his murder. However, some Midianite traders short-circuit their plan (v. 28). They remove Joseph from the pit and sell him to the Ishmaelites who take him to Egypt. Joseph is now definitely out of his brothers' hands; they no longer have any control over his future. Joseph's fate still hangs in the balance, however, because he is a slave of the Ishmaelites on their way to Egypt. This third scene eases one dramatic tension in the story only to create another over the fate of Joseph in Egypt.

The narrative sequence in vv. 27 and 28 may appear abrupt, but it captures well the suddenness of the Midianites' appearance on the scene. They may also be seen as an example of the "unexpected factor" in the development of a plot, the sort of thing that makes for good storytelling. There is a subtle irony in the picture of the brothers who are left empty-handed: no Joseph in the pit and no money in the pouch.

The reappearance of Reuben in v. 29 is equally abrupt. There is uncertainty as to whether he was present when the plan to sell Joseph was hatched and therefore acted to remove Joseph

---

46. This "farther from his father" depends on the whereabouts of Jacob (see p. 175 n. 32, on Gen 35:20). Here, following the present text, we may assume

Hebron (cf. Gen 35:27). The simple "land of Canaan" in Gen 37:1 is open to a wider range of possibilities.

before the brothers could get to him, or whether he had earlier slipped away following his original plan. In either case, Reuben's return to the pit is in keeping with his intention to rescue Joseph, as revealed in v. 22. The climactic series of events triggered by the father's plan to send Joseph to visit his brothers concludes with the account of the brothers' return to their father in vv. 31-35. In this episode the brothers successfully deceive their father into thinking Joseph is dead by presenting his robe, stained with goat's blood. Verse 35 portrays a disconsolate father mourning the death of his son.

A question that arises at this point in the narrative is why the brothers took such drastic steps to deceive their father. Why did they not simply report that Joseph was dead, or missing, or that he had never reached them? One possible answer is that the ruse with the bloodstained robe is a measure of their desperate need to put an end to the bogey of Joseph's "favored status." Their hope is that the deception will finish the matter once and for all. The irony, however, is that they must now live with a father who refuses to be consoled over the death of his son. The sight of their grieving father is a constant reminder to them of their guilt. It is not hard to see some similarity to the story of Cain and Abel here, with Jacob in the role of God, Joseph as Abel, and the brothers as Cain.

The chapter ends with the news that the Midianites had sold Joseph in Egypt to a high-ranking official named Potiphar (Gen 37:36). This report takes the story beyond the dramatic arc that reaches from v. 2 to v. 35 and prepares the way for Joseph's adventures in Egypt. Hence it is part of the overall story line. But for anyone who has followed the story with attention, the naming of the Midianites as the ones who sold Joseph clashes sharply with v. 28. This verse states that the Midianites had sold Joseph to Ishmaelites, and it was the latter who took him to Egypt. The matter is further complicated by 39:1, which claims that Potiphar (mentioned in 37:36) bought Joseph from the Ishmaelites (mentioned in 37:28). We have, therefore, clear evidence of plurality between 37:28, 36 and 39:1. At this stage we should reread Genesis 37 with an eye to other examples of duality or plurality, some of which may not be so evident in a first reading of the text.

Foregrounding Duality

In foregrounding the duality of the text, a question that arises is why the two dreams in vv. 5-11 are not distributed among different sources by Noth. There is an evident similarity of structure in the two accounts: each describes Joseph telling a dream, the rebuke that follows, and the tension that it generates.[47] Embedded in this similarity of structure, however, are distinctive features that indicate a carefully constructed progression from the first to the second dream. This is different from the duality of "doublets," which Noth regards as the most reliable indicator of the presence of sources.

The first dream, about the sheaves, is concerned with the relationship between Joseph and his brothers. It provokes the brothers to question whether Joseph will have dominion over

---

47. The introductions to each dream in Gen 37:5 and 37:9 are remarkably similar, except for the report of the brothers' hatred in v. 5. The similarity is more easily seen in a literal rendering of the Hebrew: v. 5 reads "and Joseph dreamed a dream and he declared (it) to his brothers and he said"; v. 9 has "and he dreamed another dream and he told it to his brothers and he said" For the NRSV's "told," the Hebrew uses the verb "to declare" (*ngd*) in v. 5, and in v. 9 has the verb "to tell" (*spr*). The report of the brothers' hatred is missing in the Greek text of v. 5. Without it, there are two reports of the brothers' hatred (vv. 4 and 8) and one report of their jealousy (v. 11), thus three statements of their hostility toward Joseph. With it, there is a sequence of three reports of hatred (vv. 4, 5, 8), followed by one report of jealousy in v. 11.

them. The issue in this dream is power among the brothers. The second dream, of the sun, moon, and stars bowing down to Joseph, embraces the whole family.[48] The issue here is whether they will all come to Joseph, bowing before him.

The distinctive features of the two dreams power the subsequent development of the Joseph story.[49] The dramatic events that unfold in this story become steps in the realization of the dreams. Thus the issue of who has power is initially put to the test when the brothers attempt to deal with Joseph on their terms, and fail (37:18-28). The failure of their plans provides an inkling of the truth of the dreams, in particular the first one with its focus on the relationship between Joseph and his brothers. The full realization of this dream occurs in Genesis 42, which portrays the brothers prostrate before Joseph in Egypt (42:9). But this scene also alludes to the second dream, because both dreams share the vision of the brothers bowing down to Joseph. The full realization of the second dream takes place when the whole family comes to Egypt on Joseph's terms. The family's arrival in Egypt completes a narrative trajectory that began with Joseph's dreams and the tension they caused. A critical point in this trajectory was the brothers' journey to Egypt and the dramatic events surrounding their encounter there with the all-powerful Joseph.

The presence of the two dreams and the progression from one to the other is therefore an integral feature of the Joseph story. Without

them, the narrative would lose much of its quality as a sophisticated and beautifully crafted story.

The duality that is identified as part of the source division is significantly different. The P material in v. 2 refers to a bad report about his brothers that Joseph made to his father: no details of the report are given, but the context points to a complaint about their work as shepherds. Yet this report is not mentioned in the subsequent J text. If we take into account the addition in v. 2, then the trouble could be seen to begin with the tension between Joseph and the sons of Bilhah and Zilpah.[50] These brothers are not singled out as a particular group in the subsequent J text, however, and the issue of Joseph's report is not pursued any further. Instead, vv. 3-11 tell of conflict between Joseph and all his brothers. Embedded in this duality is yet another one created by the change in names for the father, who is described as Jacob in vv. 1-2 and as Israel in v. 3 (and also v. 12)—correlating with the source division.

Unlike vv. 5-11, the report of trouble between Joseph and his brothers in v. 2 is not integral to the plot of the Joseph story. The story could function without it. Nevertheless, as the subsequent reflections on the art of combination point out, this report can be read as part of the developing conflict within the family. As such, it enhances the narrative.

After vv. 1-11, the next examples of duality are in the brothers' attempts to rid themselves of Joseph. In vv. 21-22 there are two statements that Reuben delivered Joseph out of the broth-

---

48. The reference to the moon need not imply that the narrative presumes Joseph's mother Rachel was alive. As G. W. Coats points out, "It simply facilitates the sun–moon motif at the center of the dream as a symbol of the family" (*From Canaan to Egypt: Structural and Theological Context for the Joseph Story* [CBQMS 4; Washington, D.C.: Catholic Biblical Association of America, 1976] 14).

49. On this point, see also Coats, *From Canaan to Egypt*, 13–14.

50. It is worth noting here that, in contrast to Noth, both von Rad (*Genesis*, 345) and C. Westermann (*Genesis 37–50* [Minneapolis: Augsburg, 1986] 35) include v. 2aβ in P. See also the treatment in Adele Berlin, *Poetics and Interpretation of Biblical Narrative* (Bible and Literature Series; Sheffield: Almond Press, 1983) 48.

ers' hands and two verbal interventions by Reuben to spare Joseph's life.[51] As pointed out in chapter 3 (p. 121, n. 73), this duality led Noth to propose that the subject of v. 21 was originally Judah and that it was changed to Reuben when the sources were combined. Whether this proposal is acceptable or not, the duality is clearly present in the elements singled out.[52]

The description of events after Reuben has successfully stalled his brothers' plan to kill Joseph reveals further duality. Judah's plan to sell Joseph to the Ishmaelites (vv. 26-27) is in direct contrast to Reuben's intention to return to the pit and restore Joseph to his father (cf. vv. 22 and 29). What is intriguing in this section of the narrative is that there is no reaction by Reuben to Judah's proposal, no confrontation between these two brothers. Reuben's intention of rescuing Joseph and Judah's proposal to sell him are simply juxtaposed in the narrative.

The duality created by the Ishmaelites and Midianites in vv. 25-28 can be seen clearly enough when these verses are distributed between the J and E sources. The Ishmaelites are the foreigners who feature in the J source, whereas in the E source it is the Midianites. Nevertheless, this sequence of verses can be read as a coherent and unified account. Verse 25 reports the approach of an Ishmaelite caravan which, in v. 26, gives Judah the idea of selling Joseph to them. The brothers agree to the plan in v. 27, but before it can be put into action, v. 28 reports that passing Midianite traders drew Joseph out of the pit and sold him to the Ishmaelites.

Unity is so clearly to the fore here that it is legitimate to ask whether there is indeed a dual-ity associated with the references to Ishmaelites and Midianites. But there can be no doubting the duality when we come to v. 36, for it states that Joseph was sold in Egypt by Midianites, which clashes with v. 28's account. At this point in the narrative duality reemerges in a striking and discordant way and obliges us to reassess the earlier part of the narrative where Ishmael-ites and Midianites appear. What the present text contains is a duality, which at one point in the narrative is clearly subordinate to unity (vv. 25-28) yet at a subsequent point in the narrative is disruptive of that unity (v. 36). How these two examples of duality contribute to the overall meaning of the text is discussed below in our reflections on the art of combination.

Art of Combination

When considered in isolation, the P material in Genesis 37 does not appear particularly sig-nificant; for Noth, it comprises barely two verses. Nevertheless, the location of this mate-rial maximizes its contribution, enabling it to serve as a link between the Joseph story and the larger context and as an introduction to the Joseph story itself.

The relationship with the larger context is established by two statements in the P material. Verse 1 states that Jacob settled in the land where his father had lived before him. By means of this simple remark a link is forged with the past, and the Joseph story becomes a continua-tion of the story of Israel's ancestors. Verse 2 opens with the announcement "This is the story of the family of Jacob." A more literal rendering of the Hebrew would be "These are the genera-tions of Jacob."[53] The story of Joseph thus

---

51. The NRSV translates the same Hebrew verb by "deliver" in v. 21 and by "rescue" in v. 22.

52. This is recognized by Westermann, even though he does not accept a source division in the Joseph story (*Genesis 37–50*, 35, 42). The duality involving the respective roles of Reuben and Judah reappears later in the narrative: in 42:22 and 37 Reuben is again the one who takes the initiative,

whereas in Genesis 43–44 it is Judah who takes the initiative.

53. In Noth's view, this statement is an imitation of the Toledoth book formula (*A History of Pentateuchal Traditions* [Englewood Cliffs, N.J.: Prentice-Hall, 1972; reprint, Chico, Calif.: Scholars Press, 1981] 18 n. 53; see also p. 23 n. 4, on Gen 5:1).

unfolds within a larger horizon that includes not only the story of his brother Judah in Genesis 38 but also the story of the people of Israel—the subsequent generations of Jacob–Israel.

The P material also serves as an appropriate introduction to the Joseph story itself. The main characters in the story are announced—Joseph, who is a youth of seventeen, his brothers, and their father—and a concise description of the family situation follows. This is a family in which there is trouble, for the last part of v. 2 states that Joseph brought a bad report of his brothers to his father.

P's description of conflict in the family is surprisingly terse. We are not told what the content of Joseph's report was, and the following verses from the J source make no reference to it. It is not clear whether the brothers themselves knew of the report. Nevertheless, it is instructive to observe how well this brief description, in terms of both its location and its content, enhances the overall meaning of the first part of the Joseph story.

Verse 2 is the first of three reports of conflict in the family. The second occurs in the J passage in vv. 3-4, reporting the brothers' hatred of Joseph because he is the favored son. The third is in J's vv. 5-11, which tell of Joseph's two dreams and the hatred and jealousy these cause among his brothers. The combination of P and J material enables these three passages, each of which outlines a different area of conflict in the family, to create an overall impression of worsening conflict. The brief statement in v. 2 is appropriate as a first report. It hints at tension between the brothers but does not record any exchange, any open breach between them. In vv. 3-4, however, this tension develops into smoldering hatred. A breach opens in the relationship; the brothers cannot speak peaceably to

Joseph. In vv. 5-11 this hatred bursts into words as they openly rebuke him. Even Jacob himself is drawn into the row over the dreams. The family is now dangerously divided.

Within this sequence, the portion of v. 2 that Noth identifies as a later addition can also be seen to contribute to the overall effect. The tension, which according to this addition initially involves only Joseph and the sons of Bilhah and Zilpah, embroils all the brothers in vv. 3-4 and eventually affects even Jacob himself in vv. 10-11. Similarly, the element from E, the special robe that Joseph's father made for him, is well located in this passage. Verse 4 can be read as indicating that the brothers saw the robe as a clear sign of Joseph's favored status, hence its fate in the brothers' deception of Jacob in vv. 31-35.

Closer examination shows that v. 2 also lends subtlety to an important element of this part of the narrative, namely, the question of responsibility for the conflict in the family. While v. 2 sows the possibility of tension within the family, its very brevity creates ambiguity. Does it imply that the brothers, at least the sons of Bilhah and Zilpah, had done something evil, which Joseph reported? Is Joseph already being portrayed as the sort of sharp-eyed critic who will later on become the highly competent administrator of Egypt? From a more negative point of view, does the verse suggest that Joseph fabricated the report? On top of this there is the puzzling silence of Jacob. In relation to our earlier remarks about the possible uses of a written text in ancient Israel, it is easy to see how this sort of ambiguity could provide ample scope for development by an imaginative storyteller.[54]

Ambiguity is also evident in vv. 3-11. The brothers' hatred in vv. 3-4 may be an overreaction to their aged father indulging his youngest

---

54. This does not mean that a storyteller eliminates all ambiguity and complexity when developing an aspect of a written text. Imaginative storytellers would no doubt be quite capable of weaving into their oral performance the ambiguities and complexities that enrich a story.

son; or they may have been unduly provoked by Jacob's gesture of making a special robe for the favorite son. With such a gift Jacob could be seen to have declared his preference for Joseph in a public and provocative way, without due regard to its effect on the other brothers' standing in the family.[55]

There is a similar complexity of meaning in the account of Joseph's dreams (vv. 5-11). On the one hand, Joseph may be viewed here as the callow seventeen-year-old who recounts his dreams without being aware they are adding fuel to the fire of his brothers' hatred. He is so cocooned by his father's doting love that he does not see the larger reality around him. On the other hand, the content of Joseph's dreams could suggest that he is deliberately exploiting the privileged position his father has bestowed on him. What better way to do this than to recount dreams, which may come from God? The text does not say that the dreams do come from God, but within an Old Testament story the telling of dreams invariably raises this possibility. If the dreams have divine sanction, then Joseph is destined for power. It is surely significant that at the end of this scene the brothers' attitude has shifted from one of hatred to jealousy (v. 11).[56]

Attending to how the sources have been combined in vv. 1-11 reveals a narrative of conflict in Joseph's family that is more subtle, ambiguous, and complex than an initial reading would perhaps suggest. We can view each of the principal characters in the story—Jacob, Joseph, the brothers—from more than one perspective. We can argue that all are responsible for the conflict in the family in different ways. The duality in the text makes an important contribution to this density of meaning, which is nevertheless contained in one story line. It is legitimate to say that Gen 37:1-11 is a well-crafted literary piece in which duality has been woven into the formation of a larger unity. It is, however, also legitimate to say that the text's subtlety and ambiguity allow for a much fuller form, even several alternative forms, in oral performance. All of the possible meanings outlined are available to the imaginative storyteller.

The richness of meaning in vv. 1-11 is more than matched by the combination of J and E in vv. 21-35. As noted earlier, the elements of duality in vv. 21-24 are the two statements that Reuben delivered Joseph out of the hand of his brothers and his two verbal interventions on behalf of Joseph.[57] Within the combined text, each of these dualities acquires nuances of meaning that enhance the story overall. The dual references to Reuben delivering Joseph assume an intricate relationship to each other as the narra-

---

55. In 2 Sam 13:18, this type of robe is described as the characteristic apparel of a princess in the time of David.

56. The shift in the Hebrew from the preceding verb śānē' (to hate) in vv. 4, 5, and 8 to the verb qānā' (to be jealous) points to an intensification of meaning. The English word "jealous" may not quite capture the intensity of the Hebrew. In Westermann's commentary, v. 11a is translated as "So his brothers were incensed at him" (*Genesis 37–50*, 33).

57. According to Noth's analysis, the combination has preserved each source in this section of the story intact, the only change being the replacement of Judah as the subject of v. 21 with Reuben, to bring it into line with v. 22. The view that Reuben replaced Judah as the subject of the verb in v. 21 has been a commonplace among source critics and should therefore be taken into account. With Judah as the subject of v. 21, however, there is some tension between his intervention on behalf of Joseph here and his plan to sell Joseph in v. 27. Also, our reflections on the art of combination show that vv. 21 and 22 are able to function as parts of a coherent narrative without emendation. In making a judgment on literary-critical matters such as this it is well to recall the remark by Noth in his commentary on 1 Kings (*Könige* [BKAT 9/1; Neukirchen: Neukirchener Verlag, 1969] 246): "A literary critical possibility is however still not a literary critical necessity" ("Eine literarkritische Möglichkeit ist jedoch noch keine literarkritische Notwendigkeit").

tive tells what really happened to Joseph, in contrast to what Reuben intended. Verse 21 states that Reuben delivered Joseph out of their hands, whereas v. 22 speaks of his plan to deliver him. The subsequent narrative gradually unfolds the meaning of the statement in v. 21 and in doing so reveals a massive difference between what was planned and what eventuated. Joseph is delivered from the clutches of his brothers, but it is not at all in the manner Reuben intended. In fact, his well-motivated plan of v. 22 never reaches reality; the intervention of the Midianites sees to that. Furthermore, in vv. 29-30 Reuben ends up not even knowing whether Joseph has been delivered from his brothers' hands. The contrast between Reuben's plan and how Joseph was really delivered combines with other features in this section of the story to suggest that the fate of Joseph does not lie in the hands or the plans of any of the brothers.

Reuben's two verbal interventions in vv. 21 and 22 combine to create a progressive distancing of Reuben from his brothers. His initial plea for Joseph's life in v. 21 is made as one of the group: "Let us not take his life." In v. 22, however, he stands apart from his brothers, issuing them with instructions on what to do with Joseph. This progressive separation is taken a step further when v. 22 reveals the reason for his intervention. He plans to rescue Joseph "out of their hand" and restore him to his father.[58]

Although Reuben has deflected his brothers' murderous intention, throwing Joseph into a pit hardly provides a satisfactory release for it or for the hatred that has been seething since their father made Joseph the robe with sleeves (cf. vv. 23-24). The situation remains unresolved. The scene from J in v. 25, which describes the brothers sitting down to a meal, is the sort of pause that serves to heighten tension in a narrative.

The move to resolve the tension comes with Judah's plan to sell Joseph to a passing caravan of Ishmaelites (v. 26), a plan to which the brothers agree. The emergence of Judah into the foreground heralds possible conflict with Reuben, the dominant figure of vv. 21-24. Within the context, "then they sat down to eat," we may reasonably assume that the combined text envisages Reuben joining in the meal, perhaps to keep an eye on his brothers. Therefore he heard Judah's plan. In the light of Reuben's strong intervention in vv. 21-24, we might expect him to confront Judah, so his puzzling silence prompts reflection on a possible reason. Was he afraid of a conflict with Judah over leadership of the group, or just biding his time? Verse 29 indicates that he had not reneged on his original plan, suggesting that he was biding his time. This view gains some support from the way vv. 21-24 and 29 frame vv. 25-28. The arrangement of the E and J material implies that, although Reuben eats with his brothers, he remains outside the circle of their plotting, waiting for a chance to rescue Joseph. The separation that was signaled in vv. 21-24 would therefore seem to be maintained.

An additional complication in the portrayal of Reuben is that when he does make a move to rescue Joseph, he is too late (v. 29). Did he hesitate through fear of Judah and his brothers, or was he just unlucky to be beaten to Joseph by the Midianites? Such complications as these, or ambiguities that are uncovered by a careful reading of the text, would be grist to the mill of a competent storyteller.

Judah's plan to sell Joseph is callous but clever. He can abide by Reuben's injunction not

---

58. Cf. Ludwig Schmidt, *Literarische Studien zur Josephsgeschichte* (BZAW 167; Berlin: Walter de Gruyter, 1986) 146.

to shed Joseph's blood while disposing of Joseph permanently nevertheless. But the plan puts Judah and the brothers on a collision course with Reuben, who intends to rescue Joseph and restore him to his father. We have seen that there is good reason to accept that Reuben joined in the meal; we may assume, therefore, that he knows Judah's plan. May we also assume that Judah has guessed the reason for Reuben's intervention, and that his counter-plan is really laying down the gauntlet for a power struggle? The text does not say this directly, but it is intriguing how Judah refers first of all to Reuben's two injunctions in v. 22—not to shed Joseph's blood or to lay hands on him—and then outlines a plan that effectively cuts across Reuben's own. Added to this is the already observed silence of Reuben, which may be motivated by fear of Judah and his brothers. As the narrative builds toward a climax, therefore, it is possible to see an accompanying development of tension in the relationship between the brothers. This is another example of how the sources have been combined in a way that adds depth and interest to the story.

The climax comes in v. 28, which describes, with remarkable economy of expression, how passing Midianites drew Joseph out of the pit and sold him to the Ishmaelites.[59] What is striking about this point of the narrative is how the combination of J and E elements creates a whole new dimension in the story of Joseph that is not present in either of these sources when considered separately.

In the J version, Judah's plan works; he and his brothers sell Joseph to the Ishmaelites for twenty pieces of silver. In the combined text, the plan is short-circuited by the Midianites, who nab Joseph (v. 28a). The combined text in v. 28 also contains an ironic twist that can hardly be lost on an audience. All the effort expended by the brothers in trying to dispose of Joseph and so to convince themselves that they are the ones with power comes badly unstuck. They are left empty-handed and powerless to influence Joseph's destiny. Read in the light of the dreams in vv. 5-11 and in the light of what is to come, the brothers' failure opens up the possibility that there is a hidden power at work in Joseph's sudden "deliverance" from them, and even perhaps that this is an initial step in the realization of his dreams.

In the E version, Reuben's plan of restoring Joseph to his father is thwarted by the intervention of the Midianites. This feature is maintained in the combined text, with the added element that the Midianites sold Joseph to the Ishmaelites. What is new in relation to the E version, however, is how the combined text draws an ironic parallel between Reuben and his brothers. Although Reuben seems motivated by a genuine concern for Joseph, he is left in the end like his brothers, powerless and empty-handed. The destiny of Joseph is just as much out of his hands as it is out of his brothers' hands.

The interweaving of J and E in v. 28 also offers a number of avenues for development in oral performance. The verse reports the inter-

---

59. In the J version, the brothers are the subject of the verb "sold." In the combined text, the Midianites become the subject of the verb. The attempt by Robert E. Longacre to show that the brothers are the subject of the verb in the present text is, in our view, fanciful (see his *Joseph: A Story of Divine Providence* [Winona Lake, Ind.: Eisenbrauns, 1989] 31). W. Lee Humphreys (*Joseph and His Family: A Literary Study* [Columbia: University of South Carolina Press, 1988]

36) proposes that v. 28 is ambiguous; either the brothers or the Midianites could be the subject of the verb: "As the text now stands, syntactical ambiguity signals a breakdown in the ability of the brothers fully to shape events." Humphreys concedes that, for the brothers to be the subject of the verb, the Midianites and Ishmaelites need to be one and the same. The effect of this is to make v. 28 not an ambiguous sentence, but rather a very awkward one.

vention of the Midianites but does not describe their position in relation to the brothers or record any reaction by the brothers to what is going on. A competent storyteller could flesh out these elements in a variety of ways without compromising the story line. In developing the relative positions of the brothers and the Midianites, the pit where Joseph was confined would be an obvious reference point. A pit or well such as this would presumably be in low ground. Hence an oral presentation of the story could have the brothers retire over a rise, out of sight and out of earshot of Joseph's cries (cf. Gen 42:21). Therefore they would not have seen or heard the Midianites draw Joseph out of the pit. In another presentation, the brothers could be portrayed as so engrossed in their meal and the thought of making easy money that they were oblivious to the fact that the Midianites had taken Joseph; or, if they did see them, they were too slow to stop them and perhaps too afraid to try. Each of these options could also be enhanced by two additional elements in the story: the position of Reuben in relation to his brothers and the Midianites and the position of the Ishmaelites when the sale of Joseph was made. In short, v. 28 is a good example of how well a narrative can combine direction of story line and elasticity about detail.

The separation between Reuben and his brothers, which was introduced in vv. 21-22, continues until v. 30. In v. 29 Reuben goes alone to the pit to rescue Joseph and, on finding him gone, returns distraught to his brothers (v. 30). In v. 31, however, the text reports that "they" set out to deceive their father into thinking Joseph was dead. Granted that Reuben has to return home with his brothers and live with his father, the question that arises here is whether v. 31 includes him as an accomplice in the deception. On the basis of his intervention in vv. 21-24 and the distance this placed between him and his brothers, we may be inclined to exclude him

from such a plan. But we must also take into account another possibility exposed by our reflections on vv. 25-28 and its function in the combined text: Did Reuben's initial boldness dissolve into silent fear when confronted by the counter-plan of Judah and his brothers?

Let us reflect on the situation in the narrative at this point. Reuben's plan to rescue Joseph has failed. He is gone and, as far as Reuben knows, he may be dead. The silence that follows Reuben's lament in v. 30 suggests that the brothers themselves do not know what has happened to Joseph—that is, a version in which they did not see the Midianites. More ominously, it may suggest that they know but are concealing the truth from Reuben—that is, a version in which they did see them while Reuben was absent. Whichever of these possibilities is judged more likely, at least the disappearance of Joseph has removed the reason for the initial separation between Reuben and his brothers. With Joseph now effectively out of the way, what purpose is there in maintaining the separation?

The necessity of explaining Joseph's absence to their father may also be interpreted as a unifying factor among the brothers. To present conflicting explanations would only make life more difficult for them. Did Reuben go along with the plan they concocted because he really believed Joseph was dead, or because the alternatives were too difficult to face? Or did Reuben, the eldest brother, concoct the deception himself? These more negative interpretations of Reuben in vv. 31-32 would be not be out of step with the rest of Genesis 37, a chapter in which no member of this troubled family seems to escape the narrative's critical eye.

Verse 35 adds an ironic touch to the account of the brothers' plan to deceive Jacob. Their deception is designed to convince him that Joseph is dead and so end the matter. If they report that he is missing, it is likely Jacob will set out to try to find him. Their deception is a final bid to gain some control of events. At one level the deception succeeds, for Jacob is convinced by the evidence of the bloodstained robe. The irony is that his refusal to be consoled and his family's futile efforts to console him ensure that Joseph is not forgotten. The brothers have failed again, because Jacob's mourning makes Joseph the center of attention even more than before.

The analysis of vv. 1-35 has drawn attention to the different ways in which duality contributes to the meaning of this text. We have explored how the duality of sources has been arranged to advance the story line. We have also explored how this duality has been arranged to enhance the subtlety and complexity of the text's meaning. The ambiguity created at certain points by what the combined text leaves unsaid serves to deepen this complexity.[60] In a society where it is reasonable to presume that the written versions of stories served, among other things, as a basis for oral performance, such ambiguity allows a story to be told in a variety of ways, without necessarily eliminating ambiguity and without compromising the overall story line. So, for example, an oral presentation of the Joseph story could perfectly well proceed along the lines of the present text, right up to v. 36. But v. 36 could not be included; it would be in contradiction with what has preceded.[61]

This verse, which claims that it was the Midianites who sold Joseph in Egypt to Potiphar, is in disagreement with v. 28, where the Midian-ites sell him to Ishmaelites who take him to Egypt. Genesis 39:1 complicates matters further: on the one hand, it agrees with 37:28, against 37:36, that it was the Ishmaelites who brought Joseph to Egypt; on the other hand, it agrees with v. 36 that Joseph was bought by Potiphar. The discrepancy over the sale of Joseph in Egypt—whether from Midianites or Ishmael-ites—cannot be harmonized therefore without placing undue strain on the meaning of the texts.[62]

Despite this discrepancy, it is reasonable to expect that these texts are meant to function within the story. It would have been easy to elim-inate the discrepancy by replacing the reference to Midianites in 37:36 with Ishmaelites.[63] It would then be in agreement with 37:28 and 39:1. An editorial change such as this could have been made in v. 36 at a number of stages in the text's history of transmission. The discrepancy could also have been eliminated by suppressing v. 36 altogether and ending the chapter with v. 35. It is surely significant that neither of these options was taken up.

It is worthwhile focusing on the narrative function of 37:36 and 39:1, before returning to the issue of discrepancy. A clue to their function can be found in the analysis of 37:28. As pointed out earlier, this is a verse that advances the story line in a telling and dramatic way. A close look at 37:36 and 39:1 shows that they perform a simi-lar, if not so dramatic, function. The contribu-

---

60. Sternberg devotes considerable attention to the significance of "gaps" or points of ambiguity in Old Testament narrative (*Poetics of Biblical Narrative*). He does not, however, consider the significance these gaps may have had for the oral performance of stories.

61. To press this further: the Joseph story can be told with Ishmaelites, or it can be told with Midian-ites, or it can be told as a blend of both. All three will be different stories. The blending has to be achieved. In an oral performance, conflicting aspects would be harmonized in one way or another. Notably, the present text does not do so in Gen 37:36 and 39:1. As a further example: the Joseph story can be told with Judah as protagonist, or it can be told with Reuben as protagonist, or it can be told as a subtle blend of both. Again, all three will be different stories.

62. As does Longacre, *Joseph*, 31.

63. According to Noth, something similar hap-pened in Gen 37:21. The original subject of the verb—Judah—was replaced by Reuben to create a smoother combined text. As noted earlier, it is disput-able whether this change is desirable or necessary.

tion of 37:36 to the story line is to move the narrative on from the sorrowing Jacob in vv. 34-35 to the report of the sale of Joseph in Egypt. Contrary to what his father believes, Joseph is far from dead; he has been sold to Potiphar, the captain of Pharaoh's guard.[64] By naming Joseph's purchaser and his prominent position, v. 36 may even be foreshadowing Joseph's rise to power in Egypt. If so, it provides an ironic contrast to Jacob's conviction that he has gone down to Sheol. Genesis 39:1 is a good example of what is variously called a resumptive repetition or envelope construction. It picks up the thread of the main story, after the episode of Judah and Tamar, by recalling elements of 37:36—Joseph's sale in Egypt and the name of the man who purchased him.

If, on the analogy of the complexity observed in vv. 1-35, we now view the discrepancy between 37:28, 36 and 39:1 as another type of complexity, then some insight may be gained into how it functions in the narrative. A difference between the two types of complexity lies in the way they are signaled in the narrative. In vv. 1-35 complexity is indicated in an oblique way, by what is left unstated as much as by what is stated. This creates a richness of ambiguity in the text, allowing for alternative ways both of understanding parts of the story and of telling these parts of the story. With v. 36 complexity is indicated in a bold, even disruptive, way. However, this does not exclude it from performing a function similar to one aspect of the complexity identified in vv. 1-35; that is, v. 36 can point to a way of telling how Joseph was sold in Egypt different from that indicated by v. 28.

In support of this understanding of the function of v. 36, it may be pointed out that the story of the kidnap and sale of Joseph in Egypt can, like the flood story, be told only once.[65] This imposes constraints on the way a text that does not employ modern techniques such as footnoting is able to signal alternative ways of telling a part of the story. The inclusion of the alternatives—that Joseph was sold in Egypt by Ishmaelites (v. 28) or Midianites (v. 36)—does cause disruption in the text. But, given the likely conventions of Israel's scribes, there was probably no more satisfactory way that such information could have been incorporated within the story to perform the function outlined.

The complexity around this simple issue of the identity of Joseph's vendors is symptomatic of a deeper aspect of this kind of narrative. There is immense complexity of perspective into human conflict within a family, carefully orchestrated in the various ways that episodes are told. Questions of conflict and resolution form the primary focus of the whole Joseph story. Pursuing it further here is regrettably not feasible within the present constraints.

Conclusion

The analysis of Genesis 37 given here makes no claim to be exhaustive. Its objective has been the modest one of identifying areas of duality in the chapter, in particular those that are identified by Noth as belonging to the constitutive sources of the Pentateuch, and of examining their function within the chapter.

Genesis 37 is a dramatic narrative of conflict between Joseph and his brothers and of their

---

64. R. Alter draws attention nicely to the element of continuity between v. 35 and v. 36 but does not comment on the disruption caused by the mention of the Midianites in v. 36 (*The Art of Biblical Narrative* [New York: Basic Books, 1981] 5).

65. In contrast to the three versions of the "ancestress in danger" in Gen 12:10-20, 20:1-18, and 26:1-11, Genesis 37 is an integral part of the overall story of Joseph, too important and extensive to be told more than once.

attempts to resolve the conflict by ridding themselves of him. The arc of this narrative reaches
from the first report of conflict within the family
in v. 2 to vv. 31-35, where the brothers deceive
their father into thinking Joseph is dead. Within
this arc there is the buildup of tension between
Joseph and his brothers in vv. 2-11, the dangerous errand on which Joseph is sent by his father
in vv. 12-17, and the events in vv. 18-30 surrounding the brothers' attempts to resolve the
conflict on their terms. Verse 36 does not lie
within this dramatic arc.[66] In recounting the sale
of Joseph in Egypt to the high-ranking official
Potiphar, it moves the story forward to the
threshold of the next stage, namely, Joseph's
adventures in Egypt and his eventual rise to
power there.

Within the narrative arc from vv. 2-35, the
duality of the sources has been skillfully
deployed to advance the story line and to
enhance its dramatic quality. This occurs in the
two key areas of tension within the story: (1) the
conflict between Joseph and his brothers; and
(2) their attempts to resolve this conflict on their
terms. The sense of mounting conflict between
Joseph and his brothers in vv. 2-11 is enhanced
by the combination of P and J. The drama of the
events surrounding the brothers' attempt to get
rid of Joseph is intensified by the skillful interweaving of J and E. Of particular significance
here is the effect of combining the J and E versions in v. 28. In the J version, the brothers sell
Joseph to the Ishmaelites according to plan. In
the combined text, this plan is short-circuited in
a highly ironic fashion by passing Midianites,
who make off with Joseph and sell him to the
Ishmaelites. What looks to be a simple combination of sources in effect works a remarkable
transformation of the story, intensifying its
dramatic quality and giving it added depth and
complexity.

Duality also enhances the storytelling
potential of the text. As has been pointed out,
it is quite possible that Old Testament stories
were recorded not only for reading purposes
but also as a basis for oral performance. The
interweaving of sources stimulates reflection on
the relationship between elements in the story
at certain points: for example, between Reuben
and his brothers. It also stimulates reflection
by giving the story added complexity. At
other points it introduces ambiguity, allowing
the competent storyteller to develop the
dramatic quality of the story by exploiting
the ambiguity.

Verse 36 initially looks to be quite out of
character in such a narrative. Its report that
Joseph was sold in Egypt by Midianites clashes
with the information given in v. 28. When we
realize that it falls outside the narrative arc that
reaches from v. 2 to v. 35, however, it is possible
to see how it functions as part of the larger story
of Joseph. It moves the narrative forward from
the figure of the grieving Jacob in v. 35 to report
the sale of Joseph in Egypt. The disruptive element in the verse, the identification of the sell-
ers as the Midianites, is strategically located outside the narrative arc of vv. 2 to 35 so that it does
not affect the dramatic quality of this part of the
Joseph story. Nevertheless, this "safe" location
of the disruptive element also allows it to have a
legitimate and meaningful role. It can serve as
a pointer to another way in which a part of the
Joseph story may be told.

---

66. Von Rad (*Genesis*, 350) comments that if the
narrative did not have Gen 37:36, the reader would
expect no continuation in the story after v. 35.

Interpretation of the
Deliverance at the Sea

KEY: **Yahwist**/Priestly/*Elohist*
(Source division according to Martin Noth)

EXODUS 13:17 *When Pharaoh let the people go, God did not lead them by way of the land of the Philistines, although that was nearer; for God thought, "If the people face war, they may change their minds and return to Egypt."* [18]*So God led the people by the roundabout way of the wilderness toward the Red Sea. The Israelites went up out of the land of Egypt prepared for battle.* [19]*And Moses took with him the bones of Joseph who had required a solemn oath of the Israelites, saying, "God will surely take notice of you, and then you must carry my bones with you from here."* [20]**They set out from Succoth, and camped at Etham, on the edge of the wilderness.** [21]**The** LORD **went in front of them in a pillar of cloud by day, to lead them along the way, and in a pillar of fire by night, to give them light, so that they might travel by day and by night.** [22]**Neither the pillar of cloud by day nor the pillar of fire by night left its place in front of the people.**

14 Then the LORD said to Moses: [2]Tell the Israelites to turn back and camp in front of Pi-hahiroth, between Migdol and the sea, in front of Baal-zephon; you shall camp opposite it, by the sea. [3]Pharaoh will say of the Israelites, 'They are wandering aimlessly in the land; the wilderness has closed in on them.' [4]I will harden Pharaoh's heart, and he will pursue them, so that I will gain glory for myself over Pharaoh and all his army; and the Egyptians shall know that I am the LORD. And they did so.

[5] *When the king of Egypt was told that the people had fled,* **the minds of Pharaoh and his officials were changed toward the people, and they said, "What have we done, letting Israel leave our service?"** [6]*So he had his chariot made ready, and took his army with him;* [7]*he took six hundred picked chariots and all the other chariots of Egypt with officers over all of them.* [8]The LORD hardened the heart of Pharaoh king of Egypt and he pursued the Israelites, who were going out boldly. [9]**The Egyptians pursued them,** all Pharaoh's horses and chariots, his chariot drivers and his army; they overtook them camped by the sea, by Pi-hahiroth, in front of Baal-zephon.

[10] As Pharaoh drew near, **the Israelites looked back, and there were the Egyptians advancing on them; and they were in great fear.** The Israelites cried out to the LORD.[67] [11]*They said to Moses, "Was it because there were no graves in Egypt that you have taken us away to die in the wilderness? What have you done to us, bringing us out of Egypt?* [12]*Is this not the very thing we told you in Egypt, 'Let us alone and let us serve the Egyptians'? For it would have been better for us to serve the Egyptians than to die in the wilderness.'* [13]**But Moses said to the people, "Do not be afraid, stand firm, and see the deliverance that the LORD will accomplish for you today; for the Egyptians whom you see today you shall never see again.** [14]**The** LORD **will fight for you, and you have only to keep still."**

[15] Then the LORD said to Moses, "Why do you cry out to me? Tell the Israelites to go for-

---

67. The NRSV has been slightly modified here, following the RSV in order to mirror the Hebrew more closely.

ward. [16]But you lift up your staff, and stretch out your hand over the sea and divide it, that the Israelites may go into the sea on dry ground. [17]Then I will harden the hearts of the Egyptians so that they will go in after them; and so I will gain glory for myself over Pharaoh and all his army, his chariots, and his chariot drivers. [18]And the Egyptians shall know that I am the LORD, when I have gained glory for myself over Pharaoh, his chariots, and his chariot drivers."

19 The angel of God who was going before the Israelite army moved and went behind them; **and the pillar of cloud moved from in front of them and took its place behind them.** [20]**It came between the army of Egypt and the army of Israel. And so the cloud was there with the darkness, and it lit up the night; one did not come near the other all night.**

21 Then Moses stretched out his hand over the sea. **The LORD drove the sea back by a strong east wind all night, and turned the sea into dry land;** and the waters were divided. [22]The Israelites went into the sea on dry ground, the waters forming a wall for them on their right and on their left. [23]The Egyptians pursued, and went into the sea after them, all of Pharaoh's horses, chariots, and chariot drivers. [24]**At the morning watch the LORD in the pillar of fire and cloud looked down upon the Egyptian army, and threw the Egyptian army into panic.** [25]*He clogged their chariot wheels so that they turned with difficulty.* **The Egyptians said, "Let us flee from the Israelites, for the LORD is fighting for them against Egypt."**

26 Then the LORD said to Moses, "Stretch out your hand over the sea, so that the water may come back upon the Egyptians, upon their chariots and chariot drivers." [27]So Moses stretched out his hand over the sea, **and at dawn the sea returned to its normal depth. As the Egyptians fled before it, the LORD tossed the Egyptians into the sea.** [28]The waters returned and covered the chariots and the chariot drivers, the entire army of Pharaoh that had followed them into the sea; not one of them remained. [29]But the Israelites walked on dry ground through the sea, the waters forming a wall for them on their right and on their left.

30 **Thus the LORD saved Israel that day from the Egyptians; and Israel saw the Egyptians dead on the seashore.** [31]**Israel saw the great work that the LORD did against the Egyptians. So the people feared the LORD and believed in the LORD and in his servant Moses.**

Interpretation

Two factors are of controlling significance for presenting an interpretation of the narrative of the deliverance at the sea in our present context. First, it is revered as the narrative that has come to typify the exodus, the one experience of salvation that became symbolic above all else for Israel. Second, although "the lack of unity in the account of the sea event has been recognized for well over a hundred years,"[68] and although the Priestly and Yahwist sources identified by Noth are coherent and complete, still the text has been put together so well that its duality, although evident, can be easily subordinated to its unity.

The consistency of character in the two principal narrative threads is extremely clear. What is less clear is the necessity for dividing the text between these two sources. This is particularly the case if any credibility is given to a metaphorical interpretation of the "wall" that the waters formed on Israel's right and left, as argued, for

---

68. B. S. Childs, *Exodus* (OTL; London: SCM, 1974) 218. For a literary study of the present text, see J. L. Ska, *Le Passage de la Mer* [AnBib 109; Rome: Biblical Institute Press, 1986).

example, by Umberto Cassuto.[69] Once again, with Noth what is possible is not by that fact necessary—especially in the source analysis of biblical texts. Our first task, then, is to show that, to remain within the conventions of Hebrew narrative, it is necessary to divide the account of the deliverance at the sea between two narrative strands.

A strange irony is worth noting here. When the exodus narrative is distributed between the Priestly and Yahwist sources, the result is two accounts of two clearly miraculous events. In the P account, at God's command Moses stretches out his hand over the sea and divides the waters into two walls, piled up to either side forming a wall to right and left, and the people of Israel pass through on dry ground, whereas the pursuing Egyptians are swamped when Moses again stretches out his hand and the waters come back. In the J account, the pillar of cloud moves to provide protection while God drives back the sea with a strong east wind all night, and in the morning God from the pillar panics the Egyp-

tians so that they flee from the people of Israel and are tossed by God into the returning sea. Both accounts are clearly miraculous.

The irony emerges when a resistance to the division of the biblical text into sources leads to a desire to demonstrate that this is a single unified text. In the separation of P and J, the difference is unmistakable: P's sea is divided, forming a wall on either side of Israel, and the Egyptians are in hot pursuit when they are drowned; J's sea is blown back by the wind, therefore to one side, and the Egyptians are in full flight when they are drowned. In Cassuto's attempt to construe a unified text founded on solid and attentive exegesis, the walls of water have to be taken as metaphoric hyperbole, and the various features of the text are explained in terms of a felicitous combination of largely natural phenomena. Ironically, the endeavor to maintain the unity of the text is at the cost of reducing the miraculous deliverance, confessed in faith, to a remarkable coincidence of exceptional circumstances occurring at just the right time to save Israel.[70]

---

69. "An exceptionally low tide at the Red Sea was liable to reduce the waters of the Sea of Reeds considerably, and the east wind blowing violently all night could have dried up the little water left in the narrow channel of the lake, where the bed of the lake is highest and hardest. North and south of the strait, the waters of the Sea of Reeds remained, but in the middle a ford was created. In this way we can understand the passage: . . . *the waters being a wall to them* (hyperbole) *on their right hand and on their left*—north and south of the ford" (Umberto Cassuto, *The Book of Exodus* [Jerusalem: Magnes, 1967] 168).

70. The interpreter's intentions are not at issue, only the outcome of the interpretation. "I have no wish whatsoever to rationalize the Biblical story. The narrative clearly intends to relate a miraculous event, and whoever attempts to explain the entire episode rationally does not in fact interpret the text. . . . The miracle consisted in the fact that at the very moment when it was necessary, in just the manner conducive to the achievement of the desired goal, and on a scale that was abnormal, there occurred, in accordance with the Lord's will, phenomena that brought about Israel's salvation" (Cassuto, *Book of Exodus*, 168; see n. 69, above).

A totally unconnected Australian newspaper report on Lake George, near Canberra, quotes a local com-

ment: "You can stand in one spot one day and there'll be water everywhere, but the next day it'll be way in the distance. The explanation of this 'mystery' is that because the lake is so shallow, a good wind can blow the lake back on itself, and reduce or increase the level for an incredible distance." The report adds, "But the lake was dangerous—a stiff southerly breeze can produce big waves, and there have been tragedies. In the late 1950s a group of young men lost their lives during a boating expedition" (*The Canberra Times*, 18 April 1989). Although an event of this sort might be imagined, it is not what the biblical text describes. Cf. Martin Noth: "Even J does not, as used to be widely assumed earlier, describe the events in a basically 'natural' way, so that we cannot just make a number of deletions in his account to obtain an essentially 'rational, historical' report" (*Exodus* [OTL; Philadelphia: Westminster, 1962] 119–20).

The scientific theory confirming these anecdotal observations and explaining how such an event is possible is provided by Doron Nof and Nathan Paldor, "Are There Oceanographic Explanations for the Israelites' Crossing of the Red Sea?" *Bulletin of the American Meteorological Society* 73/3 (1992) 305–14—interestingly, without reference to Cassuto. Noth's comment stands. See the discussion at the end of this chapter.

If the walls of water are understood as "piled up" to either side, a unified text is out of the question. But the observant reader will have noticed that the "piled up" is not in the biblical narrative of Exodus 14; it echoes rather the song in Exodus 15—"at the blast of your nostrils the waters piled up, the floods stood up in a heap; the deeps congealed in the heart of the sea" (15:8). It is also reminiscent of the Jordan crossing—"the waters flowing from above stood still, rising up in a single heap far off at Adam" (Josh 3:16). Therefore the issue of duality needs to be examined against the background of Cassuto's understanding of these walls metaphorically, as two lakes protecting Israel to north and south.

Only when the duality has been clearly grasped does the unity become all the more striking and the art of the compiler the more admirable.

The bulk of this exodus account is constituted by J and P. For P, the name of the LORD (YHWH) has now been revealed (cf. Exod 6:2-9), and it is available to be freely used. The Yahwist and Priestly sources, therefore, will no longer be distinguished by their use of the divine names, as they were in Genesis. The passage has the added interest that both the P and J accounts are thought to have been preserved in their entirety. From this point of view, it is a particularly excellent example of the compiler's art.

Foregrounding Duality

The duality in the exodus account can best be seen by starting with the central core of the narrative. The thread of the narrative can be taken up with Moses' first address to the people of Israel. He calls for moral fortitude: "Do not be afraid, stand firm." He promises deliverance by the LORD, and that "the Egyptians whom you see today you shall never see again." The final assurance is that the LORD will do the fighting for Israel: "You have only to keep still" (or "to keep silent"). On Moses' part, this is exemplary leadership and an example of faith that is kept strong and sure in a threatening situation.

It is puzzling, therefore, first to have the LORD reply to Moses, "Why do you cry out to me?" The reproach is addressed to Moses himself; the "you" is singular. But Moses has not cried out to the LORD; he has exhorted the people of Israel to stand firm in faith.[71] Second, the command "Tell the Israelites to go forward" (v. 15b) is in puzzling contrast to the preceding "You have only to keep still" (v. 14b). The latter might be understood metaphorically, alongside the earlier "Do not be afraid, stand firm" (v. 13), or be taken in the literal sense of silence during the crossing of the sea. But the movement of the pillar of cloud belies this (v. 19b). The pillar of cloud moves from in front of Israel to take a stand behind them, so that the Israelite and Egyptian forces were separated all night. While one might conceivably imagine both groups proceeding forward at the same speed and maintaining the same distance, this is scarcely the case envisaged. Without the pillar, Israel lacks guidance, especially at night; the pillar now literally stands (Heb.; NRSV, "took its place") behind Israel, between them and the Egyptians.[72] Even though part of v. 20 is unclear, the picture is of two stationary camps, kept apart by the pillar all through the night.[73] "One did not come near the other all night" (v. 20b).

---

71. To appeal here, as Cassuto does, to Moses' participation in Israel's cry to the LORD in v. 10 is to indulge in covert source criticism (see *Book of Exodus*, 165). It is not an interpretation of the present text, where the people's cry has been met by a vigorous and faith-filled response from Moses in vv. 13-14.

72. "The expression *stood* instead of *went*, used pre-

viously, signifies that the pillar of cloud [after its change of position] remained stationary, not moving from its new site" (Cassuto, *Book of Exodus*, 166).

73. Verse 19 suggests that the "angel of God" and the pillar are identical, so our attention can focus on the pillar for the present.

So there is opposition, first between the portrayal of Moses standing firm in faith and Moses being reprimanded apparently for lack of faith; and second, between Israel held stationary in camp all night protected by the pillar and Israel going forward into the sea at God's command.

To understand the text here closely, it is necessary to appeal in some form to the compilation of differing traditions.

The motif of "all night" is followed up promptly in v. 21: "The LORD drove the sea back by a strong east wind *all night*, and turned the sea into dry land." At this point we have to face another difficulty. The sentence just quoted is preceded by the statement that "Moses stretched out his hand over the sea" and followed by the statement that "the waters were divided." The sequence formed is barely able to stand up to close examination.

> Then Moses stretched out his hand over the sea. The LORD drove the sea back by a strong east wind all night, and turned the sea into dry land; and the waters were divided. (14:21)

At the limit of probability, one might attempt to interpret Moses' gesture as a sign to the LORD and to read the note about the waters being divided as an explanation of how the sea came to be turned into dry land.

The only possible way of understanding a division of the waters resulting from a strong east wind would be to envisage the wind reducing the water level until it fell off to either side of a causeway.[74] Were this the picture intended, a more accurate text would have said that the wind blowing all night turned *a path through the sea* into dry land.

The insuperable difficulty for this interpretation comes from the instructions given Moses by God earlier, in vv. 15-18. There Moses is commanded to "tell the Israelites to go forward"—not to wait all night. Then Moses is told to "lift up your staff, and stretch out your hand over the sea and divide it, that the Israelites may go into the sea on dry ground." There is no mention of any action by God or any reference to the east wind. Once the sentence "The LORD drove the sea back by a strong east wind all night, and turned the sea into dry land" is removed, what God commands in vv. 15-16 is exactly what is carried out in vv. 21-22. The command and compliance then become clear and exact.

Command

> Stretch out your hand over the sea and divide it, that the Israelites may go into the sea on dry ground. (v. 16)

Compliance

> Moses stretched out his hand over the sea and the waters were divided, and the Israelites went into the sea on dry ground. (vv. 21-22*)[75]

The upshot is clear: Exod 14:21 is not a unified text. It combines elements from two accounts. In one, the sea is driven back by a strong east wind all night, the entire seabed becoming dry land. In the other, Moses follows God's command precisely: he stretches out his hand and divides the sea so that there is dry ground, with the waters to right and left. Any attempt to understand vv. 21-22 as they stand in the present text as a compliance with the divine command in vv. 15-16 is a refusal to accept the plain meaning of vv. 15-16.

---

74. This is the view of the "wall" of water on either side of the Israelites, maintained by Cassuto (*Book of Exodus*, 167–68).

75. The compliance makes no reference to Moses' staff. Not every detail needs to be repeated to the point of obsession.

Again, to understand the text here closely, it is necessary to appeal in some form to the compilation of differing traditions.

One further sequence needs to be considered.

In v. 22, the Israelites entered into the midst of the sea (*bětôk hayyām*) on dry ground, with the waters a wall to right and left.

In v. 23, the Egyptians, their horses, chariots, and chariot drivers, are portrayed pursuing after Israel into the midst of the sea (*'el tôk hayyām*), presumably the sea being still a wall to right and left.

In v. 24, it is reported that at the end of the night ("At the morning watch") the LORD in the pillar of fire and cloud looked down upon the Egyptian army (camp) and threw the Egyptian army (camp) into panic. Both times, the reference is literally to "the camp of the Egyptians," last mentioned in v. 20.

In v. 25, their chariots are having trouble and the Egyptians are quoted as saying, "Let us flee from the Israelites, for the LORD is fighting for them against Egypt."

In v. 26, the command is given Moses to stretch out his hand over the sea, so that the water may come back upon the Egyptians, their chariots and chariot drivers, the group who pursued Israel into the sea in v. 23.

In v. 27, Moses is reported to have stretched out his hand over the sea and the sea returned at dawn to its normal depth. As the Egyptians fled before it (literally: fleeing "to meet it," *liqrā'tô*), the LORD tossed the Egyptians into the sea (*bětôk hayyām*).

In v. 28, it is reported that the waters returned and covered the chariots and the chariot drivers, the entire army of Pharaoh, following them into the sea;[76] not one of them remained.

The difficulties are considerable.

The timing is out of kilter.

In v. 20, the pillar separated the Egyptian and Israelite camps "all night."

Yet, in vv. 22-23, Israel has entered the sea and the Egyptians are reported pursuing them before any mention of the morning watch (the last watch of the night, v. 24) and the dawn (v. 27).

The location is out of kilter.

In vv. 22-23, the Israelites have gone into the sea between the walls of water and Egyptians have pursued after them.

In v. 24, it is from the pillar, which in v. 20 was keeping Egyptian and Israelite camps apart all night, that at dawn the LORD panicked the Egyptians. Both time and place argue for a venue on the shore. In terms of time, the pillar was to keep the two camps separate all night—therefore, not to move during the night. In terms of place, the pillar stood between the two camps—therefore, on the shore. Of course God's action could range into the distance from atop the pillar, but that is unnecessary and out of the question since the Egyptians have been unable to move all night because of the pillar stationed between them and Israel. Instead, the natural implication is that the action takes place where the two

---

76. Literally, "coming after them into the sea." The Hebrew has a participle. In the present text, where the reference to past time is certain, the translation "that had followed them into the sea" is legitimate— the Egyptians had already turned and fled (v. 27). In a source, where the situation remains open, the natural translation would be "that was following them into the sea."

camps were kept apart all night—not in the middle of the sea but on the shore. This is reinforced by the vocabulary of v. 24 that twice speaks of the Egyptian "camp," as in v. 20. It is reasonable to assume that we are dealing with one and the same pillar (against Cassuto). Taken together, vv. 24-25 indicate that at the end of the night the LORD from the pillar panicked the Egyptian camp; as in their panic they moved or regrouped, their chariot wheels were impeded and they are portrayed choosing to flee from before Israel, recognizing the LORD's action on Israel's behalf (promised in v. 14).

Easy opportunities for removing tensions are ignored.

In v. 25, it would have been easy to follow the Egyptian proposal to flee with a note that the Egyptians turned and fled from the sea. Specifying either that they did indeed reverse direction or that they were fleeing out of the sea would have easily clarified what is left unclear. Flight from their overnight camp does not involve the same reversal of an active pursuit.

In v. 26, it would have been easy to note that Moses was commanded to extend his hand to stop the wind; instead, the association is directly with sea and water.

In v. 27, Moses is to stretch out his hand so that the water may come back upon the Egyptians; yet after he does so, it is noted that the sea returned at dawn. Naturally, it is possible for Moses to have stretched out his hand at dawn, but the sequence of command and compliance is disturbed by

the presence of two signals for the return of the water. What was noted for vv. 15-16 and 21-22 is true here, if in more muted fashion. It would have been easy to resolve the tension by altering the order—And at dawn Moses stretched out his hand over the sea and the sea returned—but the text does not have that.

Again in v. 27, the description of the Egyptians literally fleeing to meet the sea could easily have been changed to fleeing from or through the sea. The NRSV translates "fled before it"; the RSV has "fled into it"; the Hebrew has literally "fleeing to meet it," or, taken as a preposition, fleeing "toward it" or "against it."[77] It is not the most natural image to use of forces pouring back across a causeway, where the sea is still present on either side.[78] It is quite inappropriate for the situation where walls of water collapse upon the army in their midst. What it fits is the image of troops fleeing across the open seabed while the sea, which had been driven back by the wind all night, was now at dawn suddenly rushing back toward them to its place.

In v. 28, after the Egyptian panic and flight, it would have been easy to change the description of the Egyptians, since the present text is most directly understood as portraying the Egyptians in pursuit of Israel (literally: "coming after them into the sea," *habbā'im 'aḥărêhem bayyām*; the NRSV's "had followed" is forced on it by the present context). To replace "coming after them" with "fleeing from them" would have been easy.

---

77. Struggle against the sea is what the Hebrew does not reflect. "Flee against the tide" might be an appropriate metaphor for comparison, if we bear in mind that it evokes forces going in opposing directions. The Egyptians are portrayed fleeing toward the returning sea.

78. Cassuto depicts the Egyptians "endeavouring to flee from the waves that were pouring over them from both sides," without explaining how this emerges from the text (*Book of Exodus*, 171). It does not. It emerges from the context and the classical understanding of the "walls" as piled up on either side.

There are duplications without apparent literary value.

The sea returns in v. 27; the waters return in v. 28. The LORD tosses the Egyptians into the sea in v. 27; the waters overwhelm Pharaoh's army in v. 28.

There are variations in the use of language.

The Egyptian forces are referred to as "camp of the Egyptians" in v. 24 (twice) and simply as Egyptians in vv. 25b and 27 (twice); in vv. 23, 26, and 28 the Egyptians are always referred to in combination with Pharaoh and/or chariots and chariot drivers. The case of the language for the sea is more complicated and will be discussed below. Here it is enough to note that "the waters" for the sea is used only in vv. 22, 26b, and 28. An appeal to normal or artful linguistic variation is not helpful, especially when it is noted that the division of the text into two coherent narratives resolves all the linguistic differences.

Basically, the differences we see here are the continuation of the two polar oppositions discussed first. There is the continuation of the opposition between the timing and nature of events, with either the two camps that stayed apart all night or the Israelites who during the night went forward into the sea at Moses' command, pursued by the Egyptians. There is the continuation of the opposition between the means for moving the sea, either by a strong wind all night or divided by the stretching out of Moses' hand in precise compliance with God's command. This section adds a third opposition: between the panicked Egyptians in full flight from their camp on the shore at dawn and the aggressive Egyptians in hot pursuit into the divided sea at night. (Note that, in this treatment, Israel's entry into the sea by night derives from the final biblical text; it is not present in the P narrative.)

Once again, to understand the text here closely, it is necessary to appeal in some form to the compilation of differing traditions.

When these three moments in the text are assessed, it is scarcely possible to maintain that the narrative follows the conventions of a coherent and unified biblical text. It can only be regarded as a single text at the cost of major and significant distortion. Respect for the text and its portrayal of God's commands and Israel's compliance with them requires us to pay close attention to its features.[79]

These features can be identified as two different sets of phenomena that are blended in the text. When these phenomena are traced separately, two totally coherent and complete narratives are found in the text. Each narrative contains all of the phenomena associated with it and none of the others; each is fully exclusive of the other. The sets of phenomena can be simply identified; listing all the details associated with each becomes quite complex.

The first set may be identified as associated with Moses' hand; the second set may be identified as associated with God's wind.

The Priestly Narrative

In the narrative associated with Moses' hand, Israel is told to turn back toward Egypt and told where to camp by the sea (14:1-2). This divine stratagem will deceive Pharaoh and, as in the plague stories, God will harden Pharaoh's heart and win glory over Pharaoh and his army and be acknowledged (vv. 3-4).

God then hardens Pharaoh's heart (v. 8), and Pharaoh pursues the Israelites with all his horses

---

79. Close attention to such features may force us to the conclusion that we are not dealing with a *single* original text; they need not impede us in the awareness that we are dealing with a *meaningful* text.

and chariots, chariot drivers, and army (v. 9). This narrative will consistently refer to the multiple elements composing Pharaoh's force. The Egyptians overtake Israel exactly where God had told the latter to camp.

At Pharaoh's approach, the Israelites cry out to God (v. 10). God responds to the cry, commanding Moses to divide the sea so that Israel might enter the sea on dry ground (*yabbāšâ*). The Egyptians—Pharaoh, his army, his chariots, and his chariot drivers—will enter after them because God will harden their hearts to gain glory and be acknowledged (vv. 15-18). Moses complies with God's command. He stretches out his hand, the waters (*hammayim*) are divided, Israel enters the sea on dry ground (*yabbāšâ*) between the walls of water (*hammayim*), and the Egyptians pursue—all of Pharaoh's horses, chariots, and chariot drivers (vv. 21-23).

Then God commands Moses to stretch out his hand again over the sea so that the waters (*hammayim*) may come back upon the Egyptians—their chariots and chariot drivers (v. 26). Again Moses complies with God's command. He stretches out his hand and the waters (*hammayim*) return, swamping the Egyptians—chariots and chariot drivers, the entire army of Pharaoh (vv. 27-28). So Israel is saved.

The Yahwist Narrative

In the narrative associated with God's wind, Israel is given God's guidance by the pillar, whether of cloud or fire, obviating the need for divine directions (13:20-21).

Pharaoh's pursuit is motivated by a change of mind about permitting the labor force to leave (v. 5). There is no need for Pharaoh to be deceived or his heart hardened.

The Egyptian pursuit inspires fear among the people of Israel (v. 10). Moses encourages them to stand firm and see the deliverance God will accomplish for them. The fighting will be done by God. Israel's role will be passive (vv. 13-14).

Following Moses' exhortation, the pillar moves to protect Israel from the Egyptians throughout the night. During the night God drives back the sea by a strong east wind, turning the sea (*hayyām*) into dry land (*horābâ*; vv. 19-21). At the end of the night, God from the pillar throws the encamped Egyptian army into a panic so that they seek to flee from the Israelites (vv. 24-25). Finally, at dawn, the sea returns and, as the Egyptians are in flight toward it, God throws them into the sea (*hayyām*; v. 27).

Thus God saved Israel that day and Israel saw the Egyptians dead on the seashore. The people believed in the LORD and in his servant Moses (v. 30-31).

Note that there is no mention in this text of Israel's position in relation to the sea or of their crossing it. The sea serves simply as God's instrument in destroying the Egyptians. God's wind blows it back all night, leaving the seabed dry (v. 21). At dawn, the wind that has blown all night can be assumed to have stopped; so the sea returns. As the Egyptians flee across the dry seabed toward the returning sea, they are wiped out by God's action in tossing them into the sea (v. 27; cf. 15:1, 4, 21). Israel has nothing to do except stay still where they had halted and observe God's deliverance accomplished on their behalf—just as Moses had said (vv. 13-14).

It is not difficult to map out a situation that would render this a feasible scenario, but because this narrative refrains from specifying geographical details and positions, there is no particular point in our doing so. It is worth recalling that, for J, the deliverance at the sea is a part of the wilderness experience. For P, it is the concluding episode in the exodus experience.[80]

---

80. See Childs, *Exodus*, 221–24.

The "Elohist" Text

The text printed in italics is attributed to sources other than P or J; Noth assigns it to the Elohist. What has been said in chapter 4 need not be repeated here under the duality rubric. When foregrounding unity, as in the following section, these passages naturally require appropriate consideration.

Foregrounding Unity

In the present text a new section of the narrative clearly begins with Exod 13:17. It resumes 12:30-33, in which the Israelites are sent forth from Egypt, and the departure itself in 12:37-41. From the outset of the Reed Sea narrative, 13:17 strikes a note of fragility. Despite the wonders that have occurred and the wonders that lie ahead in the narrative, God is still portrayed as thinking that the people of Israel might "change their minds and return to Egypt" if they were confronted by war. Its value in a unified text is to introduce a note of reality to a text that may be read too easily as glorious and marvelous. For all the experience of the plagues, the people probably feel the fear of any column of refugees, and God judges they are likely to be easily frightened. Being "prepared for battle" (v. 18), grouped in a military formation, does not eliminate the possibilities of fear and flight. The passage also sets a direction away from the intensively traveled principal route toward the Mediterranean coast.

God's leadership is specified in 13:21-22; it is provided by the pillar of cloud and pillar of fire. In the previous verses, neither the precise geographical locations nor the details of God's guidance are given, so there is no difficulty integrating the traditions, particularly if vv. 17-18 are seen as a general overview of the direction to be taken on the journey.

Placing God's words to Moses in 14:1-4 after 13:17-22 allows them to be understood as giving some verbal specificity to the guidance given by the pillar, especially in the light of the change of direction. Tension remains. The clear indications of divine guidance in 13:17-22 require that "tell the Israelites to turn back" in 14:2 is understood as a change in God's plan. However, the deception of Pharaoh by leading him to think that Israel was wandering aimlessly in the wilderness opens the possibility that the change of direction was always in God's plan. More problematic than a change of mind is the change in the form of guidance. The Israelites are not told to follow the pillar back toward Pi-hahiroth; they are told to turn back and camp there. Skillful organization of the material helps to minimize these tensions. Also, before a climactic episode in Israel's experience of God, it brings into view three ways in which God guides Israel: the unspecified leading of 13:17-18; the symbolic guidance of 13:21-22; the communicated directions of 14:1-4.

Three different formulations are again skillfully blended in 14:5-9. The basic statement, recurring in three forms, is that Pharaoh set out after Israel with an armed force. There are notable differences. In v. 5a the people have not been released but have fled; in v. 5b the minds–hearts (lēbab) of Pharaoh and his officials are simply changed; in v. 8 it is the LORD who hardens Pharaoh's mind–heart (lēb).

The differences of formulation have been used to advantage in the compilation. The E tradition could not report a change of mind on Pharaoh's part; Israel is said to have fled. Flight implies no authorization from Pharaoh and therefore no decision for Pharaoh to change or regret. This enabled the compiler to separate the report of Israel's flight (v. 5a) from the report of Egypt's mobilizing for pursuit (v. 7) and to insert between them the J report of the change of policy among Pharaoh and his officials and the readying of their forces. E's report of mobilization follows. The P tradition could be placed third, bcause it can be understood to be specifying that Pharaoh's change of mind was due to the LORD's hardening his heart and to be giving further specifics of the military force. J's pursuit note (v. 9aα) is deftly inserted into P's report between the pursuit of Israel (v. 8) and the overtaking of Israel at the sea (v. 9*). The combined text refers first to Pharaoh, then to the Egyptians, and finally to the components of the force. Verse 8 gives the basic statement; v. 9 provides its unfolding.[81]

The value of the compilation lies in the emphasis it gives to the Egyptian response to Israel's departure. The Egyptian determination to pursue Israel is both given as their own decision and interpreted as the LORD hardening their hearts. Beyond that, the threefold piling up of descriptions of the Egyptian pursuit force heightens the sense of menace for Israel: Pharaoh and his army (v. 6); six hundred picked chariots and all the other chariots (v. 7); horses and chariots, chariot drivers, and army (v. 9). There is no doubt about the danger.

The description of Israel's departure as flight (kî bāraḥ hā'ām; v. 5a) poses a puzzle. At one level it is in open contradiction with its surrounding context. Exodus 13:17 has "when Pharaoh let the people go"; literally, the verb used is "to send." Exodus 14:5 has the Egyptians "letting Israel leave our service"; again, the verb is "to send." This is in full harmony with the preceding plague and passover narratives. The hardening of Pharaoh's heart is also in a context where change is implied. At this level, then, the statement that Israel had fled may be understood to preserve a variant tradition.

At another level, however, the reference to flight may be preserving not a different tradition but a different aspect of the episode. It casts a shadow of panic over the whole Israelite movement. Israel may have had Pharaoh's permission, but their leaving Egypt was still the frightened flight of an oppressed minority. This aspect picks up and reinforces the fragility expressed in 13:17. It provides a balance to the more positive picture of Israel's readiness for battle (13:18b and 14:8b) and the LORD's guidance by the pillar of cloud and fire (13:21-22). Yet even this divine guidance has its note of urgency and flight; travel "by day and by night" certainly suggests extreme urgency, if not flight. The combination of confidence and fear is real; both can be appropriate for the experience of trust in God.

The compilation in vv. 10-14 is, again, cleverly done. The J text has: "The Egyptians pursued them and the Israelites looked back, and there were the Egyptians advancing on them; and they were in great fear." The first part of this is back in v. 9a, at the start of the pursuit; so the P equivalent, "As Pharaoh drew near," can replace it at the start of v. 10. The P statement of Israel's cry to the LORD follows. The E tradition in vv. 11-12 serves to unfold and flesh out P's inarticulate cry, though addressed to Moses rather than to God. That, however, permits the use of Moses' response to the people from the J tradition.

The tension left is slight. In v. 10b the Israelites cry out to the LORD. In v. 11a they speak to Moses. At the level of the present text, this may be understood sequentially: the address to Moses follows the cry to the LORD; or, alternatively, what they say to Moses is to be understood as the substance of what is called crying to the LORD. The sequence is a trace out of the ordinary, but it is scarcely intolerable.

The sequence of the next verses is, as we have

---

81. The sequence in the Hebrew of Exod 14:9 is more complicated than the presentation in the NRSV suggests. The Hebrew has the Egyptians pursue after them and overtake them camped by the sea; then follows the specification of Pharaoh's force—"all Pharaoh's horses and chariots, his chariot drivers and his army"—and finally the specific geographical location, "by Pi-hahiroth, in front of Baal-zephon."

seen, more difficult. It is not so much that the LORD addresses Moses after the cry has been raised by the Israelites.[82] Far more significant is the content of what the LORD says; it does not follow on Moses' admirable exhortation of Israel to faith (vv. 13-14). Instead, the LORD spells out the orders for the act of deliverance that lies ahead, as it is depicted in the P tradition.

It is here that the core of duality in this narrative is laid bare. It is appropriate that the two passages should be juxtaposed in their contrariety. In the first, it is Moses who addresses the people, and it is the LORD who will accomplish the deliverance; Israel is to stand firm and be still and see the LORD fight on their behalf (vv. 13-14). In the second, it is the LORD who addresses Moses, and it is Moses who is to perform the principal and visible actions accomplishing the deliverance; when the sea is divided at Moses' gesture, Israel is to move forward into it, while the LORD will harden the Egyptians' hearts so that they pursue Israel and give the LORD victory (vv. 15-18). In both cases, the deliverance is the LORD's; in the compilation, stillness has preceded movement. Otherwise, unity has ceded to duality.

In v. 19a the angel of God makes its first and only appearance in this narrative, at the critical moment when Israel must be protected from the imminent Egyptian onslaught. Nowhere else in this story of deliverance at the sea does the angel rate a mention. The function it performs is identical to that of the pillar. A first reading may be permitted to assume that two instruments of God or manifestations of God were active in this most critical of all moments. If our reading of Hebrew narrative conventions is right, then it is likely that this serves as a reminder that the divine guidance in the narrative may be provided by God's angel, rather than by the remoter symbol of the pillar of cloud or fire. Because one or the other may function in the story, however, there is no reason why both should not function at a key point; the first naive reading is thus confirmed.

The structure of the next section is a brilliant compilation. Two envelope structures themselves form an envelope around the separate but juxtaposed elements of the narrative center. The necessary preparation for the divine deliverance is narrated in v. 21, with the P tradition forming an envelope around the J tradition. At the core of the report of the actual deliverance, the two accounts are juxtaposed side by side (vv. 22-23 and 24-25), as they were for the instructions (vv. 13-18, above).[83] The P tradition again forms an envelope structure around the J tradition in the narrative of the consummation of the deliverance, the destruction of the Egyptians (vv. 26-28).

In v. 21 Moses stretches out his hand, the LORD drives the sea back by a strong wind all night, and the waters are divided. In search of unity, it may be postulated that Moses' gesture invokes the LORD's action, that the wind all night produces the desired effect, and that the final note on the divided waters spells out the exact

---

82. It is worth noting that this little inconsistency could be removed by the simple addition of one consonant to make the verb plural: "Why do you (plural) cry out to me?" Moses would then be addressed for what he was: the representative and leader of the people. Evidently, then, the singular here is not to be put down to carelessness. Perhaps the inconsistency was judged so minimal as to be nonexistent. Perhaps the difference from Exod 14:13-14 was felt so strongly that any attempt to harmonize more closely with v. 10 was unimportant. E. Blum insists on a lacuna in the P text here; in our view, unnecessarily (*Studien zur Komposition des Pentateuch* [BZAW 189; Berlin: Walter de Gruyter, 1990] 260).

83. This comment refers to the juxtaposition of J and P; whether Exod 14:25a was incorporated by J or was a separate addition does not affect matters substantially. These structural observations advance what was begun by Childs (*Exodus*, 227).

nature of this desired effect.[84] Similarly, in vv. 22-25, still foregrounding unity, the Egyptians follow Israel into the sea and, toward the end of the night, are panicked by the LORD and turn and flee, recognizing that the LORD is fighting for Israel.[85] In the final stage of a unified reading, vv. 26-28 portray Moses, now presumably on the far side of the sea, stretching out his hand once more; the wind that the LORD had brought up in response to the gesture now drops and, at dawn, the sea returns to its normal depth and overwhelms the Egyptians. The LORD tossing the Egyptians into the sea is the basic statement (v. 27b); how it happens is unfolded in v. 28. Such a reading is probably standard. The argument from "being" to "being possible" is irrefutable; what is can be. People do read it this way; therefore it is possible to read it this way. Unity triumphs.

Unity is entitled to triumph; the text has been deftly compiled at the same time as duality has been duly respected. Yet the text is deprived of depth and texture if we do not notice what this reading rides over roughshod.

1. There is the matter of sequence or timing. On the one hand, the two camps are separated all night, in conjunction with the wind that blows all night and the sea that returns at dawn. On the other hand, the Israelites have moved into the sea during the night and the Egyptians have pursued them, also during the night.

2. There is the matter of direction. When panicked by the LORD, the Egyptians simply say: "Let us flee from the Israelites"; and they are in full flight when they meet the returning sea. It is rather odd that there is no mention of their turning around in the midst of the sea. It is equally odd that the language of the next verse would ordinarily be understood to describe the Egyptians as those who were still following Israel into the sea (v. 28).[86]

3. There is the matter of the language used:
   a. For the Egyptians. On the one hand, the armies separated all night are both described in v. 20 as "camps" (maḥăneh), and the Egyptian army which is panicked by the LORD just before dawn is twice described in v. 24 in the same way. On the other hand, the Egyptians pursuing Israel into the sea are described as "all of Pharaoh's horses, chariots, and chariot drivers" (v. 23). When Moses is commanded to stretch out his hand again, the waters are to come back on "the Egyptians, upon their chariots and chariot drivers" (v. 26). When the waters return, they swamp "the chariots and the chariot drivers, the entire army of Pharaoh" (v. 28).
   b. For the sea. In the text associated with God's wind, blowing all night, and

---

84. The use of the passive, "the waters were divided," offers a level of ambiguity about the responsible agent that facilitates the combination.

85. When v. 25a is read as part of the present text, it has two possible interpretations. It can spell out how the LORD panicked the Egyptians, after which they decided to flee; or we can assume that, once panicked, the Egyptians turned and fled and in their flight the LORD clogged their chariot wheels. The narrative then follows a quite usual pattern: the actions are narrated before the accompanying speech is given.

For non-Hebrew readers it is worth noting one

reason for not attributing v. 25a to P or J. Verse 25a has a longer word, merkābâ, for chariot than the word rekeb used for chariot everywhere else in the narrative. The longer word stands out as starkly in the text as a white stretch limousine among red subcompacts. If, in the middle of a group of Britons discussing London traffic, a voice is heard to say, "When they are talking about cars, dear, they mean an automobile," it reveals a North American presence; so, here, merkābâ reveals another presence in the context.

86. See also n. 76, above, and the discussion in the text there.

with the army camps, the sea denotes the watery element that is blown back and, returning, deals death and destruction (*yām;* vv. 21* and 27*). In the text associated with Moses' hand, by contrast, the sea denotes the space over which Moses stretches his hand, through which Israel goes, and into which the Egyptians pursue. The contents of this space, the watery element that is divided and, when brought back, deals death and destruction, is consistently called "the waters" (*mayim;* vv. 21*, 22, 26, 28).

c. For the dry seabed. In the text associated with God's wind blowing back the sea, the dry seabed is referred to as *ḥorābâ*, translated by the NRSV as "dry land" (v. 21). In the other references, all to the texts associated with Moses' hand, the dry seabed is referred to as *yabbāšâ*, translated by the NRSV as "dry ground" (vv. 16, 22, 29).

4. Finally, there is the matter of what happens to the sea. It is not difficult to picture the sea being driven back all night by God's wind and, in the morning, returning to swamp the Egyptians in their panic-stricken flight across its bed. It is not difficult to picture the waters divided on the right and left of the Israelites and coming back to swamp the pursuing Egyptians. It

is difficult to combine the two. It is a mark of the compiler's skill that most readers surmount the difficulty with ease—usually allowing the image of the divided sea to take over the scene, rather than achieving a genuine combination.

P's conclusion (v. 29) is not part of the narrative. It is a summary of the total experience: "the Israelites walked on dry ground through the sea."[87] It is almost dryly factual. J's conclusion does not summarize the experience but describes the impact of its outcome on the Israelites: "Israel saw the Egyptians dead on the seashore . . . and believed in the LORD and in his servant Moses" (vv. 30-31).[88] It is highly theological; "thus the LORD saved Israel that day." Read as a unified text, the factual and the theological form a most appropriate combination.

Reflection on the Combination

When we seek the meaning of such a text, we have to pay attention to two clear phenomena. First, the deliverance traditions have been woven into one text, and the interpretation must reflect this unity. Second, the deliverance traditions have twice been juxtaposed in their contrariety at the core of the narrative, in vv. 13-14/15-18 and vv. 22-23/24-25, and the interpretation must reflect this duality.

The interpreter's task is to derive meaning from the text, composed in just this way. There is both close interweaving of the traditions and

---

87. The text is hardly to be construed as implying that Israel marched steadily on dry-shod while the Egyptians were being swamped behind them. Note the use of the perfect tense to achieve distance from the narrative perspective. The action in v. 28a is registered as complete in v. 28b.

88. It is possible that, for J, this was the first Israel knew of the Egyptians' destruction. "Israel remained in their camp and according to v. 30 perhaps saw nothing at all of the actual flight and catastrophe of the

Egyptians, but merely its consequence—the dead Egyptians which the sea threw up on its shores" (Noth, *Exodus,* 118). In this case, v. 31 may be read as expressing Israel's faith after seeing the evidence of their salvation. Otherwise, the two verses are structured chiastically, in the sequence "faith-perception-perception-faith." In v. 31 the movement from perception to faith is delicately evoked in the similarity of the Hebrew verbs "to see" (*wayyar'*) and "to fear" (*wayyîr'û*).

clear juxtaposition of the traditions. The text both reveals and conceals. It is redolent of mystery and also miracle: the mystery of God's will and power to save and the miracle of God's operation. Surprisingly, on close reading of the combined text, it is the mystery that is revealed and the miracle that is concealed.

What is abundantly clear is that Israel is delivered by God in an act of saving grace that can only be called mystery, at which one marvels. What becomes difficult to discover, to the point where it is in fact concealed, is precisely what was the manner of the miracle that God worked to deliver Israel.

When duality is foregrounded and the traditions are separated, the miracles can be described and the situations depicted with clarity. The mystery is more reticent, to be sought here in reflection, as in pondering the marvel of any divine wonder. But when unity is foregrounded and the text read as one, the mystery of the deliverance comes to the fore; the miracle can no longer be described and depicted with quite the same clarity.

The mystery comes to the fore. God's plan—God's guidance and direction—is present in three distinct ways: within God's thought (E), in symbol (J), and in word (P). Similarly, the Egyptian forces and their pursuit are depicted in a piling up of words and images.[89] Israel's dire straits are given urgent emotional force in vv. 11-12. The role of faith in God's will to deliver is doubly emphasized in the juxtaposition of Moses' instructions to Israel and God's instructions to Moses (vv. 13-18).

The manner of the miracle is concealed. We are left uncertain whether, in the middle of the night, Israel and Egypt are in their respective camps or on the march in the middle of the sea. When Moses stretches out his hand, the expected division of the sea does not occur at once; instead, God brings up a strong wind to drive the sea back all night. We are left uncertain whether the emergence of dry ground is the result of the sea's being driven back or divided. We are left uncertain about the Egyptian flight: Were they in the sea fleeing out of it or—leaving a camp on the seashore—were they fleeing into the space where the sea had been?

Were the traditions of deliverance to be arranged sequentially, with an Egyptian force panicked into headlong flight into a returning sea and subsequently another Egyptian force swallowed up in the midst of a divided sea, God's will for the repeated deliverance of Israel would be clear, as would the way in which that deliverance was achieved. The dramatic portrayal of repeated events would draw the focus away from the uniqueness of this expression of God's great goodwill toward Israel. With the text combined, as we have it here, the mystery of God's commitment to deliver is expressed once, in what becomes Israel's uniquely paradigmatic symbol of God's gift of salvation. In order that this faith may be given unique expression, the clear portrayal of the manner of the miracle has to be sacrificed, concealed in a reticent confusion. Theologically, it is a compelling move. The ways of God's operation remain shrouded in uncertainty. The mystery to which faith holds in clarity is God's commitment, the divine desire to deliver.

To ignore the duality so skillfully retained within the combined text would be to ignore a significant aspect of the theology of ancient Israel. Israel's compilers of this text knew that

89. Childs particularly stresses the contrast in the final narrative between the two plans portrayed, God's and Pharaoh's (*Exodus*, 224–26).

their unique expression of faith in the God who delivered them at the sea was not directly based on the raw observation of events. Instead, it was based on two depictions of history with markedly contrasting portrayals of the event, depictions that themselves may have been touched by development in story or celebration in liturgy.[90] Faith is already expressed in the depictions. For example, a strong east wind may be a matter of observation; a strong east wind from God is a statement of faith. Duality emphasizes that in the preserving of different depictions, expressions of faith are to be retained.

The recognition that Israel's compilers "knew that their unique expression of faith . . . was not directly based on the raw observation of events" is important enough to explore further. In this context, it may be helpful to look briefly at the recent "oceanographic explanations" for the deliverance at the sea. The scientific conclusions are that at the north of the Gulf of Suez, strong to moderate overnight winds could blow the sea back about three-quarters of a mile (1.2 km.) and lower the water level by about eight feet (2.5 m.).[91]

Nof and Paldor's claim is modest enough: "It will be argued that our proposed wind crossing mechanism has much in common with the original biblical description because it involves pre-event winds, receding water, and a rapidly returning wave."[92] They conclude: "Whether the above theory explains the crossing or not, it should not affect the religious aspects of the exodus. Believers can find the presence and existence of God in the creation of the wind with its particular properties just as they find it in the establishment of a miracle."[93]

That an event of this kind might form the core for the recitation and celebration of deliverance is hardly to be contested. What needs closer examination is how much it has in common with "the original biblical description." There is little in common with either the present biblical description or the P account. The present account is not to be identified with "pre-event winds, receding water, and a rapidly returning wave." It would be possible for Moses to have summoned the wind with a gesture and stopped it with another, but that is not what the present text describes, especially when its duality is taken fully into consideration. The P account, of course, has no pre-event wind at all and proceeds entirely without it. There are elements in common with only a part of the J story—the behavior of the wind and the sea. The oceanographic and meteorological events in themselves do not generate the role of the pillar in keeping Egypt and Israel apart all night or God's role in panicking the Egyptians in the morning watch. Significantly, there is the likelihood that in the J account there was no crossing at all. The "pre-event winds, receding water, and a rapidly returning wave" are fully *compatible* with the J account, but they are far from being the whole of it.

Reviewing the possibilities, there are at least four versions to be reckoned with.

---

90. For examples of this in Joshua 3–4 and 6, see Campbell, *Study Companion*, 173–82; see also idem, "Old Testament Narrative as Theology," *Pacifica* 4 (1991) 165–80. Note the comment by Childs: "It seems highly probable that the language of the Reed Sea was influenced by the Jordan tradition of the river's crossing which introduced the language of a path through the sea and the river's stoppage. Thus the exodus as the 'going out of Egypt' and the conquest as the 'coming into the land' were joined in a cultic celebration of Israel's deliverance and transmitted together" (*Exodus*, 223).

91. Nof and Paldor, "Oceanographic Explanations," 310–11.

92. Ibid., 309.

93. Ibid., 313.

1. The J biblical version, with wind-driven sea and at daybreak a panicked flight by the Egyptians—and probably no crossing by Israel.
2. The suggested modern version, with wind-driven sea and a crossing.
3. The P biblical version, with Moses' hand dividing the waters for a crossing, with the Israelites pursued by the Egyptians.
4. The present biblical text with mention of the themes associated with both the wind and Moses' hand.

In combining 1 and 3 to form 4, it is clear that the picture of an originating event is not clarified and enhanced. Any such originating event is concealed. Each of 1, 2, and 3 can be associated with an event, miraculous or not. The combination of 1 and 3 removes the event from our reach. We need to bear in mind that both 1 and 3 are already formulated as professions of faith. In 4, after appropriate reflection, the profession of faith is inescapably clear.

The Jordan can be crossed at its fords or dammed by the collapse of its banks. The sea can be blown back and suddenly return. Deliverance may be experienced in many ways. If our texts are to be associated with such scientifically feasible events, however providential their timing, complex processes and much theological reflection stretches between event and text. The texts express faith in divine deliverance.

It is not appropriate in this context to explore the validation of faith statements in relation to the phenomena of experience. It is, however, a valid exegetical conclusion to note that the present biblical text contains two different accounts of what occurred. They are brilliantly combined so as to be almost compatible—but only almost. They remain incompatible. They have been preserved that way by the biblical compilers.

The significance of this is considerable. Since it is clear that the compilers of Exodus 14 went to great trouble to combine two versions while retaining the incompatible features of each, it must be equally clear that they knew they did not have access to the raw data of uninterpreted observation. They were combining and preserving different versions from their traditions. They were professing and celebrating faith, not reporting details of fact—not reporting precisely what occurred. The final text does not function as witness to the remembered event but as witness to the faith professed. The ancient compilers knew this. They might be surprised to discover that we moderns had difficulty with it.

The maintenance of duality within this carefully combined text can only be understood as witness to the conviction in ancient Israel that Israel's history did not declare God to Israel without interpretation. Rather, Israel's theologians and people of faith read and interpreted their experience of history and declared God from it. The unity achieved in the text attests a faith that the passage from Egypt to the wilderness, from slavery to freedom, a passage symbolic of Israel's emergence from the womb of history, was a moment of such significance to Israel it needed to be focused in the uniqueness of a single story, in which Israel expressed their confession of deliverance by the God who was the source and center of their being.

Bibliography

Alter, R. *The Art of Biblical Narrative*. New York: Basic Books, 1981.

Anderson, B. W. "From Analysis to Synthesis: the Interpretation of Genesis 1–11." *JBL* 97 (1978) 23–39.

Barton, J. *Reading the Old Testament: Method in Biblical Study*. London: Darton, Longman & Todd, 1984.

Berlin, A. *Poetics and Interpretation of Biblical Narrative*. Bible and Literature Series. Sheffield: Almond Press, 1983.

Blum, E. *Die Komposition der Vätergeschichte*. WMANT 57. Neukirchen: Neukirchener Verlag, 1984.

———. *Studien zur Komposition des Pentateuch*. BZAW 189. Berlin: Walter de Gruyter, 1990.

Boorer, S. "The Importance of a Diachronic Approach: The Case of Genesis–Kings." *CBQ* 51 (1989) 195–208.

———. *The Promise of the Land as Oath: A Key to the Formation of the Pentateuch*. BZAW 205; Berlin: Walter de Gruyter, 1992.

Brueggemann, W. *Genesis*. Interpretation. Atlanta: John Knox Press, 1982.

Brueggemann, W., and H. W. Wolff, eds. *The Vitality of Old Testament Traditions*. 2d ed. Atlanta: John Knox Press, 1982.

Campbell, A. F. *Of Prophets and Kings: A Late Ninth-Century Document (1 Samuel 1—2 Kings 10)*. CBQMS 17. Washington, D.C.: Catholic Biblical Association of America, 1986.

———. "The Reported Story: Midway between Oral Performance and Literary Art." *Semeia* 46 (1989) 77–85.

———. *The Study Companion to Old Testament Literature: An Approach to the Writings of Pre-exilic and Exilic Israel*. A Michael Glazier Book. Old Testament Studies 2. Collegeville, Minn.: The Liturgical Press, 1989/1992.

——— "Old Testament Narrative as Theology." *Pacifica* 4 (1991) 165–80.

——— "Past History and Present Text: The Clash of Classical and Post-critical Approaches to Biblical Text." *AusBR* 39 (1991) 1–18.

Cassuto, U. *The Book of Exodus*. Jerusalem: Magnes, 1967. Hebrew original, 1951.

Childs, B. S. *Exodus*. OTL. London: SCM, 1974.

Cholewinski, A. *Heiligkeitsgesetz und Deuteronomium: Eine vergleichende Studie*. AnBib 66. Rome: Biblical Institute, 1976.

Coats, G. W. *From Canaan to Egypt: Structural and Theological Context for the Joseph Story*. CBQMS 4. Washington, D.C.: Catholic Biblical Association of America, 1976.

Coote, R. B. *In Defense of Revolution: The Elohist History*. Minneapolis: Fortress Press, 1991.

Cross, F. M. *Canaanite Myth and Hebrew Epic. Essays in the History of the Religion of Israel.* Cambridge: Harvard University Press, 1973.

De Vries, S. J. "A Review of Recent Research in the Tradition History of the Pentateuch." In the SBLSP, edited by K. H. Richards, Atlanta: Scholars Press, 1987, 459–502.

Driver, S. R. *An Introduction to the Literature of the Old Testament.* Edinburgh: T. & T. Clark, 1891. 9th ed., 1913. Reprint. New York: Meridian, 1956.

Durham, J. I. *Exodus.* WBC. Waco, Tex.: Word Books, 1987.

Eagleton, T. *Literary Theory: An Introduction.* Oxford: Basil Blackwell, 1983.

Eissfeldt, O. *Hexateuch-Synopse: Die Erzählung der fünf Bücher Mose und des Buches Josua mit dem Anfange des Richterbuches in ihre vier Quellen zerlegt und in deutscher Übersetzung darboten samt einer in Einleitung und Anmerkungen gegebenen Begründung.* Leipzig: Hinrichs, 1922. Reprint. Darmstadt: Wissenschaftliche Buchgesellschaft, 1963.

———. *The Old Testament: An Introduction.* Oxford: Basil Blackwell, 1965.

Elliger, K. "Sinn und Ursprung der priesterlichen Geschichtserzählung." *ZTK* 49 (1952) 121–43. (Reprinted in Elliger, K. *Kleine Schriften zum Alten Testament.* TBü 32. Munich: Kaiser, 1966, 174–98.)

Emerton, J. A. "An Examination of Some Attempts to Defend the Unity of the Flood Narrative in Genesis." Part 1, *VT* 27 (1987) 401–20; Part 2, *VT* 28 (1988) 1–21.

Engnell, I. "The Pentateuch." In *Critical Essays on the Old Testament.* London: SPCK, 1970. Swedish original, 1962.

Eslinger, L. M. *Kingship of God in Crisis: A Close Reading of 1 Samuel 1–12.* Bible and Literature Series 10. Sheffield: Almond Press, 1985.

Fisch, H. *Poetry with a Purpose: Biblical Poetics and Interpretation.* Bloomington: Indiana University Press, 1988.

Fohrer, Georg. *Introduction to the Old Testament.* London: SPCK, 1968.

Gunkel, Hermann. *Genesis.* 8th ed. Göttingen, Ger.: Vandenhoeck & Ruprecht, 1969; reprint of 3d ed., 1910.

Hayes, J. H. *An Introduction to Old Testament Study.* Nashville: Abingdon, 1979.

Hirsch, E. D., Jr. *Validity in Interpretation.* New Haven: Yale University Press, 1967.

Hoffmann, H. D. *Reform und Reformen.* ATANT 66. Zurich: Theologischer Verlag, 1980.

Humphreys, W. L. *Joseph and His Family: A Literary Study.* Columbia: University of South Carolina Press, 1988.

Hurvitz, A. *A Linguistic Study of the Relationship between the Priestly Source and the Book of Ezekiel: A New Approach to an Old Problem.* Cahiers de la Revue Biblique 20. Paris: Gabalda, 1982.

Jenks, A. W. *The Elohist and North Israelite Traditions.* SBLMS 22. Missoula, Mont.: Scholars Press, 1977.

Kelsey, D. H. *The Uses of Scripture in Recent Theology.* Philadelphia: Fortress Press, 1975.

Kraus, H.-J. *Geschichte der historisch-kritischen Erforschung des Alten Testaments.* 3d ed. Neukirchen: Neukirchener Verlag, 1982.

Lategan, B. C. "Introduction: Coming to Grips with the Reader." *Semeia* 48 (1989) 3–17.

Lohfink, N. "Die Priesterschrift und die Geschichte." *Congress Volume: Göttingen, 1977.* VTSup 29. Leiden: E. J. Brill, 1978, 189–225.

Longacre, R. E. *Joseph: A Story of Divine Providence.* Winona Lake, Ind.: Eisenbrauns, 1989.

McCarthy, D. J. *Treaty and Covenant.* AnBib 21a; new edition completely rewritten. Rome: Biblical Institute, 1978.

McEvenue, S. E. *The Narrative Style of the Priestly Writer.* AnBib 50. Rome: Biblical Institute, 1971.

Nelson, R. D. Review of *Into the Hands of the Living God*, by Lyle M. Eslinger. *JBL* 110 (1991) 142–43.

Nof, D., and N. Paldor, "Are There Oceanographic Explanations for the Israelites' Crossing of the Red Sea?" *Bulletin of the American Meteorological Society* 73/3 (1992) 305–14.

Noth, M. *Exodus*. OTL. Philadelphia: Westminster Press, 1962. German original: *Das zweite Buch Mose*. ATD 5. Göttingen: Vandenhoeck & Ruprecht, 1959.

———. *Leviticus*. OTL. Philadelphia: Westminster Press, 1965; revised translation, 1977. German original: *Das dritte Buch Mose*. ATD 6. Göttingen: Vandenhoeck & Ruprecht, 1962.

———. *Numbers*. OTL. Philadelphia: Westminster Press, 1968. German original: *Das vierte Buch Mose*. ATD 7. Göttingen: Vandenhoeck & Ruprecht, 1966.

———. *Könige*. BKAT 9/1. Neukirchen: Neukirchener Verlag, 1969.

———. *A History of Pentateuchal Traditions*. Translated by B. W. Anderson. Englewood Cliffs, N.J.: Prentice-Hall, 1972. Reprint. Chico, Calif.: Scholars Press, 1981. German original, 1948.

Polzin, R. *Late Biblical Hebrew: Toward an Historical Typology of Biblical Hebrew Prose*. HSM 12. Missoula, Mont.: Scholars Press, 1976.

———. *A Literary Study of the Deuteronomic History*. Part 1, *Moses and the Deuteronomist: Deuteronomy, Joshua, Judges*. New York: Seabury, 1980.

———. *A Literary Study of the Deuteronomic History*. Part 2, *Samuel and the Deuteronomist: 1 Samuel*. San Francisco: Harper & Row, 1989.

Porter, S. E. "Why Hasn't Reader-Response Criticism Caught on in New Testament Studies?" *Journal of Literature and Theology* 4 (1990) 278–92.

Pury, A. de, and Th. Römer, "Le Pentateque en question: Position du problème et brève histoire de la recherche." In *Le Pentateuque en question: Les origines et la composition des cinq premiers livres de la Bible à la lumière des recherches récentes*, edited by A. de Pury. Le Monde de la Bible. Geneva: Labor et Fides, 1989, 9–80.

Rad, G. von. *Genesis*. OTL. Philadelphia: Westminster Press, 1972. German original, 1953.

———. "The Form-Critical Problem of the Hexateuch." In *The Problem of the Hexateuch and Other Essays*. London: SCM, 1984. German original, 1938.

Rendtorff, R. *The Problem of the Process of Transmission in the Pentateuch*. JSOTSup 89. Sheffield: JSOT, 1990. German original, 1977.

Ricoeur, P. "Esquisse de Conclusion." In Barthes, Roland, et al. *Exégèse et herméneutique*. Paris: Editions du Seuil, 1971, 292–93.

Rose, M. *Deuteronomist und Jahwist: Untersuchungen zu den Berührungspunkten beider Literaturwerke*. ATANT 67. Zurich: Theologischer Verlag, 1981.

Rudolph, W. *Der "Elohist" von Exodus bis Josua*. BZAW 68. Berlin: Walter de Gruyter, 1938.

Schmid, H. H. *Der sogenannte Jahwist. Beobachtungen und Fragen zur Pentateuchforschung*. Zurich: Theologischer Verlag, 1976.

Schmidt, L. *Literarische Studien zur Josephsgeschichte*. BZAW 167. Berlin: Walter de Gruyter, 1986.

Ska, J. L. *Le Passage de la Mer: Etude de la construction, du style et de la symbolique d'Ex 14.1–31*. AnBib 109. Rome: Biblical Institute Press, 1986.

Skinner, J. *Genesis*. 2d ed. ICC. Edinburgh: T. & T. Clark, 1930.

Sternberg, M. *The Poetics of Biblical Narrative: Ideological Literature and the Drama of Reading*. Bloomington: Indiana University Press, 1985.

Talmon, S. "The Textual Study of the Bible—A New Outlook." In *Qumran and the History of the Biblical Text*, edited by F. M. Cross and S. Talmon. Cambridge: Harvard University Press, 1975, 321–400.

Thompson, T. L. *The Origin Tradition of Ancient Israel*. Vol. 1, *The Literary Formation of Genesis and Exodus 1-23*. JSOTSup 55. Sheffield: JSOT, 1987.

Tigay, J. H., ed. *Empirical Models for Biblical Criticism*. Philadelphia: University of Pennsylvania Press, 1985.

Van Seters, J. *Abraham in History and Tradition*. New Haven: Yale University Press, 1975.

———. *In Search of History. Historiography in the Ancient World and the Origins of Biblical History*. New Haven: Yale University Press, 1983.

———. "Joshua 24 and the Problem of Tradition in the Old Testament." In *In the Shelter of Elyon: Essays on Ancient Palestinian Life and Literature in Honor of G. W. Ahlström*, edited by W. Boyd Barrick and John R. Spencer. JSOTSup 31. Sheffield: JSOT, 1984, 139–58.

Volz, P., and W. Rudolph. *Der Elohist als Erzähler: Ein Irrweg der Pentateuchkritik?* Giessen: Töpelmann, 1933.

Weinfeld, M. *Deuteronomy and the Deuteronomic School*. Oxford: Clarendon, 1972.

Wellhausen, J. *Prolegomena to the History of Ancient Israel*. Meridian Books. Cleveland: World Publishing, 1957. German original under this title, 1883.

———. *Die Composition des Hexateuchs und der Historischen Bücher des Alten Testaments*. 3d ed. 1899. Reprint. Berlin: Walter de Gruyter, 1963.

Westermann, C. *Genesis 1–11*. Minneapolis: Augsburg, 1984. German original, 1974.

———. *Genesis 12–36*. Minneapolis: Augsburg, 1985. German original, 1981.

———. *Genesis 37–50*. Minneapolis: Augsburg, 1986. German original, 1982.

Whybray, R. N. *The Making of the Pentateuch. A Methodological Study*. JSOTSup 53. Sheffield: JSOT, 1987.

Wolff, H. W. "The Kerygma of the Yahwist." In *The Vitality of Old Testament Traditions*, edited by W. Brueggemann and H. W. Wolff. 2d ed. Atlanta: John Knox Press, 1982, 41–66. German original, 1964.

———. "The Elohistic Fragments in the Pentateuch." In *The Vitality of Old Testament Traditions*, edited by W. Brueggemann and H. W. Wolff. 2d ed. Atlanta: John Knox Press, 1982, 67–82. German original, 1969.

Index of Biblical Passages by Source

This index lists the biblical texts found in the body of chapters 2–5 of this book. It is not a reproduction of Noth's source listing, but an index to the texts indicating where they may be found in chapters 2–5. Noth's clustering of verses has been maintained, except in most cases where verse division within a source was involved. For the characterization of passages in their context, the relevant chapters must be consulted. The chapter and verse numbering here follows the NRSV; the differences involved are around Genesis 32, Exodus 8, and Numbers 16–17.

WITHIN THE PRIESTLY DOCUMENT

WITHIN THE YAHWIST NARRATIVE

WITHIN THE ELOHIST TEXTS

WITHIN THE NONSOURCE TEXTS

Index of Modern Authors

Made in the USA
Columbia, SC
16 September 2021